W9-CVZ-119

Sisters in the Blood

Sisters in the Blood

The Education of Women in Native America

Ardy Bowker

Center for Bilingual/Multicultural Education
Montana State University

WEEA Publishing Center
Education Development Center, Inc.

© 1993 by Ardy Bowker. All rights reserved

Printed in the United States of America.
No part of this publication may be reproduced, stored in a retrieval system, or transmitted, in any form or by any means, electronic, mechanical, photocopying, recording, or otherwise (unless used for communication with the author), without prior written permission of the author.

Discrimination Prohibited: No person in the United States shall, on the grounds of race, color, or national origin, be excluded from participation in, be denied the benefits of, or be subjected to discrimination under any program or activity receiving Federal financial assistance, or be so treated on the basis of sex under most education programs or activities receiving Federal assistance.

The activity which is the subject of this report was developed under a grant from the Department of Education, under the auspices of the Women's Educational Equity Act. The WEEA Publishing Center operates under contract #RP92136001 from the Office of Educational Research and Improvement (OERI). However, the opinions expressed herein do not necessarily reflect the position or policy of the Department of Education, and no official endorsement by the Department should be inferred.

1993
WEEA Publishing Center
Education Development Center, Inc.
55 Chapel Street
Newton, Massachusetts 02160

Cover design by Cynthia Bro

Cover artwork, *The Medicine Wheel,* by Louis Bowker

Cover artwork photography by Dean Miller

Dedicated to the women of all Red Nations.

Contents

Preface

Five hundred years ago, Christopher Columbus came to the "New World" and mistakenly identified the indigenous people as Indians.

Since that time, there has been considerable controversy over the appropriate designation for the indigenous people of the Americas. Some Native people endorse the label Native Americans, while others prefer First Americans; some approve the title Amerindians, while others favor American Indian or Indian.

As there is no consensus on this issue, I have respectfully chosen to use *American Indian* or *Indian* as a collective reference to the tribal women who participated in this study. Although the majority of the women referred to themselves as Indians or American Indians during the interviews, it should be noted that each tribal member preferred to be called by her tribal group name, such as Lakota, Arapaho, or Shoshone.

Acknowledgments

The study that formed the foundation of this book was funded, in part, by a Women's Educational Equity Act (WEEA) Research Challenge Grant. I am indebted to the U.S. Department of Education for providing the financial support and to Montana State University for awarding me a sabbatical to carry out the project. However, any opinions, findings, conclusions, or recommendations expressed in this book are those of the author and do not necessarily reflect the views of Montana State University or the U.S. Department of Education.

A study of this magnitude cannot be completed without the involvement of a number of people. In particular, I would like to thank Randy Hitz, Dean of the College of Education, Health, and Human Development at Montana State University, for his support in the completion of this book.

I am especially indebted to my husband, Louis Bowker, who often accompanied me to the various reservations. He was my confidant and my most enthusiastic supporter throughout this project. I am especially honored that one of his paintings, *The Medicine Wheel*, has been chosen for the cover of this book. The painting is appropriate in that the medicine wheel represents, among other things, the life cycle of the individual, a cycle that has been nurtured and protected by American Indian women in their goal of preserving their culture and heritage for future generations of American Indian children.

I especially want to thank Cheree Farlee and Minerva Allen, my colleagues, my friends, my sisters in the blood, who never let me forget the importance of this book and who were with me, if not in physical presence, at least in spirit, throughout this three-year project.

In addition, I would like to extend special thanks to Linda Eidet Heydon, who typed and edited the manuscript. Her attention to detail and her devotion to the project were unequaled. A special thanks to Judy Harrison, who edited the final copy of this book, and to Sundra Flansburg at the WEEA Publishing Center, who never failed to offer words of encouragement.

Finally, I am most grateful to the 991 women who participated in this study. Although you are not named, you know who you are. Some of your "stories" were tragic, others heartwarming, and many were hopeful. You touched my life dramatically. It is my sincere hope that your time and efforts will not go unrewarded and that educators and policymakers will listen and take appropriate action so that our sisters in the blood for generations to come may benefit from your experiences.

Introduction

Among the most serious problems confronting American Indian educators and tribal groups is that American Indian children have the highest dropout rate among all ethnic minority groups in the nation. Current statistics suggest that 50 percent of all American Indian students now enrolled in school will not graduate. Research further indicates that American Indian females are more likely to drop out than Indian males.

In examining the reasons that American Indians drop out of school, there are often as many theories as researchers, and there is a plethora of research on the dropout problem among American Indian students. For the most part, however, the majority of the research has focused on the poor self-image, cultural conflict, social disorganization, and/or socioeconomic standards of the family and child.

This so-called "within child" deficit model attributes school failure to the deficits the child brings to school, such as substandard reservation English, comparatively low IQ, cultural differences, dysfunctional home life, and poverty, and fails to look at the total context—including the school—within which the child lives and functions. This book challenges the deficit model that has been perpetuated throughout the history of Indian education and examines from the perspective of American Indian women why they were successful or unsuccessful in the school setting.

Throughout the history of education in the United States, there is a persistent theme: the education system is designed to encourage failure for some students and to ensure success for others. There is no need for an in-depth study to ascertain that this theme is persistent throughout Indian education.

In the past decade, dropping out of school has become a major political issue in this country. Almost all states have followed the lead of the federal policymakers and adopted mandates for excellence and performance standards for achievement for students within their respective states. Although such standards appear sound on paper and pacify those who would lead us to believe that American education has totally failed, these new standards may, in fact, force more American Indian children, as well as other minorities, out of school. Even more serious is the attention being paid to the economics of dropping out and the cost to our society as a whole. Not only do we read about the dismal future facing dropouts regarding unemployment or underemployment, but dropouts are being viewed in terms of a financial drain on society.

American Indians should be very wary of a system that focuses attention on the dropout problem from an economic perspective. It is a given that American Indians are the poorest minority group, both economically and educationally, in the country. But when the educators, policymakers, and leaders of the nation begin to look at a problem from an economic standpoint, we must be fully aware that such a view is closely linked to the old "cultural deprivation" and "culturally disadvantaged" theories of the sixties and seventies, which can result in a type of educational nationalism designed to justify educational policies in terms of national stability and economic competitiveness. In such a nationalistic atmosphere, equity often takes a backseat to excellence. Such results could further alienate minority populations who are already most at risk in school.

The question becomes, Are we as American Indian people willing to continue to accept this notion of success for some and failure for others? We need to ask ourselves, Is there a way we can guarantee success for all children? Can we in good conscience accept that 50 percent of our children will continue to fail in our schools? Is the middle-class Anglo culture the only yardstick we can use to measure success and failure in schools? Further, we need to ask ourselves, Is it always the purpose of American Indian schools to transmit the Anglo culture? Is it our responsibility to educate our children to give up their "Indianness" in order to be successful in school and in today's society? And finally, are we willing to accept the deficit model as a sufficient explanation for the success or failure of American Indian children in school?

This book suggests possible answers to these and other questions. In 1988–89, I was awarded a Women's Educational Equity Act (WEEA) Research Challenge Grant from the U.S. Department of Education to study the reasons for the success of some American Indian women in school and the failure of others. The study was conducted over an eighteen-month period during 1989–91. Nine hundred ninety-one American Indian females participated in the study and were representative of seven Northern Plains tribal groups, five reservations, and three Northern Plains states (Wyoming, Montana, and South Dakota). Of the participants, 327 were high school dropouts, 376 were high school graduates, and 288 had attended college for at least two years. Of the last group, 31 percent had received associate degrees, 57 percent had completed bachelor's degrees, 10 percent had received master's degrees, and 2 percent had completed doctorates. Because of the tendency of some researchers to compare tribes, which has further promoted stereotyping, I assured participants that no tribal group or reservation would be singled out, that no individual group would be compared with another, and that under no circumstances would individual comments be linked with a participant, a tribe, or a place of residence.

Personal interviews were conducted with each of the participants by the writer to further ensure individual and group anonymity. The interviews, which took approximately eighty-five minutes each, were conducted over an eighteen-month period and were arranged at the convenience of the participant.

There is great diversity in the backgrounds among those women who participated in this study. In some cases, women who would be described as being at high risk by most researchers actually graduated from high school and often succeeded in college. In other cases, girls who did not appear at high risk dropped out of school. These cases add complexity to and challenge the notion that high-risk youth share a commonality of personal and family factors that can be attributed to dropping out.

Perhaps the most painful and eye-opening result of this research will be the fact that many of the women who tell their stories in the pages of this book went to school each day and were told in both direct and indirect ways that they were not worthy or good at anything. Some rejected those continuing assaults upon their self-esteem, while others, unfortunately, did not have the internal or external resources to combat such attacks and instead became dropouts who were permanently haunted by their decision to leave school prematurely.

In writing this book, I hoped to achieve three purposes. One objective was to identify the factors that contribute to the educational success and/or lack of success of American Indian females in school. My intent was to make these factors useful to educators and school board members across Indian country by stimulating discussions and encouraging action on their part.

A second goal was to offer a theoretical framework for understanding American Indian female students and their unique position within their tribe and their schools. Such a theoretical basis can serve as a useful tool in the development of school reform that better accommodates the American Indian student.

Finally, my third purpose was to influence federal, state, and local policymakers, who are in a position to make decisions about American Indian schools. It is my hope that the stories related in this book will convince policymakers that schools can make a difference in the lives of children.

This book is divided into three parts. Part 1 consists of five chapters. Chapter 1 presents an overview of the dropout problem in America and briefly addresses the "minority dropout problem" in general. Chapter 2 discusses the history of American Indian education, its uniqueness, and its development, which differed from the historical development of public schools and the education of other racial/ethnic groups in America. Special attention is given to the types of schools established for American Indian youth, including missionary schools, off-reservation boarding schools, Bureau of Indian Affairs (BIA) day schools, BIA on-reservation boarding schools, public schools, and contract schools, all of which continue to serve Indian students to varying degrees.

Chapter 3 of this section addresses the origins of racism and stereotyping directed at American Indians and how research has reinforced stereotyping in the schools.

Chapters 4 and 5 review past research on American Indian dropouts and discuss the uniqueness of the American Indian child, the culture, and the school. As the reader will note, much of the research focuses on the personal and family characteristics of the dropouts themselves. The assumption often offered by this research, the "within child" deficit model, is that the American Indian student is the problem. While I acknowledge that a student's home and personal problems often contribute to failure in school, the case is also made throughout this book that schools and teachers contribute in a number of ways to student failure.

Part 2 of this book emphasizes the stories of the women who participated in this project. You will be allowed to vicariously experience the failures and successes of the women who speak in these pages. Throughout this section, you will learn how American Indian women have persevered and survived in a world where their behavior is often misrepresented or misunderstood by outside researchers and mainstream society in general, both of which operate from a different cultural perspective than that of the American Indian female.

Chapter 6 provides background on the processes and procedures used in the study. Subsequent chapters examine personal and family factors that contribute to the problems encountered by adolescent females, including substance abuse, child abuse, motherhood, and peer pressure, and factors that are closely linked with the school or treatment of individuals within the school, including racism and discrimination, cultural discontinuity, self-esteem/tribal identity, achievement, teacher expectations, and suspension, retention, and absenteeism.

Part 3 of this book provides a search for a solution to the dropout problem among American Indian female students, develops a theory about effective practices to reduce the high dropout rates among American Indian youth in general, and offers recommendations to policymakers and educators.

When I set out to write this book, my intention was to in some way draw attention to the success/lack of success among American Indian women in school and to influence practices within American Indian schools. To achieve this objective, I realized that it would be necessary not only to influence building-level practitioners, school board members, and tribal leaders, but to influence the policymakers at the state and federal levels toward reforms benefiting American Indian students.

This book goes far beyond its original intent. The messages relayed in these pages are important to the nation and the general public at large and should serve to benefit all youth, regardless of ethnicity or gender. There is no question that dropping out of school is a universal problem in this country, but for American Indian tribes the issue is perhaps more critical. Just as we must all accept part of the responsibility for the status of American Indian education, so must we also accept the responsibility for solving the problem. It is my sincere hope that this book will contribute in some small way to a renewed commitment on the part of educators, tribal leaders, and local, state, and federal policymakers to develop reforms benefiting students at risk. In the end, I believe that schools that are sensitive to the needs of their female students will also be responsive to the needs of all students, male or female.

Part 1

Education in Native America

Chapter 1

Dropping Out in America: A National Dilemma

> Disadvantaged students are not a new phenomenon in U.S. schools. However, the size of the disadvantaged student population will assume unprecedented proportions in the coming years. Failure to anticipate the coming changes in the composition of the student population and to plan appropriate responses will leave us not with the same educational problems we face today, but perhaps with problems so severe and so widespread as to threaten our economic welfare and even our social and political stability.
> —A.M. Pallas, G. Natriello, and E.L. McDill, "The Changing Nature of the Disadvantaged Population: Current Dimensions and Future Trends"

Prior to this decade, concern over the dropout rate in America has waxed and waned. Currently, there is a renewed interest in the number of students who leave school before graduation, for a number of reasons:

- *An increasing dropout rate.* The year 1990 marked the first time in twenty-five years, since the turn of the century, that the dropout rate increased in America. In 1979, the Carnegie Council on Policy Studies and Higher Education conducted a historical review of dropouts in America, using data from the Census Bureau and the National Center for Education Statistics. The final report indicated that the national dropout rate steadily declined in the United States until the mid-1960s. Specifically, in 1900, 90 percent of school-age children dropped out of school before receiving high school diplomas; by 1920, the nongraduation rate had decreased to 80 percent; and by the 1950s, it had plummeted to 50 percent. By 1960, the national dropout rate declined to 40 percent and continued a downward spiral until 1965, when it reached its lowest level, at 25 percent. This rate remained steady until 1990, when the dropout rate increased to 28 percent. Even more alarming was that the proportion of white male dropouts had increased by over 3 percent. With dropout rates increasing, educators, economists, businesspeople, and politicians joined ranks in sounding an alarm to decrease the dropout levels and to reform schools.

- *A changing economic structure.* Secondly, the current dropout rate signifies a serious social problem in a nation with a changing economic structure. Economic indicators predict a decrease in jobs that rely on muscle and nontechnical skills and an increase in those dependent upon brainpower and critical thinking skills. Even fewer jobs will be available to the high school dropout in a technological society.
- *An aging society.* A third factor, and one not often discussed, concerns the politics of an aging society. America is increasingly becoming a nation of older people. For the first time in our nation's history, people over the age of sixty-five outnumber teenagers. Increased life span has created some concern about the future of the quality of life for retired Americans. The problem is further complicated when the characteristics of retired Americans are examined as a group. The older population is primarily from the dominant white society. The younger population comes more and more from the ranks of the minority and disadvantaged groups who have been denied opportunity and access to the institutions and resources that allow them to be contributing citizens. This aging "white" population will make heavy demands on societal resources. On the other hand, the younger population may be reluctant or unable to pay the taxes and support the legislation necessary to maintain the standard of living expected by an aging population. Some writers suggest that such a situation is a threat to the economic and social stability of the nation.
- *The political factor.* A fourth reason is strictly political. Educational leaders at the state and federal levels have developed a series of "indicators" to measure the performance of the nation's schools. The U.S. Department of Education publishes education "wall charts" to compare state systems of education. These include high school completion rates. This effort has resulted in increased attention not only to the dropout problem, but to how to reduce it. At the same time, the media have not only latched onto information about dropouts; they have also reminded parents, educators, and government officials of how poorly American students rank with students around the world. This has brought about a surge of nationalism in regard to education.
- *A changing society.* Finally, current demographic trends indicate that future public school students will increasingly consist of the poor, the disadvantaged, and the minority—groups that the American educational system has historically failed. In contrast to the white population, minority populations in the United States are younger and will continue to grow, and the children coming into the schools will be more ethnically and linguistically diverse than ever before in the nation's history.

With dropout rates on the increase and fewer jobs for the dropout in a technological society, and with an aging population that will make large demands upon the nation's resources and a youthful population comprised more and more of persons from disadvantaged or minority backgrounds, some writers suggest that not only the economic welfare but also the political and social stability of the nation are threatened. This in itself has generated a national interest among educators, business leaders, policymakers, and the public in addressing the dropout problem.

At-Risk Students of the Nineties

We reject the implication raised in current public debate that excellence in education for some children can be made available only at the expense of other children. Indeed, it is our deepest belief that excellence without equity is both impractical and incompatible with the goals of a democratic society.
—National Coalition of Advocates for Students, *Barriers to Excellence: Our Children at Risk*

Until the decade of the eighties, the terms *at-risk* and *high-risk* were not used as descriptors in literature about dropouts. As the terms imply, much of the literature today seeks to identify the at-risk student or the potential dropout before s/he leaves school, in an effort to provide intervention strategies.

Generally, researchers identify three types of at-risk students: (1) children who come from different cultural backgrounds or minority students, (2) children from limited-English-speaking families, and (3) children from poor families.[1] Henry Levin described at-risk students as those defined in past literature as being educationally disadvantaged. He characterized these students as ". . . those who lack the home and community resources to benefit from conventional schooling practices. Because of poverty, cultural obstacles, or linguistic differences, they tend to have low academic achievement and high dropout rates. Such students are heavily concentrated among minority groups, immigrants, non-English speaking families and economically disadvantaged populations."[2] Levin's characterization of at-risk youth is a popular one. Throughout the research, "at risk" is often another code for "culturally deprived" and is frequently no more than the continued relabeling of disadvantaged students.

Research in the last decade contributed significantly to the public's perception of dropouts and has been responsible for the recognition of the depth of the problem; much of the literature addresses the dropout problem and its future impact on the country.

Concern over the political and economic future of the country is not new. As early as the 1970s, researchers predicted that the absolute numbers of at-risk students and the degrees of their disadvantage would increase in the nation's schools within the next twenty years. Many researchers noted concerns about the growing, youthful minority population in America and the lack of success of minorities in school. Based on an analysis of the U.S. population, Harold Hodgkinson projected that by the year 2000, one-third of the nation's schoolchildren would be minority. Other research showed that dropout rates vary significantly by ethnicity and class and that these rates are highest among American Indians, Blacks, and Hispanics. One national study examined the dropout rate from the sophomore to senior years using ethnic classifications and revealed that the dropout rates ranged from a low of 3.1 percent for Asian Americans to a high of 29.2 percent for American Indians. White students dropped out at a rate of 12.2 percent, Blacks at 17 percent, and Hispanics at 18 percent. More recent research reports that 8.9 percent of students from the highest socioeconomic class dropped out of school, while 22.3 percent of the dropouts came from the lowest socioeconomic class. These studies serve to demonstrate that the dropout problem in America is not restricted to the poor, inner-city minority youth, but that it is diverse in ethnic as well as class characteristics.[3]

Much of the literature on at-risk students or dropouts speaks to the impact of the problem on the country and society in general. It has been noted that youth who drop out are more likely to become economic burdens on society and are more likely to require public assistance. Business leaders and policymakers alike predict that the public will pay heavily for the high proportion of youth who drop out, creating an increased need for social and welfare programs. Educators argue, often unsuccessfully, that the investment required for dropout prevention would be substantially less than the eventual loss in productivity to the nation.[4]

Considerable attention has been paid to the labor market and the at-risk student. In the past, an economy existed to provide an orderly transition from dropping out to entry into numerous labor occupations. Such an economy no longer exists; therefore, dropping out of school often leads to no employment, or to underemployment in low-paid, often part-time jobs. Other researchers suggest that General Educational Development (GED) certificate-holders do not do as well in the labor market as high school graduates. In 1986, the U.S. General Accounting Office reported that males who drop out of high school are estimated to earn $441,000 less during their lives than males who are high school graduates. Given the low salaries earned by dropouts across their working career, the nation stands to lose $71 billion in social security, predicated on a 25 percent dropout rate.[5]

Some researchers have reported that not only are high school dropouts expected to be a massive drain on society through their dependence on welfare programs, but they are more likely to be involved in juvenile courts and prison systems. Since 1960, delinquency rates of teenagers have increased by 130 percent. In fact, it has been demonstrated in some research that failure to graduate from high school is a predictor of adult criminal activity.[6]

Other research points to a number of social problems in American society that place youth at risk. In 1984, the Alan Guttmacher Institute reported that each year 1.1 million teenage females become pregnant. Approximately 40 percent of the females who drop out of school do so for reasons related to pregnancy and marriage; however, the majority (60 percent) of females drop out for a variety of other reasons. In 1986, the National Center for Health Statistics reported that between 1950 and 1984, the rate of suicide among individuals between the ages of fifteen and twenty-four had increased by 178 percent. Research has consistently demonstrated that the relationship between inappropriate attitudes toward health and self is strongly related to dropping out of school. In 1988, the University of Michigan's Institute for Social Research reported that 58 percent of high school seniors have had experience with illicit drugs and that the increasing drug of choice is cocaine. The institute also found that nearly two-thirds of high school seniors reported using alcohol.

Gender and the Dropout

As the intellectually demanding and precariously balanced world of the 21st century comes into view, it seems clear that the mission of education must be not to train people to serve the purposes of others, but to develop their capacity to question the purposes of others.
—M.H. Futrell, "Mission Not Accomplished:
Education Reform in Retrospect"

Females have received little attention in dropout research until the last decade. The gender-related research of the eighties may in fact be due to the changing times. Fifty-nine percent of the children born in 1983 will live with only one parent before reaching the age of eighteen. This parent is most likely to be female. A Centers for Disease Control study reported that 25 percent of the children born in the United States in 1987 were born to single mothers, as compared to 4 percent in 1950.[7]

Forty percent of the adolescent girls who drop out of school in this country report that they do so because of pregnancy or marriage. Clearly, young women who drop out of school face serious economic disadvantages. It has been estimated that 49 percent of the families headed by female dropouts live in poverty. Furthermore, whereas women in general earn 64 percent of what men earn, the female dropout will earn only 29 percent of what a male graduate will earn. It is estimated that over 60 percent of the American Indian children in this country live in poverty, as compared to 36 percent of Black children and 12 percent of white children.[8]

There is insufficient research on gender and dropping out. Most researchers have found that males and females reported similar reasons (when the variable of pregnancy was eliminated) for leaving school. Other research shows that while there are many similarities between sexes, socialization factors play a major role in why boys drop out and why girls drop out.[9]

Researchers of female dropouts in general isolate four major factors that place girls at risk: (1) the socialization process, (2) teacher interaction, (3) cognitive differences, and (4) curricular choices. These factors addressing the female experience are very different from those addressing the male experience.

Society in general has placed females at risk by limiting their options. Girls in our society define their roles by forming bonds with others and by learning through cooperation, which is in contrast to the situation of males, who are urged by adults to be more assertive and to explore their environment. This stereotypical view of female and male roles, learned in childhood, is used as a means of coping with pressure and self-identification in adolescence.[10]

Research on teacher interaction with students indicates a more favorable attitude toward male development and independence. Girls, in fact, are more invisible in the classroom than boys and receive much less teacher attention and fewer rewards.[11]

Gender differences in cognitive orientation have been well researched. Studies demonstrate that girls learn through cooperation, whereas boys are more competitive and work more independently than girls. Such differences influence a student's academic achievement because of the way schools and classes are structured.[12]

Research has indicated that females of all ethnic minority groups are underrepresented in science and engineering fields. This underrepresentation is often a result of the quality and quantity of curricular choices in their secondary education experiences. Despite the research addressing this issue, females and minorities have not been encouraged to take traditionally "male" courses such as math, science, and computer education courses.[13]

The Minority Student in Our Schools

Our society is a diverse and heterogeneous one, in which we embrace a variety of subcultures delineated by ethnic, linguistic, racial, geographic, educational, and socio-economic earmarks. Within each of these subcultures, social standards vary, ... rising magically out of the middle-class pillars of society.... This, then, is the stereotypical target toward which our institutionalized educational system tends to socialize all of its participants, regardless of the adult subculture to which they are bound, and regardless of the relevancy or irrelevancy of these values and habits to each one's own real world.

—J. McDavid, "The Teacher as an Agent of Socialization"

Schools in America are geared to success, not failure. Historically, minority students from their earliest school experiences have been labeled as potential failures, their language criticized, and their origins suspect. Some researchers report that certain indigenous minorities have developed a culture of resistance to school and suggested that an "apathetic dominant society" has historically excluded the American Indian from the dominant culture. This in some ways has become a double-edged sword, in that frequently American Indians have chosen to exclude themselves, thus exacerbating the situation.[14]

Research clearly indicates that Blacks, Hispanics, and American Indians are more frequently alienated by school than Asian Americans and other new immigrants. In fact, it has been found that Asian Americans and other new immigrants regard the school experience as a major path to success. Some researchers maintain that the nation's tolerance of exceedingly high dropout rates among certain minority groups is a manifestation of a social strategy designed to keep minorities out of the political decision-making process. Given the fact that typical high school dropouts participate minimally in the political structure, they are less likely to become involved in political decision making as adults and are therefore far less able to shape their own fates.[15]

There has been inadequate justification in the research for the differential achievement levels among minorities. Some researchers present genetic or biological factors as an explanation for minority underachievement. Others maintain that cultural factors, along with socioeconomic structural factors, provide an adequate explanation. It may be that students' resistance to learning should be viewed as rejection of the cultural values of the school and society; if they perceive the school as oppressive and destructive of their culture, the effects on students are devastating.[16]

Several researchers report that the use of culturally and linguistically congruent instructional approaches smooths the transition from school to home, whereas others suggest that such approaches are culturally incongruent or meaningless.[17]

Many researchers conclude that minority youth experience more factors associated with dropping out than the general population, such as poverty, school failure, family problems, and involvement in the criminal justice and social welfare systems. In addition, they note that minority youth are more likely to come from families or environments with high rates of drug and alcohol abuse; therefore, they have a greater chance of residing under conditions that are conducive to dropping out of school.[18]

Two researchers, Signithia Fordham and John Ogbu, examined Black students' underachievement in school and proposed "fictive kinship" as a framework for understanding how a sense of collective identity enters into the process of schooling and affects academic achievement. The fear of being accused of "acting white" causes social and psychological situations that diminish Black students' academic efforts—leading to underachievement and, in many cases, dropping out.[19] There is some evidence to support that a similar force is at work with American Indian students.

Current research on dropouts in America demonstrates the diverse racial, ethnic, and class characteristics of at-risk youth. Most studies have inaccurately led us to believe that dropping out is linked only to minority populations. Recent research reveals that the problem is much more widespread.

Summary

The current focus upon dropouts in America is undoubtedly timely. However, in American Indian educational circles, this issue is not a new concern. Historically, American Indian students have dropped out of school at higher rates than any other minority group in America. Despite its seriousness, little attention has been given to empirical analysis of the problem. Instead, many writers and researchers have explained the lack of success of American Indian students as falling into four major categories: (1) cultural differences between American Indians and the white system, (2) social disorganization within tribal groups and families, (3) poor self-concept of American Indian students, and (4) low socioeconomic status.[20]

This book will seek to go beyond the generally accepted premises of cultural discontinuity and the "within child" deficit models of home and family and will examine not only the factors often attributed to dropping out, but also factors generally not discussed in American Indian dropout research. For example, there is some evidence that American Indian students do poorly in school because of racial bias, discrimination, and ambivalence on the part of teachers. This factor will be examined further in parts 2 and 3 of this book; however, it is important to note that historically, underachievement on the part of American Indian students may have resulted because white teachers and administrators refused to acknowledge that American Indian students were capable of intellectual achievement. Subsequently, American Indians began to doubt their own potential and began to define academic success as a "white man's" prerogative. As a result, American Indian students began to discourage their peers from emulating the "white man's" academic success by shaming those who were successful.

American Indians traditionally have been provided with substandard schooling, based on the Euro-American perceptions of the educational needs of American Indians. To provide further understanding of the significance of the historical impact on American Indian students, chapter 2 will present an overview of Indian education in America.

Chapter 2

An Overview of the History and Politics of Indian Education in America

> Indians are today greatly different from what they once were. They have adopted many of the cultural traits brought by the invaders, and have participated in further changes and evolutions of the national societies in which they are located. Yet there remains what is termed "an Indian Problem" and an enduring image of an unchanging Indian. The Indian appears to be a problem because he does not change—at least, not in the way and at the rate that they think he should.
> —M.L. Wax, *Indian Americans: Unity and Diversity*

Although Murray Wax wrote those words twenty years ago, they are as applicable to the American Indian of the nineties as they were when first written. To fully understand "the Indian Problem" as it relates to the American Indian student, it is important to briefly review the history and politics of Indian education in America.

Missionary Period

Education policy for American Indians parallels the conquest and colonization of America. During the Colonial period of history, many European nations were involved in bringing Christianity and civilization to the various Indian tribes, which included the responsibility of formal schooling.

Jesuit missionaries, who are credited with establishing the first school for Indians in the Americas in 1568, actively pursued "civilizing" the Native populations for 200 years. Following the orders of Louis XIV, they sought to teach both Christianity and the French culture and language to the American Indian during the seventeenth century. The Franciscans, who were mostly Spanish, were involved with Southwestern tribes in California, New Mexico, Arizona, and Texas. Roman Catholic missionaries were most active throughout the Midwest and Northwest. The Protestants established schools for American Indians under the direct order of King James in 1617. Dartmouth College was founded for the education of American Indians, Harvard was established for educating both Indians and English youth, and both Hampton Institute and the College of William and Mary set up special branches for American Indians.[1]

In all cases, the education of American Indian youth during the Colonial period was for the purposes of bringing Christianity and civilization— "civilization" in this case meaning the extermination of the Native culture and the assimilation of the American Indian into the dominant white culture. There were no efforts made during this period to incorporate the Native languages, culture, or history into the curriculum.

Treaty Period

The Constitution of the United States conferred upon the federal government the right to make treaties, regulate commerce, and control the public lands occupied by Indians, which established the legal framework for the reservation system. Indian tribes maintained the status of sovereign nations with whom the United States fought and entered into treaties. During the period from 1778 to 1871, the federal government entered into 389 treaties with American Indian tribes. These treaties generally provided for the cessation of land to the federal government with the promise to allow American Indians to keep certain lands as inalienable and tax free. In addition, most of the treaties included agreements that the federal government would provide education, health, technical, and agricultural services to the tribes. The Fort Laramie Treaty of 1868 was one of the last treaties signed by the federal government. This treaty, between the U.S. government and the Lakota Sioux Nation, established the Great Sioux Reservation as the permanent home of the Lakota Sioux and encompassed all of what is now western South Dakota, including the Black Hills. Two articles from the Fort Laramie Treaty illustrate the attention of the federal government to education as a "civilizing" process:

> ARTICLE 7. In order to insure the civilization of the Indians entering into this treaty, the necessity of education is admitted, especially of such of them as are or may be settled on said agricultural reservations, and they therefore pledge themselves to compel their children, male and female, between the ages of six and sixteen years, to attend school. . . .

> ARTICLE 13. The United States hereby agrees to furnish annually to the Indians the physicians, teachers, carpenter, miller, engineer, farmer, and blacksmiths as herein contemplated, and that such appropriations shall be made from time to time, on the estimates of the Secretary of the Interior, as will be sufficient to employ such persons.[2]

During the treaty period, a number of the treaties called for specific provisions for educating the American Indian; however, missionary groups administered most of the Indian schools with funds provided by the federal government. For example, in 1802, Congress approved an appropriation "not to exceed $15,000.00" to promote "civilization among the savages." In 1819, Congress passed an act that apportioned funds among various missionary societies to provide education to American Indians. This act once again reiterated the policy of assimilation: "The President may . . . employ capable persons . . . for teaching Indian children in reading, writing, and arithmetic . . . for the purpose of . . . introducing among them the art of civilization."[3]

These annual appropriations continued until 1873, two years after the end of the treaty period of history. No specific mention is made regarding the use of the English language in either the 1802 or 1819 appropriations. Both provisions promoted "civilization." That the English language was the "civilized" tongue and the Native languages "barbaric" was implied, but not stated.

Use of the English language in the education of Native youth was first mentioned in the report of the Indian Peace Commission, a body appointed by an act of Congress in 1867 to make recommendations for the permanent removal of the causes of Indian hostility. The report of 1868 stated that ". . . in the difference of language today lies two-thirds of our trouble. Schools should be established which children should be required to attend; their barbarous dialects would be blotted out and the English language substituted."[4]

This report sparked a heated controversy in Indian education. Missionary groups who had been given the responsibility of educating Native youth supported a bilingual instructional policy. In 1870, President Grant harshly criticized the practices of the missionaries, denouncing their insistence on using Native languages in their schools. In 1879, two missionary societies were threatened with the withdrawal of federal funds unless they complied with government regulations on language. The missionaries won a minor victory in 1888, however, when the government approved the use of the Bible translated into the Native languages in the schools.

Government Involvement in the Education of the Natives

In 1871, Congress prohibited further treaties with Indian tribes. By this time, Indian tribes were now confined to reservations where the government promised to feed, clothe, and house them until Congress determined that they could care for themselves.

In the same year, Congress included in the Appropriations Act for Indian Education a section requiring the establishment of day schools on reservations; however, day schools were not favored by those educators and politicians who viewed assimilation as impossible when students were subject to the influence of their reservations. In 1873, the Board of Indian Commissioners reported, "It is well-nigh impossible to teach Indian children the English language when they spend twenty hours out of the twenty-four in the wigwam, using only their native tongue. The boarding school, on the contrary, takes the youth under constant care ... and surrounds him in an English-speaking community."[5] The Senate and House Indian Affairs committees furthered the idea that Indians should be assimilated into mainstream society in the *First Annual Report to the Congress of the United States*, 1874, which stated that "the goal of Indian education should be to make the Indian child a better American rather than to equip him simply to be a better Indian. The goal of our whole Indian program should be, in the opinion of our committee, to develop better Indian Americans rather than to perpetuate and develop better American Indians. The present Indian education program tends to operate too much in the direction of perpetuating the Indian as a special-status individual rather than preparing him for independent citizenship."[6]

Efforts to suppress the Native culture can also be found outside the school setting. For example, in 1881, the federal government banned the Sun Dance among the Plains Indians and, in 1885, extended such policies to all religious ceremonies. In 1886, Indian men were ordered by the government to cut their hair in an effort to make them appear more like white men.

The first major financial commitment that the federal government made to boarding school policy was initiated by the efforts of Richard Henry Pratt, a U.S. Army officer, who founded the Carlisle Indian School in 1879. This school, like others soon to be established, removed the children from the reservation and placed them in a boarding school, often several hundred miles from home. Pratt, who was often referred to as the "Red Man's Moses," was the architect of the federal boarding school. His philosophy, which formed the basis for Indian education for years, is best expressed in his own writing: "In Indian civilization I am a Baptist because I believe in immersing the Indians in our civilization and when we get them under, holding them there until they are thoroughly soaked."[7] The Secretary of the Interior, speaking about boarding schools in 1883, reported that "... if a sufficient number of manual labor schools can be established to give each youth the advantages of three to five years of schooling, the next generation will hear nothing of this difficult problem, and we may leave the Indian to himself."[8]

In 1887, Congress passed the Compulsory Indian Education Act, further promoting an educational system of boarding schools, which has been compared by many historians to a penal system. Native children were separated from their families and culture, and attempts were made to indoctrinate them into the white man's culture. The off-reservation boarding school became the dominant force in the education of American Indian children until the 1930s.

Unlike that of the early missionary schools, the curriculum of the boarding schools was industrial in nature and had little or no application to the reservation. The language of the schools was English; the use of the Native language was forbidden, and any use of the Native language resulted in cruel and unjust punishment. Despite the problems with the boarding schools, they became an entrenched part of American Indian schooling that continues to the present day. Many of the schools established, following the success of Carlisle, are still in operation, including Forest Grove, Oregon (1880), which is currently known as Chemawa; Santa Fe, New Mexico (1890), which is known as the Institute of American Indian Arts; Haskell, Kansas (1884), known as Haskell Indian Junior College; Pierre Indian School (1891) and Flandreau (1893), both in South Dakota; and Chilocco (1893) in Oklahoma.

Historically, these schools were infamous for their treatment of Native youth. Children were forbidden to speak their own language, and discipline often included ankle chains and solitary confinement. In addition, children were housed in overcrowded dormitories and required to perform manual labor in support of the schools. They were forced to attend these schools, often without parental consent. In many cases, parents who refused to send their children to boarding schools were arrested, or their rations of food were decreased or eliminated. Other boarding schools, established and managed by missionary groups, are still in existence today and actively recruit students from reservations throughout the country.[9]

Mary Crow Dog, a product of the St. Francis Boarding School in South Dakota, shared in her autobiography the contents of a poster given to her grandfather by the missionaries at a boarding school. Ten rules were presented to guide the life of an Indian child (and obviously to encourage assimilation):

1. Let Jesus save you.
2. Come out of your blanket, cut your hair, and dress like a white man.
3. Have a Christian family with one wife for life only.
4. Live in a house like your white brother. Work hard and wash often.
5. Learn the value of a hard-earned dollar. Do not waste your money on giveaways. Be punctual.

6. Believe that property and wealth are signs of divine approval.
7. Keep away from saloons and strong spirits.
8. Speak the language of your white brother. Send your children to school to do likewise.
9. Go to church often and regularly.
10. Do not go to Indian dances or to the medicine men.[10]

As would be expected, there was much opposition to the off-reservation boarding schools among the American Indians themselves.

Despite the efforts to educate Indians, most jobs on the reservation were held by whites. Standing Bear was one of the most outspoken critics about such conditions: "Despite the fact that Indian schools have been established over several generations, there is a dearth of Indians in the professions. It is most noticeable on the reservations where the numerous positions of consequence are held by white employees instead of trained Indians. For instance, why are not the stores, post-offices, and Government office jobs on the Sioux Reservation held by trained Indians? Why cannot Sioux be reservation nurses and doctors; and road-builders too? . . . Were these numerous positions turned over to trained Indians, the white population would soon find reservation life less attractive and less lucrative."[11]

Before the turn of the century, a new alternative was introduced into Indian education that included on-reservation boarding schools and/or day schools. Native parents were much less hostile to this type of schooling, as their children remained on the reservation and in many cases remained at home and were transported to school. Boarding schools were established on the reservation to provide an education for those who lived at too great a distance or because inadequate roads prevented daily transportation.

From the beginning of its involvement with American Indian tribes, the federal government was reluctant to administer schools; however, the questioned constitutionality of financing church groups to provide education for Indians finally brought about a change in attitude. The Bureau of Indian Affairs (BIA), which was established in 1836 under the War Department, was shifted to the Department of the Interior in 1849, and began placing teachers and physicians on reservations in 1892.

The Dawes Act and Education

In 1887, Congress passed the Dawes Severalty Act (Allotment Act), which became the framework for white settlement of the reservation land. This policy continued until 1934. The Dawes Act provided that each Indian head of family would receive 160 acres of land set aside within the reservation borders. The Allotment Act and subsequent statutes established procedures that resulted in the transfer of some 90 million acres from Indian to white owners in the next forty-five years. The philosophical relationship between educational policy and land policy of this period is clear, but there was a financial tie as well. The surplus reservation land was to be sold, and the funds were to be used, among other things, for the education of American Indians. Needless to say, this period of history brought about an era of bitterness between the federal government and Indian tribes, which is perhaps best illustrated in the words of a Lakota Sioux elder in 1891: "They made us many promises, more than I can remember, but they never kept but one; they promised to take our land and they took it."[12]

In 1896, W.N. Hailman questioned the government's policy of education in the boarding schools regarding culture and language, noting that "the great majority of Indian teachers have labored under the delusion that they can hasten the acquisition of the English language on the part of the pupils by compulsory measures, visiting more or less severe penalties upon the unfortunate children who were caught in the use of the Indian speech. . . . To throw contempt upon the child's vernacular . . . is so manifestly unreasonable and so pernicious in its perverting and destructive influence upon the child's heart-life that it is a wonder that it even should have been attempted by the philanthropic fervor of workers in Indian schools."[13]

The philosophy of the federal government toward Indian education, however, remained the same and is typified in the report of the Commissioner of Indian Affairs in 1903: "To educate the Indian in the ways of civilized life, therefore is to preserve him from extinction, not as an Indian, but as a human being. As a separate entity he can not exist encysted, as it were, in the body of this great nation. The pressure for land must diminish his reservations to areas within which he can utilize the acres allotted to him, so that the balance may become homes for the white farmers who require them. To educate the Indian is to prepare him for the abolishment of tribal relations, to take his land in severalty, and in the sweat of his brow and the toil of his hands to carry out, as his white brother has done, a home for himself and family."[14]

As whites moved onto the reservation, they brought with them the need for public schools; however, on reservations that were not allotted (most reservations in the Southwest), public schooling did not become an issue. As a result, compulsory school attendance was introduced, and American Indians were enrolled in a number of public schools. In fact, by 1901, the states of South Dakota, Wisconsin, California, Michigan, Idaho, Montana, Nebraska, Nevada, Oregon, and Oklahoma had federal contracts to educate Indians in public schools.

In 1916, the federal government instituted a uniform curriculum in all BIA Indian schools, but there was little application of the policy. In 1918,

Congress passed the Act of May 25, 1918 (40 Stat. L. 564), which had enormous implications for Indian education and continues to the present: "Hereafter no appropriation, except appropriations made pursuant to treaties, shall be used to educate children of less than one-fourth Indian blood whose parents are citizens of the United States and the State wherein they live and where there are adequate free school facilities provided." This act eliminated the responsibility of the federal government for the education of large numbers of Indian children who were born and raised on the reservation and who, in most cases, considered themselves Indian. With this legislation, the government set in motion a system of segregation and discrimination whereby the degree of Indian blood determined services and rights to an education for the individual.

In 1928, *The Problem of Indian Administration*, commonly known as the Meriam Report, was published. The report severely criticized the federal government's handling of Indian affairs, including education, the operation of boarding schools, poorly trained teachers, and low salaries. The Meriam Report acknowledged the goal of public school education for American Indians; however, it warned against such a move as a way "to save money and wash its [the government's] hands of responsibility for the Indian child." The report further recommended establishing adequate secondary schools, loan programs for higher education, and a cadre of specialists, rather than administrators, to administer educational programs. It also recommended eliminating boarding schools for elementary children and increasing the number of day schools: "The philosophy underlying the establishment of Indian boarding schools, that the way to 'civilize' the Indian is to take Indian children, even very young children, as completely as possible away from their home and family life, is at variance with modern views of education and social work, which regard home and family as essential social institutions from which it is generally undesirable to uproot children."[15]

Although sympathetic to Indians' involvement in the direction of their lives and schools, the Meriam Report recommended a general Indian education policy that did not depart from the previous policies of the federal government:

> To achieve this end the Service must have a comprehensive, well rounded educational program adequately supported, which will place it at advancement of a people. . . .
>
> The fundamental requirement is that the task of the Indian Service be recognized as primarily educational, in the broadest sense of the word, and that it be made an efficient educational agency, devoting its main energies to the social and economic advancement of the Indians, so that they may be absorbed into the prevailing civilization, at least in accordance with a minimum standard of health and decency.[16]

Further, the report suggested that such a plan would be the most efficient way of ending the relationship between the federal government and the American Indian tribes: "The belief is that it is a sound policy of national economy to make generous expenditures in the next few decades with the object of winding up the national administration of Indian affairs."[17]

The Indian Reorganization Act and Educational Commitment

The Indian Reorganization Act of 1934 ended the allotment period of history, confirmed the rights to Indian self-government, and made Indians eligible to hold BIA posts, which enabled the hiring of Indians in schools. The act also authorized loans for Indians to attend vocational schools and colleges. During this period, there was a special effort to encourage the development of community day schools; however, public school attendance for Indian children was also encouraged. The Johnson-O'Malley Act of 1934 was passed, which provided for the reimbursement of the states for the education of Indian students in public schools. This act, commonly referred to as JOM, was to be amended several times over the ensuing years, but is still a source of support for the education of Indian students.

In 1944, the House Indian Affairs Committee made recommendations calling for a return to the policies that the Meriam Report had discredited; however, by 1948, Congress had begun to cut funds for Indian education.

In 1950, Congress passed two bills that became known as the federally impacted legislation (P.L. 874, 64 Stat., 1100, and P.L. 815, 64 Stat., 967–78). Both laws provided federal funds to compensate school districts for the financial burdens placed on them due to federal activities. Public Law 874 provided funds for general operating expenses in lieu of local and state taxes. Public Law 815 was to provide funds for school construction in areas that were federally impacted. At the time these laws were passed, they did not include American Indians, but were designed for areas impacted by military installations. In 1953, the laws were amended to include Indians. Section 14 was added to Public Law 815 to provide federal funds to school districts in need of facilities for Indian students.

Termination Period

In 1953, Congress passed House Concurrent Resolution 108, which implemented a new direction in federal policy toward Indians. Senator Arthur Watkins (Utah), the major spokesperson for Resolution 108, expressed the philosophy of the termination policy: "Philosophically speaking, the

Indian wardship problem brings up basically the questionable merit of treating the Indian of today as an Indian, rather than a fellow American citizen. . . . 'As rapidly as possible' we should end the status of Indians as wards of the government and grant them all the rights and prerogatives pertaining to American citizenship."[18] This period, often referred to as the "Termination Period," provided the mechanism for ending federal aid and protection for American Indians and was met with suspicion in Indian country. As Herbert Aurbach and Estelle Fuchs have noted, "A reversal of the government's Indian policy directed at curtailing Bureau activities and eventually termination of all federal protection sent a new wave of anxiety and suspicion of the white man's intent over the Indian country. The economic and political developments and activities of Indian communities were retarded or obstructed."[19]

In 1951, the federal government implemented a policy for relocating Indians to urban areas and away from their home reservations. The Menominees of Wisconsin became the first tribe slated for termination by the federal government in 1954. By 1960, sixty-one tribes had been terminated. During this period as well, the BIA ended operation of federal schools in four states: Idaho, Michigan, Washington, and Wisconsin. In addition, California and Oregon assumed responsibility for educating Indian youth. Despite the BIA's position of encouraging Indians to attend public schools, the bureau's boarding schools expanded during this time, basically to meet the needs of the rapid increase in student enrollment. In the latter years of the Eisenhower administration the emphasis on termination abated, and when the Kennedy administration entered office, it conveyed to American Indians its desire for reversal of the termination policy.

In 1965, Congress passed the Elementary and Secondary Education Act, commonly referred to as Title I (79 Stat., 27–36), to meet the "special education needs of children of low-income families." The criteria allocated funding based upon the number of children in a school district whose families were receiving Aid to Families with Dependent Children (AFDC) or had an income of less than $2,000 per year. Indian students, mostly coming from low-income families, were eligible for participation.

In 1966, the White House Task Force on the American Indian submitted a report calling for the economic development of tribes and for an improved educational system for American Indians. During the same year, Senator George McGovern (South Dakota) introduced a concurrent resolution in Congress calling for a policy of Indian self-determination and economic development.

In 1968, President Lyndon Johnson's message to Congress on Indian affairs called for federal support of Indian involvement in Indian affairs and an end to the termination policy: "I propose a new goal for our Indian programs: a goal that ends the debate about termination of Indian programs and stresses self-determination; a goal that erases old attitudes of paternalism and promotes partnership self-help."[20]

Further, Johnson directed the BIA to establish American Indian school boards for all BIA schools: "To help make the Indian school a vital part of the Indian community, I am directing the Secretary of Interior to establish Indian school boards for Federal Indian schools. School board members selected by the communities will receive whatever training is necessary to enable them to carry out their responsibilities."[21]

American Indian Activism and Self-Determination

During the late 1960s and the 1970s, Indian educators, often assisted by civil rights advocates, became increasingly active in promoting the rights of American Indians and calling national attention to their plight. In 1969, a group of individuals calling themselves "Indians for All Tribes" occupied Alcatraz Island, demanding that the island be turned into an Indian educational and cultural center. In 1972, members of the American Indian Movement, commonly known as AIM, occupied the BIA headquarters in Washington, D.C., demanding that attention be paid to their grievances. Later that year, AIM took over the village of Wounded Knee in South Dakota, again resulting in national attention to Indian concerns. At the same time, AIM members staged sit-ins and walkouts in high schools, demanding greater curriculum relevance and increased Indian involvement in school administration.[22] During this period of "Indian activism," a number of American Indian organizations were established, including the National Indian Education Association and the Coalition of Indian Controlled School Boards, in an effort to address the educational concerns of Indian tribes from a Native perspective.

Many of the grievances of the Indian activists had already been documented in Congress. In 1969, a special Senate Subcommittee on Indian Education issued a report, *Indian Education: A National Tragedy—A National Challenge*, on the federal government's policy toward American Indians. Chaired by Robert Kennedy and later his brother, Senator Edward Kennedy, this report (which is also known as the Kennedy Report) issued the following declaration on the state of education for the American Indian child:

> The dominant policy of the Federal Government towards the American Indian has been one of coercive assimilation . . . resulting in . . . the destruction and disorganization of Indian communities and individuals; a desperately severe and self-perpetuating cycle of poverty for most Indians; the growth of a large, ineffective, and self-perpetuating bureaucracy which retards the elimination of Indian poverty; a waste of federal appropriations.

The coercive assimilation policy has had disastrous effects on the education of Indian children . . . which has resulted in . . . the classroom and the school becoming a kind of battleground where the Indian child attempts to protect his integrity and identity as an individual by defeating the purposes of the school; schools which fail to understand or adapt to, and in fact often denigrate cultural differences; schools which blame their own failures on the Indian student and reinforce his defensiveness; schools which fail to recognize the importance and validity of the Indian community—the community and the child retaliate by treating the school as an alien institution; a dismal record of absenteeism, dropouts, negative self-image, low achievement, and, ultimately, academic failure for many Indian children; a perpetuation of the cycle of poverty which undermines the success of all other Federal programs.[23]

As a direct result of this report, the decade of the seventies was to witness major legislation aimed at implementing a new direction in Indian education. The policy of the new administration was revealed by President Richard Nixon in 1970, when he called for a new Indian policy of "self-determination without termination." The message included the following:

We have turned from the question of whether the Federal government has a responsibility to Indians to the question of how that responsibility can best be fulfilled. We have concluded that the Indians will get better programs and that public monies will be more effectively expended if the people affected by these programs are responsible for operating them.

The Indians of America need Federal assistance—this much has long been clear. What has not always been clear, however, is that the Federal government needs Indian energies and Indian leadership if its assistance is to be effective in improving the conditions of Indian life.[24]

In response, Congress passed the Indian Education Act of 1972 (P.L. 92-318, 86 Stat., 334–45), which was commonly known as Title IV (renamed Title V in 1988). Title IV was a major victory for American Indians. This act provided funds to school districts for the "special educational needs of Indian children." Divided into five parts, Title IV provided for Indian control in a much broader manner than previous legislation. Part A mandated parental and community participation in the establishment and direction of impact-aid programs. Further, by allocating up to 10 percent of the entitlement funds to schools that were not local educational agencies, the act encouraged the establishment of contract schools. Part B of the act authorized a series of grant programs that stressed bilingual and bicultural curriculum programs. Part C provided grants for adult education programs. Part D established an Office of Indian Education within the U.S. Office of Education. Part E provided funds for training teachers for BIA schools, with preference given to Indians.

Perhaps the most far-reaching legislation passed by Congress in the 1970s and signed by President Gerald Ford was the Indian Self-Determination and Educational Assistance Act of 1975 (P.L. 93-638, 88 Stat., 1910–14). This act allowed Indian organizations to contract with the BIA for any service the bureau provided to Indians, including schools. Whereas the Indian Self-Determination Act ensured American Indian tribes of the opportunity to determine their own futures, it became increasingly apparent that this goal could not be realized without an educated population. Included in the act was the "declaration of a national goal" by Congress that committed the U.S. government to providing ". . . quantity and quality educational services and opportunities which will permit Indian children to compete and excel in the life areas of their choice, and to achieve the measure of self-determination essential to their social and economic well-being."

The intent of the act was to provide an opportunity for Indian people to control their own affairs. Upon entering into a contract, the local Indian organization would manage the program, although the funding for the program would be funneled through the BIA. Should the organization fail, the BIA would resume control.

Critics of the act suggested that it was no more than another form of colonial domination. Phyllis Young, an AIM activist involved with efforts to establish alternative schools, called "Survival Schools," stated in retrospect:

> The government had spent several generations "educating" a sector of the Indian population to identify its interests with those of the colonial status quo. These people have been trained to see themselves and their nations through the eyes of the colonizer. . . . Now, these, without exception, were the people placed in charge of Indian education by the Education and Self-Determination Act of 1975. . . . So nothing really changed . . . aside from some cosmetic alterations like the inclusion of beadwork, traditional dance, basket weaving and some language classes, the curriculum taught in Indian schools remained exactly the same, reaching exactly the same conclusions, indoctrinating children with exactly the same values as when the schools were staffed entirely by white people. Only now it was supposedly more credible to grassroots people, because people who were visibly Indian were doing the teaching and administering. . . . It's really a perfect system of colonization, convincing the colonized to colonize each other.[25]

In 1978, Congress passed the American Indian Freedom of Religion Act (P.L. 95-341), which eliminated the barriers to free expression of traditional Indian religious rites and beliefs, and the Tribally Controlled Community College Assistance Act (P.L. 95-471), which provided federal funding for Indian community colleges throughout the country.

In 1978, President Jimmy Carter signed into law the Title XI Education Amendments. Part A provided for amendments to Public Law 874 Impact Aid, which allowed Indian parents and tribes to express their approval or disapproval of programs funded under Public Law 874. Furthermore, it allowed tribes participating in the program to file a complaint against a local educational agency, whereby the tribe could contract with the BIA to provide the appropriate programs. Part B had five major sections, providing for (1) the minimum academic standards for American Indian children, which could be waived by local school boards or tribal governments; (2) the implementation of national criteria for dormitories in BIA and contract schools; (3) line authority for the director of the Office of Indian Education over educational personnel; (4) equitable and direct funding for BIA and contract schools; and (5) qualifications and selection procedures of educational personnel. Part C of the Title XI Education Amendments provided for amendments to the Elementary and Secondary Education Act and the Indian Education Act.

The Decade of the Eighties and Beyond

The election of Ronald Reagan to the presidency in 1980 brought about major social budget cuts that affected many American Indian programs, including Indian education. James Watt, Reagan's Secretary of the Interior, shocked Indian country with an interview in 1983:

> We have tremendous problems on the Indian Reservations. I frequently talk about it by telling people if you want an example of the failures of socialism, don't go to Russia—come to America and go to the Indian Reservations. We have 50 million acres of Indian Reservations, 1.4 million American Indians, and every social problem is exaggerated because of socialistic government policies on the Indian Reservations. Highest divorce rate, highest drug rate, highest alcoholism rate, highest unemployment rate, highest social diseases . . . because the people have been trained through 100 years of government oppression to look to the government as the creator, as the provider, as the supplier, and they've not been trained to use their initiative to integrate into the American system.[26]

Once again, American Indians were reminded of days past and policies of assimilation, acculturation, and termination. To add to the concerns of American Indians, Ken Smith, appointed as the Assistant Secretary of the Interior for Indian Affairs by Reagan, reputedly held the attitude that Indian students belonged in the competitive environment of the public schools. Boarding school closures, which had begun under the Carter administration, continued with the Watt-Smith tenure.[27]

In August 1990, a Special Senate Investigating Subcommittee advised the Secretary of the Interior of the need to take aggressive action to improve deficient programs for Indians. During a year of investigative work and weeks of public hearings, the subcommittee reported evidence of the following:

- Corruption in contracting federal projects on Indian reservations
- Child abuse in BIA schools
- Poor management of the Indian Health Service
- Failure by the government to protect land granted to Indians by treaty from encroachment by non-Indians
- Federal projects for non-Indians that had depleted resources on Indian reservations

Senator Dennis DeConcini (Arizona), Chairman of the Senate Subcommittee, stated in response to child abuse in BIA schools, "The BIA has been grossly negligent in protecting the resource that American Indians care about most deeply—their families."[28]

As a result of their investigations, the Special Senate Investigating Subcommittee requested that President George Bush appoint a staffperson in the White House to be in charge of Indian Affairs, but no action was taken on that recommendation.

Jimmie Durham, the founding director of AIM's International Indian Treaty Council, questioned the purpose of Indian education in a speech at Alfred University: "If Indian education really had anything at all to do with the imparting of vocational skills, Indian unemployment wouldn't still be running above sixty percent. . . . The same with 'academics.' They never teach you anything you can do anything with. They just pound enough bogus information into you to get you seriously confused about who you are, who your friends are, how the world really works and what you can or should do about it. As long as you're confused in those ways, you can never pose a threat to those who wield power over you, your people, your land, your future generations. . . . That's the purpose of the Indian education system in this country, and it always has been."[29]

In early 1990, President Bush appointed an Indian Nations At-Risk Task Force to study the status of Indian education in America. In 1992, at the White House Conference on Indian Education, this task force submitted a report on the status and needs of Indian education. President Bush did not address or appear at the conference and made no comment about the report.

Indian education has not been a priority of presidential administrations for the past two decades. At a time when the Indian student population continues to grow, the Congressional Research Service reports that federal funding for Indian education has suffered from a steady decline since 1975.[30] American Indians are hopeful that the policies of the last two decades will be reversed under President Clinton's administration.

Summary

Currently there are 106 BIA elementary and secondary schools and 60 tribally controlled elementary and secondary schools in the country. In 1985, 13,245 Indian students were enrolled in boarding schools. The majority of Indian students, however, are enrolled in public schools.

Despite the changes in government policy from the Colonial period to the decade of the nineties, American Indian tribal groups have maintained their diversity, their culture, and their languages. For the first time in history, many American Indian tribes have local control over their schools as a result of the Indian Self-Determination Act and Title XI. The future is promising, but only time will tell if American Indians can, in fact, effect the changes in education that four centuries of government leadership have not provided. Estelle Fuchs and Robert Havighurst summarized the current situation in Indian education as follows:

> The experiences of the Indian people in recent decades have encouraged dynamic change. The increasing numbers of Indian children in school, the growing enrollment of Indian youth in institutions of higher education, the impact of shattering events such as World War II and the more recent wars in Asia, urbanization, improved communication and transportation, the civil rights movement of the 1960's, and the accompanying federal programs of the 1960's and 1970's—all of these have contributed to the growth and concerns among Indians for education.[31]

Chapter 3

Racism and Stereotyping in Native America

No Indian can grow to any age without being informed that her people were "savages" who interfered with the march of progress pursued by respectable, loving, civilized white people. We are the villains of the scenario when we are mentioned at all. We are absent from much of white history except when we are calmly, rationally, succinctly, and systematically dehumanized. On the few occasions we are noticed in any way other than as howling, bloodthirsty beings, we are acclaimed for our noble quaintness. In this definition, we are exotic curios. Our ancient arts and customs are used to draw tourist money to state coffers, into the pocketbooks and bank accounts of scholars and into support of the American-in-Disneyland promoters' dream.
—P.G. Allen, *The Sacred Hoop: Recovering the Feminine in American Indian Traditions*

The Origins of Stereotypes

There are two key concepts that form the basis of racism. The first is based on the belief that the inherited physical attributes of a particular racial group influence their psychological and intellectual characteristics, as well as their social behavior. Secondly, there is the belief that some racial groups are inherently superior genetically, while others are inherently inferior genetically.

Racism is generally perpetuated through a system of unequal power relationships in private and public institutions and is manifested in the form of prejudice, discrimination, and stereotyping.

A stereotype is an exaggerated set of beliefs about the nature of a particular group of individuals. Thus, race-role stereotypes are beliefs about the nature of individuals within a given racial group. In actuality, these stereotypes do not describe how a racial group differs from the rest of society, but rather how society perceives a particular group or thinks its members behave.

Stereotypes about American Indians often refer to personality traits, which range from such characteristics as being stoic, quiet, strong, and loyal to such traits as being untrustworthy, dishonest, lazy, and indolent. Stereotypes can also be used to describe situations, such as "They all drop out of school," "They all get a monthly check from the federal government," or "They all are drunks."

Similarly, race/sex-role stereotypes are generalizations applied to males or females within a given racial society. Common stereotypes about American Indian women speak to both personality traits and behaviors, such as "They all are passive and submissive" or "They all get monthly welfare checks."

Some stereotypes have no basis in fact, while others may be based at least on a small element of truth. Unfortunately, stereotyping of American Indians, which began at the onset of European contact with indigenous populations, has led to many inaccurate and misleading generalizations that are present in contemporary American society. In order to understand racism and stereotyping and their impact on the women of Native America, it is important to examine various stereotypes and their origins.

A "Vanishing" Race

From the time the Europeans arrived on the North American continent, the Native inhabitants of the Americas were regarded as "primitive" or "savage." Some writers have described this attitude of the whites as one in which the Native populations were perceived as one and the same with the untamed country.[1] Others suggested that the Europeans viewed Indians as morally and spiritually inferior people who were deficient intellectually and culturally.[2] Such prevalent and "acceptable" views regarding the Native peoples of the Americas allowed the Europeans to promote the position that, along with the wild and untamed country, the Native people should also be crushed with the advancement of Western civilization.

While the majority of the white settlers and frontierspeople advocated the taking of lands inhabited by American Indians and the destruction of the people in that process, the federal government opted for a policy directed at educating the American Indians to the ways of the white culture. This policy of assimilation began as early as 1790, when George Washington urged Congress to pass the first Trade and Intercourse Act, designed in part to civilize the Indian people. (A review of the government's efforts to civilize through education is presented more completely in chapter 2.)

The reservation system, which in itself established the segregation of the American Indians from the white population, was an attempt to prepare Indians for entrance into white society.[3] The whites believed that civilization would prevail and that the Indians and their cultures were doomed to extinction through the process of human progress.[4] The Dawes Act, which opened reservation land to white settlement, was further designed to force

American Indians to accept the white culture by coercing them to give up their cultural heritage and to learn farming and other "acceptable" trades.

According to this philosophy, American Indians would either "vanish" into mainstream society or become extinct.[5] This philosophy was further promoted by the establishment of boarding schools around the country, wherein American Indian children were forcibly removed from their parents and reservations and taught the white man's way. Some reformers during this period questioned the boarding school concept as an effective means of acculturation; they felt the schools trained too few Indian youths at too great a cost to the government. This situation was exacerbated by the fact that the majority of the youth returning to their reservations were the objects of ridicule, and their training had little or no application to reservation life. The consequences of this civilized education were poignantly expressed by Zitkala-Sa, an Indian female: "For the white man's papers I had given up my faith in the Great Spirit. For these same papers I had forgotten the healing in trees and brooks. On account of my mother's simple view of life, and my lack of any, I gave her up, also. I made no friends among the race of people I loathed. Like a slender tree, I had been uprooted from my mother, nature and God. . . . But few there are who have paused to question whether real life or long-lasting death lies beneath this semblance of civilization."[6]

The Artist and the Athlete

Despite attempts at civilizing or Americanizing the American Indian in the boarding schools, tribal languages and cultures prevailed to varying degrees on reservations throughout the country. This survival caused many whites to regard the American Indian as racially backward.[7] Others believed the retention of culture implied limited mental capabilities.[8]

When the Bureau of Indian Affairs (BIA) began to implement day schools and on-reservation boarding schools in lieu of off-reservation boarding schools, vocational instruction was given a higher priority than academic curricula. At about the same time, some boarding schools began promoting American Indian arts, such as basketry and painting, as an alternative to vocational courses. This trend was a result of the government's belief that Native arts and crafts could prove remunerative and therefore help support the schools.[9] It was at about this time that the stereotype of American Indians as artists became common among the public. Other observers maintained that Indians excelled in many civilized sports, thus promoting another racial stereotype, in athletics.[10] These stereotypes, with origins in the nineteenth century, continue to label American Indian populations today.

Welfare Ward of the Government

Along with the need to civilize the Indian, the federal government perpetuated the stereotype that the American Indian was incapable and unable to handle his/her own affairs and needed the protection of the government. This image of the childlike savage who is a welfare ward of the state, receives a monthly check from the federal government, and does not have to work is a false stereotype that is commonly held today in mainstream society. This stereotype is fostered today by many in positions of power within the federal government. In 1969, Edgar Cahn pointed out the powerlessness of the American Indian by illustrating the attitude of the "Great White Father" to his "children": "From birth to death his home, his land, his reservation, his schools, his jobs, the stores where he shops, the tribal council that governs him, the opportunities available to him, the way he spends his money, disposes of his property, and even the way in which he provides for his heirs after death—are all determined by the Bureau of Indian Affairs acting as the agent of the United States Government. . . . The BIA defines who is an Indian. It defines tribes and can consolidate tribes at will."[11]

Some writers have observed that freedom for the individual is completely reversed on Indian reservations. This inability to handle one's own affairs perpetuates the stereotype that Indians are incapable of making decisions and managing their own affairs. Warren Cohen and Philip Mause pointed this out succinctly: "Although the normal expectation in American society is that a private individual or group may do anything unless it is specifically prohibited by the government, it might be said that the normal expectation on the reservation is that the Indians may not do anything unless it is specifically permitted by the government."[12]

The "Drunken Indian"

Another source of stereotyping regarding the American Indian, and one that is currently held, has centered on the use of alcohol. This subject has received considerable attention from educators, historians, anthropologists, sociologists, and those in the medical profession. A popular conception held by the white society is that "all Indians are drunks." Early historical works recorded the uncontrolled manner in which otherwise "well-behaved" Indians acted when intoxicated: "One of the first important commodities to be used by the early settlers in trade with the Indians was intoxicating liquors. The Indian was unable to drink in moderation, . . . for the sensation of drunkenness was to him the most attractive feature of the white man's liquor, which was readily able to turn the most peaceful Red Man into a savage of the most ferocious type."[13]

Contemporary studies have further reinforced the stereotype of the "drunken Indian." According to Philip May, "Many behavioral scientists have not questioned the old stereotypes and explanations of behavior extensively enough, and in not doing so they have inadvertently served to reinforce them. These descriptive works coupled with a dearth of explanatory theory have indirectly served to prolong the image of the 'drunken Indian.'"[14]

Others have examined the stereotype of the drunken Indian and found evidence that the stereotype was inaccurate and unsupportable. Just as with other groups, American Indians possess a variety of drinking patterns, and include total abstainers, ex-drinkers, and drinkers.[15] Joseph Westermeyer pointed out that a stereotypical Indian drinking pattern consists of binge drinking over many hours or several days of group party drinking. Although he concurred that this pattern often existed, he was quick to assert that ". . . it has also prevailed among non-Indian groups—frontiersmen, men living together away from a family setting (such as soldiers and lumbermen), conventioneers in a strange city, adolescents and young adults, and homeless single men without regular jobs. Thus, it is not only an 'Indian' pattern."[16]

Westermeyer further suggested that this stereotype has become accepted by both the Indian and the non-Indian, whereby the Indian male has become depicted as ". . . a hopeless, powerless figure who had no alternative to drunkenness with which to cope with poverty, the destruction of his culture and the undermining of his family."[17]

Furthermore, according to Westermeyer, by focusing on alcoholism as the biggest problem among Indians, urgent political and economic issues are ignored. Consequently, this popular stereotype has been perpetuated to the present day.

The "Princess" or the "Squaw"

Throughout history, male scholars and Christian philosophers have often cited the Bible as the basis for concluding that women are inferior to men. Such arguments generally tend to postulate that Eve, who was created from Adam's rib, placed women in a secondary position to men.

Contrary to the masculine deities found in Christianity, Islam, and Judaism, and the corresponding belief in masculine supremacy, virtually all indigenous religions are characterized by feminine elements. Thus, the identity of American Indian women is closely linked to the cosmology and religion of the tribal groups. Attitudes toward gender among tribal groups demonstrate that in both tradition and religion, American Indian females are a primary force. For instance, Grandmother Turtle (Iroquois), Sky Woman (Iroquois), Corn Woman (Cherokee), Spider Woman (Hopi), and White Buffalo Calf Woman (Lakota) serve as a few examples of the importance of females in the tribal societies. Almost every tribal group throughout the Americas has depicted females in similar roles.

The early writers about American Indian life and tribal societies were males who most often came from the ranks of missionaries, explorers, government agents, and trappers. When ethnographers arrived on the scene, they too were male. Therefore, Indian life was recorded by males about males. Even when Indian women were mentioned, it was most likely a stereotypical view influenced by the cultural biases of white upper-class male writers, who held preconceived ideas about the roles of women and their inferiority to males.

Typically, the Indian woman was either glorified as a princess, as in the tale of Pocahontas, or denigrated as a squaw. Indian females were most often described as passive, submissive, and inferior. Their work was trivialized as menial and monotonous, and they were considered beasts of burden or the property of savage males.

Aside from the supposition of unequal status, inherent in this stereotype as well is the racist theme that because one race and sex, namely the white male, is superior to another race and sex, intermarriage will somehow improve the status of the lesser, inferior American Indian female. The roots of this racist thought once again have their origins in Christianity. Racial theorists during the seventeenth and eighteenth centuries argued that people of color were not descendants of Adam and Eve. By the late nineteenth century, scientists suggested that the human race could be divided into biologically distinct races, which were unequal in intelligence and genetics. These scientists, obviously, placed whites at the top of the racial hierarchy, with the right and responsibility to dominate others. The so-called "white man's burden" was a racist mandate for the whites to civilize the savages while at the same time justifying the annihilation of the Indian societies. Although few of today's scientists adhere to the premise of biological inequality among races, the white male-dominant society, the so-called "Good Old Boys," continues to dominate organizations and institutions that promote inequality.

Social scientists Michael Omi and Howard Winant maintain that colonization became a justification for domination of people of color: "At stake were not only the prospects for conversion, but the types of treatment to be accorded them [people of color]. The expropriation of property, the denial of political rights, the introduction of slavery and other coercive forms of labor, as well as outright extermination, all presupposed a worldview which distinguished Europeans . . . from others. Such a worldview was needed to explain why some should be 'free' and others enslaved."[18]

There were a number of reasons for intermarriage between white males and Indian women. First of all, there was a scarcity of white women. Secondly, some believed that intermarriage such as that between John Rolfe and Pocahontas, who was "saved from savagery," could result in salvation for other Indian women. Another reason was the economic benefit to the white male through ties with Indian families; this was especially true of the fur traders. Still another reason, one often suggested, is that marriage (amalgamation) is the final and desired form of total assimilation into the mainstream society.

Despite the varied reasons offered for intermarriage, such unions generally were never condoned. One prominent view, which is still visible today, is the idea that white blood uplifts or improves the Native races. On the other hand, some early writers suggested that the offspring of a mixed marriage exhibited the worst characteristics of both races. Many educators attempted to show that mixed-bloods scored higher on intelligence tests than full-bloods, a finding that has been dismissed as irrelevant, since intelligence tests measure the degree of acculturation more than ability.

While many Americans hated the half-breed, others perceived the offspring of interracial marriages between white and Indian as a marginal person who was caught between two worlds and accepted by neither. Among the fur trading society, half-breed women were the most desirable as mates.

There were those in the American society who believed that racial mixing was contrary to God's teachings and the Bible. Such proponents of racial purity maintained that God had created the white, red, yellow, brown, and black races and that it was a sin against God and his intentions to mix the races. From this perspective, Indian and white marriages were condemned.

This racist, Christian ideology resulted in three distinct stereotypes that to some degree are present in contemporary society, depending upon the geographic region and the social orientations and prejudices of the mainstream group within that region. These stereotypes included "squaw," a derogatory reference to an Indian woman that carried with it the connotation of a demeaned slave; "squawman," a white man who cohabitated with an Indian woman; and "half-breed," the offspring of a union between white and Indian.

While intermarriage between a white male and an Indian female has received much attention in both literature and other media, little has been said about the intermarriage of a white woman and an Indian male. Such relationships were highly condemned and are rarely discussed in journals and writings about gender relations. A commonly held notion, at least among the males in society, was that no self-respecting white female would ever take an Indian man as a husband. Glenda Riley wrote, "Perhaps the topic of white male sexuality is relevant. If a white woman chose of her own free will to marry a native man . . . what was the attraction that influenced their decision . . . women did not stand to gain status, wealth, power, or the approval of society. Could it be then that the supposedly inferior native male, with his assumed minimal ability in the sexual realm, was really not so impotent after all? . . . If white men admitted or even recognized this possibility, their views of their own superiority could be damaged. It might force them to admit that Indians were not so inferior after all, and thus one of the primary rationales for their destructive anti-Indian policies might be undermined."[19]

What is missing from fiction and nonfiction is the description of the Indian female from an Indian perspective. This perspective is very different from the long-established Euro-American view that males are somehow intrinsically and universally dominant and females are intrinsically and universally subordinate. From the Indian perspective, women were regarded as neither inferior nor superior to men. They were simply regarded as different. Both sexes were valued for the contributions they made to their society, and their roles were regarded as complementary rather than competitive. Ella Deloria, a Sioux anthropologist, wrote, "Outsiders seeing women keep to themselves have frequently expressed a snap judgement that they [Indian women] were regarded as inferior to the noble male. The simple fact is that woman had her own place and man his; they were not the same and neither inferior nor superior. The sharing of work also was according to sex. Both had to work hard, for their life made severe demands."[20]

The Indian of the Media

A review of contemporary studies reveals that as a group, American Indians continue to be labeled in misleading, inaccurate terms, which are often derogatory in nature. Many books and "classic" movies depict American Indians in such roles as the "Indian princess," the "white man's helper," the "warrior," and the "noble savage."

Some writers suggest that the Hollywood Indian of the twentieth century was a continuation of the stereotype created in dime-store novels, whereas others argue that the motion picture industry has become more sympathetic to the American Indian since 1950, via increased use of Indian actors and the production of Indian documentaries.[21]

Historically, stereotypical Indians were featured in fiction because the white readers expected certain types of characterizations. The majority of writers presented Indians as drunks, savages, and nomads. Romanticists, however, described them as noble savages or children of nature. C. Adrian Heidenreich suggested that the stereotyped images of the "savage Indian" and the "drunken Indian" in such novels (and subsequent movies) as *Catch-22* (Heller, 1955), *Stay Away, Joe* (Cushman, 1953), *The Big Sky* (Guthrie, 1947), and *Nobody Loves a Drunken Indian* (Huffaker, 1967) have created misunderstanding about the American Indian.[22] For example, scalping, which has been depicted in both films and books, was never attributed to the French and English, who introduced scalping to America. Instead, most contemporary Americans continue to believe that scalping was a tactic of war, attributed to the bloodthirsty savage. There are few Americans who realize that many colonists made a living collecting bounties for scalps, including those of women and children. This part of American history has been conveniently eliminated from books and movies.

Although Hollywood producers in the eighties made some efforts at accurately presenting American Indians and their culture in a more sensitive light, for example, Kevin Costner's *Dances with Wolves*, others perpetuated elements of the stereotypical images, such as in *War Party*, a film whose characters include a drunken medicine man and a group of reckless, suicidal youth, and *Pow Wow Highway*, whose main character is misunderstood by the public and lauded by critics as the "Rainman of Indian Country." More recently, *The Last of the Mohicans*, which has been critically acclaimed as a potential Academy Award nominee, has come under scrutiny by American Indian scholars. The movie, which is loosely based on the popular James Fenimore Cooper novel of the same name, promotes the theme of a "vanishing race," a commonly held belief in Cooper's time, but one that is inappropriate in contemporary society.

Stereotyped Image of Self

Some researchers have maintained that the Indian's image of himself/herself depends upon the image held by the dominant white society.[23] This is apparent in the Pan-Indian movement, which has been described as a synthesis of elements that are considered Indian by all tribes; however, these elements are often closely linked to the white man's stereotype of the Indian. An example of Pan-Indianism is the Plains Indian headdress of eagle feathers, which has become a symbol for all Indians, regardless of their tribal affiliation. Thus, in accepting the headdress as a common symbol, Indians have come to see themselves through the eyes of the white stereotypes.

Other researchers have suggested that because the white man generalized about Indians and identified them with stereotypical characteristics,
factionalism developed among tribal groups. This process perpetuated
another stereotype: that Indians cannot get along with one another and will
always be warlike. Ralph West offered the following comment: "Among
the obstacles to Indian unity are dissensions arising between the Canadian
Indians and the Indians of the United States; between Indians from Michigan and Indians from other sections of the country, between the full-bloods
and mixed-bloods, between Indians with good jobs and Indians with
menial jobs, and between Indians with more schooling and Indians with
less schooling."[24]

Factionalism among tribes and within Indian communities has been
reported by a number of researchers. It has been suggested that factionalism
developed in an effort to preserve tribal identity, but has resulted in
destructive forces within tribes and among tribal groups. Brewton Berry
quoted Don Talayesva, a Hopi, who spoke on the factionalism within his
village around the turn of the century: "Our ancestors had predicted the
coming of these Whites and said that they would cause us much trouble. But
it was understood that we had to put up with them. . . . Those who would
have nothing to do with the Whites were called 'Hostiles' and those who
would cooperate a little were called 'Friendlies.' These two groups were
quarreling over the subject from my earliest memories."[25]

The Problem of Past Stereotypes Promoting Current Ones

Although Indians are a diverse group with vast differences from one tribe
to another, many other generalized stereotypical characteristics are often
commonly attributed to American Indians in contemporary society, including having a relaxed attitude toward work, lacking time consciousness,
possessing stoic bravery and a sense of individual freedom, being oriented
to the present, being emotionally nondemonstrative and reserved, and
living in harmony with nature. Although these generalizations, based
largely on field observations by anthropologists, have little empirical proof,
they have served as a means to conceptualize the differences between
Indians and whites to the present day.[26]

In actuality, there are many misconceptions about American Indians in
contemporary society, including such commonly held perceptions as these:
that Indians lack humor, that Indians are physically indistinguishable from
one tribe to another (in other words, they all look alike), that Indians are
drunks, that Indians are stoic and warlike, and that Indians don't work but
instead live off monthly government checks.

Clearly, past negative stereotypes continue to promote current ones. Although there is some indication that the stereotyping of the American Indian has changed as a result of the development of cultural anthropology, which has promoted cultural pluralism and cultural/moral relativism in twentieth-century America, the new Indian stereotypical paradigm has tended to reinforce the past and traditional Indian stereotypical paradigm.

At the forefront of controversy today in Indian America is the stereotyped Indian mascot used by professional sports teams. Probably no team is more infamous than the Atlanta Braves, whose loyal fans participate in "Indian chants" and the notorious "tomahawk chop" as a means of psychologically terrorizing their opponents. President George Bush managed to incense American Indian tribal groups when he joined Atlanta Brave fans in the "tomahawk chop" during a campaign trip through Georgia in October 1992. Indian writers point out, and rightly so, that if stereotypes about American Indians are to diminish, it will take sensitivity on the part of many people, and especially the President of the United States.

Schools and Stereotyping

Prevalent throughout the history of the education of the American Indian is the philosophy that the Native culture or lack of culture greatly inhibited the academic achievement of Indian students. Murray Wax and his coauthors referred to this belief as the "vacuum ideology," a philosophy of white educators that Indian children come from culturally disadvantaged homes that do not serve as a basis for scholarly activity. Thus, it becomes the responsibility of educators to remove the Indian culture from the student, and to fill the newly created vacuum with Americanized Anglo heritage that would allow for education to occur.[27] Edgar Cahn explained this attitude as one in which failure was expected of the American Indian child and thus the expectation was self-fulfilling. He noted, "If the Indian child fails, it is because he is Indian."[28] In this way, the school insulates itself from taking any of the blame for the failure of American Indian students.

One needs only to examine the early education efforts of Indian females, however, to determine the skills that the dominant society believed essential for the female. Domestic skills, such as sewing, cooking, and homemaking, were the focus of the curriculum in schools for Indian girls. It was believed that this type of education would turn Indian girls into the stereotyped ideal of white womanhood. Any other attention given to the education of Indian women during this early education period was usually for the purposes of promoting civilization among the men. Generally, the attention was prefaced with a description of the deplorable state of Indian women as inferior and second-class citizens to the Indian male, followed by a plea for improving the status of women, which would eventually lead to assimilation. Reverend Jedidiah Morse, who was commissioned by Congress in 1822 to study the "Indian condition," proposed future directions for the education of Indian women. In his report, he suggested that the status of Indian women should be improved: "It is essential to the success of the project of the Government, that the female character among our native tribes be raised from its present degraded state, to its proper rank and influence. This should be a *primary* object with the instructors of Indians. By educating female children, they will become prepared in turn, to educate their own children, to manage their domestic concerns with intelligence and propriety, and in this way, they will gradually attain their proper standing and influence in society."[29]

In retrospect, it appears quite ironic that a white man should raise concern about the status of Indian women. It had been the Euro-American male in prereservation history who had refused to recognize or deal with Indian women who held positions of power in their societies. In addition to Morse, other writers suggested that Indian women should be provided with an opportunity to assume their proper roles in society. Obviously, the "proper roles" were defined as the feminine roles appropriate to Euro-American women: "The savage woman is debarred of the prerogatives, and deprived from exercising the virtues, of her sex, by her wandering life. . . . We would elevate the savage woman to her legitimate place in the social system, and make her the unconscious but most efficient instrument in the civilization of her race."[30]

With the Indian Reorganization Act, new educational opportunities were opened to Indian females. Prior to this time, Indian males and females were totally segregated in schools; however, with the Indian Reorganization Act, education was restructured along more liberal lines. Academic classes were available to both girls and boys. As a result, girls began learning clerical, nursing, and teaching skills, and consequently became more qualified for professional and administrative positions than the males, who were trained mostly in vocational areas such as carpentry and agriculture.

Among the popular stereotypes found in educational research about American Indians are such characteristics as pride, strength, courage, independence, stoicism, and self-sufficiency. In addition, such traits as disliking competition, valuing family relationships, and having little regard or desire for material possessions are commonly addressed in the literature. Research demonstrates that such stereotyping has strongly influenced teachers' attitudes toward Indian children. George Spindler and Louise Spindler reviewed autobiographies and psychologically oriented studies and concluded that there were certain characteristics widely attributed to American Indians, including reserve and self-control, ability to endure pain, positive valuation of bravery and courage, and a fatalistic dependence on supernatural power.[31] All of these characteristics have found their way into the schools and have, over the history of Indian education, contributed to the stereotypical view of teachers and others who work with American Indian populations.

Summary

There were several hundred American Indian tribes living in the United States before the arrival of the Europeans. Each of these tribes had its own language and traditions; however, because of their life-styles, there has been a tendency for American Indians to be regarded as one group in America. In a modern-day perspective, there are 550 Indian tribal and Alaska entities living in the United States today; 509 of those entities are recognized by the federal government. At the same time, it is important to keep in mind that less than half of all people living on reservations today are American Indian. This is mostly the result of federal policy and laws that opened up reservations to white settlement from 1887 to 1934, resulting in the transfer of 90 million acres of reservation land to white people.[32]

That American Indians differ from other minority groups in the United States is best illustrated by three major points:

1. American Indians were the first Americans. They did not arrive in the Americas seeking new identities or new nationalities, as was the case with immigrant groups who settled this country. (Obviously, this distinction does not apply to African Americans, who were forcibly brought to the United States.)
2. American Indian groups have a multitude of distinct languages and cultures, which are different from those of the Europeans who later settled the Americas.
3. Most American Indian tribes hold special treaty relationships with the federal government and are regarded as sovereign nations within the boundaries of the United States.

That the American Indian experience is categorically different from that of the Europeans who settled America is obvious. From the time the Europeans settled the Americas, education for the American Indian has been controlled by the government, with few rights given to parents or tribes. The government promoted the stereotyping of a race of people through policies and educational activities. The Indian Self-Determination Act of 1975 has changed the concept of Indian education. In part, the act recognized the destructive policies of assimilation and termination and validated the right of self-government and control of Indian education by Indian tribes.

Although the impact of the legislation has not been fully realized by American Indian people, for the first time, the transmission of Native languages, culture, and history are legitimate, fundable activities within the context of Indian education. This does not mean, however, that the language, culture, and history of the respective tribal groups have been embraced by the teachers, administrators, and school boards in Indian schools or that stereotypical views within schools have ceased to exist. In fact, within many school districts, there is tremendous resistance to the inclusion of culture, language, and history within the curriculum, and in many others, only minimal accommodations are made. Furthermore, this study demonstrated that stereotypical views about Indians continue to exist in schools and, in turn, impact the views that Indian girls hold about themselves.

Chapter 4

American Indian Dropouts: What the Statistics Say

> When it is considered that our schools are placed among a wild people, who, from the oldest down to the youngest, have never known any control, but have lived independent, idle lives, with no higher law than the whim of the moment, that Indians unfriendly to civilization are constantly instilling into the minds of our pupils suspicion and dissatisfaction, and that "all outside" seems as home to an Indian child habituated to a wild, roving life, and that the runaway is never at a loss, therefore, where to flee to, we may congratulate ourselves that our losses by desertion have been no more than they have been.
>
> —Board of Indian Commissioners, *Report to Congress, 1873*

Despite all the research, we know very little about what makes some American Indian students successful in school and what makes others fail. We know even less about the American Indian female dropout. We do know, however, that dropout rates among American Indian youth have been historically the highest of any minority group and that American Indians are the poorest, have the lowest educational level, live in the worst housing, have the shortest life expectancy, and are the most poorly nourished minority group in the nation. Furthermore, we know that American Indians have the highest infant mortality rate among all ethnic minority groups in America. In 1970, L. Madison Coombs reported that "Indian people have been badly miseducated, have not progressed educationally, and, as a result are at the absolute bottom of the barrel among the country's ethnic minorities and socio-economically disadvantaged groups."[1] The situation, as described by Coombs, has not changed dramatically in the past 20 years. Others have suggested that the ramifications of the lack of education among American Indians guarantee the continuation of poverty and the demise of the American Indian people.[2]

Studies on Indian Dropouts

In 1959, the Bureau of Indian Affairs (BIA) conducted a study on Indian dropouts in BIA boarding schools and concluded that a majority of Indian students drop out because of "poor adjustment to school." Comprising this category were factors of overage, homesickness, parental request, AWOL, and drinking. Students themselves indicated that they dropped out of school because of "financial need" and a "dislike of school." Some students indicated they dropped out because they disliked the teachers or because the teachers were not interested in them. Many of the dropouts reported that they were unable to take part in the social life of the school or to participate in extracurricular activities. A number of the dropouts reported being harassed and embarrassed by other students because of financial needs.

A 1966 study of American Indian students in federal schools showed not only that the dropout rates were high, but that in some schools the dropout rates were traditionally and consistently high, and in others few students finished the eighth grade.[3]

In 1968, the Northwest Regional Educational Laboratory conducted a study on Indian dropouts and reported that the largest percentage of dropouts cited lack of encouragement from the home as the major cause for dropping out; however, lack of encouragement from the school also ranked as a major cause for dropping out. Other causes mentioned included poor financial and home conditions, lack of financial support, misbehavior resulting in expulsion or jail, irrelevancy of school to life, and problems with alcohol or drugs.[4]

Estimates of American Indian dropout rates vary from study to study; however, there is overwhelming evidence that American Indian students claim the distinction of experiencing the highest dropout rate among all ethnic groups.[5]

In 1969, the Senate Subcommittee Hearings on Indian Education reported the national dropout rate for Indian schoolchildren in all types of schools to be about 60 percent. In 1973, the Washington State Commission on Civil Rights estimated that the dropout rate for American Indians ranged somewhere between 38 and 60 percent. The National Advisory Council on Indian Education (1974) listed dropout rates in Nome, Alaska, at 90 percent; in Minneapolis, at 62 percent; and in parts of California, at 70 percent. This was at a time when dropout rates nationally had peaked at 25 percent.

Recent statistics offer little improvement. Testimony at the Governor's Conference in Rapid City, South Dakota, in 1989 reported the dropout rate for the Lakota Sioux Indian students (located on nine reservations) in that state at "more than 50 percent." The State Department of Education in Wyoming (1988) listed the projected American Indian dropout rate within that state at 57.2 percent, as compared to the state average for non-Indians of 20.4 percent. The state of Montana, which has nine language groups and seven reservations, does not report statewide data; however, reports from individual school districts within the state range from 14 to 85 percent.

Theodore Coladarci reported on one high school district in Montana where, in 1980, 60 percent of the American Indian students (who comprised 90 percent of the district's student population) dropped out of school. The dropout level for non-Indians in the state of Montana is less than the national average, hovering at or near 12 percent.[6]

Currently, the American Indian dropout rate has been reported at 30 to 65 percent nationally, depending upon which study one reads. Regardless, this places American Indian youth with the highest high school dropout rate of any ethnic minority group in the country. Researchers have also reported that Indian students who attend boarding schools have especially high dropout rates.[7]

In a national study, *High School and Beyond*, it was reported that of all ethnic groups in America, the dropout rates for American Indians were the highest, at 29.2 percent. Most American Indian educators, however, use caution when quoting this statistic. The study addressed what happened to students from their sophomore to senior years.[8] Educators who work with American Indian students recognize that a high percentage of American Indian dropouts never get to the tenth grade, dropping out somewhere between the seventh- and ninth-grade levels. A Los Angeles dropout study found that 14 percent more males left school earlier than females and that the common reason noted for dropping out among eleventh- and twelfth-graders was overage. On the other hand, a Montana study explored factors relating to American Indian dropouts and reported that the decision to drop out was most often related to teacher-student relationships and teacher attitudes.[9]

A 1986 study of the Oklahoma City Public Schools reported that the most frequent time for students to drop out of school was during the ninth or tenth grade. Of the dropouts, over half were from families with a low socioeconomic background, and the students' most frequent reason for dropping out was lack of interest. Achievement scores of the Oklahoma City dropouts also indicated a history of below-average achievement. Jerry Cavatta reported that male students dropped out more frequently than females and that American Indian students, at least in New Mexico, experienced their highest dropout rate during the tenth grade. In a subsequent study, Cavatta and Albert Gomez reported that American Indian students experienced their highest dropout rates during the ninth grade.[10]

In 1984, researchers reported the seriousness of the dropout problem among American Indians, using the status of New Mexico youth as an example: "New Mexico can serve as a microcosm of the conditions of Native Americans in the United States as a whole. . . . Thirty-two percent of young Native Americans aged 16 to 19 were neither working nor attending school. Less than half of Native Americans older than 25, in fact, had completed high school, compared to more than three-fifths of New Mexico's Blacks and almost three-fourths of whites. Native Americans, indeed, were the only racial/ethnic group in the state whose median level of education was below high school graduation."[11]

Karen Giles argued that cultural conflict is a major factor contributing to dropping out: "As the child becomes increasingly aware of cultural and racial differences, he falls progressively below grade level norms. When the adolescent Indian internalizes his/her differences, feelings of inferiority and hopelessness corrode and disintegrate once-held dreams for a positive future. . . . The Indians' eventual reaction to this cultural differentiation often manifests itself as alienation, poor self-image, withdrawal and, in a word, 'dropout.'"[12]

The social and economic implications of the American Indian dropout have had little impact on the nation as a whole and have therefore received less attention by economists, educators, and politicians. The federal government, which is responsible for the funding of education for American Indians, even to varying degrees in public schools, has not chosen to publicly make an issue of the failures of an education system under its supervision. Politicians, who do not view the American Indian population as a strong political force, have long ignored the issue. American Indians themselves, in the last two decades, can share part of the blame for participation in an educational system that has perpetuated failure among their people.

Norbert Hill, an Oneida educator, reported that the American Indian high school dropout rate exceeds 65 percent nationally and that between 75 and 93 percent of postsecondary Indian students drop out; he pointed out that these statistics are only for students who leave school, and suggested that there are hundreds who "effectively drop out of school and physically never miss a day." Hill attributed dropping out to apathy and anomie: "Our survivors as well as our drop-outs of the formal education system have been forced into compliant, obedient roles which delimit the skill and confidence to manage the complexity of their lives and our future. . . . The drop-out problem is a problem of the dysfunctional education system which marginalizes students because of a narrow and discriminatory social, political and economic agenda."[13]

The American Indian Female Dropout

Inquiry was initiated in 1975 on educational equity for Indian women and girls in . . . federally funded programs by the National Advisory Council on Women's Education Programs. Testimony . . . indicated that Title IX,

the chief federal law prohibiting sex discrimination in all federally-assisted education programs, was neither understood nor enforced.
—O. Anderson, Ed., *American Indian–Alaskan Native Women's Caucus Newsletter*

Although there is a plethora of research that attempts to explain the lack of success of the American Indian in the educational system, research on American Indian females within the educational setting is almost nonexistent.

The National Center for Education Statistics study *High School and Beyond* surveyed 30,000 sophomores and 28,000 seniors in high schools throughout America. The purpose of the study was to provide descriptive information about the dropout rates among various subgroups in the country. The study reported dropout rates for American Indian males and females, along with other racial/ethnic groups, including Hispanics, Blacks, whites, and Asian Americans. Results of the study indicated that whereas American Indians have the highest dropout rate in the country, American Indian females have the highest dropout rates for all groups, whether male or female. The study reported the dropout rate for American Indian females at 31.8 percent, followed by Hispanic females at 18.0 percent, Black females at 14.1 percent, white females at 11.5 percent, and Asian American females at 2.7 percent. In addition, the study reported a 27.2 percent dropout rate for American Indian males.[14] Current estimates place the overall dropout rate of American Indians at 50 percent or above. It has also been estimated that American Indian girls constitute approximately 54 to 60 percent of those statistics.[15]

Given research that demonstrates the correlation between high school graduation and future income, it is not surprising that the majority of American Indian women fall below the poverty level. Twenty-five percent of American Indian females in 1980 had not completed high school or a GED, as compared to 16 percent of white women.[16] It is a given that minority women in America face double discrimination in the workplace, and employment opportunities for American Indian women are affected by their educational background. Statistics show that 86 percent of American Indian women, more than any other racial/ethnic group, earn less than $5,000 per year.[17] Whereas it is often noted that the white female in America earns 59 cents for every dollar a man earns, the American Indian female earns only 89 percent of what white females earn. In addition, almost two-thirds of American Indian women hold part-time jobs, while at the same time facing the highest rate of unemployment in the nation.[18]

According to data from the 1980 census, only 35 percent of American Indian women are employed in the work force, the lowest percentage for any racial/ethnic group. In addition, 25 percent of American Indian families are headed by a single parent, compared to less than one-fifth of all families in the United States. Further, it was found that American Indians have the highest birthrate of all minority groups in the country, and that American Indian families are three times more likely than whites to live in poverty.[19]

Few studies on American Indian students have distinguished between male and female attitudes, achievement, or perceptions. Estelle Fuchs and Robert Havighurst found that on the whole, American Indian adolescents felt slightly more favorable toward their teachers than Anglo-American youth of approximately the same socioeconomic status. However, their study indicated that American Indian girls were more critical of teachers than boys. Other researchers report that Indian girls are more likely to drop out than males, and that pregnancy is a major factor for dropping out among Indian females, with 12 percent of the dropouts occurring between the eighth and ninth grades.[20]

In the area of self-concept, American Indian girls appear more likely than boys to show a significant decrease in self-esteem from preadolescence to adolescence. Further study demonstrates that American Indian girls also rate themselves less favorably on self-concept measures than Anglo girls. In addition, there seems to be a tendency for Indian girls to be more self-critical and self-doubting than Indian boys on self-concept inventories. Other researchers have observed that among white, Mexican, and American Indian youth, American Indian females reported a more negative self-esteem. In a study of Sioux children in grades four to eight, results indicated that boys possessed higher self-esteem than girls at all grade levels except for the fourth grade. Further, it has been found that American Indian girls attending public schools had lower self-esteem than Indian girls in BIA schools.[21]

Interviews conducted with forty-six Indian students who had dropped out of school in Montana indicated that American Indian female dropouts reported more frequently than boys that teachers did not care about them. However, 48 percent of the females reported problems at home as a salient factor in dropping out.[22]

Some researchers maintain that the major factor contributing to the at-risk status of American Indian females is the abuse of alcohol. A review of the Indian Health Service records shows that three out of every seven teenage alcohol abusers are female. National drinking patterns survey data suggest that more Indian boys drink than girls and that among fifteen- to seventeen-year-olds, 60 percent of the males drink, compared to 40 percent of the girls. It is commonly reported that there are no significant attitudinal differences between sexes about drinking, although there are behavioral differences. It appears that there is a stronger community sanction for young Indian women that mitigates displays of drunkenness. Some researchers report that a child's gender affects parental standards regarding drinking and note that Indian parents maintain more restrictive standards for their daughters than for their sons.[23]

Today, Indian country is attempting to address alcohol abuse among young Indian women of childbearing age, which may lead to another dilemma: the increasing number of Fetal Alcohol Syndrome (FAS) and Fetal Alcohol Effects (FAE) births on Indian reservations. It has been estimated that in excess of 10 FAS births per 1,000 births could be attributed to Plains Indian groups. FAS is believed to be the second most frequent cause of birth defects in the United States and the leading cause of mental retardation. This fact alone contributes to a concern that Indian education, which has historically been burdened with high dropout rates, may, in fact, be further taxed by the entry of a population into the schools who will require special services and perhaps even institutionalization at the expense of limited educational budgets.[24]

Summary

Although American Indian youth, male and female, experience many of the same pressures as other minority groups, the history of Indian education in America and the unique position of American Indian tribes allow insight into the condition of the American Indian female. As a result, the issue of the status of at-risk American Indian youth will be discussed thoroughly in chapter 5, in an effort to shed some light on the factors that researchers claim have a major impact on the American Indian student.

Chapter 5

What Places American Indian Students at Risk?

Life for Indian adolescents is not easy. They are faced with poverty, poor educational systems, prejudice from the majority culture, and in general a disheartening outlook for the future. . . . It will be extremely difficult to change the future of these young people—to offer them a reasonable chance for personal and economic success.
—F. Beauvais, E.R. Oetting, and R.W. Edwards, "Trends in Drug Use of Indian Adolescents Living on Reservations: 1975–1983"

In a national longitudinal study of eighth-grade students in 1988, Harold Hodgkinson identified eight major factors contributing to the dropout problem for American Indian youth:

1. Twenty-nine percent of the Indian eighth-graders had repeated a grade at least once.
2. Nineteen percent of the Indian eighth-graders expected to drop out of school before graduating.
3. Eleven percent of the eighth-grade Indian students missed five or more days of school during a four-week period.
4. Only 17 percent of the eighth-grade Indian students were planning to enroll in a college preparatory curriculum, as compared to 37 percent for Asian Americans, 31 percent for whites, 25 percent for Black Americans, and 22.5 percent for Hispanics.
5. Thirty-one percent of the Indian students reported living in single-parent homes, as compared to 17 percent of the white children.
6. Limited English was reported by 8.6 percent of the Indian students, as compared to 8.8 percent for Hispanic students, 7.1 percent for Asian Americans, and 1.6 percent for Black Americans.
7. Fifteen percent of the eighth-grade Indian students reported having an older sibling who had dropped out of school.
8. Nineteen percent of the Indian students reported being home alone more than three hours a day.[1]

In many ways, American Indian students who drop out mirror the larger society of student dropouts. They come from a distinct ethnic group;

they are often from low-income families; they frequently come from one-parent homes; the educational levels of their parents and older siblings often stop short of high school completion; they have often experienced repeated failure in school; they may be the products of dysfunctional families and physical and emotional abuse; they may come from homes where a language other than English is spoken; they may come from a family where drug and alcohol abuse is present; they may have experienced a variety of forms of racism, stereotyping, or discrimination from early childhood; and, for female students, they may become pregnant during their adolescent years. On the other hand, many of the students who stay in school and graduate and even complete college come from identical backgrounds.

What Researchers Say about Indian Dropouts

Most of the literature on American Indian education and the dropout problem has been confined to qualitative, ethnographic studies. A common theme throughout the research addresses the cultural differences and/or "cultural deprivation" of the American Indian child, the racial biases of white teachers, the negative self-image of American Indian children, drug/alcohol abuse, and language barriers.[2] American Indian students have often been the subject of cross-cultural research in which a comparison of the American Indian cultural values and the dominant American cultural values is made. Often this research suggests that American Indian students fail in school because of a value system that is different from the ideology within the school system. Other researchers maintain that the educational goals of schools are fashioned toward the competitive achievement orientation of the American middle class and the attainment of material wealth. There is some evidence to support the fact that American Indians are willing to compete with their own past performances, but not with the performance of others. One researcher reported that while American Indian students often desire material things, the means to the end is vague, and that the delayed and obscure rewards of education are not associated with academic achievement in school. Some have gone so far as to maintain that scholastic competition is not valued in many American Indian homes, and thus failure in school is a given. Still other researchers have addressed the patterns of socialization of American Indian students and how these patterns differ from those of the white dominant society, thereby further undermining the American Indian child within the school setting.[3]

The Correlates Associated with Dropping Out

There are literally hundreds of sources in the literature that discuss American Indian dropouts; however, there is relatively little research that addresses the reasons for dropping out. Nationally, there are three general correlates identified with dropping out. One correlate addresses personal problems of youth that tend to be independent of class and family background, including the following:

- Substance abuse (alcohol and/or other drug use and abuse)
- Problems with the law
- Low self-esteem and lack of self-identity
- Peer pressure
- Mental health problems such as depression (suicidal tendencies)
- Pregnancy

A second correlate shows the relationship between dropping out and family background, including these factors:

- Socioeconomic status
- Educational level of parents
- Child-rearing practices
- Single-parent families
- Dysfunctional families (including those in which child abuse occurs)

The final correlate addresses school factors, including these:

- Bilingualism
- Cultural differences and cultural discontinuity
- Academic achievement and failure, including grade retention and tracking
- Attendance: truancy, absenteeism, detention, and expulsion
- Teacher attitudes and expectations
- Racism, discrimination, and prejudice

It is important to examine the research related to the three major correlates addressed in dropout literature (personal problems, family background, and school factors), as these are often attributed to the failure of American Indian youth. More importantly, however, a review of this literature serves to demonstrate that for each major correlate and subtopic area, many of the studies overlook the complex nature of school failure for

American Indian youth. For example, simply correlating the presence of alcohol-abusing parents with dropping out does not mean that such students will drop out; yet a student with such a home background will often be targeted as high risk by educators relying upon common identifiers of high-risk youth. Similarly, students who do not possess these common identifiers are often overlooked, although they may be at risk as well. Furthermore, an examination of past research demonstrates the notion that dropping out is often explained by pointing to factors inherently wrong with the child and not the system. This is particularly true of research conducted on American Indian dropouts.

Correlate 1: Personal Problems of American Indian Youth

A number of factors have been identified as personal problems of youth at risk of dropping out of school. These factors (substance abuse, problems with the law, low self-esteem, peer pressure, mental health problems, and teen pregnancy) impact a high percentage of American Indian youth, if not directly, often indirectly. A review of the literature in each of these areas is pertinent to understanding the research conducted into the world of the American Indian child.

Substance Abuse

Substance abuse is clearly a problem among American Indian youth, as is the case with other racial and ethnic groups, including the mainstream, dominant society youth. Some research indicates that American Indian youth are particularly at risk due to biological predispositions, as well as environmental factors wherein a high percentage of the adult population drinks or uses drugs. An examination of the research conducted in this area provides insight into the use and abuse of alcohol and drugs among American Indian adolescents and why some researchers suggest that substance abuse contributes to dropping out.

Alcohol Use and Abuse. Alcohol is clearly the most abused substance among American Indian youth and has been linked to the high rates of suicide, accidents, crimes, dropping out, and birth defects. Over 75 percent of deaths among the American Indian population are related to alcohol abuse.

Still, there are tremendous gaps in the research about the extent and nature of alcohol abuse among American Indian youth, and much of the research conducted before 1983 is characterized as inconclusive, lacking in detail, and inadequate for either theoretical or practical purposes. Furthermore, it was conducted on adult males rather than adolescents.

The most extensive study about American Indian adolescents and alcohol has been conducted by researchers at Colorado State University. They have reported that more than a third of American Indian adolescents use marijuana and alcohol on a regular basis, compared to 5 percent regular users among non-Indians.[4]

Other researchers have reported that Indian youth often begin using alcohol between the ages of eleven and thirteen and that between 56 and 89 percent of Indian youth from most tribes report experimentation with alcohol.[5]

Adult substance abuse is common and visible on the reservations, exposing American Indian youth to negative adult role models. Reportedly, there is a strong correlation between parental drinking and student drinking, and children who have older siblings who drink are more likely to abuse alcohol and drugs. Some researchers have observed a statistically significant relationship between high levels of family drinking and alcohol abuse among these families' children in later life, whereas other researchers have maintained that substance abuse may not be regarded as deviant behavior among American Indian youth, due to the frequency of exposure in their daily lives.[6]

Two studies in Montana found alcohol to be a major factor in the high dropout rates among American Indian males. In a survey of seven reservations in Montana, 33 percent of the juveniles ages nine to twelve were regular drinkers, and alcohol abuse was listed as the main reason that one in every two American Indian students in Montana did not graduate from high school. In another Montana study, approximately one-third of the dropouts reported peer pressure in the use of drugs and alcohol as a salient factor in the decision to drop out of school. Other researchers have reported heavy drinking to be the reason that one in two American Indian students nationwide never finish school.[7]

Some researchers have suggested that drinking patterns among Indian adolescents point to the stresses of acculturation and maintain that Indian youth have a negative self-identity as a result of their acculturation experiences. Generally, the highest levels of alcohol abuse occur among American Indian adolescents who are acculturated and identify with non-Indian values, and the lowest levels of abuse have been found among students who express an adaptability to both Indian and non-Indian values. It is generally believed that American Indian adolescents from tribal groups with strong cultural identification are less apt to be involved in substance abuse.[8]

There is little research on alcohol abuse and American Indian women or girls. One researcher wrote, "In the case of women, the attitude is quite different. In some situations and among some groups women are also under pressure to drink. In general, however, the woman who does not drink is respected and the woman who drinks is criticized."[9]

One important consideration in the relationship of Lakota males and females is the pressure of the peer group for the male to continue drinking. This behavior often leads to the dissolution of the male-female relationship. There is some indication that the male-female drinking relationships begin in the adolescent years, although it is reported that women drink less than men.[10]

It is well known that adolescent drinking is common among neglected children, and that children with drinking parents often drink with them. It has been estimated that approximately 50 percent of married couples drink, with 40 percent of those marriages ending in divorce. The loss (death) of a relative is often an acceptable occasion for adolescent drinking, but it is generally noted that heavy drinking by teenagers occurs at high school weekend parties and that the drinking remains intermittent until the student graduates from or drops out of school.

Researchers have also found that there is a great deal of social pressure to drink. This pressure is often applied in the form of joking or teasing. According to Joyce Stevens, who conducted a study on drinking among the Blackfeet for her master's thesis, "Not to drink with a group is a public indication that one wishes not to be associated with its members which, in turn, is an indication that these individuals are of inferior station, since traditionally one avoided association with one's social inferiors."[11]

A number of researchers have reported strong peer support for substance abuse and have observed significant relationships between peer associations and alcohol involvement. In addition, there is an indication that peer groups among American Indian youth not only sanction drinking, but expect it.[12]

Other influences related to drinking among American Indian youth have been suggested. Some researchers have attempted to show the relationship of culture and the use of alcohol and suggest the rationale for drinking among the Sioux is linked to the concept of "power." Among the Sioux, the search for power was a process of self-actualization. Through religious ceremonies, which included fasting, the senses were altered to bring about a vision. It has been suggested that drinking substitutes for the visionary experience; however, most American Indians disregard such theories. Other researchers have related the high incidence of alcohol abuse to instability in the home and family or the exorbitant amounts of free time, which results in substance abuse as a means of coping with boredom among reservation youth.[13]

More than any other minority group in America, Indian adolescents suffer from more substance-related problems, such as unemployment, trouble with the law, increased morbidity and mortality, lack of opportunity, hopelessness, poverty, and dysfunctional families.[14] How these factors contribute to dropping out among American Indian females is discussed in part 2 of this book.

Other Drug Use and Abuse. Most research has shown that Indian youth on the reservations use drugs more frequently than non-Indian youth, particularly marijuana, inhalants, and stimulants; however, reliable research on drug use and abuse among American Indians is not readily available, in most cases. A few studies have indicated the seriousness of the problem.[15]

Drug abuse and dependence have been reported to be the fourth most frequent reason for Indian Health Service (IHS) outpatient visits, and those under the age of thirty-nine account for 72 percent of the visits. Research among military inductees from ages seventeen to twenty-two indicates a higher rate of drug use among Indians when compared to other racial and ethnic groups. After alcohol, marijuana is the next most popular drug among American Indian youth. Although studies indicates that there is a wide intertribal variation, between 41 and 62 percent of American Indian adolescents have tried marijuana, as compared to 28 to 50 percent of other youth.

In a study of marijuana use among American Indian and Caucasian youth, researchers concluded that whereas drug attitude was the best predictor of drug involvement for white adolescents, grade level and peer-group patterns were the strongest predictors of the level of Indian youth involvement. "Certainly the Indian youth is faced with many of the same pressures of adolescent life that confront his or her Caucasian counterpart," the researchers noted. "But there are more. He or she is a minority group member growing up in a hostile social environment. A growing awareness of the limitations and restrictions that society has placed on him or her—combined with conflicts involving parents, peers and the law about drugs—may result in lowered perceptions of the risks of marijuana smoking. The end product of these processes conceivably is an isolated, frustrated, disoriented individual who might turn to drugs as an escape from both a disintegrating and depressing aboriginal world, and an uncaring and disinterested outside world."[16]

In an IHS survey, 59 percent of Indian seventh- to twelfth-graders in 1985 reported marijuana use. Other researchers have observed that Indians experience a lifetime preference for marijuana at twice the level of non-Indians and that marijuana use approaches the level of alcohol use in the adult Indian populations.

Inhalant abuse has been identified as a problem in American Indian communities and in Bureau of Indian Affairs (BIA) boarding schools.

Widespread gasoline sniffing among American Indian children has been reported. This problem has most often been identified with younger children to whom other drugs are not available, generally occurring at about the same time as cigarette smoking. American Indian youth reportedly have the highest prevalence rates of usage. It is estimated that 17 to 22 percent of Indian youth use inhalants, compared to 9 to 11 percent of non-Indians. Between 1983 and 1985, the use of inhalants decreased among Indian youth, although it continued to be more prevalent than in the non-Indian population. Recent research, however, has reported an increase in inhalant abuse.[17]

The prevalence of inhalant abuse is a major concern, in that adolescents who begin substance abuse with inhalants are more likely to become involved with more serious drugs than those whose first experimentations are with alcohol or marijuana.[18]

There have been some suggestions that the American Indian culture bears a relationship to the use of drugs among the youth. Most American Indian tribes, like other native cultures, practice rituals of healing that have included drug use; however, these drugs have rigidly prescribed roles in religious and healing ceremonies. Tobacco, for example, was a ceremonial, not a recreational, drug in early American Indian traditions. There is no place in the traditional American Indian cultures for the recreational or personal use of drugs, and such explanations for drug use among American Indian youth should be discounted. As noted by Lewayne Gilchrist and colleagues, "High levels of drug and alcohol use are not the result of anything inherent in Indian tradition."[19]

Although culture may in fact contribute to drug and alcohol use, the impact of culture on different groups must be considered carefully. For example, some observers note that "angry Anglo youth" tend to be more deviant and use drugs more frequently. In contrast, studies show that "angry American Indian youth" most often have greater pride and self-esteem and are less likely to use drugs. In fact, it has been found that whereas marijuana use among whites was related to liberal attitudes, it was not so for Indian youth.[20]

Likewise, it has also been suggested that American Indian youth take drugs because of the stress created by acculturation in the Anglo society or cultural conflict. However, much research clearly shows that the same factors causing drug abuse among other minority groups in the United States cause high drug use among American Indian youth, including peer pressure, poverty, racism, family problems, and dysfunctional behaviors. For example, it has been found that Indian youth readily shared their drugs and alcohol, since the major reasons for their use of these substances were social ones and peer-group acceptance/pressure. These findings are consistent with those regarding other racial groups in the United States.[21]

A number of researchers have noted strong support for drug use among peer groups. It appears that Indian youth are confronted with a dual problem of having many peers who encourage them to use drugs and many others who do not stop them from using drugs. It is generally agreed that peer use, peer attitudes, and peer acceptance are probably the greatest determinants in drug use by Indian youth. Dysfunctional families also appear to be a strong influence in drug abuse among adolescents.[22]

It has been noted that inhalant abuse is most prevalent in isolated communities, including Indian reservations, suggesting that drugs are often a solution to boredom for Indian youth.[23]

Problems with the Law

In 1775, Benjamin Franklin wrote in *Poor Richard's Almanac,* "The savages have a society where there is no force, there are no prisons, no officers to compel obedience or inflict punishment."[24] The lack of crime among the American Indian tribes has often been reported by missionaries and historians, who came into contact with Indians prior to the reservation system. A number of tribes had codes of justice requiring that a tribal member make repayment for an injury or a wrong caused another tribal member. Stan Steiner noted that the Indian "owed no debt to society" as such. Instead, an indemnity was paid that was thought of as justice to the wronged, not as punishment for the wrongdoer. However, as Steiner noted, this situation has changed since postreservation days: "Long ago these laws of the ancients ceased to govern the Indians. The legal codes of the modern tribes are ruled and judged by the rituals and laws of the white men, or by imitations. Economically and politically the needs of the dominant society have been successfully imposed upon the tribes—and the tribal morality has had to accede to these. . . . Laws, in any event, are enforced that require the Indians to conform to the necessities of technological life. And they do, at least on the surface."[25]

Research is vague, conflicting, and in many cases nonexistent about American Indian youth and their problems with the law. The majority of arrest rates on or near reservations are the result of excessive drinking or driving a car while intoxicated. Similarly, automobile accident records involving citations and sometimes resulting in death for drivers and passengers are frequently reported as the consequence of alcohol. Domestic fights, or simply "fighting," are among the second highest cause for arrests on the reservations. And although violence in the form of "fighting" or "quarreling" is regularly recorded, even among the youth, violence rarely results in murder, maiming, or serious injury to another individual.

A number of researchers have demonstrated the correlation between dropping out of school and juvenile delinquency. Others have found that failure to graduate from high school is a predictor of adult criminal behavior. Not only does research on American Indians indicate that their arrest rates are higher than those of the population at large, but much of the research reveals that the high arrest rates off the reservation are often closely related to discrimination, racial prejudice, or behaviors that may be acceptable within the Native culture but unacceptable to mainstream society.

The Indian arrest rate per 100,000 population is twelve times that of the white race and three times that of the Black race.[26] One writer pointed out appalling facts about American Indians and the prison system, including that (1) one out of three Indians will be jailed in his/her lifetime; (2) every other Indian family will have a relative die in jail; and (3) in areas where Indians live, despite the fact that they may be the minority, they often represent the majority of arrests. One county in Nebraska was found to have an Indian population of 28 percent but a county arrest record that was 98 percent American Indian. The National Clearinghouse on Alcoholism has indicated that almost 100 percent of all crimes for which an Indian is incarcerated were committed under the influence of alcohol.[27]

Juvenile Delinquency. Uniform Crime Reports, which is published annually, indicates that delinquency rates for American Indians are higher than for the general American population; however, this generalization should be treated with extreme caution, as the majority of court appearances for Indian youth are for relatively minor offenses. When comparing juvenile delinquency rates in the nation as a whole, American Indian youth have the lowest rate for serious offenses.

Very little research has been published on juvenile delinquency or crime within the contemporary American Indian culture; however, some researchers have found that delinquency rates are higher when compared to those among the general population but that offenses committed by Indian youth are misdemeanors or petty offenses. Other studies have found that alcohol played a major role in Indian delinquency; still others have related social and economic problems to crime.[28]

Some of the research on American Indian delinquency has been conducted in BIA boarding school settings. An examination of rule violations among three tribal groups of students in a southwestern boarding school found that violations were consistently related to tribal background. Sixty-four percent of the violations involved the use of alcohol. The authors suggested that their findings supported a tribal cultural deviance interpretation of Indian crime and delinquency, rather than family disorganization or failures of socialization. The most frequent categories of offenses for reservation youth were drunkenness and disorderly conduct. Unlike the high rate of auto theft among juveniles in the general population, this category was extremely low on the reservation.[29]

Other studies on boarding school populations have found that delinquent behavior increased with exposure to cultural conflict. For example, in an Alaska Native boarding school, violence and antiwhite militancy increased when the Native school was consolidated with a town high school.[30]

Other attempts at explaining the inordinately high rate of juvenile offenses have focused on alcohol. In fact, the public versus private nature of Indian adolescent drinking "parties," in part, seems to explain the high arrest rate among Indian youth. Others have suggested that the youthfulness of the Indian population contributes to delinquency. Seventy percent of the American Indian population is below the age of thirty, which would account for higher rates of crime relative to those of other populations, whose members are older.[31]

Researchers have found that fear of arrest from using drugs is often a deterrent for white youth, but that just the opposite is true in dealing with American Indian youth. American Indian youth are unlikely to accord much respect for drug-control laws, which they define as the "white man's law." This attitude is a result of lack of full integration by the Indian into the white society. It is often suggested that the high racial visibility off the reservation and close community life serve as primary controls to limit and deter juvenile delinquency, and in reservation communities with increased juvenile delinquency, such offenses may be the result of the loss of communal discipline. It is a well-known fact that although the nuclear family members guide children in good behavior, they do not force them, as coercion is alien to Indian familial traditions.[32]

A study on the Wind River Reservation in Wyoming compared Anglo and Indian self-reports of delinquency among high school students and found that they did not differ significantly, except that Indian girls ran away from home more frequently than white girls and Indian boys reported more school-centered offenses than white boys. However, Indian youth court appearances were about five times as high as the general U.S. rate, although the Indian youth in the study did not engage in more delinquent acts than the whites. A vast majority of the appearances were for misdemeanors.[33]

Cultural Differences and Crime. There is some evidence that a cultural phenomenon exists within the Native cultures among Indian youth in their teens to early twenties. This group, which one researcher characterized as "people who like to raise hell," refers to youth who engage in activities that carry a risk of encountering trouble or adversity. These difficulties not only are physical dangers, but also include legal entanglements. This self-identified group did not engage in these activities all of the time, but during their leisure hours they tended to look for "the action," which was found in bars and at drinking parties. They asserted their toughness by possessing qualities for effective fighting, including strength, speed, coordination, and mastery of fighting techniques. The researcher concluded that often what results in trouble with the law for American Indians is acceptable behavior within their culture, but unacceptable to the mainstream culture. This premise is generally accepted by researchers who point out that American Indians are often arrested for alcohol-related behavior that they consider socially and morally acceptable but that the dominant society considers unacceptable and deems illegal. Therefore, it can be concluded that the arrest rates of American Indians indicate intercultural discontinuities, as well as other factors.[34]

Vandalism by American Indian youth has been explained by some as a conflict between the white man's obsession with the value of material objects and the Indian's indifference to material things. It has been maintained that material objects have little value to Indians and that parents will watch passively as their children vandalize objects. Others have suggested that the vandalism in school is a "testing of reality," in that the authorities tell the Indians that the school is "theirs," but that American Indian youth doubt the statement and, as a result, expose the pretense by engaging in vandalism of the school and school property.[35]

The Justice System and the American Indian. The administration of justice constitutes an area where Indians have reportedly encountered significant civil rights problems. There have been a number of studies that have involved the administration of justice by law enforcement officers. For example, the South Dakota Advisory Committee of the U.S. Commission on Civil Rights found evidence of selective law enforcement, harassment, searches without cause, and discourtesy toward Indians by police officers. Further, studies have revealed allegations of abuse of Indian prisoners in jail. There have also been allegations that some towns and cities, where Indians are routinely arrested, use Indian prisoners as cheap labor.

Other practices of the criminal justice system that serve as disadvantages to American Indians have been studied. In the Dakotas, studies showed that Indians are not as likely as others to become jurors, because juries are selected from voter registration lists or licensed drivers lists.[36] Results of studies indicated that lawyers believe the routine exclusion of Indians from juries negatively affects the ability of Indians to receive a fair trial. Studies in border towns near reservations showed disparate patterns in fines and sentencing, to the detriment of American Indians. In the state of Washington, for example, arrest rates are reportedly higher among American Indians than among any other racial group, and Indians in that state are the least successful group regarding parole situations. It has also been documented that Indians in most states receive longer sentences than whites.[37]

Most crime-related activities among American Indians are often attributed to "marginality." Indian males in their twenties or early thirties who are experiencing problems with social adjustment and tension and who drink alcohol are most likely to be arrested. Discrimination within the justice system is also a major problem. Two researchers studied the types of sentences given to whites and Indians and concluded that the differences in sentencing were related to ethnicity. In other words, an American Indian is more likely to receive a harsher sentence than a white.[38]

Given the research, I contacted administrators in state prisons in Wyoming, Montana, and South Dakota (three states with large Indian populations and the location of this study) to determine if there was a disparity among Indian and non-Indian prison populations and to identify data on the educational level of prisoners. Responses to inquiries varied considerably, from helpfulness to indifference. According to 1988 Wyoming State Penitentiary statistics, American Indians represent 5.3 percent of the prison population, which is more than twice the Native population (2 percent) in the state. Of the American Indians imprisoned, 58 percent had not received a high school diploma. The American Indian population in the South Dakota prison system is approximately 35 percent of the total prison population, which is more than five times the total Indian population of the state (approximately 6 percent). No data were available on the educational level of the prisoners; however, over 50 percent were reported to be involved in a voluntary GED program. The state of Montana reports that information concerning ethnicity of the state's prison population is strictly voluntary, and detailed records of the American Indian prison population or their educational levels were unavailable.

There are little data regarding delinquency on the reservation, and what data are available are often subject to varied interpretations. Informal discussions with police officers and judges indicate, however, that a high percentage of these American Indian youth do encounter problems with the law, and adults incarcerated in state prisons have more often than not dropped out of high school. When consideration is given to the studies that demonstrate disparity of treatment of Indians by law enforcement officers and the court system, and the cultural acceptance of behaviors considered inappropriate to mainstream society, American Indian youth become even more at risk.

Low Self-Esteem and Lack of Self-Identity

Success in school is often highly correlated to self-concept and self-identity. Research generally indicates that American Indian students have lower self-esteem than students from other racial/ethnic groups and that they have more difficulty in establishing ethnic and tribal self-identity and pride in their Indianness.

Low Self-Esteem.   Poor self-esteem has frequently been attributed to the failure of American Indian children in school.   Howard Bahr and his colleagues described the problem of poor self-esteem of American Indian youth as follows: "There is much evidence that Indian students feel despair, disillusionment, alienation, frustration, hopelessness, powerlessness, rejection, and estrangement, all elements of negative views of the self."   Other researchers have discovered that Indian youth had far less conviction that they could affect their own environments and futures than other racial groups.[39]

Many of the studies on self-esteem and the American Indian have compared the American Indian child to a white counterpart.   This research consistently reports that American Indians have lower scores on conventional tests of self-esteem than whites.[40]   Other researchers argue that such differences are misleading because the attributes assessed by the self-esteem tests are important to white students, but not to American Indian children.   Some researchers report that dropping out of school results in short-term improvement in self-esteem.[41]

Others have suggested that American Indian children are unable to cope with feelings of inferiority and hopelessness, the result of increasing awareness of cultural and racial differences, and therefore drop out of school before graduation.[42]

Estelle Fuchs and Robert Havighurst concluded in a national study of American Indian youth that the great majority of Indian youth saw themselves as competent individuals within their social world.   Their study showed that American Indian youth look to their futures with optimism and hope and that there was no evidence that they suffered from feelings of alienation, frustration, and hopelessness.[43]   In another study, a high majority of Indian youth saw themselves as competent individuals within their own social world but demonstrated some self-doubts in the non-Indian world.   As the researchers noted, "The self-esteem and self-concept data from our study indicate that the great majority of Indian youth see themselves as fairly competent persons within their own social world. This social world is characterized for the majority of these young people by Indianness and by poverty. If they come into contact with expectations by teachers or others from the social world of the urban-industrial and middle-class society, we should expect them to show some self-doubts about their competence, and we should expect their self-esteem score to be lowered."[44]

In a 1970 study on the Pine Ridge Reservation in South Dakota, the Minnesota Multiphasic Personality Inventory was used with American

Indian adolescents, and it was concluded, when comparing this experimental group with a control group of white adolescents from the same area, that the Oglala Sioux youth consistently revealed feelings of rejection, depression, and paranoia, and that they were more socially, emotionally, and self-alienated than the control group.[45]

Clearly, the issue of self-esteem and the American Indian has received considerable study, but few researchers have attempted to identify the differences between males and females. In general, most researchers agree that low achievement in school leads to low self-esteem, which increases the chances of absenteeism, dysfunctional behaviors, and dropping out of school.

Research on American Indian youth tends to indicate that students show a decline in self-concept with increasing age. Some studies indicate that full-blood Indians achieve at lower rates than mixed-blood Indians. One study of Oglala Sioux students found that the greater the degree of Indian blood, the greater the chances that a student would have feelings of depression, alienation, and rejection. Another researcher reported in a study conducted on the Pine Ridge Reservation in South Dakota that full-blood Indians, who often look more "Indian" than those of mixed blood, faced more discrimination at school and in the job market. Thus, some researchers maintain that self-esteem is lower for full-bloods than for mixed-bloods.[46]

Harold Hodgkinson reported that 19 percent of eighth-grade students expect they will drop out of high school. He noted that expectations are self-fulfilling promises, especially among youth. Therefore, such expectations no doubt contribute to dropping out.[47]

Lack of Self-Identity. According to American Indian writer Darcy McNickle, the treatment of the Indian from the time of the European colonization to the present day has resulted in the loss of Indian ethnic, tribal, and self-identity.[48] Erik Erikson described identity formation in adolescence as dependent upon a youth's ability to integrate identifications from previous experiences with his/her current drive, abilities, and opportunities. He maintained that vital to obtaining a sense of self-identity formation was the assurance that there is consistency between an individual's self-image and the image others have of the individual. According to Erikson, developing a sense of self-identity is so vital to the adolescent that there is no feeling of being alive without it. Therefore, should an adolescent feel that his/her environment deprives him/her of the forms of expression that allow development of a self-identity, the child may resist with the strength and courage of a cornered wild animal, which could result in delinquent or psychotic behaviors.[49]

Other researchers on Indian identity indicate that Indian youth go through a period of identity diffusion and describe the young American Indian as the "marginal man," fitting into neither the white nor the Indian culture.[50] One educator observed, "The cultural impact has taken its toll in obstructing the development of the young Sioux personality. The young Sioux people meet the demands of the dominant culture with a passive resistance. This in itself, however, causes hostility, withdrawal, and a general feeling of rejection. They cannot turn back and are not motivated to go forward. They are truly caught between the cultural stresses of the old world and the new."[51]

George Spindler and Louise Spindler maintained that the Indian personality type, which they referred to as "reaffirmative native," was ambivalent to the white culture. Fred Voget noted that certain Iroquois, whom he called "native modified," were alienated from the dominant culture and that they made no attempt to identify with either the American or the Canadian culture.[52]

Assimilation is associated closely with the concept of Indian identity. Assimilation may be divided into three stages: acculturation, social integration, and amalgamation. Acculturation is defined as the process whereby Indians adopt white cultural traits; social integration, as increased interaction between Indians and whites; and amalgamation, as the biological mixing of the two races, especially through marriage. Total assimilation occurs when an Indian identifies himself/herself as a member of the white society.[53]

Other researchers have noted that Indian youth who seem to succeed are either total traditionalists or totally acculturated: "There is a failure in psychosocial development of Indian adolescents. That failure is the nonresolution of the identity crisis. Its determinants are the failure to provide an atmosphere of psychohistorical meaningfulness and personal worth in being Indian."[54]

Some researchers report that, in contrast to white children, American Indian children demonstrate more of an emphasis on family ties in self-identity tests, greater emphasis on traditional customs and beliefs, and less emphasis on formal education and material possessions.[55]

Studies of urban Indian youth and self-identity present some interesting conclusions. In order to resolve their identity crisis, urban Indian youth generally take three directions: polarization of Indian youth toward the white model, polarization of Indian youth toward Indian traditions, or a synthesis of the two models. Many youth resolve identity conflict through the synthesis of the two models, but in order to do this, the Indian youth has to be able to maintain ties with adult Indians and relatives and, at the same time, establish positive relationships with significant white adults and peers.[56]

In a longitudinal study of Oglala Sioux students, Indian adolescents who internalized the social values of white middle-class America in terms of school achievement and the "Calvinist work ethic" found this ideological framework inappropriate when applied to themselves and their lives. It was found that Indian students reacted with pessimism to the prospect of work and achievement when confronted with the poverty and dependence on the reservation and the stereotyping of the Indian in the media.[57]

In another study, academically high-achieving Indians were found to be more similar to whites in their value orientation than low-achieving Indians. The study concluded, however, that "Indian" is more valued among Indian youth than "white" is among white youth.[58]

There is some indication that the civil rights movement and the Indian activism of the late 1960s and the 1970s have resulted in a search for Indian identity. Results of these efforts can be seen in curricular and other techniques throughout schools with Indian enrollments. One researcher suggested that one of the first signs in the search for Indian identity was the return to long hair among young Indian males, which "may uniquely be identified as Native American" because of their ancestral heritage. Renewed religious ceremonies, including the Sun Dance among Northern Plains tribes, have also been attributed to the search for Indian identity.[59]

Peer Pressure

Peer pressure is often cited in the literature as having a negative impact on at-risk students and may in fact contribute to students engaging in a number of dysfunctional behaviors, including dropping out of school.

Some researchers point to peer influences among American Indian tribal groups, which involve a pattern of self-grouping at work, wherein youth with common problems and needs (including those with low self-esteem) congregate together and share mutual experiences. In many cases, these peer groups encourage others within the group to drop out of school.[60]

In a Montana study, over one-third of the American Indian students reported dropping out of school due to a desire to be with other dropouts. Others have suggested that American Indian youth, heavily exposed to negative adult role models, are influenced as well to participate in activities that often lead to drinking or dropping out. Adolescent drinking among the Oglala Sioux has been viewed as a group-reinforced behavior. "Older younger" adults make drinks available to school-age friends and relatives, and drinking among urban Sioux adolescents is a social activity, rather than a solitary one.[61]

Strong peer-group support for drug use has also been found among American Indian youth by a number of researchers. Other researchers have noted that the behaviors and attitudes of young male Indians are tied closely to socialization patterns that are reinforced by peer groups. The "warrior syndrome," which has been discussed in several ethnographic monographs, continues to the present day and includes powerful sanctions for American Indian youth.[62]

In a study of Oglala Sioux boys, Rosalie Wax noted that loyalty of the adolescents was to their peers and not their teachers in school. She reported that students joined in a series of devices: unanimous inattention, inarticulate responses, whispered or pantomime teasing of students called upon by the teacher, and refusal to go to the blackboard. She noted that these activities were a result of a need for social approval by peer groups. Others have found that mutual rejection by teachers and students results in strong peer groups that lack adult supervision.[63]

Mental Health Problems Such as Depression (Suicidal Tendencies)

Mental health problems have been a strong interest of those who have researched Indian education. Studies from the mid-1930s throughout the 1960s sought to dispel the theory that American Indian children were mentally incompetent. In a 1936 report on a mental hygiene survey of eastern Oklahoma Indian children, children who had been previously diagnosed as "mentally defective" were identified as suffering not from antisocial behavior, but rather from a lack of opportunity. Other research showed that the overt fears of Dakota Sioux children were no different from those of rural white children. Most researchers agreed that lack of opportunities, rather than predisposed attitudes and motivations, was responsible for the barriers to social and economic development for Indian children.

Others studied personality disorders among Indian students and reported that mobility of families and the necessity to conform to changing standards led to confusion and disorganization of the child's personality.

Some researchers have suggested that American Indian children perform lower academically than whites because they suffer higher emotional disturbances; that is, poor school performance may be an effect rather than a cause of mental disorder. Other researchers found that low-achieving students exhibited low self-esteem and anomie, and one report stated that 75 percent of the children in an Alaskan boarding school had emotional problems.[64]

Such studies suggest that American Indian children, when they enter school, are exposed to cultural discrepancies. Under such conditions, either they are labeled as shy and noncompetitive by the majority culture, or they are considered rebellious, destructive, and aggressive.

The amount of research on suicide and the American Indian illustrates the magnitude of the problem. Official statistics on suicide rates among American Indian youth, however, are conflicting and, in many cases, inaccurate. Estimates have been made setting the rate at two to seven times as high as in the majority of society, and yet it is important to note that the suicide rate varies from tribe to tribe. Most researchers report that approximately one in every 200 Indian youth has attempted suicide and that the suicide rate is four times as high for Indians as for non-Indians.

Unlike the case in mainstream society, where the risk of suicide increases with age, Indian suicide is mostly confined to younger people, with the vast majority occurring between the ages of fifteen and thirty-nine, but peaking at age twenty. Researchers have also noted different patterns of suicide: females commit or attempt suicide by ingesting drugs and toxins, often as a result of an argument with a significant other. On the other hand, Indian females commit suicide at about half the rate of other American women. Several researchers have identified familial disorganization as a major contributor to suicide among young Indian males. Others have also noted that having more than one caretaker before the age of fifteen, being arrested, experiencing losses by divorce or desertion, and attending a boarding school at an early age were all factors in suicide among young males.[65] One major study on adolescent suicide concluded:

> The data presented clearly indicate statistically significant differences between individuals who commit suicide and the control group. The subjects in the suicide group were cared for by more than one individual during their developing years, while control subjects were almost always cared for by a single individual. The primary caretakers of the suicide group had significantly more arrests during the time they were caretakers of the subjects. The suicide group also experienced many more losses by desertion or divorce than the control group. The individuals who suicided were arrested more times in the years prior to their suicide than were the controls. . . . Many of the completed suicides were sent off to boarding school at a significantly earlier age . . . and they were also sent more frequently to boarding schools. . . . All of the data point to a chaotic and unstable childhood.[66]

A high percentage of suicide attempts occur in conjunction with alcohol or following crimes against friends or relatives and other misfortunes as a result of drinking.[67]

Cultural conflict and social disorganization have also been linked to suicide. Suicide and suicide attempts among Indian youth are often precipitated by domestic quarrels and marital strife within one's family. Some discredit the idea that the suicide rate is directly related to the kind of schooling that American Indian children receive and suggest that the suicide rates are closely correlated with disorganized family life, alcoholism, and loss of friends or relatives by death. There is some evidence that the destruction of self-esteem has led to suicide, as well as to alcoholism and homicide.[68]

"Cluster suicides" (one suicide triggers other suicides) are reported to be higher among American Indian youth. Alcohol seems to be one major cause; yet suicide rates are lower today than during the peak years of 1970–77.

Despite the plethora of research on suicide and the American Indian, suicide remains a major concern of educators working with Indian youth. Although research exists, progress in preventive techniques and strategies is often questionable. Six years ago, I worked with an American Indian school district where twenty-three suicides had been attempted; three were successful. The suicide victims were eighth- and ninth-graders. More recently, I was on an Indian reservation where two teenage boys had committed suicide. In response to a request from a parent, I met with her son, a friend of the deceased teenagers. During our conversation, the young man revealed that he regarded his friends who committed suicide as courageous. "They are my heroes," he said.

Pregnancy

Unlike the situation for other ethnic groups in the United States, little data exist on the percentage of American Indian girls who leave school due to premature pregnancy. Most needs assessments conducted by school districts on Indian reservations speak to the need for sex education and alternative educational programs for teenage mothers. Many American Indian schools offer alternative programs for the pregnant teen, including home-schooling programs and child care programs, and some have even experimented with nursery school programs for the children of teenage mothers. National statistics report that 40 percent of the girls who drop out of school do so due to pregnancy, and there is no reason to suspect that the statistics for American Indian girls would be different. In fact, there have been reports that would indicate teen pregnancy is higher among American Indian females. One school district in Montana reported that sixteen of the twenty-three female students in the eleventh and twelfth grades were pregnant. One small South Dakota reservation community (population 150) reported that twenty-seven females between the ages of fourteen and twenty were pregnant. In addition, there are many reports of girls who have two and three children before the age of nineteen, which is consistent with national data. Organizations such as the Children's Defense Fund and the Center for Population Options, which have developed programs for teenage mothers, view teen pregnancy as the result of a lack of sufficient options. In the case of the American Indian girl, the lack of a promising future may, in fact, contribute to the high rate of pregnancy.

Bea Medicine, a Dakota Sioux anthropologist, cited an example of cultural socialization pressure among Sioux males and females that may contribute to teen pregnancy. According to her, Sioux females are not fully recognized as mature women until they have produced a son, and males feel inadequate until they have fathered a son. Medicine pointed out that "Giving birth to a child is somehow equated with adulthood . . . this status is extended to the increasing numbers of 13 and 14 year-old girls who produce illegitimate children. The Dakota phrase 'towa cinca tayesni' (literally, 'whose child no one knows') which was a tremendous mark of shame several generations ago, does not have great significance in present day systems of social control."[69]

Of primary concern to American Indian educators are statistics that speak to the number of Fetal Alcohol Syndrome (FAS) and Fetal Alcohol Effects (FAE) children being born on the reservations. There is a wide range in the incidence of FAS among tribes, from 1.3 per 1,000 live births among the Navajo to 10.3 among the Plains tribes, many of which are located in South Dakota, Montana, and Wyoming.[70]

Michael Dorris, in his recent best-seller *The Broken Cord*, reported that on some Indian reservations, Indian social workers maintain that one-fourth to one-third of Indian children are affected by FAS or FAE.[71]

Although research is almost nonexistent on pregnancy and its impact on dropping out among American Indian females, there is no question that premature pregnancy is the cause of a high percentage of girls leaving school early. The severity of the problem for American Indian girls and its implications for their futures and the futures of their children have not been researched.

Correlate 2: Family Background and Dropping Out

Various factors within the family background have often been discussed in terms of American Indian students' failure in school. Research indicates a high correlation between dropping out and the socioeconomic status of the family. Other researchers have suggested that one-parent families, dysfunctional families, child abuse, and child-rearing practices have high correlations to school failure. This section will discuss each of those factors and their relationship to the American Indian student.

Socioeconomic Status

American Indians are the most poverty-stricken ethnic group in the nation, according to the 1990 U.S. census figures. In fact, the statistics indicate a growing trend of economic inequality among minorities over the past decade. More than half of Indian households earn less than $20,000 annually, and Indian children are three times more likely to live in poverty than white children. In addition, the census figures show that Indians have the highest unemployment rate in the country.[72]

It is currently reported that 38 percent of Indian children live below the poverty line. Throughout the literature, many researchers have noted the poverty conditions of the Indian child.[73] Other researchers have reported that Indian students come to school poorly clothed and malnourished. Estelle Fuchs and Robert Havighurst noted that the majority of Indian students are reared in poverty-stricken families and that poverty is a disadvantage to school achievement.[74] A ten-year study of Indian students in California reported that not only were there high dropout and truancy rates, but there was a high incidence of health problems, much of which was attributed to crowded living conditions and isolation.[75] Several studies have indicated that the government-supported hot lunch programs increased school attendance among Indian students because of inadequate food in the home environment. Others have found that low levels of achievement are associated with low economic and social levels.[76]

The economic conditions of reservation life are very precarious. Unemployment among American Indians was listed at 65 percent in Wyoming and 64 percent in South Dakota, as compared to 7 percent and 6 percent, respectively, for whites. On one reservation where this study was conducted, 85 percent of the jobs were held by females. Among the Northern Plains tribes, male employment often falls into the category of ranching, farming, arts, and crafts. Women are more likely to work in clerical, educational, and social service areas.[77]

A BIA study of 635,000 American Indians living on or near reservations in 1989 showed that one-third were unemployed, and over one-third of those who were employed earned less than $7,000 per year.[78]

It is evident that more American Indian children are growing up in poverty than is true of any other racial/ethnic group in America. Unemployment plagues tribal groups throughout the country. That poverty and dropping out of school are regarded as highly correlated to socioeconomic status is a matter of concern in Indian country. Children who are labeled as coming from "disadvantaged" homes due to poverty may have one strike against them before they begin school.

Parents' Educational Level

Some researchers have attributed the low educational levels of the American Indian adult population to the poverty levels. Again, reports varied from tribe to tribe; however, available statistics indicate that the high school graduation level of adult Indian populations on some reservations is as low as 27 percent, compared to the national average for non-Indians of 86 percent. A study conducted in 1981 of 4,000 American Indian adults revealed literacy scores, as measured by the Adult Performance Inventory, lower than those of any other ethnic or racial group, excluding recent immigrants.[79] Scores of American Indian participants were comparable to those of individuals in underdeveloped nations. It was also reported that 59 percent of the adult Indian population had neither a high school diploma nor a GED. Of adults over the age of twenty-five, 16 percent had less than five years of schooling.[80]

Researchers repeatedly show the correlation between families' socioeconomic status and students' dropping out of school. Estelle Fuchs and Robert Havighurst reported that school achievement and socioeconomic status of the family proved to be more influential than school characteristics, except in cases where the family could not provide much help to the student because of lack of education. Specifically, they were addressing the issues of poverty and illiteracy on the part of the parents as contributing to an environment unconducive to learning, such as the absence of books and reading materials in the home and a quiet place to study. In such cases, they argued that the school may actually compensate to some extent, maintaining that many Indian parents have little formal education, resulting in their children becoming more dependent upon the school for academic instruction than children from families where parents can assist them with their education.[81]

Whether or not the educational level of parents is a major factor to dropping out has not been fully researched.

Child-rearing Practices

Child-rearing practices of Native tribal groups are noted throughout the literature as one of the major conflicts between home and success in school. In 1634, a Jesuit priest, Father le Jeune, described the frustration of disciplining Indian children in his missionary school: "These Barbarians cannot bear to have their children punished, not even scolded, not being able to refuse anything to a crying child. They carry this to such an extent that upon the slightest pretext they would take them away from us, before they were educated."[82]

Researchers have noted that although the political and economic structures of the American Indian culture have largely been destroyed, child-rearing practices and personal relationships have undergone a slower transformation. Such practices, which are characterized by permissiveness and indulgence, with little stress on noncompetitive behavior, are at odds with the school setting.[83]

Other researchers have discussed the child-rearing practices of Indians, stating that "Children are punished relatively seldom by parents. Instead, they are warned, when they are naughty, that people will talk about them. Or they are warned of punishment by supernatural beings. . . . Thus much of the children's experience of punishment comes from outside the home and comes from persons whom they do not love."[84]

Bernard Spilka maintained that the child-rearing practices of American Indians tend to foster failure in schools for Indian children, including three particular problems: (1) a preschool environment at home that does not include or display the early educational teaching by parents, common in white middle-class homes; (2) materials in school that are alien to Indian children; and (3) teacher-child relationships that are quite different from those experienced outside of school. He suggested that this discrepancy between home and school resulted in a feeling of alienation and a negative attitude toward school.[85]

Other researchers have found that Indian children are taught self-control by their parents, that parental focus allows children to learn for themselves, and that physical punishment is rare. They have also observed that authority figures are distributed among many people in the family and that individual autonomy and collective group responsibility encourage control over oneself and not over others. As such, Indian children are most often disciplined as a group, rather than individually.[86]

Some researchers maintain that culturally different children often come to schools where there is a different expectation of behavior than was established in their home. Thus, children act in ways that are judged as appropriate at home, but in school, they discover that their behavior is inappropriate.[87] For example, interruption of parents and other adults by the Indian child is not considered misbehavior, but in school, the teacher labels such behavior as inappropriate. One study of American Indian children in school and in community life identified nonacceptance of "student talk" by teachers in early grades as a determinant of failure for Indian students. The researcher noted that because different standards were experienced in the home and the school, students began very early exhibiting "learning difficulties and feelings of inferiority." This phenomenon was attributed to child-rearing practices.[88]

Some researchers have suggested that parents are perceived to be the strongest influence on a student's schoolwork. One study of Cree families reported that educational success for children was important, but that the Cree culture and heritage were equally important. Others reported that Indian parents internalized feelings of inferiority that affected their children's academic performance. On the other hand, others found little difference between parental behavior and student attitudes toward education in Indian and non-Indian students.[89]

Dick Little Bear, a Northern Cheyenne educator, maintains that the exclusion of Indian parents from the education of their children by federal government policies has not worked and has created a mistrust for education: "Indian parents were systematically excluded from participation in the education of Indian youth. Excluding Indian parents . . . has made Indian parents very suspicious of modern American education. . . . This misuse of education produced education-hating Indians. Schools are still associated with punishment and deprivation."[90]

Other researchers have noted that behavior the non-Indian culture often regards as "apathy" is actually a traditional reluctance on the part of parents to interfere in the affairs of others, including those of their own children. Permissiveness on the part of Indian parents has been the subject of a number of studies.[91] On the Wind River Reservation in Wyoming, one researcher found that Arapaho parents thought their children should make up their own minds about whether they should go to college, while another study concluded that the permissive attitude in the Shoshone home was a detriment to academic achievement.[92]

Some researchers note that child-rearing practices indirectly encourage substance abuse among American Indian youth and target the laissez-faire child-rearing practices—which were long-established Siouan cultural edicts—as fostering parental tolerance of substance abuse.[93] Others note that Indian children often go unsupervised for long periods of time, thus escaping effective controls in the home. Faced with controls in the school, American Indian children often react by at first disobeying, then skipping school, and finally dropping out.

In a study of Blackfeet children, it was found that obedience to elders is demanded, but otherwise the child has a wide range of personal choices and autonomy. Efforts at controlling the child take the form of lectures, rather than physical force or threats.[94]

The research is relatively clear that traditional child-rearing practices, which have survived at a time when other aspects of the culture have diminished or changed, impact the American Indian child's life tremendously. Furthermore, research supports that acceptable behaviors within the home are often unacceptable in the school, thus creating a feeling of disorientation in young children, and may result in dropping out in later years.

Single-Parent Families

It has been reported in various demographic studies conducted on American Indian tribes that anywhere from 24 to 50 percent of American Indian youth are growing up in homes with only one parent. In a report based on 1980 census data, it was found that 25 percent of American Indian children were growing up in single-parent homes, as compared to less than one-fifth of children in the population as a whole. These data, which are often falsely reported or not reported at all, refer to the absence of a husband, spouse, or father of the child in the home.[95] It is important to note, however, that in a high percentage of American Indian homes, the child is not growing up in an environment that is devoid of other adults. Due to family relationships and the extended family structure of American Indian tribal groups, a high percentage of students grow up in homes where other relatives or friends are living in the household.

Dysfunctional Families

The institution of the American Indian family has been drastically altered over the years. Many children suffer from unpredictable home environments that include loss in their family through divorce, separation, or desertion; arrest of parents; domestic quarrels and other marital strife; and alcohol abuse. In a study of one Indian group in which rapid change and breakdown in extended nuclear families had occurred, there was a high suicide rate among the youth.[96]

Some researchers have observed that the traditional community and family structures are decreasing among American Indians. Others have noted that among some tribes, the men's continued involvement in sharing alcoholic beverages and their participation in peer groups beyond adolescence has proved counterproductive to the family and marriage and leads to marital discord among American Indians.[97]

Although child abuse and neglect among Native populations has received considerable attention in the last decade among social service workers and health care providers,[98] little research exists on the subject. Part of the problem is created by inaccurate reporting, lack of community cooperation, and inconsistent definitions of child abuse and neglect.[99] Within American Indian communities, these problems are further complicated by cultural variations.[100] One research profile suggests that child abuse and neglect among American Indian populations is often defined in a cross-cultural context whereby "such behavior is somehow made understandable and, hence, acceptable."[101]

Studies on child abuse and neglect reveal a number of findings. In a small Alaskan village, one study reported that nearly all children in the community were neglected, and attributed the neglect to the absence of the traditional child-caring practices that had disappeared.[102] Sixty-nine percent of the referrals to Indian child welfare programs are reportedly due to physical abuse, neglect, and abandonment.[103]

There appears to be a wide variation in the incidences of child abuse and neglect among tribes. Approximately 50 percent of the child abuse cases and 80 percent of the child neglect cases are related to alcohol abuse. In a study among the Cheyenne River Sioux, sexual abuse was found to be less frequent than the national average, but physical abuse was more serious and often resulted in the death of a child. Others have reported that neglect occurs more frequently among American Indians than any other group in America.[104]

In a study among the Blackfeet, one researcher reported that babies and young children are given small amounts of alcohol when the adults are drinking.[105] Phyllis Old Dog Cross reported that the amount of violence against women, alcoholism, and abuse and neglect by women against their children and aged relatives has increased in the American Indian community.[106] In a study of families of neglected Navajo children, researchers found that the families had a significantly higher percentage of single, widowed, or divorced mothers than was true for a nonneglected control group.[107] Other researchers[108] have pointed to the deterioration of the family, which was once the cornerstone of Indian society, as one of the problems facing American Indian youth today.

Child abuse and neglect are often concentrated in dysfunctional families, frequently characterized by multiple problems, including suicide, homicide, desertion, alcohol abuse, educational problems, and health problems.[109] Alcohol abuse is related to almost every deviant behavior among American Indians.[110] A study of abuse and neglect cases at a Southwest Indian health hospital that served twelve reservations reported that alcohol abuse was present in 85 percent of the neglect cases and 63 percent of the abuse cases. In 65 percent of the cases, child abuse and neglect occurred simultaneously. The study also showed that children were likely to be abused by more than one person in the family, that girls were more likely to be abused than boys, and that 30 percent of the abused/neglected children had a history of disability or handicap.[111]

The research on American Indian students consistently reports that home environment has a major impact on the success of students in school. The research is also clear that children who abuse alcohol and drugs, children who commit suicide, and children who drop out of school often come from homes where the parent is absent or where the parent has little or no control.

Correlate 3: School Factors

A number of factors relating to school have been studied by researchers in an attempt to identify the reasons for the lack of success and/or the success of Indian students. Until the 1980s, the majority of this research focused on the deficit model; that is, the behaviors, characteristics, and cultural differences that the child brought with him/her to school were the accepted explanations for poor academic achievement, absenteeism, and dropping out. This research will be reviewed, in that it has a major bearing, even today, on the way schools deal with children. At the same time, current literature will be reviewed that seeks to identify the school's role in students dropping out of school.

This section will address the factors related to school, which include bilingualism/limited English proficiency; cultural differences/cultural discontinuity; academic achievement/failure, including grade retention, course failure, and tracking; attendance, including truancy, absenteeism, detention, and expulsion; teacher attitudes and expectations; and racism, discrimination, and prejudice.

Bilingualism

In 1899, a well-known magazine editor wrote that the American Indian should learn English as a protection against the white man: "It is well that [the Indian] should learn to read and write, and get what comprehension he can of this nation's laws and genius, and acquire our language—all of these things being valuable to him chiefly as some protection against being robbed by our rascals."[112]

From the beginning, the European settlers, and later the U.S. government, have attempted to bring the Indian into the mainstream of America through education. In the 1880s, the BIA issued orders that the English language was to be the language of instruction: "The main purpose of educating them is to enable them to read, write, and speak the English language and to transact business with English-speaking people. . . . Every nation is jealous of its own language, and no nation ought to be more so than ours, which approaches nearer than any other nationality to the perfect protection of its people. True Americans all feel that the Constitution, laws, and institutions of the United States, in their adaptation to the wants and requirements of man, are superior to those of any other country. . . . Noth-

ing so surely and perfectly stamps upon an individual a national characteristic as language."[113]

Thus, the decision to obliterate Indian languages and to replace them
with English was approached as a nationalizing purpose. Government
officials and educators rejected the notion of the coexistence of English and
the Indian languages as compatible with nationhood. Furthermore, it was
suggested that the use of English among American Indians would create
patriotism and loyalty and somehow facilitate national integration. Obviously, the assault on the Indian languages and culture has produced, over
the years, a legacy of bitterness and hatred among Indian tribes. Government policies that imposed alien standards on Indians and forced separation of parents and children induced both hostility and subtle resistance.
Force had to be used to keep students in school, as illustrated in the
following report: "I have at all times assisted the Superintendent in keeping
the school filled up with pupils, and sometimes have had to send the police
over the reservation to gather up the scholars; also have had to frequently
send the police after the larger boys, who would run away from the
schools."[114]

Accounts of the unjust treatment of Indian students can be found
throughout the literature, but the ban on the use of the Native languages
appears almost ludicrous at times: "The schools the children were forced to
attend were strict and authoritarian beyond what anyone not incarcerated
would put up with today. They were also, although perhaps not intentionally, cruel. Children were rarely allowed to go home to visit their families;
moreover, upon arrival at the boarding schools, they were forbidden to
speak their native languages and were required to remain silent until they
could speak English. That one could learn to speak by remaining silent is
a pedagogical triumph not readily encountered."[115]

The policy of the government toward Indian languages was not without its critics, and the BIA often found itself in the position of defending its
strategies from the growing number of complaints against the English-only
rule. In response to such criticism, Commissioner of Indian Affairs Atkins
stated, "To teach Indian school children their native tongue is practically to
exclude English, and to prevent them from acquiring it. This language,
which is good enough for a white man and a black man, ought to be good
enough for a red man. . . . Is it cruelty to the Indian to force him to give up
his scalping knife and tomahawk? Is it cruelty to force him to abandon the
vicious and barbarous sun dance, where he lacerates his flesh and dances
and tortures himself even unto death?"[116]

The Native languages continued to be banned from BIA schools until
the 1930s and 1940s, when some action was taken to provide for the use of
the language, as well as instruction in it, among Indian students: "It has not

been many years since the use of the native language was forcibly discouraged in government schools, and native dialects were often held up to ridicule. . . . Under the present administration the native languages have come to be recognized, not as encumbrances and impediments to the progress of the native peoples, but as definite tools to be fitted into the educational program."[117] This strategy was short-lived, however, and was discontinued with the advent of World War II.

It was not until the 1960s that bilingual education became an issue with Indian children. Testimony before the U.S. House of Representatives Subcommittee on Education concerning the Bilingual Education Act pointed out that "When you come to the Indian child, given what seems to be the fact that he cherishes his Indian status to a remarkable extent, and given the fact that his cultural patterns are markedly different from those of the dominant American group, he is not simply cheated out of a language that does not matter internationally anyway, he is not just damaged in school: he is almost destroyed. As a matter of fact, historically, that is what we tried to do with them: destroy them. All you have to do is read the accounts to know that."[118]

In 1968, the Bilingual Education Act, which was Title VII of the Elementary and Secondary Education Act, became law. This act was a compensatory education program for "disadvantaged" non-English-speaking students. In 1974, the low-income provision was removed, and in 1978, the act was amended to include funding for "Limited English Proficiency" Indian children and the participation of up to 40 percent of monolingual English speakers so that the programs did not segregate students. The act was amended in 1984 to fund maintenance and transitional programs, which emphasized the development of English language skills in non-English-speaking students.

Even today, many Indian children begin school with little or no skills in the use of the English language. The Human and Civil Rights Committee of the National Education Association (1983) reported that 25 percent of American Indian children begin school unable to speak English. Although the majority of Indian children in the country may speak English, and often only English, it is important to note that it is usually a substandard English, which is not the English of the classroom and of textbooks. Judgments about lack of intelligence are made about people who do not use standard English, such as "A child who uses correct language is presumably neat, polite, well groomed, and a paragon of virtue, whereas a child who uses incorrect language probably falls asleep in church, plays hooky from school, dissects cats, and takes dope."[119]

The language handicap for Indian students appears to increase as they move through school. The loss of the Native languages is one of the most critical issues confronting tribes and has been attributed to a breakdown in communication between children and their grandparents and the subsequent loss of heritage.[120]

Some researchers report that Indian students in South Dakota who speak their Native language are not as high achievers in school as those students who are English-only speakers. Others have tested the linguistic maturity of Indian students and found lower patterns of development than those of white children.[121] On the other hand, in a study of Canadian Indians and Metis, inadequate exposure to English, instead of the use of their Native languages, was found to be at the root of language problems.[122]

It has been noted that often Indian children make satisfactory progress in school until they reach the fourth grade. The explanation for this phenomenon lies in the fact that the textbooks in the first three grades are written in "talking" or conversational vocabulary, while upper-grade texts shift to a "comprehension" vocabulary.[123]

L. Madison Coombs reported on a study of 14,000 Indian students and concluded, "Investigation of the data reveals an amazingly consistent relationship between the degree of Indian blood and pre-school language on the one hand and level of achievement on the other. With only one exception, the smaller the amount of Indian blood in a group and the greater the amount of English spoken prior to school entrance, the higher the group achieved."[124]

Even on reservations where English, and English only, is the language, there are still the problems of low achievement, high dropout rates, and absenteeism. It may be that the language problem is a symptom, rather than the cause, of scholastic failure. A number of schools have incorporated the use of the Native language into the curriculum. Probably the most famous is the Rock Point Community School on the Navajo reservation. Graduates of this school test out on English-language standardized achievement tests as superior to Indian students who have not had bilingual education.[125] In Chicago's bilingual, bicultural Little Big Horn High School, dropout rates were reduced from 95 percent for American Indian students to 11 percent.[126] Many researchers maintain that students do better in school if their language and culture are a part of the school's curriculum.[127]

Bilingual education is controversial on many reservations. Often tribal members and teachers join forces in preventing the use of Native languages in the classroom, and yet there is reportedly no tribe that has used the Native language as a substitute for the English language; nor have they let the Native language restoration outrank the importance of teaching English.[128]

Over the years, language has played an important role in success in school. Most linguists agree that the truly bilingual child (fluent in two languages) has higher achievement in school than children who speak or understand two languages at varying degrees. American Indian children, who often understand, but do not speak, the Native language and who often enter school using substandard English, present a different situation for teachers, one that clearly warrants further research.

Cultural Differences and Cultural Discontinuity

Most researchers agree that Indian children are affected by both the white and Indian cultures. Some scholars maintain that Indian children are often torn between two cultures. Others point out that some students accept one culture and reject the other, whereas many maintain that Indian students attempt, often unsuccessfully, to participate in both cultures, but since these are so very different and contradictory, such students must develop the skills to compartmentalize their behaviors dependent upon the society in which they are functioning.   Such individuals are often referred to as bicultural.

Erik Erikson noted in his observations of Sioux children that the traditional enculturation process must be recognized so that the transition to school can be based on the Indian child's childhood.[129] A number of studies have discussed the consequences of formal education and the cultural conflict arising from the child being educated in a traditional society and the school setting.[130]

Estelle Fuchs and Robert Havighurst cited family background as being a handicap to school achievement for Indian students. In their national study, they were not only speaking to a family background with low economic status and low educational levels of the parents, but also addressing the degree to which American Indian parents continued cultural and Native language practices in the home. They maintained that family background influences success for Indian students, in that the Indian culture is often discontinuous with the demands of schooling. They included such characteristics in the Native culture that are in conflict with the urban-industrial culture as close family solidarity, support for relatives, belief in the values of a tribal tradition, belief in tribal religion, and a tribal language. These values, they pointed out, are sometimes in conflict with the competitive and individualistic achievement demanded in schools.[131]

Others have maintained that there are considerable differences between the Indian culture and the white culture that have resulted in conflict for the Indian child: namely, to stay with the traditions and accept the old ways or to give up their values and suffer hostility from friends and family and join the white society, which does not welcome them. For example, in the Indian culture, there is very little consideration of the future. Children grow up in an environment where the adults live for the here and now. This strongly affects success in school and vocational choices. Furthermore, adolescents growing up on a reservation find that their culture and way of life can be lived only on the reservation, which for many of them means subsistence on welfare, with few material comforts. If they leave the reservation, they find that any departure from the traditional way of life, such as refusing to share one's paycheck, will result in hostility from relatives and friends.[132]

The traditional cultural values allow for an enormous amount of independence for Indian youth. Many observers maintain that somewhere between the ages of eight and ten, Indian youth begin making decisions about where they will go to school, who they will live with, and when they will eat. It is not uncommon for parents to know nothing of the whereabouts of their children, although the absence of parenting is a more recent occurrence in the culture. As a result of lack of parental guidance, the decisions made by young Indians tend to be based on the need for immediate gratification.[133]

Rosalie Wax reported that alcohol abuse among Indian students was embedded in a broad social milieu within the culture. She maintained that self-determination, which promotes individual autonomy, fosters parental tolerance of adolescent substance abuse. She further noted that even though adults may personally disapprove of drinking, it is assumed that the individual must take care of himself/herself, and therefore adults do not intervene in adolescent drinking.[134] In general, there is a social acceptance of drinking as a shared recreational activity, which serves as a means for self-expression and assertion of ethnic identity.[135] It has been reported that the Indian is allowed to do almost anything when drinking, as the drinker knows that the alcohol, and not the drinker, will be blamed for the behavior. This behavior serves to advertise to non-Indians that the drinker can still "act Indian" in a way that the majority society cannot influence.[136]

Other researchers have cited cultural conflict as an explanation for Indian students' failure in school.[137] They have suggested that Indian youth do poorly in school because the educational system historically has served as a battleground in the confrontation between the Indian and white worlds. Since schools are typically the purveyors of white values and Indian ones are excluded, Indian students, who are raised with more traditional values, tend to drop out. A study of the effects of acculturation on intergroup competition and cooperation among Indian and non-Indian children found that Indian children who attend an integrated school become more competitive and that non-Indians in an integrated school become more cooperative.[138]

Others have addressed social disorganization as a serious problem for American Indian youth. They have noted that Western culture has led to rapid social change and a breakdown in traditional sociocultural systems, which has resulted in a rapidly changing, disorganized system in which values and roles are unclear. This situation, according to many researchers, has created an environment that is predisposed toward self-destruction. As such, cultural conflict is a source of stress for Indian youth in the schools. The pressure is both overt and covert. In the school and media, there is pressure to acculturate and become "more like everyone else in America," but at the same time, there is pressure from within the culture to "remain an Indian."[139] This results in a situation wherein the Indian is caught between two different existences and is marginal in each.

Brewton Berry contended that "there are some who maintain that the Indian today possesses a civilization of great antiquity, to which he is deeply attached, and which he is determined to perpetuate. He has succeeded thus far. . . . The school, the Indian rightly suspects, is a device for hastening his assimilation, and he resists it as best he can by withdrawal, indifference, and non-cooperation. . . . At the other extreme there are those, including some Indians, who conclude that the old cultures have been shattered and can never be revived."[140]

A considerable amount of research[141] has reported that midadolescence is the age when young people become exposed to the stress of cultural conflict. Joseph Trimble and his colleagues observed, "Indians persist both as heterogeneous culture groups and as a separate segment of American society."[142] As a result, Indian youth demonstrate a lack of integration into either traditional Indian or modern-day American life. Other research illustrates, however, that cultural conflict does *not* inevitably result in passivity or aggression. Although living in both cultures may create risk, it can also create opportunity. The individual who masters this situation can move between cultures and incorporate elements of both.[143]

A number of researchers have sought to explain the reasons for the American Indian child's problems with school as cultural conflict. One researcher summed up his findings somewhat succinctly by referring to the Indian student as the "marginal man." In defining the marginal man, he explained that this was "a person who participates in two different cultures without being totally committed to, or accepted by, either."[144]

Much of the literature on the American Indian dropout treats the significance of cultural discontinuity between school and home as an explanation for the high dropout rate. In response to this explanation, many scholars have suggested that "culturally relevant" curricula will alleviate the high dropout problem.

The cultural discontinuity hypothesis is predicated on the assumption that culturally based differences within the Indian students' homes and the Anglo culture of the school lead to conflicts and ultimately failure and dropping out by students.[145]

John Ogbu, an anthropological theorist, is very critical of the cultural discontinuity theory as an explanation for minority student failure in schools.[146] He notes that although the theory sounds quite plausible, since cultural differences have implications for human behavior, anthropologists are making such suggestions prior to any serious ethnographic research in the schools. Perhaps his strongest criticism of the cultural discontinuity theory concerns its failure to explain the success of immigrant minority children in American schools, who experience cultural discontinuity between home and school at least as severely as American Indians and Blacks.

Although little research explicitly supports the cultural discontinuity theory, there is a plethora of research that posits cultural conflict, cultural differences, and cultural discontinuity as the explanation for failure and makes assumptions about the need for cultural relevance in curricula. In a Milwaukee study of urban Indian dropouts, one researcher applied the cultural discontinuity theory and stated, "Considering the disproportionately high Native American dropout rate, one can reasonably assume that certain culturally-based Indian characteristics exist that clash with the urban public school environment."[147]

Many scholars assume that cultural discontinuity between the Indian culture and the school culture causes academic failure, and thus creates a dissonance within the student, resulting in dropping out. Several researchers have conducted interviews with students specifically about the importance of cultural relevance in the schools. One Montana study reported that high school dropouts cited the lack of relevance of the school curriculum in terms of both future employment and the Indian culture as a reason that significantly influenced their decision to leave school.[148] Another study of urban American Indian students found that both parents and students felt the schools to be "culturally insensitive."[149] Other researchers have related students' participation in traditional culture to their failure in school.[150] Despite the plethora of research available on cultural conflict and cultural discontinuity, cultural relevance is rarely defined in the literature, and if it is, the definitions are as varied as the tribal groups represented. Yet lack of a culturally relevant curriculum is frequently suggested as a major factor in dropping out among American Indian youth.

When explaining cultural differences as a major contributor to dropping out, it is important to look at research claiming that being bilingual and being traditional are assets for American Indian students. Some researchers have found that a student's first language (Native language) is not a determinant to success in school. In fact, it has been found that students who are bilingual are less likely to drop out of school.

Of particular importance, however, is that students from less traditional homes drop out at higher rates. In a study of urban American Indian adolescents in Phoenix, Arizona, the majority of dropouts reported positive attitudes toward school, although it was noted that some dropouts felt pushed out of school by academic and discipline problems. Although this group blamed factors within the school as contributing to their dropping out, the majority regretted their decision to leave.[151]

In a study of Navajo and Ute school leavers, Donna Deyhle found that Navajo students who came from traditional homes, spoke their Native language, and participated in traditional religious activities did not feel that the school curriculum was inappropriate for Indians. On the other hand, she found that Ute students who came from less traditional homes felt the school curriculum was not relevant to Indian students. Again, the latter group experienced the highest dropout rates. Deyhle commented, "A culturally non-responsive curriculum is a greater threat to those whose own cultural 'identity' is insecure."[152]

Although culture may be a significant factor in whether a student succeeds or fails in school, it may be that the student's cultural background, and not the school curriculum, is more significant. There is some evidence that a strong sense of cultural identity provides a student with an advantage in school.[153] This idea, which contradicts the theory that the more "white" or "acculturated" a student is, the more advantaged s/he may be in the school setting, is an extremely important issue in Indian education. It may be that the more traditional students, who have a strong self-identity and tribal identity, do better in school and that the students who are less traditional are more likely to resist school and to see less relevance in the curriculum. This may be a far more significant factor when examining the factors for success and failure in school.

Academic Achievement and Failure, Including
Grade Retention and Tracking

Research on academic achievement is varied in nature. Early researchers often attributed low achievement among American Indian students to inferior mental abilities. Some maintained that test bias was a contributing factor, whereas others saw a direct correlation between socioeconomic status and achievement.

Early studies on the intellectual abilities of American Indians tended to report inferior native ability. A number of early researchers supported a cultural difference theory to explain American Indian intelligence and concluded that American Indian children were mentally inferior.[154] Since 1935, however, most researchers have supported the theory that American Indian children are as mentally competent as children in other racial groups.[155]

However, research on American Indian students reveals a negative correlation between years spent in school and academic achievement.[156] In other words, the achievement of American Indian children declines with every year they are in school. This phenomenon, which reportedly occurs at about age nine, has been labeled the "crossover phenomenon." Specifically, prior to age nine, Indian students perform academically as well as white children, but performance begins to deteriorate in the third grade. After this, they fall behind white students.[157] One study of Oglala Sioux indicated that students exhibited a crossover phenomenon, whereby the students achieved satisfactorily until the sixth grade. After the sixth grade, there was a gradual decline in student performance.[158]

Schools throughout the United States use standardized tests to measure school success. Critics of standardized testing report that emphasis on such tests produces a built-in failure for minority students and points to the cultural bias of such tests as an inappropriate method for determining a student's knowledge and ability.[159] One criticism that is often directed against standardized tests is their language bias.[160] For example, American Indian students may have cognitive styles different from the particular cognitive style required by the test. In order to guarantee culturally fair standardized tests, it may be necessary to accept a variety of responses, rather than a single response. Most researchers consistently find that American Indian students score lower on almost all standardized measures of achievement than other ethnic minority groups do. In 1958, L. Madison Coombs and colleagues reported that American Indian children score below the national average on achievement tests and consistently score below non-Indian students.[161] This condition has not changed significantly over the past three and a half decades. John Bryde found that among a group of Oglala Sioux students on the Pine Ridge Reservation, the students scored slightly above the national norms at the fourth- and fifth-grade levels, but that their performance dropped far below the national norm by the seventh and eighth grades. He explained this phenomenon by suggesting that American Indian students at about the sixth or seventh grade become aware of being "Indian," along with experiencing the feelings of alienation and rejection that destroy their self-esteem, thus impacting their desire to achieve in school.[162]

A number of studies have focused on the mathematical and verbal abilities of American Indian students and concluded that Indian students have math skills superior to those of white students.[163] Other researchers have reported that bilingual instruction results in improved skills not only in language, but in mathematics as well; however, American Indian youth are less skilled than non-Indian adolescents in estimating time.[164] In a study of 172 non-Indian students and 88 Cheyenne Indian students on a multiple-choice test that asked students to select the amount of time required to complete a given activity, results indicated that non-Indian children scored significantly higher on the test at each of the grade levels tested.[165]

Some researchers, pointing to the fact that mixed-bloods do better on achievement tests than full-bloods, suggest that schools are designed around white values more consistent with those who are more assimilated or who are mixed-bloods. John Bryde maintained that lack of achievement by American Indian students in school is psychological. He reported that alienation and conflict between the white and Indian cultures become more focused in adolescence and cause personality disturbances that block achievement.[166] Others have reported that mixed-bloods showed higher achievement and greater popularity than full-bloods and that alienation in school increased as achievement declined.[167]

There are a number of examples of the misuse of standardized tests.[168] Perhaps one of the greatest concerns for educators of minority students is using tests to define success or failure. Since publication of *A Nation at Risk*,[169] schools throughout the country have been encouraged and even mandated to raise academic standards. These standards, which are closely tied to test results, may, in fact, force more students to leave school early. For example, higher standards defined in terms of testing results will no doubt lead to more students being retained in a grade, and students retained in a grade and overage students are more likely to drop out of school.[170] Research has clearly shown that retention in a grade does not benefit students.[171] Even retention in kindergarten is not beneficial to students. More and more, researchers are suggesting that grade retention results in students being "pushed out," rather than dropping out, of school. Some researchers have even reported that when schools push out at-risk youth, they inevitably look better in the public eye, since the average test scores are higher.[172]

Recent literature on dropping out is based in part on research on schools that effectively teach the at-risk student. According to this research, it is not the student's background, but rather the school's response to the student, that determines success in school. Gary Wehlage and Robert Rutter reported that the process of becoming a dropout is complex, because the process of rejecting an institution must be accompanied by the belief that the institution has rejected the person. Their work has focused on the ways that a student's negative school-based experiences can accumulate to the point where the student makes the decision that "school is not for me" and subsequently drops out.[173]

The literature has also reported that potential dropouts have a history of school failures. They tend to be overage for their grade, due to failures.

Many are frequently suspended from school and are often absent or truant. Gary Wehlage and Robert Rutter suggested that as a student's negative experiences accumulate, problems develop that cannot be solved, because of lack of coping skills. Thus, problems in one area often lead to problems in another.[174] These two researchers maintained that the American Indian child who comes from one cultural setting is thrown into a school setting of the mainstream culture that may result in a "values clash." This creates a situation of marginality, whereby the American Indian child lives on the margins of two cultures, having loyalties to both, but not being a member of either one. Other researchers have proposed that when the American Indian child enters school, the child's loyalties are toward the parents' values, and that in school the child encounters new values. If the child perceives that his/her values are not understood or appreciated by the school, or if the child is unable to appreciate the new values encountered, conflict often arises. The student then rebels by dropping out, failing courses, or skipping school.[175] Some researchers have observed that being successful in school can create dissonance for the American Indian student: "The native student who aspires to success is faced with the difficult and often dissonant task of marching to more than one drum. The dilemma of not rejecting one's own rich, cultural heritage while preparing to be successful in a context which at best ignores or at worst contradicts such a heritage along with its inherent values and ethics is not a simple one."[176]

Attendance: Truancy, Absenteeism, Detention, and Expulsion

Although statistics on truancy, suspension, and absenteeism vary from one American Indian school district to another, interviews with school administrators in Wyoming, Montana, and South Dakota indicate that absenteeism and truancy are a major problem.

The National Education Longitudinal Study of 1988 provided some insight into the absentee problem. The study reported that 11 percent of American Indians in the eighth grade missed five or more days of school during a four-week period, as compared to less than 10 percent for Asians, whites, and Black Americans. Harold Hodgkinson concluded that missing large numbers of school days contributed to the high dropout rate for American Indians.[177] Indian educator Dean Chavers reported that absenteeism among Indian students runs as high as 25 percent, compared to the national rate of 7 percent. He noted that often ten- to fifteen-year-olds stay home to baby-sit younger siblings.[178]

Hal Gilliland observed that tardiness and absenteeism among American Indian youth are often the result of home situations and suggested that teachers try to understand the situation and work to improve it, rather than criticize the student. "Many Indian children are continually in trouble for excessive tardiness or absence," he stated. "Tardiness is usually the fault of the parents rather than the child. If the home does not run by an urban time schedule, it may be almost impossible for the child to always be on time. If a girl is the only baby sitter when her mother has to be gone, responsibilities at home must come before school. The school needs to work with the home to try to solve these problems, but if children are continually scolded, punished, or harassed for something they cannot do anything about, they cannot be blamed if they make little effort to improve in those or other ways."[179]

It appears that one of the reasons many at-risk youth dislike school is that they are frequently placed on in-school detention or expelled from school. In a study of dropouts conducted by the Children's Defense Fund, it was found that 25 percent of all dropouts had been expelled from school before they dropped out and that 20 percent more had been identified by their teachers as having behavior problems.[180]

Two national panels, the National Board of Inquiry into Schools and the National Commission on Secondary Education for Hispanics, reported that the majority of school expulsions are the result of nonthreatening behavior. The most common infractions included "defiance of authority," "chronic tardiness," "chronic absence," and "profanity or vulgarity." The negative effect of expulsion was addressed by the panels as ineffective in encouraging discipline, and it further alienated students from school by keeping them out of class. The panels also found that in many schools, due process was neglected and a student's explanation meant very little. In addition, the panels found that minority students were three times as likely to be expelled as white students and that in integrated schools, minority students constituted a disproportionate number of the expulsions.[181]

Although detention, which is generally in the form of in-school, three-day suspensions, is less frequent, most detentions appear to be the result of absenteeism, tardiness, and truancy, thus further promoting problems of non–class attendance, such as failure of classes, low achievement, and retention in the grade. This system may contribute to what Gary Wehlage and Robert Rutter referred to as the rejection of the school by the individual student, because the school has already rejected the individual.[182]

Although some studies have indicated that absence from school may not impact achievement as much as some researchers have maintained, it appears that being absent or being placed in detention or expelled can, in fact, become habit-forming and may lead to dropping out of school.

Teacher Attitudes and Expectations

The quality and motivations of teachers working with American Indian children have been the subject of much debate. The first teachers were missionaries who sought to Christianize and convert their charges. This group was followed by government-contracted teachers who were employed to assimilate the Indian child into the white society. Neither group had knowledge of or a particular interest in the American Indian culture or language. It was not until the 1930s that the federal government required contracted teachers to have a four-year teaching degree.

Personal accounts of Indian Service teachers reported recruitment of undesirable staff by the government bureaucracy in school and dormitory facilities.[183] Throughout the history of Indian education, scholars and writers have noted the difficulty in recruiting and retaining qualified, committed teachers. Even today, the BIA reports a 50 percent turnover rate every two years among its professional staff.[184]

Some researchers suggest that the school and teachers are potential sources of emotional stress for Indian children. They have pointed to a lack of Indian role models and to curricula at odds with the child's Native culture. One Montana educator noted that teachers often refer to American Indian students as being disadvantaged, and was quick to point out that Indian students are often at a disadvantage in classrooms where the teacher does not know the culture or lacks the understanding to adapt instruction to meet the needs of culturally different children. He suggested that "teachers' actions and attitudes should never imply that one culture is superior to another. The purpose of education is not to turn all students into middle class citizens, or carbon copies of the teacher."[185] Others have noted that Indian children have little chance of being exposed to Indian teachers who can act as role models. Less than 15 percent of teachers of American Indian students are themselves American Indian, and this figure is cut by three-fourths at the high school level.[186]

A number of researchers have attributed the historically poor achievement of Indian students to white teachers who are unable or unwilling to pay attention to the cultural background and values of American Indian students: "Teachers who come to the reservation day schools often know little about the children they are going to teach. . . . Teacher orientation and training sessions pay scant attention to Indian cultural values or to problems which the teacher may encounter with children . . . who have different values and know different experiences."[187]

In a study of Indian students in New Mexico's public schools, it was determined that although white teachers were aware of the differences in language and customs, they were not aware of the more subtle, intangible differences, such as values and attitudes.[188] Other researchers have presented similar views: "The school, representing the mainstream values, seeks to assimilate the Indian pupil rather than respect his identity and accommodate him in the curriculum. It rhetorically expounds the vaunted pluralism of America, but refuses to practice it in the classroom."[189]

Hal Gilliland cautioned teachers about making assumptions concerning their students: "Teachers moving into Native American communities tend to assume that because the people have accepted modern ways of life, the old culture is lost. . . . Since each Native American tribe is a unique group, teachers cannot assume any student believes or follows all the values of a 'typical Native culture' or follows the patterns of the non-Native society. Students are somewhere in between, usually nearer one end of the scale than the other."[190]

Dick Little Bear, a well-respected Northern Cheyenne bilingual educator, maintains that there is a need for teachers on Indian reservations to work with parents: "One reason for that need is that most of those who teach Indian students are non-Indians from the dominant society. Most of their teacher training has been monocultural, with the middle-class forming their socioeconomic norm. However, teachers need to realize that when they teach Indian students they are not teaching the norm and that the students they are teaching are being impacted daily by a dynamic culture."[191]

Estelle Fuchs and Robert Havighurst have argued that the reason school achievement is unimportant to Indian students or their parents is that neither can directly relate education to the future opportunity for success. These authors noted specifically that whereas white middle-class students seem to view school achievement as an important part of their total identity, Indian students view school achievement as a separate activity, one that does not influence their view of themselves. The authors concluded that the often-held opinion that school performance is strongly linked to self-concept, which appears to be the case within the white culture, does not hold true for Indian students.[192]

Many researchers have stressed the need for informing teachers about cultural differences among their students.[193] Others have noted that Indian children are predisposed to learning cooperatively in groups, rather than competitively as individuals, and point out that Indian children placed in the "spotlight" or singled out will withdraw.[194] Anthony Brown concurred with this theory, reporting that Cherokee Indian children were more cooperative and less competitive than Anglo children in a comparison group.[195] A number of researchers have proposed that classroom organization and structure that emphasize individual competitiveness, rather than group cooperation, adversely affect the achievement of students.[196] Other investigators have reported that American Indian children often observe an activity, then review the activity in their heads until they are certain they can perform the task before undertaking it.[197] Because of the incongruities suggested by the researchers regarding learning styles and cultural attitudes of American Indian children and the school environment, a number of educators endorse a classroom organization that promotes cooperation, rather than one with a more competitive structure.[198]

Other researchers advocate the modification of classroom teaching techniques to accommodate the learning styles of Indian students, suggesting that American Indian education has traditionally emphasized attitudes of self-reliance, respect for nature and wisdom, generosity, and personal freedom, and that teachers must consider these characteristics.[199]

Some researchers have found that American Indian children passively resist authority, follow directions submissively, observe activities passively, and complain about school regimentation, rules, and regulations.[200] Rosalie Wax reported that problems encountered by Oglala Sioux boys reflected a culture that stressed loyalty and dependence on peers, physical recklessness, and impetuousness. She maintained that Sioux boys did not hold values required for success in school, and noted, "Not only is he ignorant of how to buck the rules, he doesn't even know the rules."[201]

Historically, passivity in the classroom among Indian children has been expected. The 1928 Meriam Report found that Indian children were forced to remain quiet and that the majority of the schools had locked rooms used for isolating and containing unruly students.[202] Donna Deyhle reported that Indian students are expected to sit passively in the classroom, to read and memorize information, and to listen to lectures.[203] Jim Cummins noted that most teachers use a passive method of instruction in the classroom.[204] In return, passivity is expected of students, and those who do not comply are often disciplined in terms of suspensions, promoting again the pushing-out concept often interpreted as dropping out. There is some evidence suggesting that passive teaching strategies are widely used in "low tracking" classes, where minority students are commonly placed. Compensatory programs like Chapter I have often been criticized as providing mechanical, passive instruction that results in student boredom, decreased motivation, and lack of interest.[205] In Donna Deyhle's study, she reported that Indian students often described boredom with remedial classes and uninteresting subject matter.[206] A 1989 study of Alaskan education asked high school seniors why their peers dropped out of school. Consistently, students blamed unsupportive teachers, inability to memorize information required to pass courses, and boredom.[207]

Although it is commonly assumed that Indian students who drop out are failing academically, a study of Navajo at-risk youth reported that the academic achievement of dropouts did not differ significantly from that of students who remained in school and graduated. In fact, 45 percent of the dropouts had a B or better grade average.[208]

Historically, tracking has been used with American Indian students. Part of this dates back to the early beliefs held by missionaries/teachers that Indians were lazy; that basic skills in spelling, reading, writing, and arithmetic were sufficient; and that a strong academic education for Indians promoted nothing more than indolence.[209] Therefore, teachers who have low expectations of Indian students have repeatedly counseled students into vocationally oriented curricula. This "tracking," which is more commonly associated with secondary schools, results in a substandard education for students and leads to lower-class jobs and eventually lower-class status as adults.[210] Research has demonstrated repeatedly that teachers treat lower-tracked students differently from the way they treat high-tracked students. When one considers that over 40 percent of Indian youth are in the lowest quartile on achievement test scores in math, reading, science, and history, and that less than 10 percent are in the upper quartile, it is clear that tracking impacts a vast majority of Indian students.[211] One researcher has gone so far as to suggest that tracking students into vocational education programs segregates poor minority students in an effort to preserve the academic curriculum for middle- and upper-class students.[212] While this may not be the same reason for tracking that occurs in a reservation school, it is possible that teachers at these schools support tracking into vocational programs for academically deficient students so that they can be left unencumbered to teach the "good" students. "Good" in this sense is meant to imply both academic achievement and passivity.

A number of researchers have suggested that the parochialism of the teaching staff in American Indian schools inhibits the learning of students: "Many of the teachers at the elementary level are middle-aged wives of men who have farms in the vicinity. They have lived in the area for a number of years, or in some cases all of their lives, and are acquainted with the Indians' behavior and their 'shortcomings.' They are not idealistic and are not surprised at anything the Indians do."[213]

Other researchers feel that teachers' attitudes toward Indian students are critical to success in school.[214] Hal Gilliland succinctly endorsed this view when he stated, "A teacher's attitude is . . . contagious. . . . A teacher who can earn the respect of Indian students and who can show them that they are respected for what they are is well on the road to giving those children success in school. . . . Too many teachers and other well-intentioned individuals look at the physical surroundings in which Indian students live, the prejudice they face, their problems in school, and they sympathize. They feel sorry for them. These students do not need sympathy; they need something to be proud of. Pity and pride do not go together."[215]

Much attention is given in the literature to the attitudes of teachers toward Indian children. Some researchers have found that white teachers often demonstrate contempt for Indian students, while, on the other hand, many teachers sincerely like their Indian students.[216] Estelle Fuchs and Robert Havighurst found that Indian adolescents held more favorable attitudes toward their teachers than Anglo-American students did. However, they also noted that there was a considerable amount of hostility among Indian students toward teachers whom they perceived as being prejudiced against or racist toward Indians.[217]

On the other hand, a 1990 report that compared ethnic students' attitudes toward teachers found few Indian students stating that they felt teachers were truly interested in them; nor did they feel that their teachers listened to them. In addition, Indian students reported unfair discipline from teachers.[218] In a study of Navajo and Ute students, Donna Deyhle also observed that students complained about teachers who did not care about them or help them, and suggested that minimal attention by the teacher was interpreted by students as rejection.[219]

Dick Little Bear noted that in the teacher-parent interactions, Indian parents are often judged in relation to historical circumstances by the teachers: "Stereotypes and misconceptions have been the lot of Indians since their first contact with Europeans. Many non-Indians continue to rely on these stereotypes and misconceptions—often confusing them with truth—which categorize Indians in the worst possible manner."[220] He noted, too, that this problem is not just confined to non-Indian teachers, stating that "even if teachers are Indian, they may be urban Indians with little or no knowledge about reservation cultures . . . even if teachers are from the reservation they may have unquestioningly accepted the values of the dominant society as being superior to those of the Indian."[221]

Hal Gilliland maintained that many teachers have unrealistic expectations of students: "They give them homework and penalize them if they do not get it done, without considering the home situation. . . . It is unrealistic to expect parents and extended family members who do not read for recreation, who see little relevance between school and 'life,' and who have little or no knowledge of the subject the child is studying, to shut off the TV and devote time to helping or even encouraging the child."[222]

In his three-volume work *Children of Crisis*, Robert Coles pointed out that many children enter school without obvious psychological problems but, because they are labeled as coming from so-called "disadvantaged" or "deprived" homes by teachers, they don't do well in school. Because of the socioeconomic status of their families, Coles suggested that students coming from poor homes are expected to fail by teachers, administrators, and other individuals involved in the operation and policymaking of the school:

They come from poor homes. They don't eat good food; and indeed many physicians and nutritionists and neurophysiologists would argue that a faulty diet, low in critically important vitamins, minerals and proteins, causes serious damage to an infant's brain, so that eventually he comes to school retarded, not by an accident or disease or injury, but the repercussions of a nation's social and economic problem, which becomes a very personal, everyday problem for millions of families. Yet even if poor parents can provide their children with decent meals and adequate medical care and suitable clothes . . . [d]oes the mother give her children a sense of confidence, or do she and her husband feel discouraged about life most of the time? . . . Mothers who live in broken-down, rat-infested tenements, who never quite know when the next few dollars will come, have little energy left for their children. Life is grim and hard, and the child simply has to find that out. He does, too; he learns it and learns it and learns it. He learns how to survive all sorts of threats and dangers. He learns why his parents have given up on school, why they may have tried and fallen flat on their faces. He learns about things like racial hatred . . . whether he is an insider or an outsider, whether people like storekeepers or property owners or policemen treat his family with kindness and respect or with suspicion if not out-and-out contempt.[223]

In the book *Pygmalion in the Classroom*, the authors reveal that the preconceptions of teachers serve as self-fulfilling prophecies for students.[224] Teacher perceptions and expectations negatively affect achievement in American Indian children. Research demonstrates that poor and minority students are underrepresented in programs for gifted and talented children and in college-bound curricula and are overrepresented in special education and vocational programs.[225]

The question arises about the qualities of teachers that contribute to their negative perceptions of the American Indian student's ability. One study compared teachers' family of origin's socioeconomic status with the perceptions they had about the school and students where they worked.[226] The researchers found that teachers who came from families with high socioeconomic status held lower expectations for minority students. Further, it was found that teachers' values affected their evaluation of student performance.

The power of teachers' perceptions in affecting student performance is dramatically demonstrated throughout the research.[227] In a longitudinal study of Black children, it was found that kindergarten teachers made evaluations of a student's expected abilities based on physical appearance, language style, and socioeconomic status of the child's family. Without any regard to students' academic abilities, teachers placed students into three groups, based on perceptions of whether or not they were "fast learners." It is important to note that the "fast learners" were perceived by the teacher to be clean and well-dressed, spoke standard English, interacted verbally with the teacher, and had families who were not on welfare.[228]

When an examination is made of how teachers treat "fast learners" as opposed to "slow learners" with regard to the amount of time spent on engaging children in the teaching/learning process, giving help, and providing opportunities, it is easy to understand why the gap between fast learners and slow learners increases with each year in school.

Researchers of the dropout phenomenon have consistently reported that student retention is associated with an increased probability of dropping out, rather than with improved chances for graduation. In fact, research indicates that dropouts are five times more likely to have been retained in one grade, and students who have been retained in two grades have nearly a 100 percent probability of dropping out.[229] When one considers that 29 percent of American Indian students have already been retained by the eighth grade, it is understandable why so many Indian students are at risk.

According to a Gallup poll, 72 percent of the U.S. public favors stricter grade promotion standards.[230] And yet Thomas Holmes, from the University of Georgia, recently conducted a synthesis of research on sixty-three controlled studies where students were retained and found that in fifty-four of the studies, the students who were retained actually performed more poorly on average than if they had not repeated a grade.[231]

There is considerable evidence that children perceive retention as punishment.[232] In fact, one researcher found that children rated repeating a grade more stressful than "wetting in class" or being caught stealing. The only two events identified by children as being more stressful than repeating a grade were "going blind" and "losing a parent."[233]

Basically, researchers have not been able to determine why retention doesn't work. Some have suggested that the negative emotional effects of repeating a grade inhibit subsequent learning. Others speculate that repeating the same material is an ineffective means of instruction.

Studies have found that when parents believe their children are smarter than other children, these children do better than other children.[234] If children are retained, it is likely that parents doubt their children's abilities. Thus, if parents' positive beliefs have positive academic outcomes for children, it follows that negative beliefs about ability would have negative academic outcomes. In fact, studies have shown that parents are more likely to focus on children's ability during the first half of the school year and to experience a preoccupation with retention during the second half of the year.[235]

Even though the research is inconsistent about teacher attitudes, expectations, and tracking and retention, it is obvious that the teacher plays a major role in the lives of students in how they are treated and whether they are tracked or retained.

Racism, Discrimination, and Prejudice

The placement of American Indians on reservations, where in many cases they were forbidden to leave and interact with non-Indians, was legislative racism sanctioned by the federal government. Removing Indian children from their home environment and placing them in boarding schools further suggested that the Euro-Americans considered their values, laws, and culture superior to those of the American Indian. There is a plethora of literature available on the prevailing attitude of the government throughout history in regard to the American Indian. The Indian was regarded as a savage to be eliminated or converted to the white man's way of thinking. This "civilization" of the Indian has resulted in a myriad of adjustment problems for subsequent generations of American Indians.

At a very early age, children become aware of racial differences. Several studies indicate that by the time children reach the age of five, they have a clear knowledge of racial differences. The American Indian child has often been made to feel that s/he is different from and inferior to the mainstream society, and because of these circumstances it is often difficult for the Indian child to develop coping skills adequate to meet the demands of society.[236]

A number of studies have been conducted on race and self-perceptions of children. In a study of whites, Mexican Americans, Black Americans, and American Indians, it was found that each ethnic group saw its race very favorably as a whole and saw the other groups less favorably. Other researchers studied Indian and white students to learn how they looked upon each of the two cultures and found that although Indian students rated their culture more favorably, they did not seem to identify with one culture more than the other. Socioeconomic status or social class appears to make a difference in establishing group or ethnic identity. Middle-class children showed higher rates of racial rejection than children from other social classes did.[237]

There has been little research conducted on racism, discrimination, and prejudice within and/or among American Indian groups and/or American Indians and non-Indians within the school setting; yet racism, prejudice, and discrimination clearly exist and may, in fact, be contributors to students' lack of success in the school setting.

Prior to Euro-American contact, all indigenous people were "full-blooded," so to speak. Indigenous North Americans specifically defined themselves in terms of their sociocultural membership, such as Lakota, Arapaho, Cheyenne, or Blackfoot, rather than in terms of a racial group. "Intertribal" marriages occurred during this period and the tribal societies were able to accommodate the influx of new memberships from other indigenous groups. All of this changed with the coming of the white man, who brought to the "New World" the concept of race and, through inter-marriage, the introduction of "mixed-bloods" into the tribal societies.

One needs to look no further than the boarding schools that were established to "civilize" the American Indian to find examples of racism that developed within tribal societies. Mary Crow Dog, a student at the St. Francis Boarding School, commented that the degree of Indian blood became a strategy for favoritism and acceptance and pitted students against students: "In a school like this [St. Francis Boarding School], there is always a lot of favoritism. Girls who were near-white who came from what the nuns called 'nice families,' got preferential treatment. They . . . got to eat ham or eggs and bacon . . . they got easy jobs while the skins [individuals with a higher degree of Indian blood] . . . always wound up in the laundry room . . . or we wound up scrubbing the floors and doing all the dishes. The school therefore fostered fights and antagonism between whites and breeds."[238]

One researcher who studied Navajo and Ute students reported the issues of racism and cultural maintenance as important factors in contrib-uting to students dropping out of school prematurely and noted consider-able conflict between a number of factions in the school. Reportedly, there was conflict between non-Indians and Indians, Navajos and Utes, tradi-tional Navajos and acculturated Navajos, and so on. The researcher observed that when issues of racism were coupled with academic difficul-ties, students were often the victims of negative school experiences. In addition, it was noted that many Indian students who were successful were often berated by their peers for acting like whites and were looked down on by their friends and families.[239]

Today, there is considerable disparity in the proportion of full-bloods and mixed-bloods within tribal groups. The federal government, under the auspices of the BIA, officially recognizes the American Indian as an indi-vidual who is one-quarter Indian blood or more. This strategy has resulted in keeping the aggregate number of American Indians at less than 1 percent of the overall population in the United States and thus reduces any political power that the population may have in terms of elections, lobbying power, and so forth. Further, this strategy has provided a legitimate means for the government to avoid providing educational support to students in reserva-tion schools who do not meet their blood-quantum criteria.

Thus, limited federal resources allocated by the federal government in meeting its obligations to American Indian tribal groups have resulted in tribal resolutions and constitutional amendments that enforce race codes as defined by the BIA on their own populations. This has led to excluding members who are less than one-fourth Indian blood (including children) from receiving any benefits, in order that the "real" Indians may benefit.

Thus, the question of American Indian identity has fueled the historical "divide and conquer" strategy by pitting Indian against Indian within their own tribal groups and among other groups. Some American Indian leaders have made efforts to unite their people by pointing out that these issues are not only historical, but a part of colonialism practiced by the government even today.

Tim Giago, editor of the *Lakota Times*, questioned, "Don't we have enough problems trying to unite without . . . additional headaches? Why must people be categorized as full-bloods, mixed-bloods, etc.? Many years ago, the Bureau of Indian Affairs decided to establish blood quanta for the purpose of [tribal] enrollment. At that time, blood quantum was set at one-fourth degree for enrollment. Unfortunately, through the years, this caused the Indian people on the reservation to be categorized and labeled. . . . [This] situation [was] created solely by the BIA, with the able assistance of the Department of the Interior."[240]

To illustrate further the impact that blood-quantum criteria has had upon individuals and Indian tribes, the words of Russell Means, AIM activist, are quite pertinent: "We have Indian people who spend most of their time trying to prevent other Indian people from being recognized as such, just so that a few more crumbs—crumbs from the federal table—may be available to them, personally. I don't have to tell you that this isn't the Indian way of doing things. The Indian way would be to get together and demand what is coming to each and every one of us, instead of trying to cancel each other out. We are acting like colonized peoples, like subject peoples."[241]

Dr. Frank Ryan, an American Indian educator, began during the early 1980s to question the blood-quantum criteria of the federal government for educational benefits to students and denounced them as "racist policy." He called for an abolition of federal guidelines on the issues of Indian identity without lessening the federal obligations to individual and tribal groups.[242] Other Indian leaders have suggested that the federal blood-quantum policies can be described as no less than genocide in their implications. Josephine Mills, a Shoshone activist, charged, "There is no longer any need to shoot down Indians in order to take away their rights and land . . . legislation is sufficient to do the trick legally."[243]

Perhaps no policy adopted by the federal government is so racist as the blood-quantum criteria. This policy has certainly served to exacerbate tensions among Indian people and has created divisiveness within tribal groups. As one historian noted, "Set the blood quantum at one-quarter, hold to it as a rigid definition of Indians, let intermarriage proceed as it had for centuries, and eventually Indians will be defined out of existence. When that happens, the federal government will be freed of its persistent 'Indian problem.'"[244]

Certainly, one needs to look no further than the population figures of the past two decades to discover that the numbers of full-bloods are decreasing. For example, 65 percent of all American Indian males today marry non-Indian women. Among American Indian females, marriage to non-Indians is at 62 percent.[245] As of 1970, ". . . three-fifths of all births registered as Indian list both parents as Indians [of varying degrees of Indian blood]. More than one-fourth of the remaining Indian births had only an Indian mother, and 15 percent had only an Indian father."[246]

If Indian tribes continue to allow the "divide and conquer" strategies to be enforced in terms of ethnic identification, then racism, discrimination, and prejudice are assured of continuation on Indian reservations. Schools and schoolchildren are often the most affected, not only in terms of the quality of educational programs that are offered, but in terms of how individual children deal with their own self-identity and tribal identity and how racism, prejudice, and discrimination at the hands of their "own kind" contribute to their success or lack of success in school. Perhaps the answer for tribal groups can be found, in part, by the experience of the Cherokee:

> In developing a new tribal constitution in the 1970s . . . the Cherokee Nation of Oklahoma established no minimum blood quantum for membership. Instead, one must only trace descent along Cherokee lines. . . . This comparatively generous definition has expanded the Cherokee Nation of Oklahoma population: in the mid-1970s there were only about 12,000 enrolled Cherokee . . . in 1985 there were over 64,300. There are still full-blood and traditional Cherokee, despite the myth in Oklahoma and elsewhere, of Cherokee assimilation. . . . They continue in the 1980s, insulated from American society by the much larger number of mixed bloods and less traditional Cherokee. . . . This allowed the [Nation] to reestablish itself after virtual "dissolution" and to achieve political power in Oklahoma.[247]

Summary

Although incidences of racism, prejudice, and discrimination vary from one geographic region to another and from one reservation to another, there are a number of studies that seem to support the idea that the more "white" a student appears (mixed-bloods), the more acceptable that student is to mainstream society. In the long run, this acceptability is defined in terms of more opportunities in school and employment. Therefore, the questions of racism, discrimination, and prejudice, whether practiced within the tribal groups or among mainstream society, appear to have a major impact on American Indian youth.

Part 2

American Indian Female High School Dropouts and High School and College Graduates Talk about Their Lives

Chapter 6

Introduction to the Study

Although lack of success in school has been a problem for the American Indian throughout the history of Indian education, few researchers have focused on the American Indian female, whose problems in school are often compounded by socialization and gender roles related to culture, lack of job opportunities, and lack of female role models and mentors. This study examined the lives of 991 American Indian women and their perceptions about school and the personal, family, and school factors that affected their degree of success in school.

There were two major purposes for the study:

• To identify the factors that keep American Indian females in school
• To identify the factors that result in American Indian females leaving school prematurely

In developing the research approach, consideration was given to the uniqueness of the American Indian female experience. Unlike other female groups in America, the American Indian woman has been isolated from mainstream society by placement on the reservation. However, many scholars have noted that at the time the Europeans came to the Americas, the status of American Indian women within their societies was superior to that of the white women who settled the country. In the ensuing years the Euro-American, male-dominated culture was to have a tremendous impact upon the status of Native women, reducing them to "second-class citizens" within their families and among their tribal groups.[1] According to Stan Steiner, this was a result of the inability of the Euro-American male to understand societies in which women held equal status with men.[2]

In addition, there were other unique considerations in the American Indian female experience that I had to keep in mind:

• Participants in the study lived and had gone to high school on reservations, a setting that is often charged with providing a false sense of security to its residents, thereby limiting the individual and promoting the feminization of poverty. Although dropping out of school and poverty are interrelated in all cultures, these elements have a special significance in the study of American Indian females, who have been said to regard poverty as a "way of life."

- Given the conditions of life on the reservation (as discussed in Part 1), it would appear that, at least from a cursory examination, nearly *all* American Indian girls are at risk of dropping out; yet there are those who stay in school and graduate from high school, and many continue their education at two-year and four-year colleges—some even completing master's and doctoral programs.
- Success in the educational system, especially college graduation, has often been the subject of discussion among both Indian and non-Indian observers. Historically, the intent of education was assimilation and acculturation; therefore, many American Indians who are successful in school find that their "Indianness" is questioned among their own people. The inference is made that American Indians who succeed in school have, in fact, "bought into the white man's system," or have somehow given up part of their Native heritage in order to succeed in another system.
- All tribes are currently experiencing various levels of modernization and social change. However, tribes today have been influenced by the domination of Euro-American political and social systems, so that in the areas of education and equal employment opportunities, even within their own tribes, American Indian women face the same barriers confronted by non-Indian women.

The Purpose of the Study

The purpose of this study was twofold: (1) to determine the factors that contribute to the success of American Indian females who stay in school and graduate, and (2) to determine the factors that contribute to the lack of success of American Indian females who drop out of school and do not graduate.

Another major intent of the study was to seek solutions to the dropout problem that might replace current practices in American Indian education with better alternatives. Historically, the purpose of Indian education has been to facilitate assimilation. There is no question that this approach has failed. Over the past two decades, a number of strategies have been attempted; however, the dropout rate has not declined nationally, and while some areas have recorded dramatic increases in high school graduation, others have reported increases in the dropout rate.

As most administrators admit, they often must make policy decisions based on personal judgments of what seems to work. I selected research questions whose answers would have implications for school boards and other policymakers, school districts and their administrators, foundations, and local, state, and federal agencies.

This study was conducted over an eighteen-month period between 1989 and 1991 in three states, among residents of five reservations and members of seven tribal groups. Nine hundred and ninety-one women participated in the study. Because some tribes have encountered negative stereotyping as a result of the release of survey data, I assured all cooperating individuals that data about tribal groups, individual reservations, and community locations would not be released.

Data-gathering Methods and Procedures

The data collected for this study were gathered through individual interviews, using a set of predesigned questions. The study employed a cross-sectional design in which interviews were conducted with 991 females residing on the reservation. Participants were categorized according to level of education achieved: (1) high school dropout, (2) high school graduate, or (3) holder of a college degree (including women who had completed associate degrees, bachelor's degrees, master's degrees, and doctorates). A stratified random sample of females was interviewed; these were females who graduated from high school, or who should have graduated had they stayed in school, during a fifteen-year period between 1971 and 1986. Ages of the women in the study ranged from seventeen to thirty-six.

The interview method was chosen over other methods because it provided for the flexibility of participants to respond freely and in depth to the questions, to express their responses in their own words and in their own way, and to clarify and/or explain at length any responses. An "open-ended interview" process was used. For example, each participant was asked a series of predesigned questions that could have been answered "Yes," "No," "I don't know," "I can't remember," or "I prefer not to talk about that topic." If a respondent, for example, replied, "I prefer not to talk about that topic," her wishes were honored and that particular line of questioning ceased. If the respondent answered "Yes" or "No," I took the opportunity to ask further questions, which probed for more information, feelings, attitudes, perceptions, and opinions.

For three reasons, I chose to conduct the interviews personally, rather than use research assistants: (1) I had worked at or lived on each of the five reservations, had been "adopted" into three of the tribal groups, and had knowledge of the Native cultures and tribal groups; (2) I had worked with high-risk youth and had provided personal and family counseling to parents, families, and children, thus earning a reputation for maintaining confidentiality and trust that was critical to the study; and (3) through previous work, I was regarded as an advocate for women, but not as a feminist (as defined within the majority culture).

I conducted all interviews at the convenience of the participants. Interviews took place in the participant's setting of choice. Fifty-nine percent of the interviews were conducted in the privacy of the individual's home, 27 percent were conducted in a job setting, and 14 percent were conducted in the home of a relative or friend or at such neutral settings as a park or drive-in or in a natural, country setting. The interviews were conducted at the convenience of the participant in terms of time. Thirty-six percent of the interviews took place in the evening, 23 percent were scheduled on weekends, and the remainder took place during the daytime or working hours.

Prior to conducting the interview, the researcher spent approximately twenty-five to forty minutes (dependent upon the individual) with each potential participant for the purpose of explaining the nature of the study. Generally, this period included rather informal discussions of common acquaintances, relatives, and friends; introductions to others in the home; and conversations relating to my professional career and personal life, including such topics as tribal affiliation, marriage (spouse's tribal affiliation and family), and children. Often the individual related instances of indirect or direct knowledge of me.

Once these informalities were completed, I reviewed with the individual the major correlates and subtopics included in the study, explaining that questions would be asked concerning each of the topics and citing the reasons these topics had been included in the study. The potential participant was encouraged to ask questions at any point. It was further explained that were a question or topic too sensitive, the interviewee could choose not to discuss that particular subject. Each participant was guaranteed personal and group anonymity, and time was taken to discuss any misgivings she might have about confidentiality; stereotyping of American Indian women, their tribes, and their reservations; and any knowledge of or negative experiences the interviewee may have had with other researchers. Once this stage was completed, the individual was asked if she would be willing to participate in the study. If she refused, her decision was respected without any type of pressure or encouragement for involvement.

Although time-consuming, this stage was considered critical to the success of the study for two reasons: (1) it provided an opportunity for the potential interviewee to think about whether she wanted to participate in light of the sensitive, personal, and confidential nature of the questions; and (2) it gave the potential participant a chance to assess or "size up" the researcher for trustworthiness, sincerity, and honesty. Although many interviewers attempt to maintain a formal manner with participants, this approach was considered inappropriate due to the nature of the study. For American Indian women to discuss the issues addressed by this study requires a level of trust that can be achieved only through informal conversations and adequate time to assess personal feelings and the interviewer's intent. Without this approach, respondents are more likely to limit their responses to "Yes," "No," and the like—which would have defeated the purposes of the study.

The interviews ranged in length from forty-five minutes to one hour and forty minutes, depending upon the individual's willingness and/or inclination to respond to the questions. Of the 991 interviews, 980 participants gave permission for the interviews to be tape-recorded.

At no time did I move on to another series of questions before the participant had ceased discussion of a specific topic. In addition, I did not schedule interviews within a limited time frame. This avoided the problem of "hurrying" a participant. In many cases, the interviews were extremely emotional, but at no time was an interview terminated by the participant.

After the interview stage was completed, several hundred pages of notes and over 1,000 hours of tapes had been collected for analysis. In the chapters that follow, many of the women's responses, in their own words, are quoted to illustrate the intensity of their answers.

Content Validity

The interview instrument was designed using the most current research on gender, at-risk youth, and high school dropouts. The instrument included sections on the correlates relating to success and lack of success in school, including the following:

1. Personal problems
   - Substance abuse (alcohol and/or other drug use and abuse)
   - Problems with the law
   - Low self-esteem and lack of self-identity
   - Peer pressure
   - Mental health problems such as depression (suicidal tendencies)
   - Pregnancy
2. Family background
   - Socioeconomic status
   - Educational level of parents
   - Child-rearing practices
   - Single-parent families
   - Dysfunctional families (including child abuse)

3. School factors
   - Bilingualism
   - Cultural differences and cultural discontinuity
   - Academic achievement and failure, including grade retention and tracking
   - Attendance: truancy, absenteeism, detention, and expulsion
   - Teacher attitudes and expectations
   - Racism, discrimination, and prejudice

Upon completion of the interview instrument, university faculty, Indian educators, school administrators, counselors, community service workers, law enforcement officers, and health workers were asked to review the questions and provide input. At this point, the suggestions were reviewed and appropriate modifications were made to the interview instrument.

The next step, field testing of the interview instrument, was then begun. Thirty-three American Indian females volunteered to participate. This group included eleven high school dropouts, eleven high school graduates, and eleven college graduates. The study was explained to each volunteer. A discussion of the major research questions and the correlates to be addressed was provided. Prior to the field-testing interview, each participant was given an opportunity to ask any questions. Each interview was conducted at the convenience of the volunteer, in a setting of her choice, and under the same conditions as described earlier regarding time, sensitivity to cultural factors, and concern for the dignity of the individual. Following the interview, however, each volunteer was asked to freely discuss the interview questions with the researcher. Comments on appropriateness, sensitivity, and the controversial nature of the questions were solicited. Analysis of the wording of each question was performed for purposes of understanding and appropriateness. The discussions also included a review of the personal nature of the questions, the probable difficulty of tribal women in discussing some of the issues, and the pros and cons of rewording, adding, or deleting questions.

Following this stage, the final interview questionnaire was completed and on-site visits to the reservations were conducted.

The remaining chapters within this section will report the findings of the study. The chapters have been organized around major topics, such as peer pressure, racism and stereotyping, substance abuse, and teacher attitudes. In some cases, it may appear that the accounts provided by the women "overlap" and could have been more appropriately placed in another section. Since dropping out of school or staying in school is most often the result of a number of interacting factors, I simply had to make an arbitrary decision as to where the accounts were most suitable.

Chapter 7

Profiles of Dropouts, High School Graduates, and College Graduates

There is no one characteristic that describes the women in this study who dropped out of school, just as there is no one characteristic that could describe those who stayed in school and graduated. Indeed, there was no one set of descriptors that could be used to characterize those who succeeded in school or those who dropped out. To illustrate this point, this chapter contains profiles of thirty women who were interviewed. Ten of the women were high school dropouts, ten were high school graduates, and the remaining ten graduated from college. As the reader will note, some of the women who dropped out would not have been considered high risk by educators, while others who stayed in school and graduated did so despite the odds that they were among the candidates whom researchers and educators describe as potential dropouts.

Profiles of Dropouts

Although most of the factors discussed in this book have been researched by others, but perhaps with different results, no one has ever conducted a major study on the American Indian female dropout. It is obvious from this study that no scholarly analysis of reasons for American Indian girls dropping out of school is sufficient to understand the complex nature of the dropout problem. Each girl must be considered as an individual. There must be a thorough examination of her home background and her school performance, and a complete assessment of her behavior and personality factors. Only then can an effective plan for intervention be implemented. In order to demonstrate such a need, I have chosen to profile some of the women who participated in this study. Their case studies document the complex nature of their decision to leave school and suggest the magnitude of the efforts that must be expended in order to prevent American Indian girls from dropping out of school. With each of the women profiled, fictitious names are used.

MARY. Mary dropped out of school in her junior year because of pregnancy. Both of her parents were college-educated and held good jobs in the community. Mary was the youngest of three children, but was considered very mature for her age. She had already met with a guidance counselor and was making plans for college. She planned to be a doctor. Mary's parents always attended school activities and parent-teacher meetings, and encouraged Mary to participate in extracurricular activities that interested her. In Mary's home, there were rules she and her sisters were required to follow, including curfew, cleaning their room, no dating on school days, and no alcohol or drugs. Her closest friends were her sister (older by one year), two cousins in her class, and another girl who came from a family of professional parents. Since the second grade, Mary had been a part of the same group. Mary now stays home with her baby. Her friends are planning to go to college. Mary hopes that someday she will get a GED and go to college. Mary noted that she always wanted to be a mother, "but not at seventeen."

BETH. Beth's parents were both alcoholics. She claimed her parents had put alcohol in her bottle when she was an infant to keep her from crying. By the time Beth was nine, she was drinking from half-empty beer cans left after her parents and their friends had passed out from drinking. Beth had two younger siblings who required her care much of the time. At the age of ten, Beth was sexually assaulted by her father. At eleven, she ran away to live with an aunt, but returned home when her father threatened to molest her younger sister. Until she was fifteen, Beth was the object of her father's unwanted attention. Her mother ignored her pleas and beat her when she told about her father's assaults. She also told her aunt, who refused to believe her. Beth missed a lot of school. She always felt that her teachers rejected her for that reason. Beth dropped out of school after her sophomore year. The next year, she had a baby. She went on welfare. Over time, Beth has had a series of lovers, most of them abusive or alcoholic. She has also had three other children, all by different men. She doesn't speak to her father; her mother died two years ago. She hopes her children will stay in school and graduate. She wants them to go to college.

LYNN. Lynn ran away from home when she was seven. A police officer found her, and the courts placed her in a boarding school. A few weeks later, her parents came and picked her up. Lynn's family moved twelve times during her school years. Three times, she was court-ordered to boarding schools, and each time her parents came for her. Neither of Lynn's parents worked. Her father was an alcoholic. He was abusive to Lynn's mother, but never to her. Frequently, her parents took her out of school to accompany them on trips. Many times, Lynn simply did not get up and go to school in the morning—she was too tired from listening to her parents argue. At sixteen, Lynn ran away from home and went to the city. A few months later, she returned to the reservation. She completed her GED, has taken courses at the tribal college, and holds a job as a secretary. No one in the school ever intervened in Lynn's life. The courts never stepped in when Lynn was taken from school by her parents. Lynn felt that the school, the social workers, and her teachers never cared about her.

KATHY. Kathy was deserted by her mother when she was two. She lived with her grandmother, who, by the time Kathy had reached high school, had little energy to deal with a teenager. Kathy resented her mother and most other adult females. At eleven, she began drinking. By thirteen, she had graduated to drugs. She frequently stole money from her grandmother to buy alcohol and drugs. When her grandmother questioned her, Kathy reported hitting her and threatening to kill her. Kathy repeatedly got into arguments with female teachers. She walked out of their class, talked back to them, and called them names. At fourteen, Kathy had her first sexual experience. It was with a high school shop teacher nearly three times her age. Reportedly, the event took place in the teacher's classroom and was repeated frequently throughout the next year. In return for sex, the teacher gave her money, which she used for alcohol and drugs. When she dropped out of school the first semester of her sophomore year, no one from the school questioned her absence.

LISA. Lisa dropped out of school and was married at fourteen to a man who was nearly thirty years older than she. She described her childhood as one of hunger for food and love. She was frequently abused by alcoholic parents. She was responsible for cleaning the house, cooking the meals, and taking care of her younger siblings. She recalled approaching a teacher once, whom she trusted, preparing to tell her about her family life. When she told the teacher that she had a problem, the teacher replied, "We all have problems, don't we?" After that, she never reached out to anyone in the school. Lisa said she will never forgive that teacher.

SUE. Sue was the oldest of nine children. "My mother was a whore," she explained. "Men of every size and description visited her all hours of the day and night. When I was young, I called them Daddy. They brought me presents to get rid of me so they could be alone with my mother. I wanted to go to school. I wanted to graduate so badly. I remember one day sitting in class while this teacher rattled on about her visit to Paris and the kinds of people on the streets, the cafés, the shops. I became furious. Paris had nothing to do with me. I was hurting inside, but no one cared. I never went back to school after that. I was seventeen and a senior. When people ask me why I dropped out of school, I tell them, 'It was all because of Paris.'" Sue married after three years in the military and lives on a small ranch on the reservation. She completed her GED in the service. She is the mother of two small children and is adamant that they will go to school and graduate, even if she has to sit in class with them to make sure they attend.

BETTY. Betty was expelled from school as a result of an accumulation of infractions, including excessive truancies, disrupting class, and fighting. She was happy to be expelled from school and considered her plight "a badly needed vacation." Her parents had no reaction to her expulsion. While on her "vacation," she began staying out at night, drinking, and using drugs. Her parents never reprimanded her for her behavior. When her suspension ended, Betty never returned to school. By the age of twenty-one, Betty was a self-proclaimed alcoholic with three children. She lives with her mother and an elderly aunt; they take care of her children when Betty "goes on a binge." She has been to treatment twice, but has always returned to drinking. Betty talked about getting a job, going back to school, and getting a home for her children.

JENNY. Jenny was a cheerleader and a popular girl in school. She always made the honor roll. Her parents were very supportive and provided a good home environment. When she was a sophomore, she met an "older" boy (six years older) at a basketball game. "He was so good looking, but I knew my parents would disapprove," she recalled. Jenny enlisted the help of a cousin so she could meet the young man without her parents' knowledge. She fell in love immediately. Several weeks later, Jenny attended a party with her new boyfriend and some of his friends. She smoked marijuana for the first time. Later that night, she was raped by her boyfriend and his friends. "Afterwards, I lost interest in school," she said. "It no longer had any meaning. You [this writer] are the first person I have ever told about this. I was too ashamed. Now I realize that all of them should have gone to prison." To escape her friends and school, Jenny feigned illness. Later, she started skipping school and her grades dropped. She left home one night during her junior year. Although she called her parents a few days later (she had gone to visit a cousin out of state), she stayed away for nearly three years. "I did a lot of waitressing and baby-sitting," she explained. At the age of twenty, Jenny completed her GED and enrolled in the tribal college. As for her former boyfriend, Jenny added that she hears about him: "He deals drugs and goes from one reservation to another. I guess he has set up other girls like me. At least, that's what I've heard."

ANNIE. Annie was always big and overweight for her age. "I was a fat baby," she commented. She lived at home with her parents and grandparents, who doted over her and gave in to her every whim. She didn't like going to school and leaving her family. School was never a happy place for Annie. She was teased and picked on by other children because of her weight. The teachers seemed to distance themselves from her. "I was always treated different. Most of the time I was ignored. I hated school and the teachers," she observed. Annie spent most of her time eating candy bars and reading romance novels. She didn't have any friends, except for one cousin; later, that relationship ended when Annie realized that her cousin didn't want to be around her. Annie dropped out of school her junior year. She got married when she was seventeen, to a widowed rancher, but the relationship was short-lived. Her parents talked her into coming back home. Annie has never returned to school. She still lives with her parents and grandparents. She still reads romance novels. She will be thirty her next birthday.

TERRY. Terry was small for her age and often got into fights to protect her rights. "I came into this world fighting, and I'll go out fighting," she boasted. She was an above-average student in school and rarely missed a day. Despite her scrappy behavior, Terry recalled being a favorite of teachers and peers alike. She was a self-acknowledged class clown who got away with a lot because she was "funny, little, and smart." "It all changed when I started smoking marijuana," she explained. After Terry's introduction to marijuana, she started skipping school to be with friends who smoked. "During my junior year, I missed seventy-eight days. That's close to half of the school year. I never went back for my senior year. I still smoke once in a while," she told me, "but I don't stay stoned so much anymore. For four years, I was stoned every day." Most of Terry's days are spent visiting with her female friends on the reservation.

An examination of these profiles reveals a myriad of factors that impinge upon the decision for a girl to drop out of school. Some are related to school, some to family, and some to the environment or community. In considering all the factors, it is clear that there is no panacea for reducing the dropout problem. It will require a broad-based response from teachers, administrators, researchers, parents, community agencies, law enforcement, the judicial system, and the tribal government working together as a team.

Profiles of High School Graduates

Many of the women who graduated from high school reported that their parents were middle-income, did not suffer from alcoholism, and were supportive parents. On the other hand, many reported coming from poverty and dysfunctional families, and being victims of child abuse. Others reported that neither their teachers nor their parents cared about them. And yet many of these women stayed in school and graduated. They were at risk, but they managed to survive. In selecting the following profiles of these women, I expect to demonstrate that many of the girls who are successful in school also need extra help and assistance along the way. Again, all the names used in these profiles are fictitious.

TAMMY. Tammy's father was Indian; her mother, white. For the most part, she took after her mother's side. Her mother dropped out of school in the tenth grade; her father dropped out in the ninth grade. Her father was a blue-collar worker for the BIA. Her mother baby-sat for extra money. Tammy's two older siblings had dropped out of high school. One joined the service, and the other still lives on the reservation and frequently moves back home for a few weeks at a time. Tammy had problems in school with some of the girls. She was often teased for looking white. She had a boyfriend who was often in trouble with the law, mostly for drinking and fighting. She was not very close to her mother and admitted to little communication with her father. She often skipped school to be with her boyfriend or to just stay home and watch television. She repeated three classes in high school and attended summer school so she could graduate with her class.

JUDY. Judy was an abused child. Her parents were both alcoholics. Sometimes she never got to do her homework, because her parents partied all night. There was often little food in the house. There was very little love or attention. Judy says that when she was about eight or nine years old, she made up her mind to have a life different from her parents'. She decided her only escape was to get an education. Although she sometimes got F's for failing to turn in homework, she concentrated on doing well when she was in school. She missed school at least once a week, sometimes more often, but she always tried to make up her work if her teachers would let her. On the day of her high school graduation, she moved out of her parents' house, got her own place, and took a job at a grocery store. She is planning to marry within a few months, when her fiancé graduates from college.

SHIRLEY. Shirley transferred seventeen times during her school years. She talked about loneliness and the inability to make friends in school. "We never stayed long enough for me to have friends," she recalled. When she was in the ninth grade, she moved in with her aunt and remained in one school until she graduated. Her aunt was very sick. Shirley was her caretaker. Every Friday, Shirley missed school because she had to take her aunt to the Indian Health Service. She never got to go out with friends or to school activities, as there was no one else to look after her aunt. She missed her high school prom. She admitted to being shy and not speaking up in class, and for the most part considered the teachers uncaring. Shirley graduated from high school with honors, but, because of her aunt's health, was unable to go to college. She plans to go to college in the future.

MABEL. Mabel lived in an isolated area some sixty miles from her high school. She spent nearly four hours a day on a bus. Her parents were very traditional people, and Mabel grew up speaking her Native language. Her parents had not gone to high school. No one from her part of the reservation had ever graduated from the reservation high school. All of her siblings—seven of them—had dropped out of school. When Mabel entered school, she spoke only a few words of English. There was no one in the school who spoke the Native language, so Mabel spent much of her first three years learning the English language. Mabel often missed school, especially in the winter and spring, when snowstorms or floods prevented the school bus from traveling the dirt roads that led to her home. Some of the "town" girls teased Mabel about her shabby clothes. A high school teacher bought Mabel a dress for graduation. All of her family came to see her graduate. Her parents held a feast for all of the neighbors to honor her. Mabel is divorced and has three small daughters. She lives with her parents on their ranch. She wants her daughters to go to college.

JOANIE. Until Joanie was ten years old, she lived in a very loving home with her mother and father. She had two younger siblings. On a cold, stormy December night, Joanie, her sisters, and her parents were returning from a shopping trip. They lived in a remote section of the reservation, and the blizzard made the trip hazardous. Several miles from their home, their car stopped. Her father got out of the car and started walking for help. Her mother followed him. When the father returned with neighbors, her mother was not along. The next day, she was found dead from exposure. Shortly thereafter, her father placed Joanie and her sisters in a boarding school. He said he was unable to care for them and work, too. At first, he picked them up every weekend, and those times were joyous for Joanie and her sisters. But after six months, her father got a girlfriend who did not like having the girls around. His visits became less frequent, until generally he stopped by the school only on Sunday mornings. Joanie became very resentful. She felt that her younger sisters took too much of her time; at ten, she was their mother. Joanie started drinking and using drugs around the age of twelve. She received demerits in her dorm and often lost privileges for weeks. She ran away four times, only to be returned by the police. There was some discussion about sending her to a girls home. In the ninth grade, Joanie met a teacher who took a special interest in her. On weekends, the teacher often took her for outings with her own children. For birthdays and Christmas, she bought Joanie presents. She kept telling Joanie she must stay in school and work hard. Joanie admits she did her work to please her teacher. On graduation day, Joanie joined the navy.

SARA. Sara came from a poverty-stricken home. They had no running water, no radio, no TV. She lived in a four-room house with fourteen other relatives. They survived on welfare and commodities. There was little privacy in Sara's home and she had no place to study. She rarely had pencils or paper. Her clothes were hand-me-downs. During the winter, Sara stayed home from school because she had no coat to wear. She admits that quitting school would have been the easiest route, but she wanted an education: "Somewhere in the back of my mind, I had this idea that if I could get an education, I would be able to have a better life." Sara excelled in writing. In high school, she met an English teacher who was impressed by Sara and gave her a journal to record her thoughts. The teacher, who was also single, visited Sara's family and asked for permission to take her on trips and to stay overnight at her house. At the teacher's house, Sara was introduced to the world of books, travel, and life off the reservation. She took her first bath in a tub of hot water. Sara cleaned house on Saturdays for the teacher. She used her salary to buy clothes and books. When she was a senior, she lived with her teacher for most of the year. Her teacher wanted her to go to college, but Sara opted for a part-time job in the schools. "I am saving my money," she told me. "When I leave here, I want to have enough money so I won't ever have to come back." The teacher, who is retired now and living in Florida, has offered Sara a home with her whenever she needs it. "When I go, I want to be independent," Sara remarked. So far, Sara has saved over $3,000. "One more year is all I need," she said.

BOBBI. When Bobbi was eleven years old, she moved out of her mother's house to live with her aunt. "My mother was not very stable," she recalled. "I can remember at least six different men she lived with. Some of them were good; others, not so good. My mother drank. The good ones wouldn't put up with her; the bad ones sometimes beat her. Mostly they were good to me, until the last one. He touched me places I didn't want to be touched, so I left home." Although her aunt didn't drink, she, too, was a single mother, and Bobbi often had to help her out with taking care of the children. Bobbi missed a lot of school. There was not much food at her aunt's house, and Bobbi often skipped meals so the younger children could eat. Bobbi made C's and D's throughout high school. "I could never read very well," she said. "My aunt helped me with my homework, or I would never have graduated. She is a wonderful woman." Bobbi has her own house on the reservation. She works for the tribe. She has taken in three of her sister's children and is raising them: "I want to give them what my aunt gave me. My sister doesn't want these kids. She abandoned them." Bobbi has never married: "I don't plan on getting married. No man is going to take my money, tell me what to do, or abuse these kids. I don't need 'em."

DIANE. Diane was raised by her grandparents. She remembers that they were ill most of the time, and by the time she was nine, she was taking care of the house, cooking, and caring for them. When she was ten, an aunt moved in temporarily with Diane's grandparents; when the aunt departed, five children were left behind. All were younger than Diane. Overnight, Diane became a mother as well. "My grades started dropping around the seventh grade. I was too tired to do my homework. I had to take care of a family. I worked hard. My grandparents always praised me. My grandma wanted me to make good grades in school," she said. When she was in the tenth grade, Diane decided to drop out. But, she noted, "My grandmother cried, so I decided to stick it out." She graduated with her class. Later, she took two courses at the community college and landed a secretarial job. "I'm still raising my cousins. Two of them have graduated from high school and joined the service. My grandfather passed on, but my grandmother is still living. I take care of her, too. My life isn't so bad. I just missed being a child," she said. "If I ever have kids, I want their lives to be different."

SHEREE. Sheree was the oldest of seven children. She was the only girl in the household. By the time she was four, she can remember being told to wait on her younger brothers. By the time she was ten, she was their major caretaker. Neither of Sheree's parents worked, and both of them frequently drank alcohol for days at a time. During those times, she stayed home from school: "The little ones had to be fed, their diapers changed. There was no one else to do it." Sheree fell in love during her sophomore year in high school: "He was the wrong kind of guy. He drank a lot, . . . drove fast, . . . fought a lot. He was too old for me." She ran away with him the next summer and got married. Shortly thereafter, her husband was arrested and sent to prison for selling drugs. Sheree returned home and went back to school. Although her family life had not changed, Sheree managed to stay in school and graduate. "It wasn't with my class," she reported, "but I graduated." Sheree works as a waitress in a nearby border town. "My husband got out of jail three months ago. I served him with divorce papers. I'm a free woman now," she said.

VICKY. Vicky was raped by an older cousin when she was twelve. When she confided in her mother, she remembers being slapped and told to keep quiet about the event. At school, she was sure all of the boys knew. She lived in fear that they, too, would try to hurt her. As a result, she withdrew: "I never stayed late after school, I never asked for help, I never went to a ball game, I never went to a dance. I was afraid someone might catch me alone. I never wanted to go through that again." When Vicky was fifteen, she was called into the counselor's office. She remembers being afraid that she was in trouble. Instead, the counselor was nominating her for an Upward Bound program at an out-of-state college. Vicky accepted. "In that program, I blossomed. I didn't know anyone there, and they didn't know me. I made friends. I went to my first dance. I held hands with a boy. He was very nice," she said. For the next three years, Vicky attended Upward Bound: "That program kept me in school. I had to stay in school in order to go back each summer. I had to keep my grades up to be eligible." Vicky graduated with her class. She wanted to go to college, but the BIA "messed up my funding." She took a job on the reservation. "It doesn't pay much, but it's something to do. One day, I want to be a math teacher," she said.

An examination of the preceding profiles reveals that there are many reasons girls who were "at risk" survived their environments and graduated from high school. In some cases, it was a caring teacher who intervened; in others, a family member; in some, an internal motivation to succeed. In all cases, the school and the community could have done more to intercede in the lives of those girls. Clearly, the women profiled had little, if any, childhood. Most were adults as children, with the responsibilities of adulthood. A caring school and a caring community can ease those burdens on females.

Profiles of College Graduates

Many of the women who graduated from college were not the typical college freshman, as the following profiles reveal. Again, all of the names are fictitious.

HOLLY. Holly's parents had both dropped out of high school. Her father was a seasonal laborer, and her mother worked part-time in the school to support the family. Although Holly's father occasionally drank a few beers, he was not an alcoholic. There were three older children in Holly's family. Two had dropped out of high school; one entered military service. Holly became pregnant during her junior year in high school and dropped out of school. Shortly after her baby was born, she enrolled in a GED night program and completed her studies. For the next three years, Holly lived with her parents and took care of her child, cleaned house, and cooked for her parents. She recalled, "That last year, I started running around on the weekends. I left the baby with my parents. I drank a lot, . . . smoked pot." Her parents never reprimanded her, but Holly knew they disapproved of her life-style. "One night, I got drunk and woke up the next day in bed with a stranger," she reported. "That was the turning point." She quit "partying." Shortly thereafter, Holly went to the tribal education office and put in an application to go to college. Holly's parents were very supportive when she went to school. During final exams, they cared for her daughter so Holly would be free to study. They often gave her food and extra money. "It took me five years to graduate, but I did it," she said, smiling. "I'm the first college graduate in the family."

JOANNE. Joanne's mother died when she was in the first grade. Her father was an alcoholic. Her older brother sent her away to boarding school. She spent the next eight years away from home, often staying with relatives during the summers. From the sixth through eighth grades, during the summers, she worked as a baby-sitter and housekeeper for a family near her school. During the ninth grade, she returned home. Her father and brothers were like strangers, and they were all alcoholics. Joanne had little supervision when she returned home: "I ran the streets, got in with the wrong crowd, took drugs, drank alcohol. I don't know how I kept from getting pregnant." Joanne liked school, not for the academics, she remembered, but for socializing and talking with her friends. When she was a junior, she was elected class vice-president "because nobody else ran." But it proved to be a turning point for Joanne. Suddenly, she began to take an interest in school, not only academics but extracurricular activities as well: "I found out I could make a difference. I changed my crowd and started running around with girls who planned to go to college. It was only natural that I started doing the same thing." She never received much encouragement from home. When her father got drunk, he liked to brag that "his girl" was going to college. The day she left for college, he was too drunk to tell her good-bye. Joanne graduated four years later with a teaching degree and is teaching in the local elementary school. "I'm still trying to make a difference," she told me.

TRACY. Tracy got pregnant during her junior year in high school. Her baby was born the summer before her senior year. When school began in the fall, her mother encouraged her to go back to school. Tracy remembers being ignored by the teachers after that: "It was as though something was wrong with me. Most girls had babies and didn't go back to school. When I graduated, my mom wanted me to go to college. I cried the day I left. My parents kept my son." She came home during vacations and every summer to be with her son, but she realized that he did not regard her as his mother: "There were times I wanted to give up and not go back. I worried about what I was missing. My mother told me I would have other children and not to worry about this one." When Tracy graduated, she came home to get a job. She worked for the tribal government. She got a house and furniture. She said, "I thought my son would live with me, but he refused. I guess it's OK, but I would have liked to have raised him. He was my firstborn, you know. My parents are doing a good job with him and I see him every day, but there is still an emptiness. The saddest part is that I had a hysterectomy during my senior year of college. There will be no more."

TINY. Tiny was a high school dropout and the mother of two infants by the time she was eighteen. Tiny's mother was a high school dropout who had become pregnant with Tiny when she was only fourteen years old. "Like mother, like daughter, they always say," was Tiny's comment to me as she talked about her life. "My mom never married my dad. He had a hard time, . . . no skills, . . . little education. We moved around a lot. We didn't pay our bills. We'd get kicked out of someplace and go to another." Her boyfriend, and the father of her children, was very much like her father: "He wanted me to marry him, but I didn't want to go through life like my mother." Shortly after her second baby was born, Tiny began a GED program: "It was a special program. They provided baby-sitting for kids while the mothers and dads went to school. It got me out of the house, and it gave me hope." After completing her GED, Tiny enrolled in the tribal college: "I had an aunt who baby-sat for free when I was in class. She was proud that I wanted to go to school." Tiny got her associate degree last year. She is currently unemployed, but has enrolled in the state university for the fall. She has received a Pell grant and a small scholarship. "I will have to borrow the rest, live on food stamps. My aunt says she'll go with me and baby-sit. I have to do it for my kids and me," she reflected.

ROSE. Both of Rose's parents were killed in a car accident when she was five years old. She was raised by her grandmother in a house with several other cousins. She remembers a carefree childhood, but missed having parents who could do things with her. Although she loved her grandmother dearly, Rose believes that her high school business teacher was most instrumental in her success in school: "His wife was the English teacher. They both liked me and encouraged me. When I graduated, they gave me a dozen red roses." A few weeks after she graduated from high school, Rose got a job at the tribal office. She worked her way up in the office, learning a number of jobs. When a new superintendent arrived on the reservation, he offered Rose a job as his assistant. Under the tutelage of her new boss, Rose demonstrated great potential. "He suggested that I go to the tribal college. He was like a surrogate father, so I did it to please him. His wife encouraged me also," she observed. When Rose graduated at the top of her class, her boss encouraged her to go to the university. Within two years, she graduated and returned to her old job: "Somehow it wasn't enough anymore. I quit my job and went back to school. I completed my doctorate last year. I can't believe that everyone calls me doctor." [At the time of her interview, Rose had just been offered a job with a starting salary of $58,000 on another reservation.] "It's finally dawned upon me," she said. "I don't have to be an assistant anymore; this time, I will have an assistant."

LOIS. Lois was thirty years old and married with three children and one grandchild when she decided to enroll in college. "I took a look at my life and decided I was going nowhere. My husband was a good provider, but he worked so hard and I knew he couldn't keep it up another thirty-five years," she said. When she told her husband she wanted to go to college, he was very supportive: "He offered to stay on the rez and work and let me go to school. Instead, I suggested he go with me and look for work. He was reluctant but agreed to try. On the third day, he found a job." Lois and her husband remained in the university town for almost five years. When she graduated, she said her husband should have received the degree: "He did all the work. He took care of me, the kids, a job, and he made sure I had time to study. Every woman should have a man like that." Lois is in her second year as a teacher in a reservation school. Her husband, upon his return, found a less demanding job physically. "It was all worth it," she said, "a dream come true. No one is ever too old to change her life."

JUNE. When June graduated from high school, she "bummed around the rez" for two years. "I partied a lot, went from relative to relative, powwow to powwow, and mostly hung out." When she was nineteen, she heard about a federal job program in another state. She decided to give it a try: "For the first time in my life, I was on my own. I had never really experienced the outside world. I liked it." Shortly thereafter, June decided to go to college. She chose one out-of-state, "far away from the reservation." After two years, she transferred to an in-state college. She graduated with honors and, upon graduation, enrolled in a special internship program for Indian leadership. [When I interviewed June, she was home on her reservation for vacation.] "I can't live here anymore," she said. "I like to visit once a year, but my life is out there. My parents don't understand that, but there is too much poverty, too many problems here. Things never change. Out there, I can be what I want to be. Here, I am still reminded of how people thought I wouldn't amount to anything. Guess I fooled all of them."

JANE. Jane got married the day after she graduated from high school, "mostly to escape my home life, although I guess I was in love." Her in-laws were rather successful ranchers "and white," Jane noted. They financed their son's college education. Jane accompanied him to school: "I had never really planned to go to school, but I liked the college environment. It was a different world for me. My husband didn't want me to go to college. He was majoring in agriculture. He wanted to go home and farm. He wanted me to be a farm wife. I realized, through exposure to other women who were going to college, that I didn't want that kind of life. I got a part-time job as a waitress, and with the Pell grant, I paid my own college expenses." After graduation, Jane and her husband divorced: "It was by mutual agreement. He had grown in other directions. I had outgrown him as well." Jane returned home to her reservation and took a job as a social worker. Jane became very disillusioned with her life. Each payday, her family expected money: "It got so hard, I couldn't support myself. If I bought a new dress, I felt guilty. Finally, I just quit and went back to school." Jane finished her master's in business administration and returned to the reservation. "Nothing has changed, except I make more money now, but I give it all away. I've put in several applications out of state. Hopefully, I will get another job and can move away. It is the only way I will ever have anything for myself. Sometimes I feel guilty for wanting more than my parents, but that's just the way I am. I can't put those feelings away," she stated.

CINDY. Cindy dropped out of high school at fifteen and married her grade school sweetheart. "I never intended to go back. School was not for me. I hated the teachers. I hated the restrictions," she remarked. Cindy had twins when she was sixteen. "That kept me busy until they were in school," she recalled. "Afterward, I felt lonely. I started riding the bus with them and going to an adult education program while they were in school. I graduated just as they were completing kindergarten. Next, I enrolled in the tribal college. I rode the school bus for the next two years with them." When Cindy graduated, she took a job managing a local store. "My husband only finished the ninth grade," she told me, "but he is a good man. He doesn't mind that I go to school. He thinks it's great. Someday, I may go on and complete my education, get a four-year degree, . . . probably when my kids finish school."

PAM. Pam grew up in a traditional home, "where being Indian was more important than an education," she reported. Pam recalled that her parents didn't like sending her to school, because "it was too white." Pam learned early in life to keep secrets from the school about her home life and secrets from her parents about her school life. "I lived in two worlds," she told me. "It was fascinating. I liked who I was, I believed what my parents taught me, but I always knew there was more." Pam graduated from high school at the top of her class and received a scholarship to college. When she graduated, she took a job in an out-of-state city: "I wasn't happy there. I needed to get back in touch with my roots. I missed my mom and dad. They are old and needed my help. So I came home. Luckily, I found a good job." Pam married a high school dropout. They live with her parents.

A review of the profiles of the college graduates reveals a number of factors that should have kept them from succeeding in school and graduating from college. None of the women fit the typical stereotype of the college student. All of them had major obstacles to confront in their pursuit of an education, but all found the inner resources to persevere. In examining the profiles, it is clear that there is no one reason women go on to college and graduate. Some did it for their children; others, for themselves; and some, "to make a difference." Many things motivated their decisions to make a change in their lives. All felt they were better for having done so, even if their "new lives" created limitations for them on their reservations.

During the interviews, I was impressed with the power and resiliency of the American Indian female, regardless of her level of education. Over and over again, women demonstrated strength in maintaining their culture, their family relationships, and their tribal identity. Without question, these women dispelled the stereotypes of the American Indian girl and woman.

Chapter 8

The American Indian Child and the Culture of Poverty

According to the 1990 U.S. census, American Indians are the most poverty-stricken group in the nation. A recent census report indicated that more than half of the Indian households earn less than $20,000 annually, and that Indian children are three times more likely than white children to be poor. The statistics further point out that American Indians are the only ethnic group in the United States whose average household income has fallen since 1980. In addition, the report shows that Indian households have not only the highest poverty rate but also the highest unemployment rates in the nation. In response to the report, Alan Parker, director of the National Indian Policy Center, commented, "The poverty on Indian reservations is pervasive and endemic. It's no secret that the government has not responded in any meaningful way to boost reservation economies or by creating tax incentives or a financial structure to address these problems. . . . It's been going on for at least 20 years and it's only getting worse."[1]

Research clearly shows that poor children are more likely to drop out of school than their more advantaged peers. Studies have consistently demonstrated the relationship between the number of poor students in a district and the number of dropouts. This does not mean that growing up poor by itself will determine that a child will drop out of school; however, it does indicate that unless the burden of poverty is alleviated by the distribution of resources and the commitment of sympathetic and dedicated teachers and administrators, such a child will find it much harder to succeed.

Unfortunately for American Indian children, that assistance has not been generally available. Instead, many educators and researchers have mislabeled the conditions of poverty as the conditions of culture and its incongruence with the school environment. Thus, it becomes very easy, as well as convenient, to blame school failure among American Indian children on these students' culture.

The fact remains that for the American Indian child growing up in a home where the parents are low-income or unemployed, or in a home with a single mother on AFDC, the chances are good that s/he will receive far less positive attention from teachers and administrators in the school, even when it is a reservation school dedicated to the purposes of educating American Indians. In any case, poverty is bad enough, but when poverty is combined with insensitive, uncaring teachers, it becomes much more difficult for an Indian child to overcome the hurdles of school.

Robert Coles, in his three-volume work *Children of Crisis*, devotes a chapter to teachers and the children of poverty. In that chapter, he describes the types of students teachers like as "well-scrubbed, eager, obedient, responsive,"[2] qualities that are often a far cry from the characteristics of children of poverty. Furthermore, he questions the larger issue of poverty and child performance in school based upon a "family's spirit":

> Does a [poor] mother give her children a sense of confidence . . . ? Mothers . . . who never quite know where the next few dollars will come from, have little energy left for their children. Life is grim and hard, and the child simply has to find that out. He does, too; he learns it and learns it and learns it. He learns how to survive. . . . He learns why his parents have given up on school, why they have tried and fallen flat on their faces. He learns about things like racial hatred . . . he learns whether he is an insider or an outsider. . . . By the time a child . . . first arrives at school he has learned so much that his knowledge might perhaps be credited to an account called "the intelligence of the so-called unintelligent as it appears in sly, devious and haunting ways." The average teacher may know all that, but find little time to dwell upon the social and psychological forces that make children so very different before they have had one day of school.[3]

An examination of various national surveys on dropouts further demonstrates the problems encountered by racial minorities. These surveys report that about 13 percent of the white students in the United States drop out of school, but surveys on minority students report that (depending on the survey) between 12 and 24 percent of Black students drop out, and that approximately 40 percent of Hispanic students and between 35 and 50 percent of American Indians never complete high school.[4] As Theodore Sizer points out, many schools in this country assume that minority students will not graduate.[5] In the case of reservation schools, a similar attitude prevails.

What is important for educators to do is to separate the impact of poverty from the impact of culture on the educational achievement of Indian children and to identify the processes by which poverty and cultural background affect success or lack of success. This chapter will deal with the impact of poverty; chapter 9 will address cultural discontinuity.

The Myths of the Culture of Poverty

What seems to be at the heart of the matter realistically is the fact that poverty is a condition that is distasteful not only to most Americans but to most educators. We do not like to talk or think about it, much less do anything about it. To further complicate the matter, the decade of the eighties witnessed a rightward shift in the public debate about social welfare regarding the defective nature of poor people, their motivations, behavior, and moral character. Although the majority of attention has focused on Black Americans, American Indians have been the subject of some media attention—a recent example being the "Tragedy at Pine Ridge," a 1991 NBC News two-part special on the social problems of the Oglala Sioux on the Pine Ridge Reservation in South Dakota. Rather than focusing on the poverty, the extremely high unemployment rates, and the lack of economic initiatives on the part of the federal government as the root of the problems, the reservation-specific culture and the pathological behaviors of alcohol abuse became the basis of the news special.

A typical example of the prevailing attitude in this country about the poor is found in the work of Isabel Sawhill, a senior fellow at the Urban Institute, who refers to the poor people of this country as the "underclass." Although Sawhill's work is based on her observations with Blacks, there is an underlying applicability of her treatise to all impoverished racial groups in the United States, including American Indians. According to Sawhill, the underclass in America exhibits behavior that is "dysfunctional," and she sets about describing the "norms" that society demands of its members: "First, children are expected to study hard and complete at least high school. Second, young people are expected to refrain from conceiving children until they have personal and financial resources to support them; this usually means delaying childbearing until they have completed school and can draw a regular salary. Third, adults are expected to work at a steady job, unless they are retired, disabled, or are supported by a spouse. Fourth, everyone is expected to obey the laws."[6]

Sawhill maintains that every citizen should meet these obligations as a part of the American "social contract"[7] and further proclaims that "the underclass is a subgroup of the American population that engages in behaviors at variance with those of mainstream populations."[8] The most common of the deviant behaviors include dropping out of school, welfare dependency, adult male unemployment or underemployment, and female-headed households.

William Julius Wilson describes the underclass within the accepted "tangle of pathology" litany as individuals involved in crime, abuse, teenage pregnancy, out-of-wedlock births, welfare dependency, and female-headed households.[9] David Ellwood characterizes the poor as those who experience "a frightening array of negative forces: deprivation, concentration, isolation, discrimination, poor education, . . . crime, drugs and alcohol, the underground economy, and welfare." He further maintains that this underclass "seem[s] to embrace values that the middle class cannot understand."[10]

The danger in the treatises advocated by Sawhill, Wilson, and Ellwood is that their ideas have been embraced by politicians, middle-class Americans, wealthy Americans, and a wide range of middle-class minority groups. These ideas have also found fertile ground among the younger generation of white Americans, who see the chance of having a better life than their parents slipping out of their reach. Since these views often regard poverty status as synonymous with minority status, they open an entirely new venue for racial hatred and bias. Therefore, the incompetent individual who is unable to find a job blames affirmative action or women or a minority group.

In recent years, politicians have fueled the anger against the poor by campaigning against welfare for poor women and children. Since the general public's perception of the welfare recipient is often defined as a female member of the significant minority group within a state or region, racial issues become intertwined with poverty. A corollary to this perception, in regard to American Indians, for example, is that Indians are poor because of their race, which is intermingled with cultural values incongruent with those of white, middle-class America. In other words, Indians are poor because they adhere to cultural values that inhibit their movement into affluency. Totally absent from this theory is the recognition that being poor is a major burden for any child to overcome, but when one adds the factor of race, the opportunities become even more limited. Josue Gonzalez, associate superintendent of the Chicago Public Schools, suggests that there are actually two school systems in the United States—one that is characterized by resources and good teachers and serves middle-class or affluent white youth, and another that is a "pauper's system" that educates most of America's poverty-stricken minority children.[11]

Poverty versus Culture

Perhaps the most significant feature about these constructs of underclass is that they all focus on behavior, values, and culture, and all center on an overlapping list of behavioral characteristics. These factors serve to perpetuate the idea that, at least as far as American Indians are concerned, Indians are locked into their current situation not by their lack of opportunities, but because of their culture, values, and traditions, which are inherently out of sync with mainstream America. In addition, an unspoken accompanying premise underlies these beliefs: that the culture itself is responsible for the poverty conditions.

Since American schools have historically been the purveyors of "American culture" and middle-class Anglo values (even among Indian reservation schools), blaming the culture of the child, the "within child deficit," has become the norm in Indian education. American Indians have also fallen victim to this type of propaganda and have accepted the cultural discontinuity theories as the reasons for their children's lack of success in school. Many researchers and educators have alleged that Indian students adhere to alien cultures and values that are incompatible with the school environment, thus creating patterns of behavior that impede success in school. Therefore, it is the child who has failed and the child's culture that has failed, not the school. I suggest, however, that the major factors impeding the success of Indian youth are neither the "alien" Indian cultures, traditions, and values nor cultural discontinuity between the schools and the home environment, but rather the state of poverty of American Indian households, the hidden curriculum of the schools, and the stereotypical attitudes toward Indian children.

American Indians have in one sense compromised their cultures by accepting these explanations for their behavior and their children's failure in school. For example, in general, Indians have come to accept characterizations of behavior as "an Indian thing" or "that's the way Indians are" rather than seeing behaviors as distinctly a "poverty thing." Whereas characterizing cultural phenomena as the cause of school failure reveals a zeal for validating the need for integration of the culture into the school curriculum and has provided countless opportunities for experts on culturally sensitive curriculum reform, it also conveys a fundamental unwillingness to look at the economic conditions on reservations and the implications those conditions may have in the schooling of children. Further, it conceals the real distinction between the behaviors that are related to culture and the behaviors that are related to poverty.

The Problem of Educability and the
Hidden Curriculum in Schools

The lack of success in school among Indian children is often blamed on the problem of educability—that is, that American Indian children do not possess the motivations, orientations, and skills that are prerequisites for schooling. These prerequisites, which are acquired through early exposure to learning tasks and positive socialization experiences, are frequently referred to as the hidden curriculum of schools. Basically, the hidden curriculum advances four elements of educability.

First, it is expected that upon entering school, children will possess a finite set of student behaviors. These behaviors are developed by providing early experiences in which children learn appropriate adult-child relationships.[12] An example might be to teach the child to respond to adult directions. Second, teachers expect that children will enter school with the development of cognitive and perceptual skills appropriate to the school setting. In other words, educators presume that parents will provide their children with activities that encourage them to explore and analyze their environment.[13] Third, educators expect that children will enter school with the motivation to achieve. This motivation is developed by parents encouraging their children to hold positive feelings toward school and about adult praise and approval. And finally, teachers assume that the child understands and speaks standard English.[14]

Throughout the literature, these four aspects of the hidden curriculum differentiate between the poor student and the good student. What is perplexing, however, is that the American Indian student who fails to acquire the prerequisites of the hidden curriculum is often quite capable outside of school, and while many American Indian students have difficulty in school, others do not.

Research on the effects of poverty on educability appears to be compromised by two factors: socialization and health. The influence of poverty on the socialization of children is not well documented; however, we know that unemployment among adults often results in withdrawal, depression, apathy, and loss of self-respect.[15] With the high rate of unemployment and underemployment on Indian reservations, we can theorize that negative parental behaviors are likely to have powerful effects on Indian children.

Furthermore, poor people have less access to the printed media and are restricted in the quality and amount of information they receive.[16] In fact, most people of poverty appear to substitute television for printed media. One researcher pointed out, "While television can be a powerful educator, its present programming supports a distorted view of reality and everyday life."[17] This distorted perception of life may be a distinct effect of poverty that affects the early socialization of the child and thus the educability of the child. Further, in poor families it is unlikely that printed materials or educational materials (paper, crayons, pencils, books) are available. This in itself is another detriment to the child of poverty, who, in order to acquire the prerequisites of the hidden curriculum, must have access to those materials in early childhood.

In general, poverty and health are strongly related. Poor people are less likely to seek and obtain proper medical care. In the case of American Indians on reservations, who depend mostly on the Indian Health Service for medical attention, the conditions are often quite bleak. Throughout Indian country, there is a plethora of accounts of understaffed hospitals, incompetent staff, and insufficient funds for providing adequate care.

Indian people suffer from the highest infant mortality rate in the nation, have the shortest life expectancy, have a greater risk of prenatal complications associated with low birth weight, and have the highest rate of FAS babies. Some researchers have suggested that poor children have an increased risk of suffering neurointegrative sensory motor abnormalities, which contribute to lack of achievement in school.[18] Other researchers have found a direct relationship between poverty and intellectual development in later life. Although severe malnutrition is not a major problem in the United States, subnutrition is a problem for poor children on Indian reservations. Researchers report that subnourished children are less attentive in school, less responsive, more easily fatigued, and unable to sustain prolonged mental and physical activity.[19] That subnutrition indirectly affects a child's motivation and cognitive skills is therefore a given.

There is no question that poverty and ethnic status are inextricably linked, in that many of the people who live in poverty come from minority groups and certainly at a higher proportion than the mainstream society. But what is important is that we separate the issues of poverty from the issues of culture. Poverty is strongly associated with health problems and socialization factors that have a profound influence on the development and education of children. Should we continue to view poverty and ethnicity as synonymous, however, we will perpetuate an ethnocentric misinterpretation of the educability of Indian children and the subsequent development of inappropriate educational interventions.

Native Women Speak Out on the Culture of Poverty

Various factors associated with family background (single-parent households, educational levels of parents, and socioeconomic status) have been attributed to the success or lack of success of American Indian students. Many researchers have demonstrated a correlation between dropping out and socioeconomic status of the family, whereas others have suggested that cultural differences between the home environment and the school environment place these students at risk. Others have maintained that parents' educational levels and female heads of households are deciding factors in premature school leaving. Since educational level is most often directly linked with economic status, and the majority of female-headed households fall below the poverty level, these topics will be discussed within this chapter. On the whole, it is a given that American Indian children grow up in an environment where poverty is much more common than affluency and where lower educational levels and single-parent families are more common than in mainstream society. Clearly, there is disagreement about what constitutes behaviors imbedded in the very nature of poverty and what constitutes behaviors attributable to culture.

All of the participants in this study were asked to classify their family's socioeconomic status during their high school years. Seventy-three percent of the women reported that they were from families who lived "at or below" the poverty level, 26 percent felt that their families were lower-middle-class, and the remainder reported that their families were upper-middle-class. Of the third group, the majority were from families whose parents were college-educated and both parents generally worked. Nearly 70 percent of the women in the "poverty level" category reported "very little," if any, income in their families. Many said that because poverty was the norm on the reservation, they didn't realize they were "poor" until they entered school.

When asked to describe significant events related to their economic status, a majority of the women appeared to confuse the circumstances of poverty with cultural differences. For example, many of the women talked about the lack of future orientation within the Indian cultures and attributed certain incidents and events to the culture, rather than to the poverty conditions of their families. Many noted that they were raised to live day to day and to confront problems and issues as they arose, rather than making plans. One female provided the following commentary, a common response offered by many of the women in the study: "Indians don't plan things like white people, because if you are an Indian, you never know what will come up that will prevent you from doing what you planned. That way, you are never disappointed. For example, you may want to go to town and eat out, but you might not get paid. Or your car might break down; somebody might die or get sick. Your dad might get drunk; he may not come home at all. It's hard to deal with such disappointments, especially when you are a child. It's more fun to get to do something when you're not expecting it."

A college graduate spoke of the frustration of her high school guidance counselor, who wanted her to apply for college:

> When I was a junior, he [her counselor] told me I had to start thinking about college. My dad said he couldn't think that far ahead. My senior year, the counselor started on me in September about college. Dad said he didn't know what was going to happen tomorrow and he couldn't think about next September. Finally, in June, I filled out the papers for admission. Dad still didn't say anything. When I got accepted, he didn't say anything. But in July, he started planning. He bought me a car and fixed it up; they took me to [nearest city] and bought me clothes. They went with me to campus in August. I know that he wanted me to go to college, but he didn't want me to be disappointed. He wanted to wait until he was sure I could go.

Several women revealed that even if they planned something, it often did not work out the way it was intended, due to circumstances beyond their control. Frequently, plans were delayed or aborted because of family responsibilities. One college graduate spoke about a recent visit to her brother:

> My sister and I planned for six months to go visit our brother for Christmas. We planned and planned. We bought presents . . . [and] saved money each month. My sister was supposed to come to my house and we'd leave at noon on this particular day. We even planned what food we would pack for our kids to eat on the trip—it was about a ten-hour drive. When the day of the trip came around, I couldn't get off from work until 4:00. My sister didn't show up until 6:00, because she had to take one of our aunts to the hospital. We finally left eight hours later than we had planned, . . . [and] we forgot the Christmas presents. Nothing ever works out the way you plan. That's just the way things are.

Other women reported that Indians often like to plan certain things (go hunting, take a trip to visit a relative, go to a powwow), and the planning is often as much fun as the actual experience, which may be aborted somewhere along the line. One woman related a story about her grandfather and his brothers:

> Every year in August, my grandfather and his brothers would sit around the kitchen table, drink coffee, and plan the first day of hunting season. They would tease each other, tell tales on one another, joke. They spent days cleaning rifles, talking about strategy, planning the big day. I used to love to listen to them. But lots of times, they never got to go hunting on that first day. Sometimes one might show up, sometimes two. But it never went as planned. They didn't have money for gas. Or the truck wouldn't run. But the real fun was in the camaraderie they shared—the getting together, the talking. Indians never expect things to work out the way they plan.

Throughout the interview process, it became very clear that what were being described by the women as traits and characteristics of American Indian cultures were not endemic to Native cultures at all. They were the consequences of poverty. Whether an individual is a reservation Indian, an African American living in the ghetto, an Hispanic from the barrio, or an Appalachian white, these behaviors are not characteristic of an ethnic group, but rather are the consequences of the culture of poverty. Therefore, when we define Indian culture as lacking future orientation and living day to day, it appears as though we have added legitimacy to the observations of outsiders who have stereotyped a people on the basis of race, rather than the economic conditions forced upon a people by segregation on reservations. Thus, when a child is late for school because s/he had to help a single working mother feed younger siblings, we define that child's tardiness as "Indian time." When someone fails to get to a meeting on time because the car broke down, we explain the incident as "living on Indian time," rather than confronting the real reason for the situation, which is most often linked to poverty.

This legitimacy of stereotypes about American Indian people was expressed in various forms by the Indian women who participated in this study. For example, many expressed the belief that "taking one day at a time" was characteristic of the Indian culture. When the suggestion was offered to a group of women that the philosophy was more characteristic of the creed of Alcoholics Anonymous, many of the women immediately connected the origins of the characteristics as being imbedded in the subculture of recovering alcoholics. This subculture can be found among all classes and racial groups and is definitely not an "Indian trait." One woman commented, "We have accepted the philosophy of living one day at a time as characteristic of Indian behavior. It is not true at all. Traditionally, Indians had to plan and look toward the future for their very survival. Food was stored, tribes moved with the seasons, social gatherings were planned because it often required travel to distant places."

Obviously, the question then becomes, What behaviors are associated with cultural values and what behaviors are imbedded in the consequences of poverty?

When the women were asked if they felt that their family's financial status in any way affected their success or lack of success in school, 43 percent of the women responded that poverty was a hindrance to their success. A high school dropout described the agony of being ignored by uncaring, unsympathetic teachers:

> Not having good clothes and not having money to do anything was always hard for me. Teachers didn't pay any attention to poor kids. On this reservation, the teachers are white, and about 20 percent of the kids in our school were white. The teachers identified with them; they were not only the same color, but their parents dressed them the way teachers expect kids to dress. When you only have two dresses to wear to school or clothes that are three sizes too big, you aren't going to get very far in school. The teachers will see to that. I wanted to be like the white kids, have nice things, go on trips. I always felt cheated because my family was Indian.

Another woman attributed her dropping out directly to her family's poverty and teachers' insensitivities: "I just got sick of being teased because of my clothes. The teachers were not understanding. I walked by the teachers' room [lounge] one day and heard them talking about me. They were arguing about whether I was clean or dirty. One teacher said all Indians were dirty, [that] it was just the nature of Indians. Only one teacher defended me. I never went back to school after that."

A college graduate recalled that teachers lavished attention on the more well-to-do students in her school and ignored those who she felt were not college material or those without influential parents in the community:

> I was in this English class. About three-fourths of us were Indian, the rest white. This teacher only talked to the white kids in the class or the breeds whose parents were important in the community. If you were Indian and poor, if you were a breed and poor, or even if you were some godforsaken white that was poor, she simply ignored you. She was interested in kids who were going to college and who had opportunities to do things. I remember sitting in class and hating her. I told myself that I would graduate and go to college and come back and make her eat my degree. How can anyone call themselves a teacher and make such prejudgments about kids? Sure, I was an Indian, and I was poor, but that didn't make me a nobody.

A high school dropout spoke about learning lessons of racism at the hands of an uncaring teacher, when the behaviors of the students were actually the result of poverty:

> I remember this one teacher, he thought he was cool. He called us "skins," short for redskins. If one of us was late for class, he said, "What can you expect of an Indian, . . . living on Indian time?" If we didn't do our homework, he related that to being Indian. He said Indians had "no appreciation for book-learning," and that's the reason we were the conquered and his race the conquerors. It didn't matter to him that some of us had to get younger brothers and sisters to school so we were late, or that we simply didn't have alarm clocks and that we got there when we woke up, or that we didn't have encyclopedias at home to do his stupid homework assignments. I get mad every time I think about him. That SOB still teaches on this reservation. Why is it that Indian schools employ teachers like that?

Many of the women discussed the powerlessness of Indian students within a reservation school setting, a factor they believed was a result of the poverty of the students. One college graduate noted:

> You know, most of our schools are run by white men—men who are a part of the establishment, the "Good Old Boys." Most of our teachers are white. Historically, it's been us against them, and it's still that way. Whites are still deciding what's best for us, still trying to brainwash our children, still trying to keep us powerless. So if you are an Indian teenager and you don't go to school, they say, "That's the way Indians are," or they say, "Indian parents don't care," or other things, like "You can lead a horse to water, but you can't make him

drink." Half of the kids on this reservation who drop out do so because even though they are going to a reservation school, it is still a white, middle-class school, with white, middle-class rules, white, middle-class control, with no understanding or sympathy for the conditions of poverty that not only impede learning but in some cases prevent kids from being in school on a regular basis. Kids in trouble have no advocates. Even the Indian teachers—there are three—act like whites. They hold themselves up as role models, only they aren't Indian role models who advocate for kids. They are the kind of role models that are acceptable to whites because they act just like them. Indian kids are labeled incorrigible because they are Indian. It's the old stereotype that we are lazy, uncontrollable savages who are trying to live in the past and have little appreciation for education.

Speaking about behaviors that she attributed to poverty rather than culture, a college graduate articulately presented her thoughts:

If I hear one more person identify multiple families living together in one house as a cultural characteristic of Indians, I am going to go on the "warpath" myself. The fact is that the people on this reservation are poor, and several family members live together simply as a means of survival. The other problem is that there is inadequate housing on this reservation, . . . not enough homes for the population. If a relative has a home, it may be necessary for another family to move in, but that has nothing to do with being Indian. It is a fact of life, a matter of poverty. White people on this reservation look down on Indians who live in houses with multiple family members. I've heard teachers remark that such housing arrangements are "unsanitary," "ungodly," or that "they are just like a pack of dogs." You can imagine how they must approach a child who comes from such a home environment. What we never really deal with is the fact that poverty is the cause of these living arrangements, not the Indian culture. The worst part of this whole thing is that we contribute to this. We say such things as, "We always look out after our relatives," or "We always take care of our extended family." Although this is a fact of the culture, it is not appropriate to housing situations. We have bastardized our culture. We have accepted the white stereotypes of what Indians are, and we have been responsible for perpetuating them.

Another college graduate told about how, as a teenager growing up, she attributed her unhappiness in school to being an Indian, rather than to poverty:

Probably the one thing I remember most was hearing two teachers discuss what some of us brought to school in our lunches. I took whatever we had at home—generally fry bread and fried deer meat. Obviously, that was not what any respectable person was supposed to eat. One teacher commented to the other, "What can you expect of a bunch of dog-eaters? That's just the way Indians are. They're a bunch of scavengers. They'll eat anything." I remember throwing my lunch away after that on the way to school. I didn't want any of the teachers thinking I was a "scavenger," which in my juvenile mind was something akin to savage, I think.

When women were asked about the availability of books and educational materials in their homes, only 3 percent reported having a daily newspaper in their homes. Less than 10 percent reported having books or magazines in their homes. Seventy-one percent said that pencils, papers, and crayons were rare items in their homes, if they were present at all. One high school dropout stated, "We never had crayons and pencils or paper at home. I used to eat my crayons. I thought they tasted good. I chewed on my pencils. I was always getting in trouble with the teacher. I had never used a pencil before I went to school. That was a real shock."

One college graduate related that her mother bought used books for her: "My mom liked books. We couldn't afford the new ones. She'd go to flea markets and buy paperbacks and anything she could find for me. She'd pay a nickel, ten cents, or a quarter. Sometimes the covers would be gone, but I learned to love the stories. Every evening, we would read our books, sometimes over and over. By the time I was in the fifth grade, I was reading westerns and romances—anything so I could read. My mom never censored what I read. She was just happy that I read."

A high school graduate reported the lack of paper and pencils in her home and how she learned to conserve: "I had a tablet with those rough, yellow papers and blue lines. I used to write on it and then erase what I wrote and use it over again. I was always afraid to ask for more paper. We didn't have much money. Paper was expensive. I used to borrow in school from the richer kids, until the teacher caught me and made fun of me in front of the whole class. She called me a 'parasite.' I didn't know what that was, but I knew it was bad."

Another high school graduate spoke about her discovery of the joy of books when she went to school and the disappointment she felt when the teacher would not allow her to take the books home: "When I was in grade school, I *loved* books. I liked to hold them and touch them. Our teacher wouldn't let us take them home, because she said they were school property and that we would lose them or they would get torn up. I wanted to take them home. I begged her, but she never let me. By the fourth or fifth grade, I quit asking."

Another high school graduate attributed her lack of interest in reading to the school environment, which prevented her, too, from taking books home: "When I was in the first and second grade, I loved books. We were never allowed to take them home. We didn't have a library—just books in the class. The teacher was afraid we wouldn't bring them back, so we never got to take them home. I wanted so badly to share them with my brothers and sisters, but she said that they would tear them up."

Thirty-four percent of the high school graduates and 23 percent of the college graduates reported that when free hot lunch programs were introduced in the schools, it made a considerable difference in their desire to go to school and stay in school. A high school graduate related, "We never had enough food. When your stomach is empty, other things don't matter. The free lunch program kept me in school. It was sometimes the only meal we got, at least during the last two weeks of the month. During the first of the month, we'd get a few groceries and commodities; our house was always full of people drinking and eating. By the middle of the month, all the food was gone. I stayed in school because at least I could eat there."

Speaking emotionally about going to school hungry and going to bed hungry, a high school graduate related:

> There were many nights during my childhood that I remember crying because I was hungry. Going to bed hungry. I wonder if anyone who has never wanted for food can even relate to the cries and feelings of a hungry child. Can you imagine that, in the richest country in the world, there are children still going to bed crying because they are hungry? I doubt that there is one teacher in our school who knows what it is like to go to school hungry. I remember sometimes being so sick in school from hunger that I couldn't even think about what was going on in class, much less do my work. I was afraid to tell the teacher I was hungry.

Women from families in middle-income and upper-middle-income groups felt that coming from families with better financial means made their school experience more bearable. Many of them recognized the sacrifices made by their parents in order to make them feel at ease in school. One high school graduate reported, "It takes money, even in a reservation school, to do things. There are trips, powwows, dances. Although I never got the most expensive dress or had a lot of money to spend, my parents always made sure that I never missed out on anything because it cost money."

College graduates came from all socioeconomic backgrounds. It was evident, however, that students with some financial assistance or other types of support from their families during their college years were often more successful at staying in school. In many cases, a college education for one person was supported by a number of family members. Seventy-two percent of the college graduates reported receiving financial support or "in-kind" support from their families. One college graduate pointed out that had her parents not been able to help her financially, she would never have completed college: "They never gave me a lot of money, . . . but enough. Sometimes I'd be short, need a book, some spending money, food. They always came through for me. I had friends whose families couldn't help. Some of them dropped out."

Another college graduate related how she and two of her cousins managed to graduate by using the financial resources of several relatives: "There were three of us . . . cousins who went to school. My dad found us an apartment and paid the rent. An uncle gave us an old car to get to school and back. My two aunts gave us commodities. Another uncle hunted; we all had deer licenses. He kept us supplied with meat. We had part-time jobs—waitressing, motel maids, cleaned houses. We paid the utilities and bought any special things we needed. We shared each other's clothes, books, and personal things. When we graduated, it was like the whole family graduated."

Similar stories were told by other women of relatives investing in their college education. One woman explained how family support not only encouraged her to stay in school, but enables her to help others today: "Everyone in my family helped me go to school—my parents, my grandparents, uncles, and aunts. I'd come home from college and they'd give me money, take me shopping, buy me food, even send me a bus ticket to come home. My whole family wanted me to graduate. Now when they need something, I can help them. That's what it is all about, . . . being Indian. I wouldn't have graduated without them. I can help them out now."

Another graduate reported, "My brother and sister-in-law helped me. They were both college graduates. I got married right out of high school, . . . broke up three years later, . . . had two babies. They told me if I would go to school, they would help me. They paid my baby-sitting, kept my car running, paid my tuition, gave me extra money every month. With the Pell grant, I made it, but it would never have been possible without them."

A college graduate, who reported growing up in poverty, felt that in many ways her children were "poorer" because they had grown up in a more affluent family:

> There were six kids in our family. My grandma and grandpa lived with us. My aunt and her three kids lived with us most of the time—all of us in a four-room house. We lived on commodities and deer meat. We didn't have much, but we were happy. When I got in high school, I realized that there was more to life than living from day to day. I wanted a college education so my children could have a better life. In many ways, my kids have missed out, though. We rode horses, swam in the river. We were more creative; we entertained ourselves. My kids watch TV, play Nintendo, and want motorized toys. Many times, I long for those old days and I wonder if I've done right by my kids.

Throughout the interviews, concern for the life-styles of the youth surfaced. Many of the women expressed concern that Indian parents, who have historically doted on their children, are swept up in the commercialism of mainstream society and unable to cope with the consumerism confronting reservation youth and its effects on them. One high school graduate suggested:

> As parents, we need to take control. We have to teach our kids that they don't need everything they see on TV. Life has changed so much since I was a girl. I never got to town, except maybe once or twice a year. My kids get to travel more, and they see things. We have TV; they want everything they see. Many parents on this reservation do without food or paying their bills so their kids can have fancy clothes and toys. Indian people used to take care of one another, . . . everybody shared. That way, everyone was taken care of. Now we do without and let our kids have frivolous things. We are teaching our kids to be selfish and greedy.

One single parent, a college graduate with a well-paying job by reservation standards, reported that the peer pressure on her children often made being a parent difficult: "I try to teach my children the value of money. I refuse to buy them expensive toys and clothes they will grow out of in six months. My three-year-old wanted a toy the other day; one of his friends had one. When I told him I didn't have any money, he told me to write a check or use a credit card. He doesn't understand that checks and credit cards require money. It's hard for kids to understand when their friends, whose parents don't work, have the latest thing and I tell my children we can't afford it. And the truth is that I can't afford it even with a decent job."

Clearly, there is a relationship between dropping out of school and poverty for American Indian females. Often teachers misinterpret poverty as a cultural attribute and explain away student behaviors as "being Indian." Perhaps even more enlightening to this discussion is the fact that American Indians themselves have embraced many of their behaviors and events in their lives as "being Indian," rather than recognizing that the basis is actually related to poverty conditions.

It is more convenient for school personnel to attribute tardiness to "Indian time," or to make negative judgments about parents' lack of interest in or appreciation for school by insinuating these are imbedded in the traditions of an oral culture and language, rather than in the Anglo written tradition. It is much easier to assign inappropriate behaviors—such as boredom, idleness in class, or daydreaming—to traditional, carefree, permissive Indian parenting than to address the attitudes of teachers or the lack of proper nutrition as the problem.

Over and over again, American Indians have allowed researchers and writers to explain away behaviors as the truths of culture. In other words, American Indians have, in a sense, cooperated by attributing their own behaviors to culture.

Throughout the interviews, there was a common theme among the discussants about how the teachers ignored them because of unsuitable clothing, food, cleanliness, and so on, and did not intervene when their classmates taunted them for inappropriate dress. Many teachers appeared to attribute lack of proper clothing and inadequate food to being Indian, rather than to the conditions of poverty.

FINDING: Poverty is a major cause of American Indian girls dropping out of school.

Over two-thirds of the women in this study spoke about the humiliation of growing up poor, inadequate food, inappropriate clothes, and unsympathetic, uncaring teachers who were quick to make judgments about them based upon stereotyped racial traits, rather than on the factors of poverty. Forty percent of the women identified poverty as a factor in dropping out of school. When this is viewed in terms of racist remarks and self-fulfilling prophecies of teachers who do not expect poor Indian girls to learn, much less graduate, the factor of poverty in the decision to leave school among American Indian girls becomes even more paramount. Poverty and its accompanying problems, such as hunger, lack of nurturing, lack of family spirit, lack of hope, and the overwhelming need for basic survival, encumber school success.

There was considerable evidence that the lack of preparation for the hidden curriculum of the school, in terms of lack of socialization and health factors, was present in the lives of many of the women in the study. Women reported the lack of educational materials in their home, parents who were unemployed, and inadequate and insufficient food. Research clearly demonstrates that poor nutrition leads to lack of motivation, fatigue, and inattentiveness. In addition, children who do not have printed materials and books, pencils, and crayons in the home are not adequately prepared for the hidden curriculum in the schools. When educators set expectations that a child coming into school will possess certain attributes and then discover that the child does not possess them, the interaction between the student and the teacher often becomes strained and further contributes to the child's alienation.

Although many of the women underplayed the impact of poverty on their lives (since poverty was described as the norm for the reservation), others viewed it as a devastating factor in their lives, one that in many cases continued to affect their lives as adults and the lives of their children. Despite the poverty conditions for many girls, they were able to survive within their peer environment because their peers were more likely to be from the same income level. Since peers are often related in Indian schools, poverty is protected within the sphere of one's own family. It is only when a girl comes into contact with the more affluent teacher or classmates that she begins to question her own self-worth.

In those cases where poverty was directly linked to dropping out, it was most often associated with teacher attitudes toward the student or the student's family.

There was some indication that government-supported hot lunch programs kept girls in school. Almost half of the women in the study felt that free lunch programs were important to their health and welfare, with the majority reporting inadequate food at home. Considering the impact of subnutrition on children, school lunch programs are invaluable.

FINDING: Family support, either financial or through other "in-kind" contributions, appears critical to the success of female American Indian college graduates.

A majority of the college graduates reported that their families, and often extended families, assisted them in staying in college. Although the support ranged from money to food supplies, the assistance also carried with it an implied moral support. Women with such strong family support appeared to feel an obligation to be successful in school. Whereas in the majority culture, a child's education is the responsibility of the parents or of the child himself/herself, contributions toward the American Indian student's education may come from grandparents, aunts, uncles, and older brothers and sisters. Instances of such family support were reported by women from the poorest of families, as well as by those from the more affluent ones.

There was some indication that lack of family support or extended family support may have resulted in girls not pursuing an education beyond high school. Thirty-seven percent of the high school graduates in the study reported that they did not have the money to go to college. Of this group, almost 20 percent reported being from one-parent homes, being from dysfunctional homes, or having drinking parents.

In many cases, it did not appear that financial support in college was as critical as the "in-kind" support. Although the majority of women reported coming from homes where there was little "spending money," they revealed that getting food donations, gas money, or a bus ticket home was often critical to their morale while in school. Again, the critical factor was the commitment of the total family in the education of the individual. On several occasions, women reported that a number of family members pooled their resources to buy a bus ticket, pay car insurance, or help them with a larger purchase.

Parents' Educational Level

Research tells us that poverty and educational level are directly related. A number of researchers have maintained that socioeconomic status and educational level of parents are more influential than school factors in whether a student stays in school or drops out.

Throughout the literature, girls whose mothers dropped out of school are reported as more at risk than girls whose mothers graduated from high school. In an effort to determine the impact of their mothers' educational level on the women in this study, a number of questions were asked.

All women were asked about their mothers' educational background. Twenty-four percent of the dropouts reported that their mothers had dropped out of high school, as compared to 23 percent of the high school and 17 percent of the college graduates. Of the last two groups, 74 percent indicated that their mothers were critical to their decision to remain in school and to go on to college. Nearly 30 percent of those women, however, reported that their mothers, even though they dropped out, had at some point continued their education, either by obtaining a GED or by pursuing vocational training; 2 percent reported mothers who had returned to school and graduated from college.

One college graduate related a story often repeated by other women: "My mother went to boarding school. She completed the eighth grade, but refused to go to high school. She wanted me to get an education. It was important to her, even though she never went to school."

Another woman commented that her mother kept very close track of her school achievement: "My mom quit school in the eleventh grade. She got behind and couldn't catch up. She never wanted us to miss school. She kept telling us that we needed an education. She wanted more for us than she could give us."

A high school dropout revealed that her mother never expected her to graduate from high school: "She always told me it was all right if I brought home F's. She had made lots of F's in school. I think because she failed, she expected me to fail."

Only 27 percent of the high school dropouts reported that their mothers voiced concern that they stay in school and graduate. When asked if there was another family member who was particularly supportive of their educational goals, 38 percent of the high school graduates cited a grandmother as being instrumental in their lives. Fifty-two percent of the dropouts reported that they made the decision to drop out of school without consulting their parents, whereas the high school graduates reported that their parents were more involved in assisting them with decision making. In fact, 13 percent of the high school graduates said that when they decided to drop out, their parents forced them to go to school.

One female, whose parents were both college graduates, related her parents' disappointment when she dropped out of school: "I got pregnant. . . . I dropped out. I know I disappointed them. Mom cried for a week; Dad never said anything. When the baby is a year old, I'm going to get my GED, . . . go to college. I know they want me to, but they never say anything. I used to tell my dad I was going to be a doctor and come back and work on this reservation. He always said I could be anything I wanted to be. I never wanted to be a mother, not at seventeen."

Another high school dropout with college-educated, working parents reported: "My mom worked, my dad worked. They were more involved with work than with us. I got into alcohol first, drugs next. I lost interest in school, . . . started skipping. By the time they [her parents] found out I was failing school, I had already quit."

The majority of the high school and college graduates felt that their parents' educational level had little to do with their own success in school. Instead, they attributed their success to their family's support and interest in their academic performance or their own internal motivation. Many reported that their success in school was often critical to the family's survival. One woman, whose parents had not completed the eighth grade, related, "My dad couldn't read; my Mom—maybe third-grade level. They made me bring books home every night. After supper, I read out loud to them. That was the evening entertainment. When I got into junior high, I read books to the whole family. My dad loved westerns; my mom, mysteries. My parents weren't dumb. They valued education. They gave me that message every night they asked me to read to them."

Other women, whose parents had an eighth-grade education or less, reported similar experiences. Many reported taking on special family responsibilities, such as handling family or legal affairs, as their skills increased. One female commented, "Every time my grandpa went to town, he made me go with him. I had to check the prices at the grocery store, go to the tribal office with him, and read his papers. I helped him with his will. He'd tell me that it was good that I was so smart. He would say that I had to stay in school so I could look out for the family. He never trusted the white man's words, but he thought they were very powerful. He was ninety-seven when he died."

One college graduate reported a similar experience in being responsible for family affairs:

> Every time my mom—she dropped out of high school—went to the tribal office on business, she would keep me out of school and take me with her. She needed help reading lease forms, filling out papers. It's a good thing I was a good student. That happened at least two or three times a month. Every time she took me out of school, she reminded me that she wanted me to get an education and not be like her. Of course, all my teachers thought she was an irresponsible mother, . . . that she was the typical Indian who didn't care about education. I only hope I can be half the mother to my girls that she was to me.

A majority of the women who stayed in school and graduated, regardless of their parents' education, reported that their parents wanted them to go to school, often talked to them about the importance of school, and helped them when they went away to college. The majority also noted that their parents attended school events and supported their participation and involvement in school-related activities such as clubs, sports, drama, music programs, and field trips. One high school graduate related, "My parents both went to boarding school. They hated it, . . . ran away, . . . were sent back, . . . [and] ran away again. That was repeated many times. But they wanted me to go to school. They wanted more for me than what they could give me. Most parents want more for their kids than they have—not money and cars, but an easier life, not living from day to day."

One college graduate reported her grandmother's response when she complained about school and a particular teacher: "She said, 'I don't want to hear bad things. Tell me only good. I send you there to learn, . . . nothing else. If she teaches you bad things, forget them. If she teaches you good things, remember them. Then you will know only good things, and that is powerful.' My grandmother never spoke English. She never once went to school to see my teachers. I knew what she expected of me. . . . She valued education. She was a powerful woman."

One college graduate, who was raised with three brothers and one sister by a widowed father, reported that her father's expectations were critical to her success: "My dad dropped out of school and went to the service. He sent money home to my grandma to help feed his brothers and sisters. He wanted us to go to school; that was important to him. My sister and I used to sit on his lap when we were little girls. He'd call me his 'little schoolteacher' and my sister his 'little nurse.' And that's what we grew up to be—a schoolteacher and a nurse. He still calls me his 'little schoolteacher' and my sister his 'little nurse.' It's all in what is expected."

Although research on dropouts indicates that the educational level of parents is directly linked to the success of children in school, this does not appear to be a significant factor among American Indian women. In fact, the majority of the women in this study who dropped out of school came from families in which the parents had completed high school or obtained a GED.

FINDING: *Educational level of parents, at least for the majority of the American Indian women in this study, is incidental to whether a girl stays in school and graduates or drops out.*

Throughout this study, parental support and encouragement have emerged time and time again as a critical factor in whether a girl stayed in school, graduated, and went on to college. It would appear that among many of the participants in this study, supportive parents were not necessarily parents with college degrees. Fourteen percent of the women whose parents had an eighth-grade education or less graduated from college. The majority of these women whose parents did not go to high school reported graduating from high school. Many of them described parents who encouraged them, reinforced the importance of school at home, accepted no excuses for failure, and set high expectations for them.

A majority of the women who graduated from high school related that their parents cared about their grades, encouraged their participation in school activities, and were involved in their lives.

From this study, it would appear that parental support and involvement are the key to a child's success in school. A parent with an eighth-grade education can be just as supportive as a parent with a graduate degree. On the other hand, parents in both of those categories can neglect their children, be too much involved in their own lives and work, and fail to recognize the importance of parental guidance and support in a child's life.

Clearly, girls whose mothers dropped out of school are more at risk than girls whose mothers graduated from high school. There is, however, another intervening factor. Many women whose mothers dropped out reported their mothers returning to school and completing high school requirements, and in some cases obtaining college degrees. This type of role modeling certainly has an impact on American Indian girls. When parents, either verbally or by modeling, set expectations for girls to complete school and reinforce that school is important, children react positively to such messages.

Given that positive role modeling does affect young women, more opportunities should be made available to adult women on the reservations. The tribal colleges on many reservations offer special opportunities for adults; however, it may be that many females are unaware of those opportunities or do not perceive themselves as candidates for a GED or a college degree. Concerted efforts by women's groups and community agencies could assist women in realizing opportunities as well as their potential. Information should be provided to adults that education is a lifelong process and does not end with adolescence.

Single-Parent Families

It has been reported by many researchers that the number of American Indian youth growing up in one-parent homes far exceeds the national norm. Research also tells us that children from one-parent homes are more at risk than children who grow up in the traditional home of two-parent families. In the case of American Indian children, although there may be only one parent in the family, there are likely to be other adults in the household, including grandparents, aunts, uncles, and even live-in mates. This study attempted to determine the impact of the family makeup on the degree of success in school attained by the women in this study.

Thirty-six percent of the women reported that their mothers were single parents. Twenty-four percent reported that their mothers had a live-in mate(s) while they were growing up. Eighteen percent of the women were raised by their grandparents. Forty-seven percent reported living in two-parent homes, with parents who were married. The remainder reported living with a relative, who was often their guardian.

Of the women who dropped out of school, 39 percent reported coming from single-parent households, homes where their parents divorced while they were in school, homes where their mothers had live-in mates, or homes where their mothers had neither married nor had a "significant other" present.

The answers were varied when women were asked about the impact of their family structure on their childhood. Many of the women spoke about the poverty of being raised in a one-parent home. One woman compared her childhood to the childhood of her father's second family: "We were raised on AFDC and commodities. I know if my dad had lived with us, we would have had a better life. . . . He married again, and his other wife and kids had a much better life than we did. He never gave child support to my mom; I don't think she ever asked. But he always had a good job."

Other women reported that mothers who were the wage earners in the family often had less energy and less interest in their school activities. One woman, whose father was killed in an automobile accident when she was a child, described her childhood growing up in a one-parent home. Her comments were representative of the remarks of other women, who spoke about how poverty affects all aspects of family life:

> Mom was always tired. She worked as a secretary, . . . raised a garden, and took care of us, our dogs, cats, and cattle. She had little time to worry about whether we were doing well in school. We had chores to do at home, but even when we chipped in and helped, Mom never had the energy to do things with us. She never went to a ball game, a school function; she never attended parent-teacher meetings. I felt cheated when I was little. I wanted an active mom, a mom that would do things with me. I didn't understand at the time that being poor and worrying about how you were going to put food on the table and how you were going to keep your family together and how you were going to get to work if the car didn't run was just about all anyone can manage when they are raising six kids without a father.

Several women spoke about home environments that included drinking and men (often a series of relationships) and that ended in bitter disappointment for both mothers and daughters. One woman disclosed, "My mom was the kind of woman who had to have a man around. When one left, she always found another. I used to pray for a daddy, but none ever came. Most of the men drank, or they took advantage of my mom. She gave them money to keep them around—money she should have spent on herself or us. When I got older and realized what was going on, I was really mad at her. I guess I never really got over it. I don't ever plan to marry or take up with a man. I spend my money on myself."

When women were asked why they felt the number of one-parent homes was higher in their culture than in the mainstream society, I received a number of responses. Many of the women attributed the independence of Indian women to the number of female-headed households: "I always wanted kids, but I never really saw a husband as a part of my life. I got two girls and no husband. I don't want one. I have a job and support my girls. We may not have a lot of things, but we got each other. I want my girls to be as independent as I am. . . . I want them to go to college. It hasn't been easy raising two girls on my salary. I dread the day when they are teenagers and things cost more."

Other women attributed the number of one-parent homes and a lack of successful marriages to the inability of the male to feel good about himself and the need to always be reassured of his self-worth, namely by going from one relationship to another. Other women saw the lack of job opportunities, which contributed to poor self-image on the part of the Indian male, as a major cause for the high divorce rate. One college graduate, who volunteered details of three unsuccessful marriages, noted, "The trouble is not in finding someone to marry; the trouble is finding someone who wants to make a permanent commitment. Indian guys have trouble finding work, . . . there are arguments, . . . [and] finally, he walks out and takes up with another woman. Maybe I expect too much. I don't think I'll ever marry another Indian. They are not faithful husbands. . . . Indian men can't be trusted. They are always trying to prove that they can get any woman they want."

Another female was more sympathetic toward the Indian male and the lack of opportunities available to men in the reservation community, a factor she felt contributed to the number of divorces and female-headed households: "I was married once. We were awfully young. He couldn't get a job. One day, he left, saying that the kids and I were better off without him. It's harder for the Indian man. There are more women working on this reservation than men, . . . more jobs for women. Half of the good jobs here are held by white men or Indians from other tribes. It's hard for a man . . . to keep his self-respect when his kids are doing without."

Given the negative influences that unemployment has on the mental health of adults, it is not unlikely that an increased incidence of divorce and unfaithfulness may result.

FINDING: *Being raised in a single-parent home may place American Indian girls at greater risk of dropping out, but it appears more likely that the poverty generally present within single-parent homes is the determining factor.*

Although being raised in a single-parent home does not mean that a girl will drop out of school, there is a correlation between dropping out and single-parent homes. However, this may be the result of the economic status of single-parent homes, rather than family structure. Many female respondents from single-parent homes graduated from high school and/or college. Others with traditional family homes (mother and father) dropped out of school. In almost all of the cases, poverty seemed to be the norm, rather than the exception, in a female-headed household.

In many cases, single mothers were very capable, strong women who managed to raise their children without the assistance of a husband. In other cases, the homes of the women in this study were so disruptive and unstable that little support was provided for the child. For some, the choice of single parenthood was a deliberate decision.

The stability of family structure appears important to all women. Women from divorced homes or single-parent homes were in some cases less likely to find the support and encouragement they needed to remain in school. Yet the absence of birth parents (girls raised by relatives or guardians) in itself seemed to be less important unless poverty was a major problem.

Girls from single-parent homes with a large number of children (five or more) seemed to drop out more frequently. Again, this appeared to affect not only the financial status of the family, but the housing arrangements as well. The majority of the women in this situation reported living in poverty and substandard housing.

While many of the women attributed high divorce rates and single-parent homes to males who had low self-esteem, were unemployed or underemployed, and abused substances, others were very defensive of males, whom they viewed as victims of the culture of poverty. While some Indian women openly stereotyped Indian males as unfaithful and untrustworthy, the majority did not.

Since single-parenting is much more common among American Indians than among other groups in the country, it is evident that support for single mothers is critical to the welfare of children. Whether this support comes in the form of tribal assistance, opportunities for increased training and jobs, or family support, it must be recognized that single-parent families are on the increase within American Indian communities and that more teenage girls are having babies. As a result, this problem is likely to increase, thus placing larger numbers of children at risk.

Summary

The question remains as to what should be done for American Indian children to reduce the dropout rate. First, it is imperative that we reject all the assumptions that poverty and race are synonymous. If we accept the fact that a percentage of all people in the United States have children out of wedlock, drink alcohol, take drugs, live on welfare, get divorced, and are unemployed, then we can recognize that such behaviors exist across all classes and all groups of people, and we can dispel the idea that race produces pathological behaviors. Throughout the research on American Indians, the discussions suggest that pathological behaviors are attributed to cultural characteristics, traits, values, and differences within tribal societies. Other writers would lead us to believe that those same characteristics found in racial groups are typically found among the poor, who also tend to be minority as well.

Moreover, as American Indians, we should distinguish between those issues and behaviors which are truly cultural and those which are not, rather than legitimizing stereotypical views of our people and our tribal groups.

Finally, we should fight for better schools for our children, for better-trained teachers and administrators, and for school boards representative of the interests of Indian children. We should fight for policy changes that will provide opportunities for our children, for better housing, for economic development of reservations, for better health care for our children and our elderly, and for the kind of treatment and rehabilitation for substance abuse that is available to the affluent in the American society. Educators interested in the problems of American Indian students must examine the effects of restricted socialization and health factors on the acquisition of the hidden curriculum and its implications for our children.

If we accept the idea that our children are unsuccessful in school because they are Indian and that our culture is incompatible with the culture of the school, then we are blaming ourselves and our children for their lack of success in school, rather than placing the blame where it rightfully belongs.

Chapter 9

Cultural Discontinuity and Dropping Out

When examining the culture of poverty and its impact on American Indian children, it is implied that the acquisition of the hidden curriculum in schools is appropriate; however, this assumption is more difficult when examining the effects of cultural differences on educability. Although there are literally hundreds of reports on American Indian dropouts that define and count the numbers of dropouts, little research speaks about the causes for so many Indian students leaving school prematurely.

Throughout the history of Indian education, there have been numerous explanations for the low achievement of Indian students. At first, a common explanation was the genetic defect: American Indian children were from a cultural background that was inherently inferior, both intellectually and morally. In the 1960s, the cultural deficit explanation became popular. Thus, the reason Indian children did not achieve was that they were not reared in a cognitively stimulating environment and were "socially disadvantaged" or "culturally deprived." The cultural deficit theory was acceptable to educators in that it enabled them to place the responsibility for school failure outside the school.

In the late 1960s, the culturally relativist position became an explanation for the academic failure of Indian students. This position blamed neither the teachers nor the students, but placed the responsibility for such failure on cultural differences in communication styles between the teachers and their students.

In the mid-1970s, John Ogbu argued that school failure was the result of inequity in access to employment. He maintained that generations of minorities who had been denied access to opportunities in the American society had simply communicated their cynicism to their children and that this factor accounted for the school failure of minority children.[1] By the mid-1980s, dropping out and school failure were attributed to multiple variables, and students possessing those characteristics were labeled as high-risk or at-risk youth. Many educators have cautioned that those terms are no more than disguised labels for students who were previously regarded as "culturally deprived" or "socially disadvantaged."

Many of the studies on Indian students suggest that there is a need for a "culturally relevant" curriculum within the schools to keep students in school. In fact, one recent study[2] presents a compelling argument for Indian failure in school by pointing to the cultural differences between Indian cultures and the Euro-American culture. Other researchers have suggested that Indian students receive messages in school that conflict with the messages of their home, thus creating dissonance within the child and a subsequent resistance to school.[3]

Although cultural relevance is rarely defined, these studies have given rise to bilingual education programs or Indian studies courses within the regular curriculum throughout Indian education, but they have not been without their critics. Gerald Wilkinson suggests:

> For all the talk about the uniqueness of "Indian education" all that has basically been created are white institutions run by Indians. . . . These institutions have not made the leap from the colonial mentality to the development of indigenous concepts based on their own self-interest as people. . . . In the area of curriculum much has been made of bilingual education. Except at the low-grade levels, bilingual education is generally taken to mean native language courses. These courses have about the same effect on the students as if they were taking Latin or Greek. The thing about language is that it can only be successfully taught if it can be used. . . . To succeed a tribe must make a cultural decision that their language is an important part of their life and their future. . . . Another example is the teaching of history. . . . The history of Indian people is not taught as Indian history but as the history of Indian/white relations. This approach gives the impression that Indians would have no past at all if it had not been for the European invasion. . . . It is difficult to see how an Indian young person could get any perspective on himself when his past is presented to him as a mere sideshow in the panorama of human existence.[4]

That a culturally relevant curriculum will ameliorate the problems of Indian students in school is rarely discussed in terms of how the curriculum will improve performance, except in regard to improved self-identity or self-esteem.

Cultural Discontinuity Theory

Basically, the cultural discontinuity theory maintains that cultural differences in the communication and learning styles of minority students result in conflicts and misunderstandings within the Euro-American culture of the school, leading to failure for students.

Underlying the cultural discontinuity theory is the assumption that language, memory, and other cognitive skills are held in common by American Indian groups or other minorities. Although the demands on the individual may vary depending upon the social, physical, and economic requirements of the group, conflicts and differences arise as a result.[5]

Researchers have therefore concluded that making the classroom curriculum more culturally relevant will mean success for Indian students.

The central argument put forth by the cultural discontinuity theorists is that teachers and students differ in their expectations of behavior and that their expectations are derived from experiences outside of school in what sociolinguists call speech communities or speech networks. According to Dell Hymes, culturally distinctive ways of speaking differ from one speech community to the next and tend to run along major social divisions, such as race, ethnicity, first language background, or class.[6] Thus, while an Indian child may speak only English, the child is a member of a differing speech community or network that has differing assumptions about ways of communicating such things as approval, disapproval, sincerity, irony, and lack of interest. Further cultural differences in ways of listening and speaking between the non-Indian teacher's speech network and the Indian child's speech network lead to recurring, systematic miscommunication within the classroom.

Susan Philips, who studied children on the Warm Springs Reservation in Oregon, examined the differences in communication and interaction patterns between the community and the school and maintained: "The children of the Warm Springs Indian Reservation are enculturated in their preschool years into modes of organizing the transmission of verbal messages that are culturally different from those of Anglo middle-class children. I argue that this difference makes it more difficult for them to then comprehend verbal messages conveyed through the school's Anglo middle-class modes of organizing classroom interaction."[7]

One of the aspects of the hidden curriculum (see chapter 8) of schools is the requirement for standard English skills. For an Indian child, the lack of standard English skills is said to result in ineffective communication and thinking skills. Some researchers have suggested that requiring standard English skills ignores the universality of languages and is the product of racial discrimination, and that standard English is not a demonstrated requirement for potential educability of minority children.[8]

Other researchers have suggested that similar conflicts have occurred between the behaviors of minority children and the expected behaviors of the teacher or the school. For example, if a teacher comes from a culture or speech network in which attention is measured by direct eye contact and a child comes from a culture in which it is impolite to look directly at a speaker, the teacher may interpret the child's behavior as unmotivated or uninterested, rather than recognizing what is happening in terms of cultural differences. As a result, the teacher further contributes to the dissonance of the child, who may react in what are considered inappropriate ways, such as withdrawal, silence, or hostility, possibly leading to a teacher diagnosis of student incompetence or inadequacy.

Researchers have reported on similar conflicts between behaviors expected in the home and those expected in the school. For example, one study looked at Hawaiian children and found that both parents and siblings were responsible for the care and safety of children within the home. Further, the study showed that Hawaiian children often look to older siblings or peer groups for help and that they watch and monitor adult behaviors, as well as those of other children. In school, however, children are expected to seek help only from the teacher or to pay attention to what the teacher is doing and saying. As a result, it was found that the teacher often interpreted the helpful nature of Hawaiian children when they consulted with other children as one of "cheating."[9] This difference between expected behaviors in school and those at home further contributes to the conflict between students and the concept of educability and is applicable to the behavior of Indian children, as well as Native Hawaiians.

Although there is considerable empirical evidence to support the communication process explanation of cultural discontinuity, there is little evidence to support the inclusion of culturally relevant materials within the classroom as a solution to improved Indian student achievement.[10] Two studies are most often cited by researchers in Indian education to support the cultural discontinuity theory.

The Kamehameha Elementary Education Project (KEEP) was developed in response to the lack of success of Native Hawaiian children as compared to Japanese, Chinese, and students of European ancestry. The project developed a K–3 language arts program based upon the socialization practices in Hawaiian homes. As a result of the culturally compatible curriculum, at-risk Hawaiian children demonstrated significant gains in reading achievement.[11] The Rough Rock Community School on the Navajo reservation in Arizona replicated the KEEP project. Even though researchers concluded that the two studies support the argument for cultural compatibility between school and home as an enhancement for school success, it was found that many of the strategies that were successful for Hawaiian children were ineffective or counterproductive for Navajo students.[12] Other educators have characterized Indian schools as offering an inappropriate curriculum that does not reflect the Indian child's cultural background and consequently results in early school leaving, even though there is little empirical evidence to support these assumptions.[13]

On the other hand, a 1983 study of Navajo youth found that the student's first language was not as important a factor to school success as the successful transition into English. The study found that students who were fluent and dominant in English or bilingual in English and Navajo were far less likely to drop out of school, regardless of their first language. Students from less traditional homes, however, dropped out at much higher rates.[14]

It is important to note, according to the premises of the cultural discontinuity theory, that the more traditional Navajo and those who spoke their language or were bilingual should, for all intents and purposes, have difficulty in school. Yet the opposite was found to be true.

In a 1989 study of Navajo and Ute dropouts, it was found that students who came from traditional Navajo homes and who spoke their Native language and participated in social and religious activities did not feel that the school curriculum was inappropriate for Indian students. Among Ute dropouts, who were less traditional than the Navajo students, it was found that they experienced the highest dropout rates and the most problems academically and socially. These students reported that the curriculum was not relevant to them as Indians. The researcher concluded that "a culturally non-responsive curriculum is a greater threat to those whose own cultural 'identity' is insecure."[15]

Cultural Differences and Educability

Perhaps one of the factors being overlooked in this debate is that the problems of educability of Indian students may be between the child's attitudes developed within one setting and the expectations and requirements of schooling. For example, schooling requires obedience and assent on the part of students. It requires students to accept that knowledge is important to their survival and their future. It may be that education is not viewed in that context by Indian students who drop out. In fact, there is evidence to suggest that Indian students have developed a resistance to learning.

With respect to the academic failure of minority students, one explanation that has received a great deal of attention in the past decade is found in the work of John Ogbu, who maintains that students, as well as their peers and their parents, are convinced that graduation from school will not help them break out of the cycle of poverty. Ogbu defines these students as members of "castelike" minority groups, such as Black Americans, American Indians, Chicanos, and Puerto Ricans. These minority groups have resided in the United States for generations in situations of oppression and share a fatalistic perspective that there will never be opportunities or jobs for them. Therefore, these students develop the attitude or belief that there is no reason to try to succeed in school.[16]

Ogbu criticizes the cultural discontinuity theory as an explanation for school failure and has suggested that the theory is a result of the work of anthropologists who conducted research for the purposes of demonstrating that cultural discontinuities caused failure, rather than looking for the causes of failure. His most powerful argument against the cultural discontinuity theory is based upon the theory's failure to explain why immigrant children are successful in school. He maintains that among immigrant children, cultural discontinuity between home and school is just as severe as that encountered by castelike minorities. However, he suggests that members of immigrant minorities are much more optimistic about their chances for opportunities in American society and that these children and their parents believe effort should be applied to school success, as it will pay off in future employment and opportunities. Ogbu further suggests that just as there are different types of minorities—castelike minorities and new immigrant minorities—there are different kinds of cultural discontinuities: "(1) universal discontinuities experienced by all children; (2) primary discontinuities experienced as a transitional phenomenon by immigrants and non-Western peoples being introduced to Western-type schools; and (3) secondary discontinuities, which are more or less enduring among castelike or subordinate minorities within Western nations."[17]

Ogbu defines universal discontinuities as the experiences all children encounter concerning what is taught and how it is taught in school versus in the home environment. Primary discontinuities result when non-Western students or immigrants attend Western schools. Ogbu believes that students who experience primary discontinuity are more motivated to overcome difficulties they encounter because they perceive success not as a threat to their cultural identity but as a means to opportunity and financial gain. Secondary discontinuities, ascribed to castelike minorities, "develop after members of two populations have been in contact or after members of a given population have begun to participate in an institution such as a school system, controlled by another group."[18] As a result, Ogbu maintains, castelike minorities define themselves in opposition to the Anglo culture and develop "coping behaviors" as a response to oppression. These behaviors, according to Ogbu, may in fact work against student achievement in school, in that students may actively resist the school's attempts to confer upon them knowledge and values they view as important to the Anglo culture, a culture that has consistently denied them access to opportunity.

The Politics of School Failure and Success

Indian students, whether in school or at home, are learning constantly. When Indian students fail in school, teachers assume they are not learning. But what this actually means is that the students are not learning what teachers expect them to learn; it does not mean that students are not learning.

According to Frederick Erickson, learning what is taught in school can be viewed as a form of political assent, while not learning can be seen as a form of political resistance.[19] This premise, posited by Erickson, a longtime defender of the cultural discontinuity theory, is based upon the acknowledgment of the strength of John Ogbu's definition of secondary discontinuity. Erickson goes on to suggest that assent to authority within the school involves trust, which he describes as a

> leap of faith—trust in the legitimacy of the authority and in the good intentions of those exercising it, trust that one's own identity will be maintained positively in relation to authority, and trust that one's own interests will be advanced by compliance with the exercise of authority. In taking such a leap of faith one faces risk. If there is no risk, trust is unnecessary. . . . To learn is to entertain risk, since learning involves moving just past the level of competence, what is already mastered, to the nearest region of incompetence, what has not yet been mastered, . . . as new learning takes place with a teacher, the student again engages risk because the student reenters the zone within which the student cannot function successfully alone. If the teacher is not trustworthy the student cannot count on effective assistance from the teacher; there is high risk of being revealed as incompetent.[20]

Erickson suggests that communication between student and teacher can often lead to an "entrenched, emotionally intense conflict" over time, resulting in regressive relationships in which teacher and student do not bond with each other.[21] Consequently, there is no trust on the part of either the teacher or the student, and, according to Erickson, students become more alienated by school, become less likely to be persistent in doing their schoolwork, and fall further behind academically. In the end, these students become either passively resistant or actively resistant, both characteristics of high-risk youth.

Moreover, Erickson acknowledges that trust and political assent are the "most fundamental factors in school success,"[22] and concludes that culture and cultural differences have varying influences on school success or lack of success:

> A much more prevalent pattern . . . is for cultural differences to make a negative influence, (1) because they contribute to miscommunication in the early grades and (2) because those initial problems of miscommunication escalate into student distrust and resistance in later grades. . . . In the absence of special effort by the school, the deep distrust of its legitimacy that increases among students as they grow older and the resources for resisting by developing oppositional identity that the school provides . . . pose serious threats to the school's perceived legitimacy. . . . Culturally responsive pedagogy is not a total solution.[23]

According to Gerald Wilkinson, much of the rebellion against authority is not a rebellion at all, but rather a struggle on the part of Indian students to create a sense of identity and a context for themselves within a global society:

> Many students learn to conceive of all learning as "honky." A great many of these students reject all formalized learning and then con themselves into thinking they have done the Indian thing. For all their rejection of what they perceive as white ways they end up falling prey to the shoddiest of the white radical ideas. They are concerned about Indian people and devoted to the Indian cause, but because they have not developed a sufficient critical ability to appraise nor gained the intellectual experience to distinguish, they fall for the radicals' worst ideas, not their best. Another group may conceive of learning as "honky" and as a result pursue it with a vengeance. They view a degree from a university not as a tool to get more involved in the Indian community but as a passport out of it. To the American mind, these people have succeeded; to the Indian mind, they are the most tragic.[24]

Native Women Speak Out on Bilingual Education and Cultural Discontinuity

In order to examine the cultural discontinuity theory and the impact that language and cultural differences had upon the achievement of women in this study, a number of questions were posed in relation to Native language fluency and school curriculum and to teacher-student communication and interaction.

All participants in the study were asked about their level of fluency in their Native language. Ninety percent of the women reported that they were not fluent in their Native language. Twenty-seven percent reported understanding their Native language, but never learning to speak it fluently. Forty-six percent reported using "Native words" and phrases in their everyday speech, but regarded their first language as English. Only 10 percent of the women reported fluency in their Native language.

When asked if their parents spoke their Native language, 26 percent reported coming from homes where their parents spoke their Native language, although 88 percent reported that their parents used mostly English when addressing them while they were growing up. Many of the women who reported that their parents and grandparents, but not they themselves, were Native speakers attributed the loss of the language to federal government policies regarding their language and the schooling of their parents. One thirty-five-year-old female lamented the loss of her Native language: "My mother—she is seventy now—she went to a boarding school. Those nuns wouldn't let her talk Indian. She had to speak English. She never spoke Indian to us kids; we never learned. Now she volunteers at the school, trying to teach the little ones Indian. Once I told her that she should have taught us, and she cried. Poor thing. It wasn't her fault."

Other women took opposition to that opinion and maintained that Indian parents and grandparents made a concerted effort not to teach the Native languages. Although this decision may have been rooted in the difficulties experienced by their parents and grandparents in English-only boarding schools, many of the women felt that their parents viewed the Native language as an inhibitor to success in school and had purposely chosen to ensure that their children spoke English upon entering school. One woman, who was raised by her grandmother, reported, "Grandma used to speak to us in both English and Indian. Sometimes when she spoke to us in English and we responded in Indian, she demanded that we answer in English. Other times she reversed the demands. She constantly reminded us that when we went to school, that we had to speak English, so she wanted us to learn to speak it, too."

Another woman, who understood her Native language but admitted to speaking it very little, commented that a good command of English was more powerful to Indian children than knowing their Indian language:

> My parents made no effort to teach us Indian. They talked to us in English. When they talked Indian, it was between the adults. I learned to understand it so I could tell what they were talking about, but I rarely tried to speak it. Sometimes my kids ask me the Indian word for something and I tell them, but I want them to learn English. If they learn English, they can help their people. I'm not sure that learning Indian will help anybody. Some people say that it improves their identity. Well, I don't believe that. My kids know they are Indian, and they are proud to be Indian. Language doesn't make you an Indian any more than Indian dancing makes you an Indian.

Other women felt language was so closely tied to the culture that the loss of the language would mean the eventual loss of tribal identity, although the majority of them could not agree on how the languages could be restored, preserved, or maintained. One high school graduate commented, "I don't speak Indian. I would like for my kids to learn it. The school is the only place where they have an opportunity to do this. Yet, I know that the language as it is taught in schools is ineffective. My kids learn words and phrases, but they will never be able to speak it. So I don't know what the answer is."

A college graduate, who felt that knowledge of the Native language added to the individual's credibility as an Indian, responded, "I don't know what the answer is. I know that if my kids are going to do well in school, they have to learn the basics and be fluent in English. Yet, I have always felt that I missed out on something very important to me and my identity because I never learned to speak my Native language. Perhaps it is the perception others have of you. If you don't speak your language, you're not really an Indian."

Several women reported that they felt the changing life-style of the American Indian woman was in part responsible for the loss of the language, in that more Indian women are working mothers. One college graduate, who spoke her language fluently, stated:

> Sometimes I feel guilty that I never taught my children to speak Indian. On the other hand, I work, and it is very difficult to teach two languages to a child when you aren't with them every minute. I had to make a choice. They needed English to be successful in this world, and that's what I taught them. I think there are a lot of Indians who have made that choice, and now they want the schools to teach their kids to be Indian speakers. That's crazy. I don't mind if my kids participate in Native language courses in school, but I am realistic. I know that they will not be fluent speakers. I resent, however, that all of the cultural activities focus on the past. It's like there is no such thing as contemporary Indians.

Another woman suggested that perhaps tribes should analyze what they really need in terms of Indian education, and proposed that alternative schools might be the solution:

> As I see it, we need two school systems. One for parents who want their children to remain on the reservation and participate in a limited fashion within the mainstream society. These children could be immersed in the language, culture, traditions, and history of our people. The second school system could prepare students to participate in the world at large. We need both kinds of citizens on the reservations. We confuse our children too much. We tell them that we want them to get a good education and to learn to compete with the white student, and then we promote all kinds of paternalistic programs and Indian preference. We tell them we want them to learn the language, and then we speak English. We tell them we want them to stay on the reservation and help their people, and then we are suspicious of them when they are successful.

When the women were asked if they felt the Native languages should be taught in school, slightly more than half felt the Native language was critical to the curriculum; however, few voiced hope that future generations would have a fluency in the language or believed that the school should be charged with the sole responsibility of ensuring the continuation of the language. A high school graduate commented, "In order for a language to survive, it must be used. What good does it do for the school to teach a language when the kids have no place to use it? They might as well teach French or German. It makes about as much sense. Besides, if we care so much about our language, we shouldn't turn it over to a bunch of white teachers and white administrators. Once they get hold of it, they will mess it up, like they have done with everything else."

A college graduate, who described herself as traditional in that she spoke her language and participated in traditional religious and social activities, responded:

> Our language will never be a spoken language again. The parents blame the school and want them to teach it, and yet the kids can't go home and speak with anyone else, because their parents don't know it. The tribe doesn't want to take any responsibility. They want to blame the school. We need to take a good look at ourselves. If the language is important, we should take the leadership in preserving it. The old people say that when the language is gone, our culture is gone. That may be, [but] I'm not sure that language alone holds a people together. If that was the case, we wouldn't be here; we have survived despite the loss of language. It may be that there are other distinguishing factors that make us Indians. Our language may never be a major force again.

A high school dropout was just as adamant about relinquishing the language and culture to the school: "Despite all the intrusions on our culture by white people, we have remained Indians. If we give up our language and culture to the schools, we can kiss that good-bye. Schools on reservations, whether run by Indians or whites, are all the same. Right now, there is a big move on to make us all act like Indians. They say we should be bilingual and bicultural. I don't trust anything these experts have to say. If we want our kids to learn Indian, we should do it within the community."

One Native-speaking female, who opposed Native language instruction in the school and was critical of the instructional methods in bilingual education programs, summed up the feelings of many:

> Kids are not going to learn a language by learning to count, to name colors, and parts of the body. If the Native language is important to us as Indian people, we should be teaching it, not the school. Our language distinguishes who we are. If the school teaches it, we have once again relinquished our power to the bureaucracy. Our survival as Indian people has been our language, our culture, and our spirituality. Once the school gets it, it becomes trivialized. It is just another subject; you can choose to take it or not. Our Native language should not be a choice. It should be a requirement!

One-fifth of the women attributed the loss of their Native language to intertribal marriages, marriages to non-Indians, or non–Native speakers within their tribes, and not to the impact of schooling on their parents. One woman, who reported fluency in the language, commented, "When my girl was born, I talked to her in Indian, sang to her in Indian. It made my husband mad. He couldn't talk Indian. Even those of us who can speak Indian aren't teaching our kids. I don't know one single kid on this reservation under the age of sixteen that can speak their language, and very few understand it. In another twenty years, our language will be gone and then they will be teaching it as a foreign language in school. After that, it will never be a spoken language again."

Another female, who married into a different tribal group, related the difficulty in using a Native language in a mixed-tribal marriage: "Both my husband and me speak our Indian languages, but I don't understand him and he don't understand me. English is our common language. We always speak English to our kids. I don't feel bad about that. Our kids need English to survive."

None of the women in the seventeen to twenty-two age-group reported speaking their Native language. Half of them wanted their children to learn their Native language, but felt that competence in the English language was far more important for success in school. One seventeen-year-old dropout objected vehemently to requiring Native languages in school: "Why should I have to take the Indian language? My parents don't speak it; my friends don't speak it. I don't care what they offer in school, but they shouldn't make the Indian language a requirement. What good is it when everyone talks English? I know several kids who took the class. None of them can even say a sentence in Indian—just words. They should make all the old people on the reservation go back to school and learn Indian. Then maybe I'd learn it, too."

One articulate, nineteen-year-old high school graduate reported similar feelings: "Our parents didn't teach us our own language. They blame the government schools. That's part of the reason, but let's face it: it takes effort to teach a child two languages. The Mexicans do it, but my parents didn't think it was important to teach me, so I am not going to try to learn it now. If it was important to them, they should have taught me. It's too late for me."

Another recent graduate, who had studied her Native language, reported mixed feelings about teaching the Native language in the schools: "I took four years of [Native language]. I never got beyond the stage of translating. I can't think in Indian. I can't speak Indian. I can say words and a few phrases. I wish I could speak, but the teachers don't know how to teach the language. Kids have to have a reason to learn something. When you don't know anyone who speaks, we don't see the importance of learning it. None of us took it serious enough—and we all got A's. It was an easy class."

When asked if their knowledge of the English language influenced their performance in school, less than 10 percent of the women revealed having difficulty in their early years understanding teachers. One woman spoke about her unfamiliarity with the English vocabulary of her teacher: "My parents both spoke Indian and English. They were more fluent in Indian. I remember that to them something was either 'good' or 'bad.' When I went to school, teachers said things like 'super,' 'great,' 'wonderful,' 'fantastic.' I had never heard those words before. I didn't know if they were good or bad."

One college graduate talked about the embarrassment of mispronouncing a word in class and poignantly revealed how an insensitive teacher can affect a child's performance in school:

> My parents spoke English—I guess you'd call it reservation English—but they didn't always say the words correctly. Once, in the eighth grade, I said the word "nabel" for navel. This teacher stopped the class, repeated what I said, and talked for thirty minutes about the correct way to say the word. Needless to say, I said very little in that classroom again. People say that Indian kids don't talk; that's a lie. Have you ever watched a group of Indian kids playing in the yard? They are like a bunch of magpies. But put them in a classroom and it's different. All it takes is one teacher like mine. You never talk again—at least, not in school.

Another woman, who did not understand English when she entered school, reported being placed in special education classes, a familiar story among language minority children: "I couldn't speak English when I went to school. When the teachers said something to me, I didn't know what to say. I was afraid. They put me in special ed. They thought I was retarded. It took me three years to learn English."

Only a small number of the women who dropped out of school attributed their difficulty in school to their inability to understand, write, or speak the English language—not to the lack of knowledge in their Indian language. One high school dropout responded:

> I got behind from the first day of school, and I never caught up. You have to read, write, and speak English to pass. I got D's all through school. My parents couldn't read, . . . [and] I can't read well, either. You have to read to be able to do well in school. I think we should forget about bilingual and bicultural education and teach kids the basics. Reading, writing, and math is what kids need. We can make the decision on an individual basis as to whether the Indian language or the culture is important. If it is, we have the responsibility as parents to teach it. Besides, how can we expect the school to do something we are unwilling to do?

When those women who reported speaking their Native language were asked if they considered themselves "bilingual" (equally fluent in their Native language and the English language), 8 percent of the two-language speakers felt they fell into that category. Among those first speakers of the Native language, who felt they were equally fluent in both languages, all of them admitted to using English more frequently. None of the women who were bilingual reported dropping out of school. Of those who reported that their parents, but not they themselves, spoke their Native language, 3 percent dropped out of high school.

Of the female respondents who reported speaking their Native language, 100 percent declared themselves as three-fourths Indian blood or more and considered themselves traditional women. In addition, almost all of the Native-language speakers reported having grown up in isolated regions or small villages (one hundred inhabitants or less) on their reservations and indicated that the Native language was the common language of communication within their families and community.

Many researchers have noted that Indian children are often torn between two cultures, that of the school and that of their home, and that this conflict affects school performance. A number of questions were asked of the participants to identify any cultural conflicts between home and school that might have contributed to success or lack of success in school. Throughout the interviews, many women reported miscommunication as the greatest problem. Most often, the problems were centered on attitudes of teachers and miscommunication with teachers, or on the values teachers promoted that were in opposition with the values of their home culture.

All of the women were asked if they felt that the school was sensitive to their culture and heritage. Nearly three-fourths of the interviewees reported that the school was insensitive to the Indian culture. Eighty-three percent felt that the teachers were not interested in their culture and made little effort to understand Indian people. Over half of the women reported that their education was no more than a formal process to transmit the white man's view of the world. One respondent commented, "Everything was conformity—stand in line, salute the flag, be a good American. We were taught to be hardworking and successful so we could have more than our neighbor. Those were our teachers' values, not our values. No wonder our lives are so screwed up now. We feel guilt if we are successful, [and] we feel guilt when we aren't."

Another female, who described herself as "cutting her teeth on Indian activism" as a result of her parents' involvement in AIM, reported that she rejected what she considered an Anglo political agenda within the school setting:

> In our fourth-grade class, every student had to take turns at being a leader. One of the responsibilities included bringing into the classroom the American flag and holding it while the rest of the class said the pledge. I simply refused to do it. I grew up seeing the American flag flown upside down—symbolic of the distress, you know, the distressful situation of the Indian nations. It would have been a slap in the face to my parents, their political beliefs, and the values I was raised with to participate in such an activity. The teachers considered me a rebel. I liked that label. It was better than squaw or a dumb Indian.

The majority of the women rejected the idea that the curriculum was a problem in their success or lack of success in school. One woman, who mirrored the comments made by many of the participants, suggested, "Kids will learn anything. Cultural relevance means nothing to children. It is all in how it is presented and how the teacher treats you and whether you like her and she likes you. If you got a teacher who thinks you are lazy or not very smart, or one that yells at you or accuses you of not paying attention, it doesn't matter what is being taught in class—you just aren't going to pay attention."

Another woman suggested that a culturally relevant curriculum was meaningless in the context of the school:

> You know, most educators believe that cultural relevance means that you talk about Indians and what they did in the old days. My son, who participates in a bilingual program at school, came home from school one day and asked me when he was going to meet a real Indian. I tried to explain to him that he was a *real* Indian, but I think between the school and me, he is totally confused. In school, when culture is included, Indians are always talked about in the past tense. It's like we do not have a viable, colorful, living culture. I don't believe in [a] culturally relevant curriculum. I believe teaching Indian children about the history, politics, and government of Indian people is fine, but in high school. Small children do not need to be confused about whether they are Indian or not. These proponents of bilingual education are trying to validate themselves. They are not helping children. I believe that we should promote a multicultural curriculum where Indian children learn about the world they live in and not just the reservation or Indian culture.

Child-rearing practices among American Indians have been considered in the literature as a detriment to success in school. Although the traditional political and economic structures of American Indian tribal groups have been mostly destroyed, traditional child-rearing practices and family relationships have undergone a much slower change, and these traditional parenting practices are sometimes at opposition with the structured, competitive nature of the school environment. Thus, conflict often develops for a child in school when s/he is forced to conform to the school standards. As documented earlier, a number of researchers have reported that this results in student misbehavior, skipping school, and eventual dropping out.

Several questions were designed to determine if the women respondents were subject to the traditional child-rearing practices of the American Indian community, and how and if these practices impacted their success in the school setting. Many women reported difficulty in not being able to conform to school rules about talking with neighbors, getting out of their seats, or talking in class. One female reported that her first major conflict happened on the second day of school in her kindergarten class:

> I was raised by my mom, my aunt, and my grandma. We all lived together, a houseful of women. I know they loved me dearly. I could do anything I wanted to; I was rarely punished. When I wanted to talk with them, they always stopped and listened regardless of what they were doing. When I went to school, I expected my teacher would be the same way. All the adults in my world listened to my questions and my needs—but not at school. On the first day, the teacher talked about raising our hands to be recognized. All that was foreign to me. I was forever getting in trouble for walking up to her and asking for help or asking a question. On the second day, I was put in the corner for asking her a question without raising my hand. I sat there and cried for an hour. School was a lonely place.

The majority of the women spoke about getting into trouble in school for socializing with others in the class. One woman, who was representative of others, talked about spending recess in class writing for the teacher:

> She [the teacher] had this rule. We were not allowed to talk to anyone in class without permission. I was always forgetting. At home we could talk whenever we wanted to. It never made much sense to me to want to say something and not be able to say it. This rule—if she caught you talking—you had to write 50 times "I will not talk in class." If she caught you again, it was 150 times. Each time, it tripled. I never got many recesses; I was always writing. When I got older, I didn't write for teachers who had such punishments. It was stupid anyway, and I discovered if I didn't write, there wasn't much they could do anyway.

One high school graduate talked almost reverently about a teacher who understood the importance of socializing among Indian children:

> She was a special teacher. We all loved her. Every day, she started class with a "three-minute news period." During that time, we could announce to the class, or privately to someone, anything that we wanted to tell. At the end of the period, when all of our work was done, she would walk around the class and visit with us. She allowed us to visit with our friends. We never got rowdy or

loud. We respected her too much. She probably spent no more than five minutes a period on such activity, but because we knew we could talk, we worked hard for her when it was time to work. I know we got a lot more accomplished than in classrooms where teachers were always stopping and correcting someone's behavior. When we had desk work, she always let us help each other. Sometimes the principal looked in and frowned, but she just smiled at him and let us keep on working together.

Other women reported a major conflict between the way they were raised and the rules in school. This conflict often resulted in girls getting into trouble in school because they helped someone out (with homework or with an answer on a test). The teachers regarded such indiscriminate help as "cheating," whereas at home these girls had been raised to help each other. One female commented:

If you watch Indian kids play, they are always taking care of each other— particularly the girls. So, if someone falls down and starts to cry, everyone runs over, helps that person up, brushes them off, and loves them. You would never walk away from someone who is in trouble. But in school, it is different. My cousin was in the same grade. She was not very good in math. I was pretty good, I guess. I would help her with her homework or let her see my paper. Sometimes I gave her answers on tests. One day this teacher yelled at us, calling us cheaters, . . . embarrassed us, . . . when all I was doing was helping someone who needed help. I found out that in school, you never help anyone who needs help.

Many women talked about the importance of grades to teachers and of being singled out in class. One woman reported that what was desirable was neither success nor failure, but rather, staying "in the middle of the road," as she called it: "If you made a good score, the teacher would announce it to the class. If you failed, the teacher would announce it to the class. None of us wanted to be singled out. At home, our parents didn't single us out and compliment us or scold us. They either complimented the whole group or scolded the whole group. It was never 'Look at this one or that one.' I discovered that as long as I made C's, I was not singled out. It was better to be average than good or bad. I know I was much more than average, but the teachers never knew it."

Another woman spoke about the privacy of praise or scolding at home, but the lack of privacy within the school setting: "My parents scolded us and praised us. But it was never in comparison with others. Sometimes the whole group got scolded or praised so as not to draw attention to one person. Other times, when more deserving, I guess, we were praised in private or scolded in private. Teachers should have used such tactics. It would have made us feel more at home in school."

Some college graduates felt that a strong sense of tribal identity and self-identity made the difference in their success in school. One college graduate suggested:

> There is a real advantage to being Indian in the school setting. At home, you know the values that are important. In school, you learn different values. I learned early that in school, there were ways of doing things, and at home there were ways of doing things. But the real advantage is that as you grow up, you have a chance to make choices and choose the best of both cultures or commingle those cultures. Curriculum doesn't make a difference; how you are treated by teachers does make a difference. I think the difference for me was that I had a strong identity and I rejected those things in the school that were in direct opposition to what I had been taught at home, but that didn't mean that being exposed to them or learning about them was a detriment to me as a human being. I think it made me a better human being.

When asked if cultural differences contributed to dropping out of school, none of the women considered cultural factors a principal reason for dropping out. Although many spoke of differences between the home and school, few felt that those differences alone interfered to the degree that they justified dropping out of school. Most noted that while they could deal with the differences in the cultures, teacher attitudes that led to their alienation in school were a major factor in dropping out.

When women were asked if they developed a cynicism toward school or felt there were few opportunities for them even if they graduated, nearly half of the dropouts responded that lack of opportunities or a future was certainly a determinant in their decision to leave school early, whereas less than 10 percent of the college graduates reported such feelings. On the other hand, nearly one-fifth of the high school graduates reported feeling disillusioned about their future, but determined to stay in the system.

One high school dropout suggested that there were few role models for students to follow in the pursuit of an education: "How can you feel hope for your future when you grow up in a home where no one works, where no one has jobs, and where there is no hope for you to get a job once you graduate? I know Indians who have college degrees and are unemployed."

Another dropout spoke quite forcefully about her attitudes toward getting an education: "You can't get a job on the reservation unless you are related to someone on the tribal council or the school board. You can't get a job off the reservation unless you are willing to be a motel maid, and then you'll get fired if a white person comes along and wants the job. What good is an education, anyway? Yeah, I gave up on school. It served no purpose to me. It was just a way of delaying getting on with my life, which had already been planned for me because I am an Indian."

Another dropout attributed her giving up on school to teachers and their superior attitudes toward Indian students:

> In school, you learn that there are the bosses and they are white, or Indians who act like whites, . . . and then there are the others, who do what the bosses tell them. If you are an Indian, it is clear that you will never be the boss, because it is the whites who are in power. I never felt good in school. I always felt like I wasn't good enough or that the teachers were doing me a favor because they were trying to teach me. As I got older, I realized that education for Indians meant nothing. There were no jobs, no opportunities. So why even try? Even if we got a job, it was still the whites, the teachers, who would be in power.

One high school graduate reported that, although she didn't believe school would provide her with employment opportunities, she did feel it would provide her with the skills to intervene in a system she considered unjust and corrupt: "I hated school. Most of the teachers didn't expect very much of us. They knew that even if we graduated, we wouldn't do anything with our education, because there were no jobs. Any good job was held by whites, and if an Indian did get a good job, they were generally run out of it by oppositional political forces within the community. By the time I was a tenth-grader, I knew that the likelihood of getting a job was almost zero, but I also knew that even as much as I hated the school, I needed an education so I could stand up for my rights or at least the rights of my children. I graduated for that reason."

Among all the issues confronting American Indian populations today, two appear to be the most controversial: (1) Native language and cultural instruction in school and (2) the importance of the Native language for purposes of self-identity and tribal identity. A number of conclusions surfaced, however, when analyzing the findings of the study.

FINDING: Native American females who are Native-language speakers do not drop out of school more frequently than females who are monolingual English speakers.

As with other language minority students, speaking a language other than English upon entry in school may impact a Native American female's achievement during early years, but it does not appear to be a major factor in whether a girl will complete high school or not. In fact, in this study there was considerable evidence that girls who came from strong traditional backgrounds or Native-speaking backgrounds were as successful as, if not more successful than, less traditional students. Although cultural discontinuity was reported in terms of communication and interaction with teachers, few of the women in this study felt that being traditional was a detriment to school success. This finding is consistent with recent research among Navajo youth.[25]

FINDING: Native language fluency is decreasing with each generation of American Indian youth.

Research tells us that women are the teachers of language; therefore, if the mother is a Native speaker, the child is more likely to speak the Native language. In this study, only 10 percent of the women reported fluency in their Native language, and none of those women (100 percent were mothers) reported teaching their children the Native language. An examination of the data about language retention and usage among the participants in this study demonstrates the loss of the Native language among each generation. The participants in this study reported that 54 percent of their grandparents spoke their Native language, and yet just a little over one-fourth (26 percent) of their parents were fluent speakers. With their generation, those numbers have decreased to 10 percent. Should this rate of language loss continue, the Native language may indeed be lost to future generations. From all indications, the present generation—the children of the participants in this study—will speak only English.

These statistics are disconcerting to many women in this study. While some felt that the language was the responsibility of the family, others felt that the school should assume the responsibility for teaching the Native language. Although a majority of the women felt that the Native language was important, they felt English was equally, if not more, important. Others reported frustration with Native language classes in schools that did little more than teach words or phrases, and even though they wanted the Native languages taught in the school, they did not feel it was a solution to the preservation or restoration of the languages.

It is clear that time is running out for some American Indian populations on the issue of language maintenance. Basically, children are not learning their Native languages; their parents either have chosen not to teach them or do not possess the skills to teach them. Should this trend continue, it is likely that the languages will disappear from usage once the women in this study reach old age.

FINDING: Classroom English may be an inhibitor to the Native American female's early success in school and establishes a pattern that is difficult to reverse in later school years, unless there is early intervention to develop vocabulary and the basic skills needed for success.

Although less than one-fifth of the women in this study reported having difficulty with the English language during their elementary school years, it is important to examine the problems that were reported. Their difficulties ranged from lack of familiarity with words used by the teacher, to humiliation as a result of the reservation English they had learned in their home environments, to being non–English speakers when they entered school. Although a number of the women reported coping skills, many more reported failure, confusion, and withdrawal in the classroom. Further examination of this problem demonstrated that their failure, confusion, and withdrawal were in part created by what they perceived to be insensitive attitudes on the part of teachers.

It is apparent that women who came from homes where standard English was not spoken had more difficulty in school. The significance of this finding cannot be overlooked. Educators often assume that if the Indian child does not speak his/her Native language, the child must be fluent in English. Many Indian children appear to be illiterate in both English and their Native language. They speak neither language fluently, although they may understand one better than the other. In any case, language and vocabulary development are critical in the early childhood years, both in prekindergarten and in the lower elementary grades, to develop language skills that will prepare children for success in school. Moreover, teachers who expect students to enter school with standard English skills (one of the aspects of the hidden curriculum) may in fact be ignoring or misinterpreting the cognitive skills of Indian children.

FINDING: Efforts at Native language restoration, preservation, and maintenance must become a family/community/tribal commitment and should not be the sole responsibility of the school.

If the Native language is to be restored, preserved, and maintained, the schools need help. Schools cannot make speakers out of children when the language is regarded as one of many subjects to be taught throughout the day; an hour of daily instruction will not make children speakers. Children will become speakers only if the language is reinforced at home and within the community and only if they perceive that it is relevant to their lives and to their self-identity and tribal identity. If parents want their children to learn the Native language, perhaps they, too, should enroll in classes and learn the language along with their children. This approach calls for a concerted effort on the part of families and the community.

Throughout the interviews with younger women, there were strong tendencies toward eliminating the Native language in the schools. Many did not see it as relevant to their contemporary lives. The majority agreed that English language competency was at least as important to success as Native language competency. As these young women will become the mothers of future generations, it is important for tribal groups to act at once if the Native languages are to survive. Schools cannot and should not be totally responsible for restoring, preserving, or maintaining the language. That responsibility, at least in part, lies with each resident of the reservation.

Moreover, the question is raised as to the issue of relinquishing the teaching of the language to the school environment. Many women questioned the motives of educators who purportedly had the best interests of Indian people in mind when they advocated Native language instruction within the schools. Perhaps for tribes to be successful in the restoration, preservation, and maintenance of their languages, they must decide as tribal groups whether the language is important to the future of their tribes. Then Indian tribal institutions or agencies could be charged with restoring, preserving, and maintaining it. Some tribes may decide that it is possible to maintain their cultural identity without the Native language; others may see the loss of their cultural identity directly linked with their loss of language.

In any event, the preservation of Native languages may be too crucial a responsibility to relinquish to schools that have traditionally held as their mission the assimilation of Indian students into the white culture. I believe that, although Native language instruction can be an important function of the school, schools should not and cannot be the sole preserver of the language and culture.

FINDING: Cultural discontinuity is not a sufficient explanation for American Indian girls dropping out of school and is not a major factor in girls leaving school prematurely.

Although the majority of the women in this study reported that there were cultural differences between the school environment and the home environment, the majority felt that those differences were not the principal cause of dropping out of school or their lack of success in school. In fact, the women were much more likely to point to secondary discontinuities (as defined by John Ogbu), rather than the school curriculum, as a determinant of dropping out. In other words, distrust of school personnel resulting from years of negative experiences, or giving up on school because it had no relevancy to their futures, was much more likely to cause girls to drop out of school than the fact that the school's language and culture differed from the home's. Many of the women cited the lack of job opportunities, the existence of few role models, and the reality that high school graduation would not provide them with a way out of poverty as factors in dropping out of school. Others viewed the school system as corrupt, unjust, and the promoter of an Anglo culture that was in opposition to their values and those of their parents.

Although much of the distrust for teachers and schools may have developed as a result of the communication and interaction between student and teacher, which is basic to the cultural discontinuity theory, a culturally relevant curriculum was not viewed as a solution to the problem. In fact, if anything, the women advocated a more contemporary curriculum that better prepared students for a global society, rather than one limited to reservation and tribal issues. This does not mean the women saw as unimportant the history, culture, and traditions of their people. On the contrary, they felt that culture had a distinct place in the curriculum, but that it was more appropriate for older students, who had the ability to discriminate between the past and the present. The bottom line appears to be this: the content of the curriculum is not nearly so important as the interaction between teacher and student and the bond the student develops with the school.

Summary

In chapter 8, I called for a separation of the effects of poverty from those of culture and race on the educability of Indian students. Researchers should use caution when interpreting the results of studies on children from poverty or children from different cultures. For instance, although poverty is a status position, it is critical for researchers to examine the intervening variables that modify the effects on education, such as socialization and health conditions, rather than assessing income levels of parents and making judgments about children. Moreover, researchers interested in the development of Indian children must further distinguish between the mediating variables of poverty and the attitudes and perceptions that may be endemic to poverty, such as distrust, skepticism, and lack of hope or motivation. For example, if children do not view education as an asset or a means to future opportunity, a culturally relevant curriculum will serve no purpose. And finally, it is important to separate the conditions of poverty from those of culture and to understand that some behaviors have become so ingrained within the cultures of poverty that we begin to accept those behaviors as a part of our respective cultures when they are nothing more than the consequences of poverty.

A major concern for educators of Indian children is to determine why children demonstrate the skills to communicate, act, and think outside the school setting, yet do not demonstrate those skills in school. Just as poverty affects the development of children, so does the culture of a child. Perhaps of equal significance are the values and attitudes children bring to school that are the result of poverty. When it is assumed by educators that all children should have the prerequisites of the hidden curriculum prior to entering school, these assumptions interfere with teachers' judgments and interpretations of students' behaviors in class. Moreover, to assume that all Indian children are going to come to school with the same set of values, attitudes, beliefs, and behaviors is erroneous.   Indian students' backgrounds are varied. Some come from traditional homes; others come from homes where radical views are espoused. Some come from homes where education is highly valued; others come from homes where education is viewed with distrust and skepticism. Some come to school with well-developed cognitive skills appropriate to the hidden curriculum; others come from homes where nonstandard English is the norm and opportunities for exposure to written and educational materials are few. Some come from homes of poverty where family spirit is minimal and survival is a priority; others come from more affluent homes where security and stability within the child's world are promoted.

It is important to recognize that Indian education has basically reflected the political position of the federal government. From the beginning, Indian education was for the purposes of destroying the Indian culture and Christianizing the Indian. Now the move is to teach the Indian to be Indian in order to save the culture. Perhaps it is important to recognize that between both of these extremes, it is generally the non-Indian researcher and the non-Indian educator who knows what is best for Indians. As Gerald Wilkinson notes, "It seems to be a permanent and required fixture in the American character that the Indian must be constantly saved from something."[26]

Much more research is needed to understand why Indian students are not successful in school. The cultural discontinuity theory has played a major role in determining the solutions in American Indian education over the past decade, although it is not a totally convincing argument for why Indian students fail. For most educators, the solution to cultural discontinuity has been the development of a culturally relevant curriculum, which is generally undefinable and at best couched in vague descriptive terms. Without question, this focus on a culturally relevant curriculum draws attention away from some of the more pressing political and economic issues faced by Indian students.

Although cultural differences may be a factor in lack of success, it may also be true that culture is a significant factor in success in school. As the research discussed within this chapter suggests, a strong sense of cultural identity may provide students with an advantage in school, thus eliminating their resistance to school for fear of losing their Indianness. If that is the case, it is certainly contradictory to the cultural discontinuity theorists' position that the differences between home and school cultures create failure for students. On the other hand, what we may be dealing with is a group of parents and students within their respective tribes who have little tribal identity and who perceive a culturally relevant curriculum as the answer to their need to enhance their own Indianness. If so, the issue of culturally relevant curricula and Native language instruction will remain controversial in Indian country.

Regardless of the position one takes, it appears that cultural discontinuity is insufficient to fully explain the reasons that Indian students are failing in school. To this extent, tribes should seriously consider how much they want to rely on the schools to transmit their cultural knowledge and what should be left to the family and more traditional Indian institutions. Dependence upon experts who come up with solutions to the failure of Indian students has done nothing to solve the problems in Indian education, but it has provided funds and new jobs, especially for researchers, consultants, and experts, who in many cases contribute to the magnitude of the problem. As Gerald Wilkinson comments, "If a tribe needs more medicine men than Ph.D.'s to survive as a people, then their educational institutions should reflect this."[27] To rely upon the solutions of those outside the Indian community is likely to continue to produce few results.

Chapter 10

Self-Worth/Tribal Identity and American Indian Women

Self-worth is something everyone needs. It increases our chances of happiness and enables us to cope with life's disappointments and changes. We need to have a good sense of self-worth in order to recognize our place in the world. Self-worth is important to our psychological well-being and affects virtually everything we say, do, and think. Many researchers have attributed the lack of success in school and the high dropout rate among American Indian students to low self-worth. In order to investigate this problem, all participants in this study were asked a series of questions relating to self, including questions about peer and parental approval and about participants' attitudes and perceptions about themselves. As the purpose of this study was primarily to identify feelings, perceptions, and attitudes at the time the participant was in high school, no standardized instrument (which is a frequent method used for determining self-worth) was used as a part of this process.

Seventy-two percent of all the participants reported "liking" themselves; however, only 61 percent said they approved of their physical appearance when in high school. Fifty-four percent of the high school graduates indicated that they had athletic or creative talents in high school and that these talents enhanced their self-worth. Slightly less than 10 percent said that "doing well in school" improved their self-worth.

The women who dropped out of high school reported a slightly lower level of self-approval than the high school and college graduates, but the difference was not significant. The majority of the dropouts reported "liking" themselves when they were in high school, although many reported unhappiness with their physical appearance.

When asked the difference between "liking" themselves as individuals and disapproving of their physical appearance, most women defined liking themselves in terms of their service to others, such as being a good daughter or a good sister, being responsible and dependable, and not doing "bad things" to other people.

As a follow-up to this question, the women were asked to describe their lack of acceptance of their physical appearance. In almost all cases, the responses from all three groups were "too fat," "skin problems," or "too dark." Fifty-seven percent of the women reported inadequate clothing as a major source of strife for them while in school. One female dropout expressed the feeling that students were favored or disfavored according to dress: "There were seven of us. Dad didn't have a job. All my clothes were given to me. Most of them didn't fit. Everyone laughed at me. The teachers didn't pay any attention to me. They knew I would never go to college because of the way I dressed, . . . too poor, too dumb. White teachers see clothes as a reflection of whether you're smart or not. I hated them for the way they treated me. They never knew that clothes didn't make a person."

Although the issue of inadequate or improper clothing was discussed by the participants as a source of low self-worth, the broader issue of self-worth appeared closely tied to poverty, which affected teacher attitudes and perceptions.

Many females reported low self-worth related to verbal abuse from teachers. One female summed up similar stories of encounters with verbally negative and abusive teachers: "This one teacher called us 'squaws' and 'baby factories.' I didn't even understand what he meant. We were only in the sixth grade. He told us all to drop out of school. He said it was a waste for us to go to school, . . . we'd just go on welfare anyway."

Another woman remembered a home economics teacher: "She spent six weeks on teaching us to cook beans. She said that's all we would ever be able to afford anyway—free commodities. She used to make us list what we ate for breakfast, lunch, and dinner. She'd go down the list, call out each girl's name, and belittle her. After a few days of that, we all made up lists from the basic food groups on the wall charts and lied to her."

A high school dropout related, "My teacher told me I was dumb. My mom told me I was dumb. My dad—he was white—told me I was going to end up getting pregnant. He said that Indian women were only good for getting pregnant. I guess I believed him. I got pregnant at fourteen."

One female expressed the pain of dealing with teachers who made her feel inferior and how one teacher positively affected her self-image: "I had this teacher in the first grade. She sat me in the back of the room. I wasn't asked to read out loud in class. I practiced reading when I went home. I read to my brothers and sisters. In the sixth grade, my teacher asked me to read out loud in class and I couldn't. . . . Everyone in class thought I couldn't read. Later, that teacher asked me to come in after school and read to her. She told me that I could be anything I wanted to be as long as I could read. I believed her. I might have dropped out of school if it hadn't been for her."

In recent years, most psychiatrists have concluded that verbal abuse may be as devastating to an individual's self-worth as physical or sexual abuse. Within the setting of the school, children should expect to feel unthreatened. Verbally abusive teachers, although not the norm, are common enough that Indian communities should be alerted to this problem. Students who are unable to trust their teachers are more likely to drop out of school. Clearly, it is difficult to trust a teacher who is verbally abusive.

It is evident that American Indian adolescent girls' self-worth is impacted by what others say about them and how others treat them, just as with girls in other cultures. Despite the research that suggests Native girls have lower self-worth than white girls, there is considerable evidence that the self-worth of American Indian girls depends less on external forces than on their families and their roles within their reservation societies.

FINDING: Self-worth is not a significant factor, either positive or negative, in whether an American Indian girl stays in school or drops out.

Throughout the research, American Indian children reportedly suffer from low self-worth, which contributes to their dropping out of school. The majority of the women in this study reported "liking" themselves. Although low self-worth may be a contributing factor for some individuals, for the majority of the women in this study, their self-esteem or self-worth was not strongly connected with success or failure in school. There were strong indicators that American Indian girls develop coping skills to deal with negative comments from teachers. Furthermore, since they do not perceive success in school as important to their image as an individual, neither high self-worth nor low self-worth appears to influence their decision to stay in school and graduate or to drop out.

FINDING: The self-worth of American Indian girls is closely tied to family relationships and approval from within the reservation society.

American Indian women draw a strong relationship between self-worth and their contributions to their family, their friends, and their tribal society at large. In fact, they define "liking" themselves in terms of "being a good daughter," "being a good sister," and "being dependable." When girls grow up in supportive family settings, it is very likely that they are receiving praise and approval for such characteristics. Even girls in dysfunctional homes may receive such praise and approval, because they often find themselves in the role of caretaker of siblings or even their parents. Being a dutiful daughter is grounded in cultural traditions and therefore is much more highly prized in terms of self-fulfillment and expectations than performing well in school, which is based in the white man's culture.

FINDING: It appears that physical beauty, in terms of the self-worth of American Indian girls, is impacted by nonreservation, nontraditional norms.

A majority of the women interviewed indicated that they were not happy with their physical appearance while in high school. This is typical of adolescent girls in most societies and may be explained as such. However, as noted earlier, another factor seems to be involved: women explained these feelings in terms of being "too fat," "too dark," or "having skin problems," and such feelings may be a result of media advertising—that is, magazine, TV, and movie portrayals that promote thinness, good skin, and, perhaps more importantly, fair skin and light-colored hair as the hallmarks of beauty. Although within the culture there appears to be a strong rejection of "clothes making the individual," there was considerable discussion by the women in this study about the impact clothes had on the way they were treated and regarded by their teachers. There are some indications, particularly when children stay home from school because other children tease them about their clothes, that nonreservation, nontraditional norms are negatively influencing these children's sense of self-worth.

Self-Identity/Tribal Identity

Researchers have often related dropping out of school to alienation resulting from the lack of ethnic identity. Some researchers suggest that Indian youth go through a period of identity diffusion, and describe the young American Indian as a marginal person, one who fits into neither the white nor the Indian culture.

This study designed a number of questions to address this issue. Eighty-nine percent of all the women reported "pride in their Indian heritage." When asked if pride in their heritage was a significant part of their identity as adolescent females, 43 percent felt that their Indian heritage was a source of pride. Twenty-four percent of the females reported having wished, when they were in high school, that they had been born white instead of Indian. When this "wish" was pursued by the researcher, many of the women reported that being Indian was a disadvantage when in high school and that those Indians who had white blood had more opportunities or were viewed as being more favored. "If you looked white," stated one full-blood participant, "the teachers treated you better and you were more popular with the boys. Indian boys liked white women—at least when I was in high school. That's the reason we [Indian girls] didn't like the breeds."

When asked if there was a social status distinction between full-blood Indians and mixed-bloods, 97 percent of the women reported that the degree of Indian blood was significant to the way individuals were treated, both on the reservation and off. One college graduate, who reported that she was half Indian, said:

I learned to take advantage of my white blood off the reservation. Because I look more white than Indian, I didn't encounter too much prejudice. If people found out that I was half Indian, that was an advantage in the white world. People like having a minority around, if you act like them. On the reservation, it is a disadvantage. You are criticized according to your heritage. If you do something people don't like, you are reminded that you are white. A lot of breeds connect up with men who look "more Indian." It's a validation of their Indianness more than anything else. There is a certain status in being married to or living with a full-blood with long braids, even if he doesn't work, . . . even if he drinks, . . . even if he beats you. It helps identify us as Indians.

When asked to what degree they had adopted values from the white culture, 77 percent of the women reported incorporating both Indian and white cultural traits into their life-styles. When asked which white traits they adopted, the responses ranged from having bank accounts, using educational training, buying nice furniture and clothes, and planning for the future, to vacationing in Hawaii. Eighty-nine percent of the mixed-blood women of one-half Indian blood or less reported adhering more to white cultural values than to Indian ones. Again, the "white" values most commonly identified were materialistic, wanting to get ahead financially, and having a comfortable retirement. A high percentage of the females spoke of wanting "nice things," which they noted was not a value in the Indian culture.

A majority of the women reported that "sharing" one's resources was a source of personal strife. One college graduate related the frustration of acculturation:

There are two things involved. As children, we are taught to share everything. We go to college and find out that no one shares. . . . You work to get ahead and to do better. When you have a job on the reservation, you are expected to share with relatives. If you don't, you are rejected. . . . It's a double bind. When you buy nice clothes or furniture, you feel guilty. Your family has nothing—so you give them money and buy them things. They expect it. If you don't, you are talked about. My house was broken into once. People said if I hadn't had so many "things," it wouldn't have happened. It's like it is OK to steal if you steal from people who have too much. I should really move off this reservation.

One female, who reported that she rejected the white culture of materialism as inappropriate to Indian people, expressed a concern that was voiced by other women: "I tell my kids that they don't need everything they see on television. It's hard to keep them from being influenced by the outside world. They want toys, pump-up sneakers, clothes. I have a four-year-old who wants designer jeans. I try to tell them that those things aren't important to Indians, . . . [but] they don't listen. TV has changed this generation. It's hard to raise children to be Indian today."

A more philosophical respondent offered her assessment of materialism among contemporary Indians:

There is no such thing as "true Indian" today. Indians are like everybody else. They want cars, clothes, money. It's just that they buy junkers [used cars], and they break down, and they spend their money on fixing them up. They buy clothes from Kmart that fall apart after three washings. They spend money on new ones. They buy toys for their kids. They tear them up, and they buy new ones. We want the same thing as white people—only poverty and lack of education prevents us from getting it. Lack of education breeds more poverty. Indian or white, it doesn't matter. Poor whites behave the same way as poor Indians. It's a vicious cycle.

Another Indian female spoke of family discord created because of cultural conflicts:

I'm married to a white man. His parents were poor but hardworking. They were strict with him. He is strict with our kids. My family doesn't like that. They don't think our kids should have to work around the house. They don't like it when we don't buy them candy and pop. I finally had to tell them to stay out of our business. They do, not because they like it, but because he is my husband. In the summer, we let the kids stay with my parents for a couple weeks. It is a treat for them. . . . They have no rules—they can stay up, eat candy, drink pop, watch anything on TV. My husband used to get mad about that, but he is better now. I tell him that that's what grandparents are for—to spoil kids. I agree with him, you know. I wish Mom and Dad had been stricter with me. . . . I wish they had told me they expected me to go to college.

Another woman spoke of how differing values within her family resulted in the deterioration of a brother-sister relationship: "My brother married this white woman. . . . She was in graduate school; she helped him go to college. They both have good jobs, live in a fancy white man's house, drive new cars, travel. He's changed. She's changed him. I wish he'd divorce her and come back to the rez. We could be together like we used to. My kids need an uncle to look up to. He sends us money. He buys clothes and presents for my kids. . . . But it's not like having him living here. That woman [her sister-in-law] has made a white man out of him."

Clearly, there appears to be a distinction between self-esteem and self-identity among American Indian women. Whereas self-esteem relates to one's self-worth, self-identity is defined in terms of one's level of acculturation and assimilation, and the degree of one's Indian blood.

FINDING: *It appears that American Indian women who strongly identify with their Indian heritage and those who strongly identify with the white culture do better in school than those who have no strong ethnic identity.*

Women who had a strong sense of tribal and ethnic identity or a strong sense of identification with the white culture were equally successful in school.

This study indicated that degree of Indian blood was not a factor in school success. Some women who were less than one-fourth Indian identified strongly with their Indian heritage and considered themselves more Indian than white. Other women who were less than one-fourth Indian identified more frequently with the white culture, but this did not seem to prevent them from being successful in school. It would appear that whether a female is a full-blood Indian or a breed matters very little as far as staying in school is concerned. What does seem to matter is that adolescents have a strong sense of who they are and that they take pride in their heritage.

There appears to be an identity factor at play, however, in the adult lives of some females who form relationships with Indian males who display their Indian heritage physically, such as by wearing long braids. It is as though the assimilated or less culturally oriented female somehow obtains her "place in society" vicariously, that is, by association with a male who has a strong Indian identity.

FINDING: For most American Indian females, "pride in their Indian heritage" is not a major part of their self-identity as children or adolescents.

There was evidence that, as children or young adults, many American Indian women did not have a strong sense of being Indian or pride in being Indian. This pride in their heritage seemed to develop with adulthood. Many reported a desire, during their adolescence, to be white, as they felt that breeds had more opportunities and were favored. Perhaps white teachers inadvertently identify with children who are "more white" in physical appearance and therefore give them more positive attention. As there are few Indian role models within the school, students who are more Indian often have no one to relate to and believe that if they looked or were more white, their lives would be considerably different.

This desire in children to be more white often translates into contempt for breeds in adulthood. Part of this may result from the fact that breeds are seen as favored, and because they are more white, they have more opportunities in both Indian and non-Indian worlds.

FINDING: Social status within the Native American female's own tribe appears to be based, at least to some extent, not on educational or economic success, but on the degree of Indian blood or one's adherence to the traditional culture.

Whereas social status within the white society is often loosely based on a person's economic wealth, wealth has little to do with status within most Indian societies. In fact, it has just the opposite effect. Economic success means "being white," even if one is a full-blood Indian. Although a majority of American Indian women appear to function in a world that incorporates both Indian and white cultural values, reverence and admiration for others in the Native societies are often confined to those who are reported to "follow the Indian ways." For the most part, efforts by breeds to practice the "Indian ways" is looked upon unfavorably, unless, in the case of women, they are married to a man who can give them that degree of credibility.

In the case of the college-educated female, there appears to be another factor at work, one that has been ignored by previous researchers. Although a college degree carries with it credibility, many successful American Indian women marry men who do not have comparable educational backgrounds. In fact, 17 percent of the college-educated women participating in this study admitted to marriage or cohabitation arrangements with men who were high school dropouts. An additional 32 percent had married high school graduates or men who had completed GEDs but had not pursued any postsecondary education. Less than 3 percent of the women with master's or doctoral degrees had marriage partners or live-in mates with college degrees. High school graduates (11 percent) had, however, married or lived with males who were college graduates. None of the dropouts reported marriage or involvement with college-educated spouses or mates.

Throughout this study, there were strong indications that the college-educated female was regarded (or at least perceived herself to be regarded by her tribal society) as less traditional. In other words, to be successful, an Indian female relinquishes her "Indianness," at least in part. To deal with this situation, it appears that a high percentage of these females opt for personal involvements with men who are perceived as "more traditional." This often translates into marriage or cohabitation with a male who is far less educated, who is perhaps unemployed or seasonally employed, and who in some cases may be an alcoholic or abuser. In this way, it appears that the college-educated female reestablishes her connection with her tribal group through marriage or association with the male who has strong cultural ties. Such an alliance may also serve to validate her with other females, since she is choosing a personal life that is no different from that of the women who dropped out of high school or those who chose to stay on the reservation and assume more traditional roles. This phenomenon, which appears commonplace among college-educated American Indian females, does not seem to apply to the educated American Indian male. In fact, researchers have noted that college-educated American Indian males most often marry non-Indian women, thus reducing, for the educated Native female, the number of eligible American Indian men with similar backgrounds.

Again, the double standards applied to acceptable behavior within the culture dramatically affect the life of the adult female, whether she is a high school dropout or a college graduate.

Suicide and Self-Worth

A number of researchers have studied the high rate of suicide among American Indian adolescents, estimating that suicide is seven times higher for Indian youth than for adolescents in the majority society. In turn, suicide victims are often described as those individuals who have low self-worth.

Although American Indian females reportedly attempt suicide at about the same rates as non-Indian girls, I posed several questions to elicit information from the participants about their inclination toward suicide. Twenty-nine percent of the females in the study admitted to thoughts of suicide while they were in high school. Nineteen percent reported that their home situation (parental drinking, fighting, death in the family) resulted in such feelings.

Twelve percent reported having attempted suicide; of that group, 7 percent indicated they had more than one caretaker in their younger years and 6 percent reported having attended boarding schools when they were young. Of the 12 percent who indicated they had attempted suicide, the overwhelming majority had taken sleeping pills. Eleven percent of that group reported that the pills were ineffective and that no one in their family knew they had even tried to commit suicide. The remainder reported such suicide techniques as excessive drinking and reckless driving, or trying to freeze themselves to death by staying outside in subzero temperatures. Only three women in the study admitted to attempting violence against themselves, which included using a firearm and cutting their wrists.

When the participants who admitted to having but not pursuing suicidal thoughts were asked the reasons for not following through, they most often described their depression as temporary. The majority (69 percent) said they had broken up with a boyfriend and considered suicide as a way of handling their pain. As with other adolescent girls, most noted that their depression was temporary and said those feelings disappeared when they found a new boyfriend or got involved in some school activity.

Among the group who noted that suicide had never been a consideration, the majority (91 percent) reported "enjoying life too much" to consider suicide. When asked to define this characteristic, the majority reported substantial involvement in school activities. Even the women who had dropped out of school (53 percent) reported that they enjoyed school activities (ball games, clubs, field trips, dances) and social interaction with their peers. Several women voiced concern that suicide was like other problems that can get out of hand when left unattended. In the words of one respondent, "Suicide is like an epidemic. One person kills himself and then a whole bunch does the same thing. I think it's because these kids see how much attention someone gets when they kill themselves. They think they will get the attention. It sure is bad when we give more attention to the dead than to the living. Maybe that's cultural—but the same thing happens to whites, too, doesn't it?"

Another woman suggested that "spiritual forces" had been responsible for suicides on her reservation: "We had several suicides here a number of years ago. One happened, then another, then another. These kids became obsessed. Finally, one boy told his uncle that he was being told to kill himself and join the others. His uncle went to a medicine man. Several elders got together and decided that a bad spirit was involved. They held ceremonies and sent 'it' away. Afterwards, no more kids killed themselves. I worry that 'it' will come back."

Several females disclosed that suicide is such a frightening subject on reservations that the adults refuse to talk about it, thus not addressing the problems of the youth and/or learning skills for coping with the problem, even with their own children. One college graduate stated, "It's called denial. They think that if they talk about their fears, it will become a reality. It's hard to get them to address the problem. Parents blame themselves. They don't want anyone to think they are bad parents. It's frustrating. If you have a workshop on suicide, people stay away and say things like, 'Why are they talking about suicide? It just makes people think about it when they talk about it.' We need to talk about suicide with parents and with kids. That's the way to prevent it."

When asked if they remembered having any feelings of hopelessness or despair about their futures when they were in high school, only 16 percent of all the participants reported having felt that going to school was useless. The majority (14.4 percent) of those who voiced such concerns were from the seventeen to twenty-one age-group. Seventeen percent reported feeling hopelessness or despair in terms of their personal lives, which most often included problems with drinking parents or breaking up with boyfriends. A majority of the participants indicated that their self-worth was often closely tied to the males in their lives during high school. Breaking up with a boyfriend could be detrimental to one's self-worth. Drinking parents also impact one's self-worth; the women often reported feeling ashamed of their parents' drinking problems or blaming themselves for their parents' drinking.

Although 12 percent of the women in the study reported having made suicide attempts, most of those efforts were discreet and were not repeated. Like girls in the mainstream society, these American Indian girls chose pills as the preferred method—a choice that usually results in unsuccessful or aborted attempts and differs from the more violent methods typically chosen by males. Since little has been written on American Indian girls and suicide, the findings of this study are worthy of note.

FINDING: School failure or pressures seem to play no role in either suicidal thoughts or suicide attempts by American Indian girls.

Whereas failure in school and pressures placed on students to perform academically are reportedly a major cause for suicide attempts or suicide within the white society, those factors appear to play no role in American Indian girls' suicidal tendencies.

With American Indian girls, there seems to be a strong connection between unhappiness or despair in their personal lives and suicidal thoughts or suicide attempts. As noted earlier, American Indian girls seem to develop their self-worth from within the family structure and the reservation environment. Should a distressing event occur, such as parental drinking or fighting, or the loss of a loved one or a boyfriend, it may be that self-worth is affected to the point that thoughts of suicide or suicide attempts result.

FINDING: The number of caretakers and removal from the family and reservation environment (boarding school) are significantly related to suicidal thoughts and suicide attempts among American Indian girls.

Again, in a society where girls' self-worth is often measured by their position within the family and the community, removal from that setting, even when the home setting is negative, may result in such loneliness or despair that suicidal thoughts and suicide attempts become more of an option. In addition, girls who do not have a stable home environment often seek love from others. A majority of the women in this study noted that breaking up with a boyfriend had been instrumental in their thoughts about suicide, although this reason may be more prevalent among girls who are removed from their family circle and their reservations.

Summary

Many researchers have maintained that low self-worth causes failure in school. Among the women in this study, there was no evidence that self-worth was a contributing factor. Tribal identity and self-identity seemed to play a much greater role.

Chapter 11

American Indian Females and Substance Abuse: A Self-fulfilling Prophecy or a Social Anomaly?

There is no question that substance abuse impacts the majority of American Indian females, whether directly or indirectly. Many researchers have identified drugs and alcohol as a major reason for students leaving school before they graduate. This study did not find substance abuse to be a significant factor in school leaving or staying, although the girls who drank or used drugs were more likely to drop out.

Each participant was asked a number of questions about drug and alcohol use and abuse during adolescence and adulthood, and about substance abuse within her immediate family and among her peer group. These questions examined the individual's introduction to alcohol, the nature and extent of use/abuse among family members and peer group, the individual's attitude toward alcohol abuse, and the impact alcohol had on her life as an adolescent and as an adult, if appropriate. Each major topical question was followed by "probing" questions to determine feelings, perceptions, attitudes, behaviors, and knowledge.

Responses about substance abuse revealed some interesting findings often overlooked or not addressed in previous research.

FINDING: American Indian female adolescents do not appear to drink in excess of their white female counterparts, even though they themselves perceive they have a "drinking problem" and believe they drink more than white female adolescents.

It is extremely important to note that 67 percent of the women in this study reported they *did not drink* while in high school. This finding is particularly significant, since research often reports that upward of 89 percent of the adolescent Indian population on reservations drink alcohol and that American Indian youth drink at two to three times the rate of white adolescent comparison groups.[1] Only 14 percent of the women in this study reported drinking once a week or more while in high school. This finding is in striking contrast to other research, which reports that 40 percent of American Indian girls use alcohol regularly.[2] These current findings indicate that alcohol use/abuse among American Indian females somewhat mirrors national statistics on alcohol use/abuse among the female majority culture.

This does not mean, however, that American Indian adolescents do not have access to alcohol, or that they have not had "some experience" with alcohol by the time they reach high school. Eighty-eight percent reported "experience" with alcohol, which ranged from "tasting it," "drank a beer," and being given "lemonade or Kool-Aid laced with alcohol" by a friend or relative, to simply having "tried it."

Despite the fact that American Indian girls appear to drink no more than girls in the mainstream culture, they themselves perceive that Indian teenage girls drink more than white teenage girls. In addition, a majority of the women, many of whom were infrequent drinkers while in high school, felt that they had a "drinking problem"—whether they drank alcohol once a year, twice a year, or more than once a month. This finding certainly suggests that American Indian females may consider themselves to have a "drinking problem" during adolescence, when in actuality they do not. It would also appear that the prevalent attitude that "all Indians drink" and that drinking is not considered a deviant behavior may influence adolescent females' perceptions about drinking and the guilt associated with even infrequent drinking; thus, if they drink, no matter how little, they must have a "drinking problem."

One female, who reported the guilt associated with taking an occasional drink, related a humorous account of how she decided to seek help through Alcoholics Anonymous because she felt she had a drinking problem:

> I decided I must be an alcoholic. I told my husband that I was joining AA. He said, "Why are you going to AA? You're no alcoholic. I'm the alcoholic." I told my sister I was joining AA. She said, "You ain't no alcoholic. I'm the alcoholic. If anyone goes, I should go." My other sister agreed. She felt she was an alcoholic, too—but she wasn't joining no AA. I was shocked. My husband wasn't an alcoholic. My sisters weren't alcoholics. Maybe I wasn't no alcoholic. Maybe it was guilt. Maybe because I drank once in a while, I had come to believe I was an alcoholic. I never did go to AA. I never was an alcoholic. I just thought I was.

In further discussions with the participants, it became very clear that not only did the majority of the women believe that Indian girls have problems with alcohol, but the women themselves may have contributed to that perception. Seventy-three percent of the women reported "exaggerating" on substance abuse surveys about their alcohol and drug use, as well as on questions about sexual behaviors. One college graduate confided, "It became a game to us, . . . to see who could tell the biggest story. We meant no harm. It was just that about once a year, some white man would show up at the school and ask us to answer all these questions about alcohol and drugs. We didn't know who he was. We figured he thought we were all 'lost causes' anyway, so we spent a great deal of time proving to him that we were. That was terrible, now that I think of it. None of the people who came were ever Indian. We decided it was all right to lie to a white man. After all, they had lied plenty to Indians."

Another woman, who attended boarding school for a few years, reported, "Twice a year, the nuns would hand out questionnaires about drinking, drugs, smoking, and sex. We always looked for the worst possible response and checked it. It was fun. We didn't know people were writing books about us. We were playing jokes on them [the nuns]. . . . We wanted to shock them. . . . [I] guess the joke's on us."

Clearly, something is amiss when American Indian female adolescents perceive themselves as potential "alcoholics" or as a group with a "drinking problem" when, in fact, they drink no more than white females or other ethnic minority females in their same age-groups. In all forms of media, American Indian youth are confronted with the dismal statistics, research, myths, and stereotyping of American Indians and alcohol abuse. It may be that American Indian adolescents, who are not only the objects of such information but the subjects of such research, believe what they read and are told. Such information continually imposed upon youth may become a self-fulfilling prophecy. That is, if "all Indians drink" or if occasional drinking is translated into a "drinking problem," it may be that American Indian youth are fulfilling an expectation set by researchers, educators, parents, and particularly mainstream society.

FINDING: Culture may play an indirect role in American Indian female adolescents' drinking behavior and attitudes toward drinking.

This study found strong evidence that culture may play a role in the drinking behaviors and attitudes of American Indian females. In fact, the findings indicated that the female socialization skills and parental child-rearing practices, based in the traditional culture, are in part responsible for female adolescents' attitudes and behaviors in the consumption of alcohol. It is noted at the outset, however, that traditional cultural practices were in no way found to promote alcohol abuse.

Within the American Indian cultures, generosity is a highly valued trait. Indian females are socialized in the art of generosity at a very early age. This socialization process includes the offering of food, drink, and shelter to relatives and friends and the reciprocal acceptance of food, drink, and shelter when in another's home. This type of "hospitality" or generosity is practiced by the poorest of families, as well as by the more well-to-do.

Nearly three-fourths of the participants in this study who drank while in high school reported that family members introduced them to alcohol.

Outsiders often view such reports as an example of the debilitating nature of the Indian cultures as a whole; however, within the Native culture, it may be that both the act of generosity and accepting the generosity of others have a major bearing on alcohol consumption among Native females. For example, if part of the socialization process is to accept what others offer you, regardless of whether you like or want what is offered, very confusing messages may be sent to the American Indian female who is offered an alcoholic beverage. The behavior of giving and accepting alcohol appears to be strongly rooted in the socialization process and is reinforced through cultural practices such as giveaways, feasts, and honoring ceremonies (which involve providing food, gifts, and tobacco to those in attendance).

One female expressed an attitude voiced by many of the women: "How do you tell a relative that you won't take a drink? All of our lives, we are told to eat and drink what is put before us. Why do you think so many Indians are overweight? We eat when we aren't hungry, because we don't want to hurt other people's feelings. . . . The same applies to alcohol. We drink even when we don't like it. I never realized until it was too late that people who offered me alcohol were not my friends; they only wanted me to be just like them. I drank for ten years . . . lots . . . used drugs. I quit two years ago. . . . I don't have many friends now."

Furthermore, there is strong evidence that child-rearing practices of American Indian parents may have a profound impact on females' attitudes and behaviors concerning drinking. A high percentage of the participants consistently reported that their parents did not care if they drank. Many reported frustration with parents who did not punish them or reprimand them when they drank. Many interpreted the lack of parental intervention as a signal of lack of interest or concern by the parents.

One female, who identified herself as a "reformed drinker" and a "hell-raiser" in high school, spoke about the frustration with her parents, who never interfered in her life: "I drank a lot in high school. Both of my parents knew. I was a hell-raiser in high school. I got in lots of fights, [with] both boys and girls. I got kicked out of school for fighting. My folks never said anything about it. At first, I really felt good about getting kicked out. Later, I wanted them [her parents] to make me go back to school. They didn't. I couldn't go back unless they made me—pride, you know. I spent most of the next two years high—drugs, alcohol, inhalants, whatever. Then I got pregnant."

Another female voiced an often-reported opinion, one suggesting that culture and child-rearing practices play a major role in the drinking habits of female adolescents: "I know my parents knew I drank. They had to get me out of jail a couple of times. Once my dad had to come pick me up because I was drunk. He never said a word. When I was younger, I thought they didn't care what I did. Now I know it was just their way."

Traditionally within Indian cultures, parents did not punish or reprimand their children; nor did they interfere in children's exploration or experimentation. Childhood and youth were a period for self-learning. Researchers often refer to this practice as noninterference and define it as a belief that no individual has the right to interfere in the lives of others. In the traditional American Indian cultures, parents provided unconditional love to their children. Others, who were part of the extended families (aunts, uncles, grandparents), established the limits of behavior and reprimanded children when appropriate. American Indian societies rarely used physical punishment.

This system proved very effective within prereservation societies. However, by the time Native populations were confined to reservations, extended family units had suffered many losses due to warfare or the placement of close relatives on different reservations or at great distances from one another on the same reservation. As a result, a tremendous void was created in the traditional child-rearing practices, which included the discipline and guidance of children. Despite this loss, there is substantial evidence that the role of parenting did not change. Parents continued to practice noninterference, providing unconditional love and avoiding the role of disciplinarian.

Outsiders have often viewed such parental practices as irresponsible. Others have labeled such behaviors as "laissez-faire child-rearing practices" or parental apathy. Indeed, I would be the first to admit that increasing numbers of American Indian parents are irresponsible and neglect their children—as in the mainstream society. However, I reject the generalization of irresponsible parenting when applied to all Indian parents. It appears that child-rearing, at least as practiced by many parents, is one of the remaining vestiges of the traditional culture.

American Indian youth, on the other hand, who are more influenced by the media and contacts outside the reservation and in school, may have come to define a caring person as one who "interferes" in their lives, reprimands them, and punishes them for misdeeds. Most educators would agree that students often misbehave in order to get attention. Thus, when American Indian females drink alcohol, they expect punishment or a reprimand, and when this expectation does not materialize, they are confused and interpret parental behavior as uncaring.

These findings have serious implications for educators and parents. Over the past decade, a plethora of drug and alcohol intervention and prevention programs has been implemented in American Indian schools. All have an overriding goal of raising the self-image of the American Indian child and enhancing skills to "just say no" to drugs and alcohol. It would appear, however, that "just say no" and similar strategies, such as "walking away," would prove ineffective in a culture that promotes and encourages both giving and accepting graciously. Furthermore, it is much easier to "just say no" to a stranger than to a relative.

FINDING: *The level of parental support and supervision and the home environment (drinking or nondrinking) have a major impact on American Indian females' self-image and attitudes toward school.*

Findings of this study clearly indicate that females who are raised in home environments where there are rules, where there is less incidence of alcohol abuse, and where encouragement and support for academic achievement and school activities are given are more likely to stay in high school and graduate and even go on to college. Among those girls who were successful in school, 81 percent reported strong mother-daughter relationships or grandmother-granddaughter relationships.

Approximately 10 percent of the females who graduated from high school or college reported a drinking parent, whereas 36 percent of the girls who dropped out of high school reported that their parents drank. In addition, girls with drinking parents reported a higher incidence of running away from home, living with other relatives, and fighting with parents.

Dropping out of school appears to be only one problem associated with American Indian females who grow up in alcoholic homes. Ninety percent of the females reported feeling "guilty" or blaming themselves for their parents' drinking. There was considerable evidence that guilt feelings, developed during early childhood or adolescence, continued to affect their adult lives and were often manifested in drinking behaviors and patterns consistent with their parents' life-styles. There is a multigenerational influence on female adolescent drinking. Females who grew up in homes where drinking was commonplace were more apt to drink as adolescents and as adults. Furthermore, family members contributed significantly to adolescent drinking, at least initially. It does appear that acceptance of alcohol from a relative or friend may be closely tied to a culture where children are expected to accept food and drink regardless of whether they want it or like it. In families where drinking is the norm, children are learning behaviors that have serious implications for their adult lives.

FINDING: *Alcohol use is more prevalent among adult American Indian women than among adolescent Indian females.*

Sixty-seven percent of the women reported that they did not drink in high school, but that from their high school years to their adult years, alcohol abuse nearly doubled. Whereas 14 percent reported regular drinking (once a week) while in high school, 27 percent reported regular drinking during adulthood. A main factor contributing to the increased usage in adulthood appears to be related to the "significant other" in the female's life. Women feel compelled to drink with husbands, live-in mates, and boyfriends. Often those women believe that joining their male partners in drinking is the only way to maintain the relationship.

When the participants were asked how they viewed women who drank with their husbands, 83 percent sympathized with those women and said they felt that men were the main reason adult women drank. The majority of the women reported conflicting attitudes toward female drinking. One woman spoke at length about this conflict:

> The lowest person on this reservation is a female alcoholic with kids. Their kids are neglected, go to school hungry, dirty—nothing is lower. The next lowest person is the single female alcoholic who uses sex or bums money for drinks or tries to hock things. Male alcoholics who neglect their children or beat their wives are not regarded in the same way. Excuses are made for them. No excuses are made for women. Women who drink with their husbands are pitied. People say that she wouldn't drink if her husband didn't drink; in probably 75 percent of the cases, they are probably right. Women don't want their man to find another woman to drink with him. . . . At parties, there are always women who are willing to drink with your man and sleep with him. Women drink to protect their property [the man]. There are some women who get their men to drink—not many, maybe 5 percent. Then there are those couples who are drinking couples; they are both alcoholics. Women who drink have a much harder life, regardless of the circumstances.

FINDING: In American Indian families, different standards are applied to male and female children, as well as to male and female adults.

Many of the responses throughout the interview process included references to the "acceptable male role" and the "acceptable female role" within the Indian societies. The majority of respondents reported different rules and standards for male and female children. Ninety percent of the women stated that parents made greater demands on the female children in the household in terms of job responsibilities and that higher expectations were imposed on them.

In discussing their relationships with their parents, although the majority of the high school and college graduates reported close relationships with mothers, grandmothers, and aunts, 91 percent felt that their mothers, grandmothers, and aunts treated their brothers and other males (including boy cousins) more favorably. Women described their brothers with such terms as "pampered," "got their own way," "babied," and "never had to do anything." This behavior may be traced, at least in part, to the confinement of the American Indian population to the reservation.

Although both women and men suffered confinement to the reservation, part of the traditional role of the Indian women continued in their activities as mothers and wives. Men, on the other hand, lost their role as provider and protector within the family, resulting in a total loss of identity and purpose. It may be that this dramatic role change for males was viewed sympathetically by women, resulting in the lack of expectations for males. Out of this sympathy, women placed few demands on their male partners and subsequently their sons. As a result, Indian females, whether consciously or subconsciously, have perpetuated a cycle of nonexpectation for males, resulting in double standards for male and female children. Parents set higher expectations for their daughters than for their sons. Thus, twice as many Indian females go to college and twice as many women graduate from college when compared to their male peers.

It is also apparent that double standards are applied to adolescent male and female drinking. In many cases, the females in this study reported strict discipline from their fathers.

One nondrinking female related a humiliating event that made her a confirmed "teetotaler":

> My older brother drank. My cousins drank. My parents didn't like it, but they didn't do anything about it. Several times they got my brother out of jail. I know my dad felt guilty, 'cause he drank when he was young. When I was sixteen, I got in a car with a guy at a powwow. He was from another reservation. He was really good-looking . . . about ten years older than me. He brought me back a few hours later. I was drunk. My father went nuts. He loaded me up and took me to the IHS. He had the doctor to check me out to see if I'd had sex. I thought I would never forgive him. I was so embarrassed. He took me home and sat up with me all night long. I was sick. I've never taken another drink—[that was] my first and last.

Women frequently reported that whereas the "reformed" male drinker was looked upon with respect, "reformed" female drinkers received little praise or recognition, and that despite years of abstinence, people frequently remembered their past transgressions. When women were asked to explain such contradictory attitudes, their comments often included socialization and cultural factors. One nondrinking female suggested, "Indian women can do anything—well, almost anything—as long as they are good mothers. There is no expectation for Indian men to be good fathers. There is an expectation for men to be good grandfathers. So, you see, men can drink from their teenage years to their forties or fifties. . . . When they become grandfathers, they quit, and suddenly they are good grandfathers. A woman is either a bad mother or a good mother. She can never completely redeem herself—even if she is a good grandmother."

Another woman spoke of male and female roles within the culture:

Indian women are expected to have children and to take care of their children. . . . Men have no responsibility in raising children. That's the way we are raised. That's the way it was done by our parents. Our mothers took care of everything. They taught us the language, they played with us, they sat with their friends and let us play and run around, they fed us and put us to bed; they made our dance outfits, refereed our fights, pampered us, told us secrets, gave us money; many worked at full-time jobs. [On the other hand,] Dads went to town, they talked to the council, they visited their friends, they rode horses and rodeoed, they went to powwows, they were cowboys and ranchers, they cut firewood and hung out with the guys. Men who drink do not do things with their children. With men, it makes no difference. They don't participate in raising children. Drinking is worse for women for that reason. This is a sexist society. It's not just men who are sexist; women are, too. They [other women] don't like women who don't conform to the female role. If you are a professional woman, you still have to be a mother. That validates you as a woman.

One college graduate, the only female child in a home with six brothers, reported the inequities in her home life that have continued to affect her adult life and the lives of her siblings:

Indian girls are taught to take care of babies—in my case, two younger brothers. I had to wait on the older ones. I learned to cook, to clean house, to shop. My brothers had no responsibilities. They played basketball, ran track, rodeoed, and danced at powwows. Sometimes they came home drunk. Each time, my parents would remind me, "You'd better never come home drunk." I resented being a girl. Boys got to do everything. . . . My brothers got all the attention. When they did something wrong, I got the lecture. Now I get most of the attention. I'm the only one who went to college. My brothers are still playing basketball and fancy dancing and rodeoing . . . and drinking. My parents complain because they take off from work and go to a basketball tournament or on the powwow or rodeo circuit. They all have families to support. My parents help them out every month. Then I end up helping my parents. Now I'm the one that gets the praise. My parents don't even see the irony in the situation. . . . I'm raising my children differently. My son washes dishes, makes his own bed, washes clothes. My daughters do the same. There is no favoritism in my house. I am not the typical Indian mother. Most of my friends—even professional women—cater to their sons. The daughters are always last.

There appears to be little or no support for the abused female on the part of relatives and friends. Societal expectations, in fact, place women in a position of accepting poverty, abuse, unfaithfulness, and neglect at the hands of an alcohol-abusing spouse, lover, or partner. Women who have been socialized with these beliefs have come to accept them as a part of the

"Indian way" when, in fact, history repeatedly records that Indian women were never placed in those roles in Native societies prior to Euro-American contact. Furthermore, it appears that women who have been socialized in this manner have a great deal of difficulty in devising plans for escaping their fate. Many hold on to the belief that things will get better and that in some vague, distant future (often middle age), their lives will change when their "significant other" quits drinking.

One woman reported the hope, despair, and tragedy heaped upon generations of American Indian families—a common story, only with different characters: "After all, my kids are his kids, too. A father shouldn't have to live without seeing his kids. When he is sober, he is a good father. Someday, he will change. His father drank when he was young. He quit ten years ago. If I just wait, he will quit, too. I knew he drank when I married him. I thought he would change. It's just taking longer than I thought. . . . My dad was an alcoholic. He never got a chance to quit. He died of cirrhosis at fifty-four."

While women are socialized to accept and even expect their fates, it would appear that Indian men may be victims of that same socialization process. For example, it appears that fewer parental rules are applied to males. It may be that through this process, males directly or indirectly receive the message from their families and other adults that there are no expectations for them to behave responsibly. This attitude seems to carry over into adulthood in their social interactions, in their marital relationships, and in a lack of incentives to assume or redefine the male role within the society. Even when attempts are made to redefine the male role, such efforts appear to be directed more toward defining their Indianness (e.g., through Indian dancing or participation in ceremonies) than at assuming responsibility for their families or even themselves. It may be, however, that this process—the redefinition of Indian maleness—is preliminary to accepting responsibility. From an educator's perspective, it must be remembered that individuals who feel good about themselves are more productive; therefore, it may be that with time, these activities will in fact create the pride and improved self-esteem of the Indian male to the point where he is able to assume his rightful role as father, brother, son, and mate.

Although women willingly admitted that alcohol was a source of family strife, abuse, and poverty, very few of them felt that divorce or separation was the solution to the problem of an alcoholic partner. Once again, this seems to be strongly rooted in societal values. Furthermore, it was very clear that the female alcoholic was considered the scourge, the "lowest of the low," of all people on the reservation, whereas no such standards were applied to men. As alcoholic behavior was closely connected to one's ability to perform the duties of wife and mother, Indian women who ignored these responsibilities were severely criticized by other women. A large percentage of the women chose to drink with their husbands rather than risk losing them to another woman. Whether this attitude is created by low self-concept on the part of the female, by fear of family disapproval, or by a combination of both, American Indian females find themselves trapped in a situation without solution until their "significant other" quits drinking.

This study clearly pointed out the degree and extent to which alcohol abuse impacted the lives of female children, adolescent girls, and adult Indian women—whether they were high school dropouts or college graduates. Women from all classes of society, from all educational levels, and from all types of families appear to have suffered the consequences of alcohol abuse in one way or another. Whether it is the college-educated female who marries the alcoholic male or the high school dropout who marries her high school boyfriend, there is little difference in their reasons. Both want to be accepted within their culture and to receive approval from their family and friends.

FINDING: American Indian female adolescents do not regard intoxication, excessive drinking, or alcoholism as deviant behavior.

The majority of the women interviewed indicated that at some time during their childhood or early adolescent years, they had formed the opinion that drinking alcohol was the "norm" or that "all Indians drink."

When follow-up questions were asked to determine the origins of such attitudes, responses and stories varied widely; however, all the responses had similar themes. One high school graduate spoke of her early attitudes toward drinking: "When I was in elementary school, I remember thinking that all Indians drank . . . and whites didn't. I never saw a white drunk. I remember thinking that when I grew up, I would drink, too. I didn't think that drinking was bad. It was like . . . if you were born Indian, you would drink, just like if you were born an Indian, you lived on a reservation. When I took my first drink, I remember thinking drinking was bad. I really felt guilty. I still feel guilty when I drink, even when it's just a beer."

Another woman reported that not only was drinking condoned in her family, but that she received messages from her mother that anything could be forgiven or overlooked if alcohol was involved:

> The thing I remember most was my dad coming home drunk. He never hit us or anything. He was funny and kissed us. He never hugged us or kissed us when he wasn't drinking. One night he didn't come home. I was maybe eight. A tribal policeman brought him home the next morning. He had wrecked the car. I started crying . . . because he had promised to take me to the carnival. Our

plans were ruined . . . so I cried. Mom really got mad. Later she told me that Dad couldn't help wrecking the car, because he was drinking. . . . Things like this happened all the time in our house—Dad getting drunk, Mom making excuses. I grew up thinking it was OK to do anything as long as you were drunk. A boyfriend could sleep with another girl if he was drunk because he didn't know what he was doing. You could break into somebody's house and get away with it if you were drunk. It was OK to wreck a car if you were drunk. During my sophomore year, I drank on the weekends a lot. I remember staying home from school on Mondays. I didn't feel good. I couldn't help it—I had been drinking all weekend.

A twenty-nine-year-old woman, who had recently enrolled in college, spoke of how she had personally accepted drinking as a "way of life" as a teenager and related her personal battle with overcoming such strongly ingrained ideas:

I wanted to get married when I was seventeen. Mom didn't want me to. She said Tom [fictitious name] was too wild and that he drank too much. I told her that she had lived with Dad all these years and he drank. She let me get married after that. Five years later, I had four kids, one right after another. Tom hung out with his friends a lot. . . . I heard he was sleeping with other women. He got one pregnant. Still, I stayed. One day, my friend Shirley [fictitious name] came to see me. She said I should divorce Tom. I got really mad at her and told her off. I said something like . . . Indian women were supposed to have a hard life, . . . and she looked at me and said that being Indian didn't mean we had to be stupid. It took another four years before I would admit to myself that she was right. I left Tom. I've never seen Shirley since. . . . Sometimes the truth hurts too much.

Clearly, the acceptance of alcohol abuse (learned in childhood) has contributed to the attitudes and opinions Indian women struggle with in their adult lives.

The use of drugs among adolescent American Indian females varies dramatically from the use of alcohol. This study brought to light concerns about drug use and abuse not addressed in other research.

FINDING: American Indian women consider drugs far more dangerous than alcohol to the health and well-being of future generations of Indian youth.

Although among adult Indian women, drug abuse appears to be less of a problem than alcohol, there exists a greater concern among American Indian women about the prevalence of drugs, the variety of drugs, the availability of drugs on the reservation, and the lack of law enforcement regarding the sale of drugs and its potential impact upon future generations of American Indian children. In probing for the source of their fears, one issue kept surfacing: the belief that drugs are more destructive to the individual because involvement with drugs seems to result in the loss of free will. At least among the population of this study, women did not perceive alcohol as having such an effect.

One female, who reported using marijuana only once, described the effect it had on her: "It scared me to death. When I drank a beer, I could still walk around, dance, drive a car. Grass made me feel lifeless—I couldn't move. I sat for hours until it wore off. Everyone was laughing around me. I never knew why. I never smoked again. I stayed with alcohol after that. I still don't drink much. . . . I don't allow grass in my house."

However, when the data are analyzed, it is clear that whereas the use and abuse of alcohol increased with age, at least as far as the participants of this study were concerned, the use of drugs diminished with age. One seventeen-year-old scoffed at the idea that drugs were more dangerous than alcohol: "Grass is not addictive . . . alcohol is. I know a lot of people who used to smoke grass. They don't anymore. You outgrow grass. Most people never outgrow alcohol."

Their perceptions of drugs may be based on a lack of knowledge or on a general disregard for alcohol as an addictive substance. It may be that because the use and abuse of alcohol have been a major problem within the Indian culture since its introduction by the white man, there is a general acceptance of its consequences upon the lives of the people. Drugs, on the other hand, were alien to the culture until approximately twenty years ago. In addition, alcohol is a legal substance, whereas drugs are considered illegal substances and the very purchase of drugs involves breaking the law. It may be, too, that becoming intoxicated is regarded as a part of "growing up" and "everyone does it," whereas drugs have not become a part of that accepted norm and thus are regarded with greater fear and suspicion.

FINDING: The use of drugs appears to be gaining popularity with Native American female adolescents on the reservations.

Younger participants (seventeen to twenty-two age-group) in the study were five times more likely to have used drugs than the older participants (thirty to thirty-six age-group), primarily because drugs are more available today on reservations than they were ten or fifteen years ago. In contrast to their experiences with alcohol, the majority of the females reported that their first introduction to drugs was from an acquaintance, a friend, or an outsider at an intertribal function. This fact, in part, would indicate that drugs are often brought onto the reservations from the outside. Furthermore, the sale of alcohol is forbidden on some of the reservations where this study was conducted. In most cases, however, bars and liquor stores are readily available in border towns to the reservation populations, so that bootlegging is not as popular as it once was on dry reservations. In contrast, drugs appear to be readily available on the reservation; almost all of the women could identify a "pusher" living among them on their respective reservations. One woman, a self-described activist member of the American Indian Movement, reported a concern that was voiced in one way or another by many of the women: "Everyone knows who sells drugs—the police, the FBI, the tribal council. Nobody does anything. Even if they arrest someone, they generally get a few months in jail and they're back doing the same thing the next day. The government doesn't mind if we're stoned. Stoned Indians don't stand up for their rights. Big politicians don't have to worry about stoned Indians. It's ironic: the government has been trying to destroy us for 500 years, but we are doing the job for them with drugs and alcohol . . . and not one gunshot will be fired, not one arrow."

Another woman, who voiced the concerns of many others, spoke of the fear of reprisals from family members of "dealers" peddling drugs on the reservation: "This reservation is a small place. . . . Even the police know the dealers. Some are related to them. People turn their heads the other way when their relatives are involved. I would never report a dealer. The relatives might come after me. It's not like living in a big city. I don't think they would kill me, but they might beat me up . . . vandalize my house, my car . . . make threats. I have to live here. My kids have to live here. I would be alone if I tried to do something about it. It's a sad thing. . . . I don't know what will happen to the next generation."

Availability of drugs and fear of reprisals from drug dealers may account for the fear among women that future generations are more in danger of drug addiction than alcohol addiction. One female recalled a party where she caught her children smoking marijuana: "They were imitating the adults—passing the joint from one to another, choking and coughing, laughing. My boys were involved. That's the first time I ever spanked my kids. . . . I was mad and scared. They were just kids—six, seven, eight. The oldest might have been ten. I never took them to any parties again. I quit going myself. I felt bad that I had hit them. I had set a poor example. Someone should have beat me instead."

Drugs, which are sold on the reservation, appear to be more readily available to preadolescents than alcohol, thus contributing to parental concerns.

FINDING: American Indian adolescent females who use drugs while in high school are more likely to drop out of school than those who do not use drugs.

Although few women directly identified drugs as a major factor in dropping out of school, it appears that drug abuse played a part in dropping out, even though there was not a statistical significance. Again, denial was common among women who participated in such activities. Twenty-seven percent of the women who admitted to using drugs in high school eventually dropped out of high school prematurely, as compared to 21 percent who admitted using alcohol on a regular basis.

One female, who admitted to drinking and using drugs in high school, spoke about how she considered herself very lucky in becoming drug-free:

> I started drinking when I was a junior—just an occasional beer or two on the weekends. It was no big deal. I never got really drunk. I made good grades in school . . . never did anything crazy. Then I smoked my first joint. Grass was different. It took away all motivation. I didn't care about school, home, my appearance—nothing. I almost flunked out of high school. I went to college, and that was worse; everyone was smoking. I got put on probation the first quarter. It took that for me to realize what I was doing to myself. . . . I just quit. I'm lucky. Some of my high school friends are still smoking. . . . It has affected their memory; they're paranoid; they care about nothing else.

FINDING: Outside peer pressure seems to play a major role in the American Indian female adolescent's decision to use drugs.

The women in this study who used drugs during adolescence appeared to use them under circumstances different from those involving their use of alcohol. Introduction to alcohol and continued use of alcohol seemed to be more related to family activities and were often condoned or supported by family members. Drugs, on the other hand, pushed adolescents away from their family groups and involved nonrelated friends or acquaintances from outside their respective reservations. Another apparent difference between alcohol and drug abuse was that the women who frequently used drugs reported associating with other drug abusers. This was not always the case with alcohol abusers. Female alcohol abusers, at least during their high school years, often reported having "sober friends" and "drinking friends."

Some women spoke of their obsession with drugs (noting a different effect from that with alcohol) and wanting to stay "high." One woman commented, "It made me forget that I wasn't the most popular girl in the school. In fact, it made me feel pretty. After my first joint, I could handle anything—not that I did, 'cause nothing mattered but staying high. I wanted to be with friends who smoked. They were all older than me . . . or had dropped out of school. I dropped out, too. I guess they all had dropped out, now that I think about it. I spent eight years of my life 'high.' I don't use nothing now. . . . I don't remember those eight years, either."

In the case of drug usage, girls, at least in a party or celebration setting, often participate in the use of drugs because their friends are involved or they are encouraged to do so by outside pressures, such as an older male who is not from their respective reservation. This would also explain why girls appear to experiment at a later age with marijuana than with alcohol. It appears that, until she approaches young womanhood and is in settings where she associates with males in a male-female relationship, the American Indian female has less opportunity to experiment with drugs.

FINDING: Native American females who use inhalants during their preadolescent years appear to be more susceptible to adult use of drugs and alcohol.

Women in the study who reported inhalant abuse as preadolescents most often reported moving from inhalants to alcohol, and often into smoking marijuana. These same women, as adults, continued to be the most frequent users of alcohol and marijuana.

One mother of five recalled, "I sniffed gasoline at three. I used to get so dizzy I'd fall down and pass out. My older brother—he was seven—taught me how to put a rag in a gas tank and sniff. By eight, I was drinking and smoking. I have awful headaches. I think it did something to my brain. Is that possible?"

Clearly, inhalant abuse is much more serious than many parents, educators, and tribal leaders may believe. If inhalant abuse is a predictor of substance abuse in adult life, which it appears to be, strategies must be developed for early intervention.

Summary

There is no paucity of research on substance abuse and American Indians. As documented earlier, many researchers have reported the extent and frequency of abuse among Indian youth. Others have reported that one in every two Indian students drops out of school because of alcohol abuse. Although substance abuse was a problem for the women in this study, it is impossible to attribute dropping out of school to substance abuse. Such abuse may, in fact, serve as a contributing factor among a list of many other factors, but substance abuse in itself was not a significant factor in dropping out.

What is significant, however, is that American Indian girls do not view alcohol abuse as deviant behavior and that they themselves seem to have accepted the stereotype that "all Indians are drunks." It also appears that they believe the research suggesting that Indian adolescents have problems with alcohol. Self-fulfilling prophecies often have a great impact on youth, and in the case of American Indian females, it would appear that research may have had a direct impact on their attitudes and behaviors regarding substance abuse.

Further, it would appear that child-rearing practices and parental noninterference have contributed to the problem. Double standards for girls and boys are apparent within the socialization process and add to the frustration of females.

To change these attitudes and behaviors will take a major community and tribal effort. It is unlikely that alcohol education programs developed for mainstream society will have any primary impact on Native youth and their families. In fact, the key for prevention is so closely linked with the family that any program should include a plan for education of the family unit. Such an effort should involve not only the school, but community organizations and tribal agencies.

It would appear that a redefinition of the traditional culture also may be necessary. Clearly, American Indians have always taken care of the needs of the family; however, that did not include the "enabling" of family members to drink and be irresponsible. With the introduction of alcohol and drugs into the Native societies, many individuals have interpreted being "traditional" as supporting family members for behaviors that should plainly be unacceptable, especially when they involve substance abuse, child abuse, spouse abuse, and/or neglect. As Native peoples, we must recognize the difference between traditional culture and enabling individuals within our family unit to behave in inappropriate ways.

Finally, it may be necessary for Native people to become their own researchers. Most of the research conducted on substance abuse and Native people speaks to the frequency and level of use and the substances of choice; however, little attention is paid to the causes or remedies. There is a question, at least in my mind, as to the validity of much of the previous research. Clearly, it would appear from the interviews with the women in this study that they more often than not reported incorrect answers to "outside" researchers who delved into their private lives. Although it appears that this technique was used by many of them during their adolescence as a means of rebelling against the "white establishment," the fact remains that the results of such studies are highly publicized and may indeed contribute to the self-fulfilling prophecy of substance abuse among Indian youth.

Chapter 12

Adolescent Pregnancy and Motherhood: Sanctions within the Culture

Adolescent pregnancy is a widespread problem, and virtually all tribal groups report that the problem is growing. According to the last two census reports, American Indian females marry earlier, have children earlier, and have larger families than the general population. Few statistics are available, however, on adolescent pregnancy among Indian girls. Fifty-one percent of the participants in this study who dropped out of school reported dropping out as a result of pregnancy. Among the Indian women who had graduated from college, 9 percent reported getting pregnant before marriage. Among those who graduated from high school, 17 percent reported having a child prior to marriage, but not before graduation. Only 7 percent of the women who reported getting pregnant and dropping out of school indicated they had married the father of their child. None of the women who reported getting pregnant during their teenage years chose abortion as a solution to their pregnancy, although four of the participants in the study admitted to having abortions during their adult years. Seventy-one percent of the women reporting premature teen pregnancies said they used drugs or alcohol during the sex act.

Participants who reported pregnancy prior to marriage were asked a number of questions to determine their feelings about unplanned pregnancies. Their feelings ranged from depression, loneliness, and a sense that their lives were over, to a reaction of pleasure and satisfaction at being a mother. Seventy-one percent reported feeling "cheated" out of their youth. Eighty-nine percent said that their lives changed dramatically and that they were not ready for adult responsibilities. Fifty-one percent lamented losing touch with peers who were still in high school. Although a majority of the women indicated that their parents were not upset when they discovered they were pregnant, one-fifth of them indicated "hiding" their condition from their parents until they could no longer do so, due to their physical appearance. Over half of the women reported that their first child (born to them as teenagers) lived with their parents or that the child spent more time with the grandparents than with them.

When asked if anyone ever encouraged them to return to school after they had given birth, only 3 percent of the females said they received such encouragement from school officials or parents. Nearly one-fourth of the women reported getting GEDs once they were in their twenties, but considered the decision to be self-motivated. Others, after receiving their GEDs, went to college and graduated. One college graduate reported: "I dropped out at sixteen. When I was twenty-one, I got a GED. I started taking night classes at the tribal college. I liked school. The next year, I enrolled at [four-year college]. My parents supported my decision. They raised my son. He [her son] asked me if I regretted having him, when he was about ten. I told him that I was glad I had him. I told him he could live with me if he wanted, but he said he wanted to stay with my mom and dad."

When women were asked about abortion as an option, only four of the participants confided they had had an abortion. One female explained that abortion was not a realistic option within the culture: "The white man tried to make us white. When they couldn't, they killed women and children. . . . Indian women, even if they aren't married, think it's better to bring another Indian into the world than to destroy a life. The white man did enough of that. Besides, if you are an Indian woman and don't have kids, people think something is wrong with you. Kids are our proof of womanhood."

One female who admitted to an abortion reported her fear of family members discovering her secret: "If my sisters ever found out that I had an abortion, they would never speak to me. I had a friend out of state, from college—a white friend. I called her and went to visit. She understood my problem and helped me. There was no one I could turn to here. My mother would die if she knew. Several years ago, she was sterilized by a doctor at the IHS. She never gave her permission; this doctor just decided that six kids were enough. You've heard about the sterilization of Indian women. If she knew what I did, she would have nothing to do with me, either."

A number of women spoke with concern about an issue that I have termed "prenatal abuse." This issue surfaced on several reservations and appears to be a growing problem among adolescent girls who become pregnant. One female spoke about it most descriptively:

> Abortion is really not an option for Indian girls. They can't even get birth control pills at the IHS unless their parents give their consent. Most girls won't tell their parents they are going to have sex, so they go unprotected. Because of the personal humiliation of abortion, . . . the lack of knowledge, . . . and no place to get an abortion on the reservation, many girls are trying to abort babies in other ways—taking bottles and bottles of Midol and aspirin, taking overdoses of diet pills, jumping off roofs, lying on the floor and having friends jump up and down on their stomachs. Who knows what they are doing to their babies? I'm not so sure that some of these babies that are identified as FAS might not be the result of the kinds of things the girls are doing to get rid of their babies.

Sixty-nine percent of the women reported having their first sexual experience while in high school. When asked to think back to their first experience, and to identify why they had become involved in early, pre-marital sexual activities, 70 percent of the women reported feelings of being unloved, which led them to seek love elsewhere. Eleven percent reported "liking sex." Others cited immaturity, lack of knowledge about sex and its consequences, or peer pressure—such as "other girls were doing it" and the lack of popularity of those who did not engage in sex.

Among the group that identified themselves as "searching for love," 79 percent revealed they were promiscuous, in that they had engaged in sex with three to five boys during their high school years. Many of the women reported a connection between alcohol and drugs and their introduction to sex: "I was fourteen. There was this boy I was crazy about. I went to this party at his house, . . . his parents partied with us. He gave me a drink, and we ended up in a bedroom, and the rest is, . . . well, history. We had sex almost every day for the next several months. Then he moved on to someone else. I did, too."

All women were asked to identify the age when they first became involved sexually. Forty-three percent reported having their first sexual experience between the ages of fourteen and fifteen, 20 percent reported having sex by the age of sixteen, and 10 percent reported having their first sexual experience at the age of seventeen. A few of the women (less than 1 percent) reported engaging in sexual activities before the age of fourteen, but the remainder of the group were seventeen or older.

Women were asked about the extent of their knowledge, during adolescence, concerning the consequences of sex. Ninety-one percent reported that their knowledge came from peers, rather than parents. Eighty-four percent indicated that their information was incorrect or insufficient, and a similar percentage said that they did not practice birth control during high school. When asked if the AIDS epidemic had affected their sexual lives, only 4 percent of the women reported being more careful about sex partners. Girls within the seventeen to twenty-two age-group reported having no fears of being infected with AIDS.

Among the varying age-groups, more women (78 percent) between the ages of seventeen to twenty-one reported having sex at an earlier age. Of that group, 54 percent of the dropouts had left school because of pregnancy, a higher percentage than for any other age-group.

Women who had become pregnant in high school were asked if they had made a conscious decision to get pregnant and drop out of school. Only 2 percent of the women reported that they had wanted a baby of their own. Thirty-one percent of the dropouts, however, reported that once they had one baby and had dropped out of school, they wanted another baby.

When asked about current practices of birth control, 64 percent of the dropouts revealed that "abstention" was their only method. Of the women who were mothers, 33 percent reported their status as single mothers, whereas 13 percent reported living with someone who was not the father of any of their children. Eighty-nine percent of the college graduates stated they used medically approved birth control methods. Nineteen percent of the total population reported having children by two to four different men. Only 5 percent of the women reported having been married and divorced. One female, a veteran of a fourteen-year marriage, voiced a concern for future generations of Indian children who were growing up in homes without any semblance of a family structure and without a father in the household: "It is acceptable to live with this man for a while . . . and then another. Our mothers didn't do that. They stayed with one man. Young women today go from one to another. I worry about future generations. Half-sisters will be marrying half-brothers or cousins. There are women who don't know who fathered their children. I worry about what will happen when those kids grow up."

An unmarried mother of three children by three different men added this perspective: "I never intended to get pregnant—not once. But I love my kids. I can't trust myself. Every time I party, I end up with some guy. Three times, I've ended up pregnant. I know the fathers of my kids, but my kids don't know. Their fathers never come around. I think they know, . . . but they are so pitiful. They can't help themselves, so how can they help their kids? I've never told my kids who their fathers are. I don't plan to."

A number of women described having become sexually involved with men who would have been poor candidates for fatherhood:

> I knew his reputation, . . . I should have known better. He has at least a dozen kids by different women. He parties a lot, runs around with his friends, . . . lives with his parents. He is good-looking and can get almost any woman. I would never live with him. He would just run around on me . . . or beat me. He's not the husband type. His parents never recognize any of their grandchildren, either. . . . They deny it; they protect him. I hated myself when I got pregnant. I went over to [a friend's] house. He got her pregnant last year. I told her what happened. We sat around and teased each other. We were both stupid.

When women were asked if economics was a factor in the decision to have a child, 90 percent of the dropouts reported that finances were not a consideration for pregnancy. Fifty-three percent of the high school graduates reported that finances were a consideration, and 73 percent of the college graduates said that they had limited their families because of economic considerations. Over half of the women attributed their larger families to the desire to have children of both genders. For example, 31 percent of the women with more than three children reported having three or four girls in succession before having a boy. The opposite was also found, although to a much lesser degree. As a result, many of the women reported having several children until they had children of both genders.

Adolescent pregnancy appears to be more prevalent within the American Indian culture than in the mainstream society. This may be the result of unspoken sanctions that are applied to teenage pregnancy and the importance of children and of reproduction within the American Indian societies.

FINDING: Teenage pregnancy is a major factor in whether an American Indian girl drops out of school.

As noted earlier, 40 percent of female dropouts nationwide report dropping out of school because of pregnancy. Among the high school dropouts in this study, 51 percent left school prior to graduation as a result of pregnancy. In addition, there appears to be evidence that adolescent pregnancy, at least among the participants in this study, is on the increase. Fifty-four percent of the women in the seventeen to twenty-two age-group reported dropping out of school due to pregnancy. There is no question that adolescent pregnancy has a tremendous impact on teenage girls. For the majority of them, it appears that the mother and the child become permanently dependent upon public assistance. Most of these girls are socially, physically, and economically isolated. To be a mother requires the assumption of parental responsibility for the care and protection of a child; however, in order to care for a child, the mother needs to be able to care for herself. For the majority of American Indian adolescent girls, this is not the case. Most often, these girls remain in their parents' homes, where they receive welfare assistance and the grandparents assume the major caretaking role for the infant. Keeping pregnant teens and teen mothers in school must become a primary goal of educators within the Indian community. If children are having children, it is unrealistic to expect them to make that transition from the selfishness of childhood to the responsibility of adulthood without family and community support systems and without an education.

FINDING: Neither abortion nor childlessness appears to be an option for American Indian females.

Abortion is not an acceptable option within the Indian culture. Few women choose that route, and if they do, they do so without the assistance (or even the knowledge) of family members. No teenager appears to see abortion as an option, or even to have knowledge that abortion is a possible option to dropping out of school. Nor is adoption considered an option for pregnant teenagers within the American Indian society. Therefore, American Indian teenage girls who become pregnant become teen mothers and most often do not return to school.

In a culture with so few options for adolescent girls, the American Indian woman is certainly limited by cultural constraints. These cultural constraints and early social environments may very well contribute to the "acceptance" or "sanction" of adolescent pregnancy among Indian girls and their parents. For example, Nancy Chodorow suggests that the early social environment is experienced differently by male and female children, and as a result, "in any given society, feminine personality comes to define itself in relation and connection to other people."[1] Virginia Woolf argues that sensitivity to the needs of others and the responsibility for taking care of others result in females listening to voices other than their own and including in their judgment other points of view. Thus, the Indian girl who learns of the genocidal practices toward her people may indeed be listening to a "different voice" from that listened to by girls in the mainstream society, who do not have similar experiences.[2] In doing so, Indian girls are in some ways making a "moral" decision that is justified, according to Carol Gilligan, "as an act of sacrifice, a submission to necessity where the absence of choice precludes responsibility."[3] In this way, according to Gilligan, the girl avoids self-condemnation and maintains an innocence that is necessary for her self-respect.

FINDING: *For the Native American female, marriage is not a prerequisite for motherhood, nor is it likely that the teenage mother will have a long-lasting relationship with the father of her child.*

Nearly half of the women in this study identified themselves as "never-married" single mothers or unmarried mothers with live-in mates. A majority of the women reported preferring such a life-style, in that they could function independently of the male, without the need to obtain "approval" or "permission" from the male should they want to do something. As far as decision making was concerned, almost all of these females made daily decisions about their lives and their children's lives independent of the male. Within this group, there was a strong perception that married women had to obtain "permission" from the males should they decide to do anything, such as go shopping, visit a relative, go out of town, or even something as minor as cook dinner. Single women, even those who lived with men, preferred this independence to marriage.

Furthermore, a majority of the women indicated that the Indian male preferred his independence, and although he might not prefer an independent female, there was often little he could do about it, especially if they were not married. Despite the abusiveness of many of the male-female relationships, there was a knowledge that if things got too difficult, the female in an unmarried relationship had more options than a married one.

FINDING: For the Native American female, the need for love, affection, and approval is a very strong factor in teen pregnancy.

An old stereotype that is often voiced about teenage females who become pregnant is that they do so in order to announce their "womanhood," or that they need "someone to love" or to love them, or that they get pregnant "on purpose," with the underlying intent of "trapping" some unsuspecting male. This is clearly not the case with Indian females. In this study, many of the women who became pregnant reported unfulfilled childhoods and teenage years. They reported neglect by parents, uncaring or uninterested parents, abusive parents, drinking parents, and parents who paid little or no attention to them. Given those circumstances, it is not surprising that adolescent girls would look outside the family circle for love, affection, and approval. Frequently, the beginnings of feeling "loved" or "part of a group" may come with drinking alcohol or using drugs to gain the attention or approval of a male abuser. Often these relationships result in premature pregnancy. For the females, these relationships have a major impact on their adult lives. As noted by many of the adult women in this study, they are still seeking that "love" denied to them as children.

The basic struggle for American Indian girls is no different from that for people everywhere. The American Indian girl needs and wants to feel loved and to be capable of loving. Her feelings about herself are grounded in the type of family life in which she grew up and strongly affect her ways of coping with her transition from childhood to adulthood. Adolescent pregnancy among Indian girls is the response to this female's unique life problems, which are closely related to her current family situation. Becoming pregnant may be the young woman's attempt (usually outside of her own awareness) to solve her problems or those of her family. She may be trying

- To solidify a relationship with a young man so that she feels loved and wanted
- To demonstrate her independence and show her parents that she has a life of her own and is no longer under their control
- To obtain attention from her family for her needs
- In the absence of a "real family" of her own, to create a baby to love her so that she will not be alone in the world

Although the last factor proved to be the least acceptable among the women interviewed, the fact that this was a reflective study may have contributed to those opinions.

Chapter 13

Racism: A Factor of Life for American Indian Women

Racism is generally perpetuated through a system of unequal power relationships in private and public institutions and is manifested in the form of prejudice, discrimination, and stereotyping.

A stereotype is an exaggerated set of beliefs about the nature of a particular group of individuals. Thus, race-role stereotypes are beliefs about the nature of individuals within a given racial group. As discussed in chapter 3, stereotypes about American Indians often refer to personality traits or are used to describe situations, such as "They all drop out of school," "They all get a monthly check from the federal government," or "They all are drunks." Some stereotypes have no basis in fact, while others may be based at least on a small element of truth. Unfortunately, stereotyping of American Indians, which began at the onset of European contact with indigenous populations, has led to many inaccurate and misleading generalizations that are present in contemporary American society.

Prejudice is unfriendly feelings directed against an individual or group because of race, whereas discrimination results in treating some people better or worse than others because of race. A number of researchers have identified racism, stereotyping, prejudice, and discrimination as explanations for the lack of success by American Indians in school. In order to understand racism and stereotyping and their impact on the women of Native America, the participants in this study were asked a number of questions related to racism, stereotyping, prejudice, and discrimination.

As a lead-in question, all participants were asked if they had ever been victims of racism. Ninety-three percent of the women reported experiencing racism from teachers and peers during their school years. Seventy-four percent of the women reported having been "put down" by white adults, who included teachers and businesspeople. Fifty-three percent stated that their experience with racism came from white peer groups, whereas nearly one-fourth of the women reported racism on the part of white adults (not connected with the school system) both on and off the reservation.

From the interviews, it was evident that peer-group stereotyping, prejudice, and discrimination occurred frequently when Indian adolescents left the reservation for one reason or another. One former athlete reported, "We played basketball teams that were white. We'd go to these little towns that had no Indians. They called us 'squaws' and 'niggers.' That made us play harder. . . . We usually won."

When asked how they reacted to racism directed at them from peer groups, an overwhelming majority reported fighting or physically attacking the person who had verbally attacked them or made critical remarks about their heritage. One woman stated emphatically, "You can call me a 'bitch' and you might get away with it, . . . but don't call me a 'squaw.' Then you are putting me down because I'm Indian. There ain't nobody—man or woman—who can get away with that!"

Over half of the Indian women in the study who described themselves as "part white" disclosed that they had been discriminated against by other Indians on their reservation. Said one woman: "My skin was fair. All my brothers and sisters looked liked full-bloods, even though they were part white, too. In school, there was these girls who never got along with my group of friends. They always called me 'white trash.' It isn't easy being different or having white blood, sometimes."

Another woman spoke of the pain of adolescence when her early feelings of being ashamed of being part white were grounded in her family and how she felt as she was later harassed by her peers for being part white: "I was always picked on. I never had any peace in school. I was quiet. Maybe that made me a target. From my earliest memories, being part white was painful. My auntie used to hold me on her lap and tell me that someday my hair would be black and beautiful like my sister's [participant's hair was medium brown]. She always cried when she talked about my hair. I knew it made me different. In school, I was picked on and called a 'white girl.' I hated my hair. I hated being part white. Anytime anyone got mad at me, they called me 'white.' They still do."

A college graduate, who remembered the taunts of childhood for being part white, commented that the federal and tribal governments have contributed to the confusion about who is Indian and who is not: "It's hard being part white, when you are a child. You are raised on a reservation. You know nothing but the reservation. You are raised to be an Indian, and then someone casts a doubt on your whole identity by saying you are white. The government has added to discrimination of Indians against other Indians by insisting on blood quantum. The tribes add to it. You can be a full-blood on this reservation, but only be counted as half Indian because your father is from another reservation. We are pitting ourselves against one another."

Another female reported, "'Apple' is a common expression here—white on the inside and red on the outside. It refers to Indians who act white more than to the color of skin. To act white is not acceptable. White can be getting good grades, doing what your parents tell you to do, or just trying to get ahead. Being called an 'apple' is a real put-down."

Discrimination by Indians against other Indians occurred both on the women's home reservation and on other reservations. Mixed marriages and/or relationships often seemed to result in discrimination against one partner or the other. A respondent, who married outside her tribal group, related, "I lived up on the [name deleted] Reservation. My husband was from there. He couldn't get a job. His relatives said it was because he was married to me. I don't know if that was true, . . . but I wanted to come home. When we broke up, he went home and got a job."

One female, whose mother was white and whose father was seven-eighths Indian, revealed:

> We made frequent trips off the reservation . . . to visit relatives . . . to go shopping. As long as my mother was along, we had no problems. If my dad and I went, I noticed that people treated us different. I think it was harder for my mom on the reservation. She seemed happier off the reservation. I felt sorry for her sometimes. My aunts [her father's sisters] would get after her about something. It was always based on race, never on what she did. I felt sorry for my dad off the reservation. He was a good father. I don't think that whites think that an Indian man could be a good father. Now that I'm grown up, I understand why they stayed together—they really loved each other and wanted to be together.

Another view of mixed marriages and its implication in terms of acceptance within society was offered by one of the women:

> There is a double standard. It is all right for a white man to marry an Indian woman in this country, . . . but I think it is harder for a white woman to marry an Indian man. Women are judged by their husbands. A white woman who marries an Indian is judged more harshly . . . unless she marries an educated Indian. If she marries an uneducated Indian, she has lowered herself to marry an Indian. Indian women who marry white men have raised their status. It's mostly the educated Indian males who marry white women. That further alienates them from the culture, and a lot of them live off the reservation or go to another reservation where they are more accepted. An uneducated Indian who marries a white woman has a harder time, . . . not completely accepted in either world. Indian women seem to fare better in both worlds.

When asked how they coped with prejudice and discrimination, nearly one-fourth of the women reported feeling angry and often reacting violently, nearly half indicated feeling shame and frustration, and nearly one-fifth reported feelings of worthlessness.

Of the women who had graduated from college, 54 percent reported rejecting racist comments or attitudes, or not personalizing them. Of that group, 30 percent said they had developed those coping mechanisms on their own, whereas 24 percent reported their parents or other relatives helped them deal with racism.

When asked how they dealt with white adults who put them down, one-fifth of the women spoke of "getting even" through a variety of ways. College graduates preferred economic pressure, for example, by boycotting a store whose owner engaged in discrimination practices, and telling others to do the same. Some even reported taking legal action against off-reservation merchants and persons who discriminated against them in housing. Other females described more vindictive tactics: "If we knew a store owner was prejudiced, we passed the word. When we went to town, we would steal from that store. I don't think none of us ever got caught."

Women who were half white or more reported fewer incidents of racism and discrimination off the reservation, but more such incidents on the reservation. Just the opposite was true of women who identified themselves as having more than one-half Indian blood. They commented that their experiences with racism came from whites living on the reservation or during travels off the reservation.

When asked if they felt their teachers were prejudiced, 71 percent of the women reported having at least one teacher who they felt was prejudiced. Twenty-one percent reported that prejudiced teachers contributed to their dropping out of school. Seven percent of the females in this study said that a prejudiced teacher was the major reason they dropped out. When asked to describe prejudiced teachers, the women gave a number of responses. Some recounted confrontational statements of teachers, such as "acting like a wild Indian," "dumb Indian," "What could I expect from an Indian?" and "Don't act like a squaw." Others identified more subtle actions on the part of teachers, such as favoring mixed breeds or white students by giving them more attention and praise, giving privileges to white students, and always blaming Indian students for problems in class.

When asked how they dealt with teachers who they felt didn't like Indians, 81 percent of the participants reported being inattentive or ignoring them in a variety of ways. Twenty-four percent acknowledged skipping classes or feigning illness rather than attending class. Sixty-nine percent believed that white female teachers were more prejudiced toward Indian females than were white male teachers. Seventy-three percent believed that white female teachers favored Indian boys over Indian girls by allowing them to be more disruptive in class, by permitting poorer performance, and by overlooking classroom infractions. Fifty-nine percent of the women felt that white male teachers favored boys over girls.

One well-educated, self-described feminist reported, "If these teachers were halfway intelligent, they'd give the girls all of their attention. It's the Indian woman who holds things together. If things ever change, it will be because the Indian woman takes charge. . . . But I don't think white female teachers or white male teachers think of Indian girls as leaders. After all, white women aren't leaders, are they? We don't get teachers who think liberally or critically. We get teachers who are limited themselves, so how could they expect great things of us?"

Other "revenge" techniques, which involved a small number of girls, were used with teachers who were labeled as racist. According to one female, "We put sugar in their gas tanks. We broke off their antennas. We stole their mirrors and hubcaps. We knew they valued their possessions more than anything else. It was the only way we knew to get even. If we complained to the principal, things got worse for us. We couldn't trust the counselor. He was a drunk. We fought back the only way we knew. In one way, we just confirmed what they thought of us anyway. Too bad."

When asked if they felt racism and discrimination were on the decrease, 94 percent of the women indicated they believed racism and discrimination had actually increased or were on the increase. One respondent with a graduate degree reported:

> Before we started going to college, we weren't a threat. Before we stood up for our rights, we weren't a threat. Every time an Indian goes away and gets an education, whites on the reservation are threatened. There is now an Indian who might be able to do his job and maybe do it better. When we stand up for our water rights, our legal rights, white people want the state or the federal government to wipe us out again. The more educated we become, the more vocal we become. That's a threat to whites. I think we can expect more racism to be directed our way. We already feel the pressures from some U.S. senators who want us to be good Indians and give away our resources to the whites. Our senator reminded us that he had always taken care of us and scolded us like children when we refused to go along with him. The message was clear—either act like Indians are supposed to act, or we will vote against you in Congress. It's the same all over. . . . Ask any Indian from Wyoming, Montana, the Dakotas. Our own representatives are against us.

A number of the women in the thirty to thirty-six age-group attributed the increase of racism to the Reagan years. A female college graduate in that age-group suggested a connection between racism and the political power of various federal administrations:

> Nixon may have been a crook, but he was good to us. Carter may have been a humanist, but he wasn't too interested in Indians. We knew that, so we knew what to expect of him. Reagan used rhetoric, which is more dangerous. He let Watt speak for him and then chastised him for speaking out. The message was loud and clear: Indians are dispensable. The average American cares more about the starving Ethiopian than the hungry Indian. The Blacks made a lot of gains with the civil rights movement. We gained nothing. . . . We were simply sent back to the reservation and told to stay there, and that's what we did.

Discussion

There is no doubt that racism, prejudice, and discrimination affect the American Indian female adolescent. The effect varies from female to female. Some develop very early coping mechanisms. Others never learn to cope. Some act out their anger in violent or vindictive ways.

FINDING: Racism on the part of a few teachers may be directly linked to American Indian females dropping out of school.

Ten percent of the females in this study who had dropped out of school reported dropping out because of a teacher they perceived as being racist or prejudiced. Nearly three-fourths (71 percent) of the women reported having teachers who exhibited these characteristics.

Adolescents, who are often very influenced by what others think about them, react in a number of ways to negative attitudes and verbal abuse from teachers. Many of them react by "fighting back," such as by destroying the teacher's property. Some avoid the teacher, skip school, or fail to do homework, actions that set them up for failure in school. Others refuse to cooperate in the classroom setting. Regardless of who is to blame, the fact that so many women report such incidents is reason enough for educational and tribal leaders to be concerned.

FINDING: A majority of American Indian women experience racism during adolescence.

Over 90 percent of the women in this study reported having had experiences with racism, both on and off the reservation. Most of their on-reservation experiences came from teachers. Off-reservation experiences ranged from incidents with merchants in participants' early years, to those with white youth their own age (in competitive sports or on field trips), to discrimination in housing and employment as adults.

Whether or not one develops coping skills, racism in any form obviously affects the individual's ability to become successful. It appears that many American Indian females are able to ignore such encounters or to compensate in other ways, while some see "fighting" or "stealing" as an outlet for their expressions of frustration and anger.

FINDING: For Native American females, prejudice and discrimination toward other tribal groups and among their own tribal members in terms of degree of Indian blood appear to be common occurrences.

Repeatedly throughout this study, women voiced concerns about prejudice and discrimination within their own tribe. Women who are "more Indian," that is, who have a higher degree of Indian blood, frequently shared their disapproval of "breeds" or "whites" on the reservation who were actually tribal members. Again, part of the basis for this discrimination against one's own tribal members may be the resentment that has occurred during preadolescent and teen years, wherein children who "looked more white" were more favored by their classroom teachers. On the other hand, "being white" does not always reflect the color of one's skin; an individual may "act white," such as becoming more acculturated (educated) or amalgamated by marrying out of one's race or by choosing to live off the reservation for a number of years and later returning to one's roots.

For the most part, I do not believe that American Indians are racist. Racism is institutional. A racist can deny equal access or opportunity to other individuals on the basis of their skin color. American Indians are not in a position to do that, as institutions are mostly white institutions. However, prejudice and discrimination do occur among American Indian populations and, as in any ethnic group, limit growth and potential associations with others.

FINDING: Racism and discrimination create a high level of dissonance and frustration in American Indian female adolescents.

Anytime an adolescent encounters racism or discrimination, it creates a certain amount of dissonance. It is not an easy lesson to learn that others perceive you in ways that are not agreeable to your way of thinking about yourself. This dissonance may take the form of acceptance; that is, the individual may come to accept what others say and think about her/him. It may result in frustration and anger or any number of coping behaviors, including the desire to prove others wrong (e.g., by excelling in sports or graduating from college), or the desire to "get even" or hurt others as the individual has been hurt (e.g., by fighting, stealing, or vandalizing). Since discrimination and racism are a fact of life for American Indian females, it appears that part of the early development and nurturing of girls should include ways of learning to cope with such encounters. Leaving them alone to survive on their own may be one of the indirect causes of dropping out.

Chapter 14

The American Indian Female: Peer Pressure or Family Loyalties?

Peer pressure is often cited as a major source of high-risk behavior for youth in the United States. Since American Indian youth are confronted with the same issues as other adolescents regarding their decisions to drink alcohol, use drugs, or drop out of school, this study made use of a number of questions to investigate peer pressure and its impact on Indian adolescent females. Although the interviews revealed that American Indian girls are indeed influenced by their peer groups, probably more significant was the finding that peer groups for American Indian females in reservation schools differ dramatically from peer groups for adolescents in the white society's schools. For Indian girls, the majority of their friends or peer group are also their relatives. As a result, peer pressure often becomes an issue of family loyalty and of maintaining family harmony, and, in terms of education, staying in school may be an expectation ascribed to family groups.

Although American Indian girls appear to be strongly influenced by peer pressure, this does not seem to affect whether or not they drop out of school. Only eight women in the study reported dropping out of school because a peer or friend had dropped out. In fact, the majority of the women reported staying in school because their friends were in school. One dropout reported that her decision to drop out, which she later regretted, was influenced by a female cousin who had dropped out: "I had no other friends in school. When Mary [fictitious name] dropped out, I was lost. It seemed like she had so much freedom—no schedules, . . . could stay up late, . . . sleep late. I dropped out. A few weeks later, I found out that Mary was pregnant. I should have stayed in school. After her baby was born, she didn't have any freedom. There was nothing for me. Soon after that, I got pregnant, too." The high school dropouts in this study discussed dropping out for a number of reasons, but dropping out to be with another dropout was not the norm.

Graduating from high school or college also appeared to be influenced by one's family group. If parents, cousins, and other relatives had gone to college, it was expected that the relatives within the female's respective peer group would also go to college.

The women who went to college immediately after high school most often reported that family members were very supportive and encouraging.

One graduate related, "People in my family always went to college; . . . [that] goes back to when [name of tribal college] first opened. There was an expectation that when you graduated from high school, you went to college. It was never discussed much. When I look around the reservation, that seems to be common. If your parents went to high school or college, chances are that you will go, too. Education runs in Indian families."

As in the case of the mainstream society, higher-educated Indian parents appear to influence their children's aspirations toward higher education. It is likely, too, that these parents may spend more time helping their children academically. In addition, it appears that girls in this study whose parents were better educated were often able to travel with their parents to conferences and were more likely to have rewarding educational experiences outside the classroom.

Women who reported a lapse between high school graduation and college enrollment indicated that friends were very influential and were often role models for them. Over 40 percent of this group felt that their peers had a major influence on their decision to enter college. Others reported peers using more indirect tactics: "I had this friend who invited me to come live with her at school. After a few weeks there, I decided I liked it. The next quarter, I enrolled, and we actually graduated together. I would have never gone to college if she hadn't kept after me to come and live with her. I would have been too afraid to go by myself. Having her there made the difference."

The influence of peers on high school and college graduation may again be directly tied to the importance of family relationships and extended family groups, both within high school and in terms of the support provided to college students. Indian relatives (cousins, sisters) may, in fact, provide the support a young woman needs to survive in the alien culture of a college campus. Ten participants who were college graduates reported attending college with their aunts. One female disclosed that she graduated with her grandmother, and two related that their mothers went to college with them. Ten percent of the females who graduated from college noted that, while in college, they often had a "close friend" who was ten to twenty years older than they and who helped them through difficult times. In all of these cases, their close friends were "older Indian women" who had returned to college after many years of living on the reservation and had decided that a college education was important to their futures and to their children's or grandchildren's futures. In this case, it appears the older Indian female became a surrogate mother or aunt to the younger Indian female, who was experiencing the white culture for the first time.

All of the women in this study, whether high school dropouts, high school graduates, or college graduates, reported that peer pressure was often involved in their behavior or misbehavior in school. Many of the women spoke openly and freely of plotting against teachers who were regarded as unjust or racist, despite the implications that their behavior might lead to suspension or expulsion from school. One high school graduate described how an entire class responded to an unjust teacher:

> This teacher picked on all of us. She didn't believe we were smart or that we would ever graduate. She was a racist. So we just proved her right. We didn't do anything—never did our homework, didn't go to the board, ignored her requests to be quiet, walked out of her class. Eventually, we all got put in detention for some reason or another. But we would go right back to class and do the same thing over again. At the end of the year, she was fired because she couldn't control us. We got rid of her, but we didn't learn anything about English. . . . We did learn that, as a group, we got something accomplished that one or two of us could never have done.

Another respondent recalled an incident where an entire class cooperatively worked together against an unfair teacher: "This woman should have never been a teacher in an Indian school. She was from a white family here on the reservation. Her family was rich. . . . Her father had taken advantage of the Indians—stole from them, paid them low wages. The family was prejudiced against Indians. About the second week of school, she got mad at us and called us 'a bunch of wild Indians.' After that, we refused to do anything for her. We became wild. We wouldn't stay in class. We ignored her. We talked back. This went on for weeks. She still lives here and still thinks we are 'wild Indians.'"

Although it is clear that in the two scenarios described above, peer pressure surely contributed to the behavior of the students involved, it should be pointed out that there were many instances when women discussed "group actions" as a means for dealing with teachers who were unjust or racist. It would appear that in Indian schools, students have little opportunity to reveal such injustices to administrators. Most often, they feel that their concerns will fall on deaf ears. As a result, they frequently resort to their own means of controlling their environments. Unfortunately, many of these students gain reputations for being incorrigible or delinquents, while others are chastised for associating with "bad" peer groups; yet it is the schools that have failed such students. Instead of the schools recognizing their contributions to inappropriate student behaviors, the blame is placed solely on the students—many of whom are labeled as troublemakers or future dropouts.

Skipping school appeared to be influenced by peer associations. In some cases, when skipping became habitual, it created a number of problems for students and in some cases may have resulted in eventual dropping out. Interestingly, when this did occur, it generally affected only one student. One college graduate disclosed, "My cousin and I skipped school in the ninth grade. We couldn't find anyplace to go. We couldn't go to my house, because my mom was there. We couldn't go to her house, because her mom was there. We finally walked over to the ball field, but my uncle saw us there and took us to school. I never skipped school again, but my cousin started doing it regularly. She eventually took up with some older kids who dropped out of school, and one day, she never came back to school at all."

A high school dropout described a similar experience about skipping school: "I talked my sister into skipping one day. She was in the ninth grade, and I was in the tenth. We took off with some other kids—older kids who had dropped out. My sister didn't like it. She was scared. After that, she never skipped again. [For] me, it became an everyday occurrence—hanging out with older kids, mostly guys. My sister graduated. I never got beyond the tenth grade."

Throughout the conversations with the women in the study, there was a consistency about skipping school. Although in many cases, the first incidents of skipping occurred between peers of the same age, skipping generally ended unless the student or students connected with older students who had dropped out of school. In most cases, habitual skipping involved a younger female and an older male.

Other women reported smoking on school grounds or skipping classes as a result of peer influence. One high school graduate reported, "I always seemed to be on the outside. Kids made fun of me. The teachers never did anything to make me feel good about myself. The only kids who ever paid any attention to me were the ones who were outcasts themselves. That's when I first started smoking. I was in the fourth grade. I hung out with them. They broke every adult rule about smoking, drinking, going to school. . . . I was in the ninth grade before I straightened up and quit hanging out with them."

Another respondent related a story similar to other stories told to me about skipping classes: "Our teacher never took roll. If you didn't give him any problems, you got good grades. My cousin and I used to sneak out of his class or not go at all and spend the hour in the bathroom or out behind the school. We never got caught. He didn't care if we skipped."

In this case, an uncaring teacher appeared to have had more direct influence on skipping classes than peers did. It would appear that students who have teachers who are their advocates, take a personal interest in them, and set high expectations for them are less likely to skip classes or become involved in other inappropriate behaviors. Although educators often attribute inappropriate student behaviors to peer pressure, it may be that they themselves are contributing to such behaviors in many unseen, untold ways.

Most reservations and reservation communities are rural and isolated. Families and relatives often congregate in these small communities. This is frequently a result of the extended family practices within Native cultures, so that it is not uncommon to travel a reservation road and find members of an entire family located within two miles of one another. This can include grandparents, uncles, aunts, and cousins. Often the world of the Indian child, prior to school, is the world of cousins (the child's brothers and sisters in Indian kinships). When girls enter school, they are in school with cousins, as well as with students from other communities on the reservation. In 88 percent of the cases in this study, however, the Indian females reported that their best friends were their cousins and sisters. Typically, these friendships develop at birth and are nurtured throughout the preschool years. In most cases, the friendships remain strong throughout adulthood.

A majority of the women reported that their first experience with alcohol was with a relative and that "drinking parties" most often involved cousins. One woman reported the difficulty of "saying no" to relatives: "They come to your house; they have a six-pack in the car. They want to go for a ride. You go. The beer is passed around . . . you drink because everyone else is drinking. Mostly when you are in high school, it is harmless. None of us had a lot of money for alcohol. The problem comes after high school. No jobs, no future. It goes from a six-pack to a case or several cases. Partying helps you forget."

When asked if their friends included both drinkers and nondrinkers, 82 percent of the participants responded that their friends included "sober" friends as well as "drinkers." One high school graduate reported that parents do not interfere with their children's peer relationships, even when they know several in the group may drink:

> In the white culture, kids choose their friends more on the basis of whether they drink or not, whether they play sports, are in the band, are in plays. Very early, white parents watch their kids and help them choose their friends. It's different on the reservation. You can't choose your relatives. Parents don't say, "Don't hang out with so-and-so, 'cause he drinks or she drinks." If they did that, everyone's relatives would be mad. Some of my friends drank; some didn't. If I wanted to drink, I knew who to hang out with. If I wanted to do something else, I knew who to hang out with. Nobody ever got mad whether I drank or not.

When analyzing peer pressure within these parameters, it takes on a very different dimension. Women reported that parents are unlikely to interfere in their relationships with peers, because the peers are often relatives, and that parents do not forbid them to associate with drinking peers, because these persons are often drinking relatives. This appears to be just the opposite among white parents, who are dealing with peer groups that are not composed of relatives. As noted earlier, when it comes to substance abuse, it is much more difficult to ignore, walk away from, or "just say no" to a relative. This situation carries over into other behaviors and attitudes of the American Indian female.

Women in this study reported having the options of drinking or not drinking and having both sober friends and drinking friends. They reported little pressure from other girls to drink, although there were indications that they drank and used drugs because other girls joined in. None of them described being teased by other girls about failure to participate in drinking alcohol or in using drugs; however, they did report fear of appearing "unsophisticated" in the eyes of out-of-town males or older males who encouraged them to participate.

Indian adolescent males, on the other hand, appear to be under heavy pressure to drink. Drinking is a form of "machismo," whereby males encourage others to drink and reject those who do not drink with them. The females in this study reported that within their peer group, they were more often encouraged to drink by boys, including boyfriends and male cousins or other male relatives. Although boys often encouraged girls to drink, most of the female respondents felt that boys really didn't like girls who drank. One college graduate spoke about the double standard within the male culture:

> Boys who encouraged girls to drink were after one thing—sex. It's the macho thing. Even shy boys were uninhibited if they had a few drinks. A lot of researchers try to explain why Indian kids drink. It's the same reason all kids drink—to feel better about yourself and to "score" with a girl . . . have sex. Boys always knew which girls would drink and have sex. They left the rest alone. Drinking, sex, and dating often went together, which was different from drinking and casual sex. Most girls didn't have sex if they didn't drink. It's the old thing—you can do anything, and it's acceptable if you drink. When you are sober, sex is taboo. We need more sex education, instead of so much drug and alcohol education. When these same boys grow up, they like women who don't drink . . . unless they are the true alcoholics. Women who don't drink are more responsible and often have jobs.

Unlike the situation with alcohol, women disclosed that they were most often given drugs (usually marijuana) by nonrelated friends. Most reported obtaining drugs from older boys or men whom they met at powwows. Although drugs were often introduced to them by "outsiders" to their community, they admitted that other females often encouraged them to smoke marijuana. One woman summed up the situation in the following manner:

At powwows, you meet guys from all over—guys that aren't your cousins. Some are really handsome. Girls hang around them like groupies. The joints appear out of nowhere. They are offered to you, . . . [and] you want to act grown-up, sophisticated. Others are doing it. You don't want to be a "baby" in front of these good-looking guys, [so] you do it, too. Sex is often involved afterwards, . . . sometimes with several guys. Maybe that is peer pressure of a sort. You want to be popular. You want the guy, instead of letting your cousin get him. Later you feel bad. But something happens with grass—once you smoke, you want to do it again. Grass is different than alcohol. . . . It doesn't make you sick; it's a better high. I never thought much about alcohol. After my first joint, I thought a lot about grass and wanted it again.

Even though it appears that adolescent males frequently expend a great deal of effort on encouraging females to drink, there is some evidence that they do not want to marry women who drink. This application of a double standard to males and females often appears to be the source of much frustration for Indian girls.

Discussion

Although all women in the study reported that peer pressure had influenced them in a number of ways, a majority denied that peer pressure contributed to their dropping out of school. It is important to note, however, that despite their denials, the women exhibited a number of inappropriate behaviors in response to peer pressure, behaviors that may have been contributing factors to dropping out, whether the women recognized those factors or not. Several findings are presented here about peer pressure and American Indian girls.

FINDING: For Native American females, peer pressure appears to have a positive effect on staying in school and graduating and on pursuing a college education.

Peer pressure as it relates to graduation appears to have a positive effect on Indian girls. Over 70 percent of the women in this study reported that peers had influenced them to stay in school and graduate.

At work here may be some factors that differentiate Indian girls from other racial minorities. First of all, reservation communities are generally small and isolated. There are few places to go and even less to do. Therefore, dropping out of school is likely to lead to boredom and individual isolation. The reservation school is generally the hub of social events and activities, in addition to its academic functions. Minimum-wage jobs are rare for teenagers, so girls do not drop out to seek employment. Furthermore, the majority of Indian girls expect to be gainfully employed and regard a high school diploma as a prerequisite for even a minimum-wage job. And finally, the social structure of Indian tribes is very closely linked to family relationships and friendships. Staying in school to be with friends and family members may be a choice based on social functions, rather than academic ones, but this factor does seem to keep Indian girls in school.

FINDING: Peer pressure involving Native American girls is often regarded as a source of inappropriate behavior within the school setting.

Clearly, peer pressure is responsible for many of the inappropriate behaviors associated with school. Women reported that skipping school, resisting and/or confronting authority figures such as teachers, and engaging in other inappropriate behaviors within the classroom setting were quite common when faced with insensitive teachers or situations over which they had little control.

Teachers, on the other hand, who did not understand the culture and were unaware of the peer relationships, often did not understand why the students rebelled against them. In many cases, the so-called peer pressure was loyalty to family members.

Skipping school appeared to be influenced by peer associations. In some cases, when skipping became habitual, it created a number of problems for the females in this study and sometimes resulted in dropping out of school. Interestingly, when this did occur, it generally affected only one student.

FINDING: For American Indian girls, peer pressure and substance abuse are often closely linked to family kinships.

The majority of the women in this study reported that their first experience with alcohol was with a relative. In over half of the cases, this relative was also a member of their peer group.

The nature of reservation life, the ruralness and isolation, combined with the presence of extended family groups living in close proximity to one another, makes the decision to "just say no" an inappropriate response for the women in this study. As reported earlier, it is much more difficult to say no to a family member. This situation carries over into other areas of peer pressure and contributes to other dysfunctional behaviors, as well.

Summary

Within all adolescent groups, peer pressure impacts the behavior of the youth in their respective societies. For the American Indian female, however, peer pressure cannot be defined in a conventional way. Because her peers are frequently family members as well, it is difficult to distinguish whether a response to such pressure is the result of loyalty to friends or is prompted by family kinships.

Clearly, there is little peer pressure among Indian girls to drop out of school. However, peer pressure does often result in behaviors that are inappropriate to or incompatible with the school setting (e.g., uncooperative, vengeful attitudes or skipping school), behaviors that may, in fact, contribute to dropping out. Peer pressure in relation to substance abuse, which has been closely linked to dropping out of school, impacts Indian girls to varying degrees, since they may be dealing with sanctions within their family groups.

For the majority of Indian girls and women, their peer groups, which are more often than not their sisters and cousins, appear to have positive effects concerning their decision to stay in school, and particularly in the decision to go to college. Modeling within families is a significant factor in the decision to stay in school and graduate. Peers within these families often provide support for one another. This fact, in itself, provides educators with a tremendous advantage in keeping girls in school. If education is important to a family group or peer group, motivating girls to stay in school does not appear to be the problem that many researchers have previously suggested.

Again, it should be noted that what we often describe as peer pressure may in fact have its origins in other problems confronting students, such as an inability to cope with the school environment or a teacher's attitudes toward students. In this instance, we need to rethink our definition of peer pressure and examine closely the roots of student behavior before making such judgments.

Chapter 15

Child Abuse: The Silent Enemy

Child abuse is a generic term that is used to describe emotional or psychological injury, sexual molestation of children by caregivers, negligence, or nonaccidental physical injury. Perhaps one of the more tragic elements regarding abuse of American Indian children is the lack of accurate data concerning the scope of the problem. Estimates of the prevalence of child abuse are generally recorded with the Indian Health Service or the tribal police force; however, to present a clear picture of abuse is often difficult. In addition, it is important to note that statistics reveal only the cases reported. Based on the experiences related by the women involved in this study, it is evident that the majority of incidents of abuse remain unreported.

Historically, child abuse research has centered on the characteristics of the abusive caregiver, with little attention focused on other variables that are frequently associated with abusive behavior. Current theories of child abuse examine the caregiver's role as only one variable (although a significant one) to be considered within a model of many interacting variables that cannot be separated or viewed in isolation.

Caregivers who abuse their children are often themselves victims of abusive behavior. Environmental conditions—which may include unemployment, household poverty, or dysfunctional family structure (e.g., alcoholism or frustration with one's own life)—are likely to trigger child abuse.

Since prereservation days, the institution of the American Indian family has changed drastically. Many American Indian children are growing up in homes where they experience a number of unpredictable events, among them abandonment by one or both parents, neglect, child abuse, imprisonment or arrest of parents, marital strife, divorce, and alcohol abuse. In addition, many researchers have reported on the breakdown of the extended family.

The responses of the participants in this study, when they were asked if they had been abused as children, demonstrate the depth of child abuse within Indian communities. Thirty-four percent of the women reported being verbally or psychologically abused as children, 32 percent reported being physically abused, and 17 percent reported being sexually abused.

Many women discussed the pain of verbal abuse, which they disclosed took place in the home, as well as in the school environment. One female described the anguish of verbal abuse, which was directed at her by her parents and had been ongoing since childhood: "My dad always called me a 'bitch.' My mom told me I was fat and ugly and that no man would ever want me. But I never had no trouble finding a man to sleep with, even though I was fat and ugly. Three years ago, I decided to change my life. I lost forty pounds, went back to school. I still get up some days and think I'm fat and ugly, . . . my mother still says so. My dad still calls me a 'bitch' when he's drinking."

Another woman talked about the psychological abuse within her family that resulted in her fear of being abandoned by her parents: "If we did something they [her parents] didn't like, they threatened to give us away . . . send us to jail or reform school. Sometimes when they went on a drunk, I lived in terror that they would never come back. I don't know why—they were lousy parents."

Other women revealed their firsthand experiences of neglect by parents who frequently left them at home alone, sometimes for hours, sometimes for days. Said one: "My parents were into drinking. They thought only of themselves. When they drank, they often would go off for days at a time. We never knew where they were or when they were coming back. I was the second to the oldest in a family of seven. My older brother and I took care of the family. Sometimes we didn't have nothing to eat. Many times I gave the babies water in their bottles to try to keep them from crying. We always tried to hide our situation from the school. We were afraid that we would get separated."

One woman spoke with great admiration of her mother, who made a decision to leave her father—a man who not only neglected his family's needs, but also abused them: "We lived in the country. My dad would sometimes go drinking for days and come back and beat us up. This one time, he left us without any food and didn't come back. I remember that my mom took us and walked to town. She found him at his brother's house. She told him she was leaving him and that he was never to come around us again. He never did. She was a determined woman. She got a job and supported us after that. We never went hungry again."

When the interview questions turned to issues of sexual abuse, it was apparent that the women in the study found it very difficult to speak about the topic. One female, who confided that she had never previously discussed sexual abuse with anyone, related:

Not very many are going to talk about sex abuse. It's here—fathers, uncles, brothers, cousins—but our ways cover it up. If you report it, the whole family would turn against you. There is no help for little girls; . . . if you lose your family, you have nothing. It's the same way with abuse of any kind. No one admits they beat their kids. Kids don't tell, either. It's not the Indian way to beat kids, to abuse them in any way. It would be like saying to everyone that this person is acting like the whites. So it's covered up, while girls suffer. Sometimes

I think about going public, like those women on TV, but then I know it would do no good. This is the first time I have ever told anyone that I was sexually abused. . . . I still feel guilty about it.

Another woman recalled an incident of sexual abuse in her family and her relatives' reaction toward her when she sought help: "I'm ashamed to tell this story. The abuser was my father. I caught him sexually assaulting my two nieces. When I told the rest of the family, they became very angry with me. Finally, I went to my uncle. . . . He was kind of the head of our clan. . . . He sent my father away . . . told him to leave the reservation and not come back. But I've never been forgiven for telling on him."

All women in the study were asked if they were subjected to physical punishment from their parents. Over half of them revealed that they had never been spanked or "hit" by their parents. In 51 percent of these cases, the women reported verbal warnings, quiet lectures, or private scoldings. Many women described private lectures. One female talked about being told to go to her mother's room: "My mom was the disciplinarian in the family. She never disciplined us in front of anyone else. At home, we were sent to her bedroom. If it was at someone else's house, it was the bathroom. We dreaded going to the bedroom, . . . but the bathroom was worse, because we were so embarrassed. Once we were in private, she talked to us. We hated those quiet lectures. Believe me, they worked!"

Other women reported nonverbal language, such as disapproving cues (frowns, shaking of the head "no," walking away by a parent, hand signals). This nonverbal correction often took place in front of other relatives, acquaintances, or strangers. One woman said that her father used a cowboy hat as a means of nonverbal discipline: "Dad always wore a black cowboy hat. He used it effectively with us. Just by pulling the front brim down slightly over his forehead, we knew to leave the room, . . . cease some behavior, . . . be quiet. He managed all this without a word. We always obeyed."

Four percent of the female respondents reported frequent spankings that "did not hurt" but were intended to "shame." In almost all of those cases, either the father or the mother in the family was non-Indian. Three percent of the women reported "isolation" from the family as a punishment for misbehavior, such as being sent outside to be alone, being left out of family activities, or being sent to another room. During such occurrences, other youngsters and adults in the family ignored them. This type of family censure, at least in the opinion of the women in this study, was most effective.

Nearly one-third of the women reported spankings that were intended to "physically hurt" or demean them as individuals. In 92 percent of severe physical punishment cases, the parents were drinking when the child was punished. The severe physical punishments resulted in raised welts (often with bleeding), cuts, bruises (including black eyes), and burns. In a book entitled *The Dark Side of Families,* a number of writers speak to the sociocultural factors that foster abusive environments within families, including violence between parents.[1] More important, however, is that the acceptance of physical punishment of children within our homes and schools and the willingness of caregivers to employ physical punishment are the most significant determinants of child abuse in America.

Nearly 50 percent of the women reported that they were the only abused child in their family, a situation that further complicated their feelings of guilt, loneliness, and helplessness. When the women were asked if anyone (teacher or relative) ever intervened to help them, 3 percent reported that a grandparent, uncle, or aunt had intervened. They related that they were often taken away from the abusing parent by these relatives, but said that they were not happy in a "safe environment." One woman shared those painful feelings from her childhood and her inability to reconcile those feelings as an adult:

> I was the oldest. When my parents drank, I always knew they were going to beat me. If one of the other kids [four younger siblings] cried, I got beat up. . . . If they argued, I got beat up. . . . If they were hungry, I got beat up. My parents were into drinking. Hunger, crying, fighting—all natural things for kids—interfered with their drinking. When I was fourteen, this old guy asked me to marry him. I was looking for a way out; it didn't matter that he was in his forties. I jumped at the chance— anything to get away from home. I knew nothing about sex . . . being a wife, but I could cook, clean house, take care of kids. He was good to me, . . . treated me more like a daughter than a wife. He died five years ago.

Many women told similar stories about the abuse of alcohol and its consequences on their lives. One woman, who carried the physical scars of her abuse, told the following story: "There were probably a dozen people drinking—all day, all night. I was so thirsty, . . . [but] I couldn't reach the sink. . . . I tiptoed in and asked my father, who was standing by the stove, for a glass of water. Instead, he poured boiling coffee on my hand. It was two days before they quit drinking and sobered up and took me to the IHS. I still have the scar [she shows it to the researcher]."

As a follow-up to the question regarding child abuse, women were asked if they had ever been abused in their adolescent or adult lives by a "significant other." The responses to this question, although much more open, were still somewhat subdued. Twenty-nine percent of the women reported being abused by a high school boyfriend. One female discussed such a relationship: "At first, John [fictitious name] was nice to me. He was always jealous, and I kind of liked that. It made me feel like he cared. . . . I never felt like anyone cared for me before. About a month after we started dating, he hit me for talking to another guy. He apologized later, and I accepted it. After that, he hit me often. I always took it. I tried to stop talking to people. But he would hit me if I even smiled at another boy."

Another woman spoke about believing that she deserved to be abused by a high school boyfriend: "When my dad hit my mom, she always told us kids not to blame him—that she had made him mad. When my boyfriend beat me up, I blamed myself. I figured I had done something wrong. All my life, I've been with men who hit me. Every time, I blamed myself."

Thirty-three percent of the women in the study reported being physically abused by a spouse. Forty-one percent reported being physically abused by a boyfriend or male friend, and 19 percent reported having been raped or sexually abused by a male friend. When asked if they had remained with an abusing partner, 53 percent of the women revealed that they had remained in the relationship. In many cases, those relationships eventually ended by mutual agreement. In a high percentage of the cases, women reported developing a subsequent relationship with another abuser. In addition, abused women came from all walks of life and from among dropouts, high school graduates, and college graduates. Education seemed to make little difference as far as forming healthy male-female relationships. A married college graduate reported, "Ten years of marriage and four kids, and he still occasionally beats me. I leave and go home to my family, but he comes after me. My mother says I should stay with him. My dad says nothing. My brother beat him up a couple of times, but it made things worse for me. Why do I stay? I guess because most of the time he is good to me and the kids. We mostly fight over money. I have a good job. He ranches, but never makes any money. I control the cash. He doesn't like that."

An unemployed high school dropout related similar problems: "We fight all the time—mostly because of his drinking and running around with his friends. My family used to take up for me, . . . his family took up for him, . . . [and] then we'd have one big fight, with everybody taking sides. No one pays any attention now. When they see my eye black or my glasses broken, they know why. I stay because there is no place to go. The rez ain't that big. He would find me. When I was little, Dad used to punch Mom in front of us. He quit after I left home. Maybe the same thing will happen to me."

Another woman related how she ultimately gained family support to divorce an abusing spouse: "From the first week of our marriage, he beat me. I told my mother, but she told me that sometimes men act that way until they get it out of their systems. I asked to come home, but she wanted me to stick it out. Then my girl was born. When he started beating her [around three years of age], my mom encouraged me to divorce him. It was OK for him to beat on me, but it wasn't OK for him to beat on her granddaughter."

A college-educated female described how she solved her problem of an abusing husband:

> Our second year of marriage, he started beating me up. . . . Finally I went home to my mother. She said I couldn't stay with her; . . . she told me I didn't have to put up with being abused. She had the solution—"Give him some of his own medicine. Beat him up!" I took her advice seriously. One night, he came home drunk. When he fell asleep, I took a stick of wood and let him have it. He didn't know what was going on. The next day, I told him, "If you ever hit me again, I'll kill you." He never has hit me again—that was ten years ago, . . . [and] he quit drinking that same night. He really turned out to be a good husband. He just needed a little discipline. [She laughs.]

Other women associated the abuse they suffered as children with their acceptance of spouse abuse as adults. One woman served as a spokesperson for others: "I keep going back to him, . . . even though I know he will beat me again. Have you ever watched an abused child? They always go to the abusing parent, always seeking approval. I've spent my life seeking approval from abusers—first my parents, then my husband. Do you suppose it will be the same for my girl [referring to her five-year-old daughter]? I worry about that. Someday I might get the courage to leave him."

Women were asked if they were supportive of other women who were physically abused by their "significant other." Seventy-three percent reported not getting involved at all. One-fifth of the women reported supporting friends who had been abused, by giving them money or a place to stay. One female revealed, "You have to be very careful. If you help out, you may get in trouble with the families. Abuse of women is so common on this reservation that it is accepted. It doesn't occur to very many women that they have any options. Alcohol is the culprit, and these women live in a fantasy world which includes a belief that someday these men will quit drinking and become good husbands or lovers. The funny thing about it [is], . . . when they get to be about forty or fifty, most of them [the men] do change."

One battered wife talked about the support she received from her cousin, who is also an abused spouse: "When Tom [fictitious name] beats her up, she [the cousin] comes over and we talk about it. I put on a pot of coffee and we talk all day. When it [abuse] happens to me, I go over and she puts on the coffee. We plot all kinds of things around this kitchen table, but we never do anything. It helps to talk. . . . I guess it's good to know you are not alone."

When asked if physical, psychological, or sexual abuse affected their self-image, 87 percent of the women who reported abuse felt that it impacted their view of themselves, both as competent individuals and as worthy individuals. When asked if abuse inflenced their decision to drop out of school, one-fifth of the females felt that abuse was instrumental in their decision to leave school. Most of the females spoke of "escaping their home environment" or "escaping abusing teachers," but not finding contentment elsewhere. Many voiced a concern over younger siblings and quit school to protect and care for younger brothers and sisters. One dropout remembered her teenage years: "I was the oldest. I have four younger brothers and sisters—three sisters, one brother. I didn't have to worry about [brother]. He was never abused. He was the favorite. If I was home to cook, put the kids to bed, clean up the house, there was less violence. Once I went to live with my grandma but came home. I worried too much about the girls [younger sisters]. My mom was crazy. I hate to say that, 'cause she's dead now, . . . alcohol. I have nothing to do with my father. He lives with my younger sister now."

The subject of verbal abuse from teachers was interjected by the women throughout the interviews. (References to verbal abuse were discussed in chapter 13 on racism and in chapter 14 on peer pressure in regard to teachers and their attitudes toward students.) During the interview process, comments about physical and sexual abuse surfaced as well. Twenty-nine percent of the women who had at some time been enrolled in boarding schools reported physical or sexual abuse. This abuse—from teachers and dormitory personnel—included beatings with a paddle, withdrawal of daily meals, solitary confinement, and sexual harassment and abuse. One victim of boarding school abuse confided:

> I've never told anyone this story before, not even my mother. There was a counselor. He had a reputation for liking Indian girls. Every new girl that arrived had to see him. Once in his office, he locked the door. . . . Then he told you what he expected. Next came the conditions. If we wanted any extras, like a candy bar, we had to let him feel our breasts. If we wanted to go to town, we had to undress for him so he could look at us. Often he would pose us in different positions. He would give us money if we let him touch us and kiss us on different body parts. Hell, . . . I was just in the eighth grade. At first, I was afraid not to cooperate. I started out with little things—the touching. Later, I kind of enjoyed it. It felt good to be touched and kissed. Later, I felt guilty. If I saw him today, I would kill him. . . . I blame him for the things that happened to me. Later, I let boys my age do the same thing. All I wanted was to be loved. Instead, I got a bad reputation for letting men do anything they wanted.

Not all abuse of Indian girls in a school setting was confined to non-Indian personnel or to the boarding school setting. Two percent of the women in the study who attended public, BIA, or contract schools on the reservation reported dealing with sexual harassment and sexual abuse. An additional 3 percent reported physical abuse from teachers, such as slapping, pulling hair, and paddling. One female told of a traditional American Indian male, employed by the school on her reservation to teach the Native culture and language, who abused girls in the school:

> He was an old man—maybe fifty, but old to us. He was a medicine man—at least, he called himself a medicine man, . . . but he wasn't. He used to catch us in the hall, always when we were alone. He'd push us into a broom closet and feel our bodies. If we fought, he would hurt us and threaten us. Most of us, after the first time, tried to avoid him, but it didn't always work. I have trouble respecting medicine men, even today, because of him. He was married and had kids, . . . but he got his kicks at our expense. There wasn't a girl in our school that hadn't been pushed into that broom closet. What is worse, he still calls himself a medicine man. He has even had meetings with presidents, been on television. All I know is that his time will come. What goes around comes around.

Discussion

Clearly, many American Indian girls are subjected to a variety of abuses and neglect that impact not only their childhood, but their adult lives as well. A number of findings surfaced from the interviews.

FINDING: American Indian girls and women suffer an extraordinarily high rate of abuse, including physical, sexual, and psychological/verbal abuse.

The interviews indicate that the traditional image of the doting, loving American Indian parent may be fallacy, at least among a very high percentage of girls growing up on the reservation. In the case of many women, although they were not physically abused, they were psychologically and verbally abused by parents. Others were sexually abused by male relatives—most often fathers, grandfathers, or brothers. In these incestuous relationships, almost all of the women reported having had no advocate.

Although abuse of alcohol was most often related to the accounts of physical and sexual abuse, results of the study indicate that this was not always the case with psychological and verbal abuse. In nearly 10 percent of the cases of psychological and verbal abuse, women described parents who were apparently frustrated in their roles, unhappy with their lives, or unable to cope with children. As a result of the parents' dissatisfaction, children became the objects of their anger and frustration.

From the interviews, there is overwhelming evidence that abusing parents and/or other relatives are seldom punished for their misdeeds. In fact, evidence supports the fact that families protect the family-member abuser, and that child abuse is ignored or covered up within family groups. Denial of such abuses has long forced American Indian girls and women to remain silent about their situation.

It is difficult to resolve such abuses without the intervention of law enforcement and the judicial system.   Abusing parents must be held accountable by their relatives, the police, and the courts.

FINDING: American Indian women are twice as likely to be abused in their adult lives as in their adolescent years.

Whereas nearly one-half of the women in this study were subjected to physical abuse as children, nearly three-fourths of the women admitted to experiencing physical violence and spouse abuse at some point in their adult lives.   Nineteen percent revealed that they had been raped during their adolescent or adult lives. The majority of women who were involved in violent relationships reported a lack of support if they were to leave the relationship.   In fact, 53 percent who disclosed such relationships either remained in those relationships or became involved in subsequent relationships that were equally abusive.

There appears to be a lack of alternatives or support for women who are abused. Seventy-three percent of the women in the study reported that they did not get involved when a female friend or relative was the object of abuse. The majority of the women revealed that their own families provided little or no encouragement for them to leave abusive relationships.

It is obvious that women on the reservations have the potential of being a strong force in the support of abused women. In many cases, I was told stories of abuse that the women had never shared with one another. In other societies, women's support groups have become a major influence in communities and in the lives of women and families. For American Indian women, this appears to be an untapped resource that desperately needs to be explored. Women can make a difference in their lives. Perhaps it is time that American Indian women, who have demonstrated strong leadership skills in other areas, assume a leadership position in halting child abuse, rape, and spouse abuse.

FINDING: Child abuse contributes to American Indian girls dropping out of school.

Although only 10 percent of the women in this study reported dropping out of school as a means of "escaping" an abusive home life or an abusive teacher, it is obvious that child abuse may be responsible for thrusting the

young female into other types of behaviors—behaviors whose consequences contribute to her dropping out of school. For example, 51 percent
of the women reported dropping out of school because of unplanned
pregnancies; yet in the majority of the cases, these women reported becoming sexually active because they needed or wanted love and mistook sexual
relationships for love. Further, many of the women who dropped out of
school reported uncaring parents, and in many cases, those parents were
neglecting or abusing ones.

*FINDING: Some American Indian girls experience tremendous psychological and
emotional problems as a result of abuse from personnel within the school setting.*

Twenty-nine percent of the women who attended boarding schools reported incidents of physical, sexual, and psychological/verbal abuse from
school personnel. In many cases, sexual favors were expected of girls in
return for privileges. Eleven percent of the women who attended school on
their reservations related incidents of sexual abuse and harassment from
teachers, administrators, and counselors. Three percent reported physical
punishments. It is likely that there has been no greater injustice suffered by
the American Indian female than the kinds of abuses reported by the
women in this study. Schools should provide a safe environment for girls,
and if they fail to do so, those employees who are guilty of such abuse and
exploitation should be prosecuted to the fullest extent of the law. School
administrators and school boards must take the responsibility for carefully
monitoring the behaviors of teachers, and the complaints registered by girls
against school personnel should be investigated and taken seriously. This
is not to suggest that a "witch-hunt" should be conducted in every school
serving American Indian youth; it does suggest, however, that there are
many abuses occurring within the school environment that cannot be
condoned, and action must be taken to prevent recurrences. American
Indian women who have been subjected to such cruelties should join
together to speak out on these issues—if not for themselves, then for their
daughters and granddaughters. The time has come to end the silence about
such injustices.

Summary

This study demonstrates, perhaps for the first time, the extent of physical,
sexual, and psychological/verbal abuse suffered by Indian women and
girls. When the home fails to provide a safe environment for the young girl,
it is expected that at minimum, the school will be a safe environment. This
was not the case for many of the women in this study.

In order to curb the accumulation of factors that contribute to girls leaving school (including child abuse), all agencies within the community—including the school, the tribal government, and law enforcement agencies—must take an aggressive role in protecting the female child and adolescent. This protection must also extend to the adult women, who clearly are in need of assistance as well.

Chapter 16

Schools and Teachers: Are American Indian Girls Dropouts or Pushouts?

In the literature, there are generally three causes identified with dropping out. One of the issues is personal problems of the individual. These problems, such as pregnancy, substance abuse, health problems, and personal abuse (physical, sexual, psychological, and verbal), are independent of social class and family background. A second cause, family background factors, relates to the socioeconomic status of the family. Because dropouts more often come from poor, minority families or single-parent homes, researchers maintain there is a strong relationship between family background and dropping out.

School factors are the third cause generally discussed in the literature as impacting the dropout rate in America. A number of factors relating to school have been studied by researchers in an attempt to ferret out the reasons for Indian students' lack of success. The most common school-related factors include poor academic achievement, an inability to get along with teachers or peers, a dislike for school in general, retention and attendance, and a culturally hostile environment for minority students. Although some of these factors, such as relationships with teachers, have surfaced in other chapters of this book, the focus of this chapter will be specific to those categories.

I did not have access to GPA (Grade Point Average) scores for the women respondents; therefore, the academic information presented in this category is strictly a retrospective account by the women who participated in the study. However, in defense of this approach, it should be noted that the women themselves are a relatively valid source of information about their own academic achievements.

All women were asked if they encountered academic difficulty in school. Twenty-one percent reported that they had failed a class at some point during their school experience; however, less than 1 percent of the women reported being retained in a grade because of poor academic performance. The majority of the women in the study reported that retention was not a problem in reservation schools. One dropout suggested that few reservation schools retain students due to community pressure and/or lack of interest by teachers: "Teachers in Indian schools pass kids; . . . you will very seldom see an Indian child who is retained. A lot of us never learned to read well in our early years. No one ever goes back and corrects that problem. The teachers know we can't read, but they ignore it and pass us anyway. By the time we reach the fifth or sixth grade, it is too late. Most teachers don't expect us to learn, so they just pass us . . . or they are afraid they will lose their jobs if they flunk us."

Of the group who reported failing a class, less than one-fifth eventually dropped out of school. When asked at what grade level they began to experience academic difficulty in school, the majority of women reported their academic problems began somewhere between the sixth grade and junior high. Although few of these women discussed academic failure in terms of grades, one-fourth of them indicated that they began to lose interest in school or that school "made no sense" to them in terms of its relevancy to their present or future lives. Other school problems were described in terms of interactions with teachers.

When women were asked to talk about their relationships with teachers, many spoke of school rules that seemed inappropriate to their age-group—for example, standing in line, raising their hand, obtaining permission to go to the bathroom, receiving demerits, or being rewarded for perfect attendance. One high school dropout noted, "By the time I reached the sixth grade, I had experienced it all—alcohol, abuse, housecleaning, cooking, taking care of babies. I probably had more responsibilities than the teachers. I know I had faced and survived more problems than they had. Raising my hand for permission to sharpen a pencil seemed stupid. . . . I rebelled. No one could do anything with me. That continued until I dropped out, in the tenth grade."

Other women voiced similar opinions. One high school graduate related her frustration at teachers' lack of knowledge or understanding about the age-group being taught:

> Indian kids are taught to be independent from the time they take their first step. By the time an Indian female is ten, she has done it all and seen it all, . . . but the teachers are still treating us like babies. A lot of teachers are totally out of contact with our lives. They drive onto the reservation in the morning, and they drive off in the afternoon. They don't realize that some of us go hungry, that some of us have spent the night fighting off a drunken relative, that some of us have to take care of our younger brothers and sisters. They don't care. I began defying them and their rules during the fifth grade. During high school, I used to get up and walk out of classes and roam the halls. No one ever did anything. Somehow, I managed to pass.

The topic of teachers, good and bad, surfaced throughout this study and has been discussed to some degree in other chapters of this book. A consensus of the research addressing the issue of school effectiveness points to competent and caring teachers as the single most critical factor in reducing the dropout rate of students. Women in this study were asked to recall experiences with teachers and if and how those teachers impacted their decision to stay in school or to drop out.

Many talked about teachers who ignored them, teachers who didn't expect them to do homework, teachers who gave them busywork and read novels or magazines during class, and teachers who criticized them as individuals.

When women were asked about their reported "dislike of teachers," 84 percent pointed out that they had teachers they liked; yet nearly 82 percent reported having teachers who negatively affected their school experience and whom they disliked. Almost three-fourths of the women reported having at least one teacher who they felt was prejudiced or racist. When asked at what grade level they began to identify racist or prejudiced teachers, 93 percent reported "somewhere between the fifth- and sixth-grade year in school." When asked the major reason for disliking teachers, 74 percent responded that their teachers were unfair, 73 percent reported teachers who practiced favoritism, and 73 percent felt that their teachers didn't care about them or didn't expect them to perform.

When the women were quizzed about how they interacted with teachers they disliked, the majority (81 percent) reported being inattentive, ignoring the teachers, discounting their opinions or comments, walking out of class, or being generally disruptive. Others reported "sleeping in class," putting their heads on their desks, or defiantly doing other work in class. One female recalled "sleeping" through her junior and senior years in high school: "I had a lot of teachers who just left you alone if you didn't make trouble. I slept through classes in high school and got straight C's. Nobody cared if I learned. They just wanted good kids—passive, I guess you call it. If you didn't make trouble, you passed."

Over 20 percent of the women in this study who dropped out of school revealed that they dropped out because of a teacher (or teachers) or because of the hostile environment of the school. Over one-fifth of the women in this study said that relationships with teachers, and particularly those that they viewed as racist and prejudiced, contributed to their overall attitude toward school.

Over half of the women talked about a school environment that was hostile to Indian students. One college graduate reported, "You would think that in an Indian school, the teachers would be sensitive to Indian students, but that is not necessarily the case. Some teachers are just outright prejudiced, and they do not even make an effort to hide their attitudes. They told us we were dumb. They suggested that we drop out. They told us we weren't going to amount to anything or that we didn't need an education to live on welfare."

Another dropout claimed that, in general, teachers encouraged students to drop out of school: "I think those of us who were not functioning well in school were mostly ignored by teachers. They wanted us to quit and leave. We were failures, and they didn't like to confront failure. They only wanted to work with the kids who came from good homes and showed potential. They never looked for potential in us."

When women were asked if teachers contributed to their staying in school, nearly 22 percent identified a teacher who had been particularly encouraging or instrumental in their decision to remain in school. A high school graduate reported that a caring teacher helped her stay in school: "I had lots of trouble at home. . . . I guess she [her teacher] sensed that. She started making special comments on my papers. Once, she took me shopping and bought me a book. She told me I could write well and I should consider writing my own story someday. I stayed in school because of her."

Another experience with a caring teacher was described by a college graduate: "She approached me one day in the hall and told me that she was proud of my work. She said that she was the first one in her family to graduate from college. She asked me if I had considered college. She kept reminding me every year that she had high hopes for me. When I graduated, she gave me $100 and told me to buy some clothes for college. . . . I did. I still go see her. She cared about me and lots of other kids."

One college graduate related overhearing a group of teachers discussing her in the faculty lounge. Their negative comments angered her so much that she made a commitment to herself to get an education: "They never expected much of me. Still, I managed somehow to stay there and learn. One day, I heard them talking about me. They said I would never amount to much—they figured I would drop out like my brothers and sisters before me. I made up my mind that I would show them. All through college, I fantasized about sticking my degree under their noses. But I never did. Somehow, after I graduated, it wasn't important anymore."

Several of the women spoke about developing long-term relationships with teachers who were special to them. One woman discussed making a trip to see a former teacher who lived out of state: "When I was in school, I could always tell her anything. She never disapproved of me, no matter what I did or what my family did. She just encouraged me. Sometimes she invited me to her house for dinner; . . . sometimes she took me on picnics with her kids. I felt like I was one of her kids. I stayed in school because she cared about me and wanted me to get an education. Last year, she got sick. I drove to Denver to see her. She said my visit made her well."

Twenty-nine percent of the women in the study suggested that reservation schools attracted more than their share of undesirable teachers. Many noted that teachers with "problems," including alcoholism, drug abuse, and psychological problems (abusive), had more anonymity on an Indian reservation. Eleven percent of the women reported having seen a teacher intoxicated at school or at social events within their communities.

A high school dropout related how she and a group of friends had gathered evidence on an alcohol-abusing counselor and suffered the consequences. This story was corroborated by three other females from the same reservation: "We had a high school counselor. Some of the kids saw him drinking in the school parking lot. We got into the school and searched his office. We found two pints in his desk drawer. When we told the principal, we got kicked out for breaking into the school, and he got promoted to assistant principal. He was always picking on us, watching us, threatening us. I dropped out because of that SOB. I am out, but he's still there. That's justice—white man's justice."

When asked if they respected teachers they suspected of abusing alcohol, 89 percent of the women reported that they did not. One woman commented, "I think we deserved better. Do you think those white communities would allow an alcoholic to teach their kids? It was like . . . we were all going to end up alcoholics because we were Indian, so anybody was better than nobody. I ask my kids about their teachers. If I hear something I don't like, I go to the school board. . . . They don't listen. How can they fire an alcoholic teacher when some of them [board members] are alcoholics?"

One woman told a story of being introduced to marijuana by a high school teacher. Several others from the same reservation reported similar stories: "He invited us to his house; . . . he was our favorite teacher; . . . he gave us beer and grass. He was from back east somewhere. He said he didn't like white kids, because they didn't know how to have fun like Indians. I heard when he left here he went to Alaska to teach Eskimos. He probably got half of his class high. We never told on him. Can you imagine a teacher doing a thing like that? There should be a law against teachers doing things like that to kids. We didn't know any better. If the teacher said it was OK, then it was."

One female, who had completed graduate school and was herself an educator, described at great length the types of individuals attracted to teaching on reservations:

> During my senior year in high school, . . . some of my friends got together one night at my house and we started categorizing teachers into groups. We tried to list every teacher we had since we started school. Six basic categories surfaced. There were teacher dropouts. . . . Maybe they were good teachers at one time, but not anymore—they had dropped out, . . . just put in their time, . . . made us do paperwork or nothing at all. There were the incompetents. They couldn't get a job anyplace but an Indian reservation. . . . We knew more about the subject than they did; . . . they got angry and punished us when we pointed

out mistakes. There were the rednecks. Both women and men fit into this category. They owned farms or their husbands owned farms on the reservation or in the area. They hated Indians; . . . they expected nothing of us; . . . any misdeed or failure on our part just reaffirmed their feelings that whites were superior to Indians. There were the sickies. They were the alcoholics, the drug users, the sexual perverts, who preyed upon students, both male and female. There were the missionaries. They spoke with eastern accents. . . . They bought us presents; they took our pictures and wrote stories about us. Sometimes they were rich, and their friends and family would send us Christmas presents or clothes. . . . They never expected us to learn—we were too pitiful. Finally, there were the real teachers—those who expected us to work. . . . They praised us for good work and told us quietly we could do better when we failed. Their classes were filled with laughter and learning. Unfortunately, all those categories still exist. . . . Maybe the kids have different labels for them, but they are still teaching in Indian schools. I think that today there are more in the "teacher category," . . . but we have more than our share of the others as well. It's frustrating. Most are tenured—almost impossible to fire, thanks to government bureaucracy.

When asked about the curriculum, the majority of the women (71 percent) reported that somewhere between the fifth and sixth grades, they began to question the classroom activities and their relevance to their lives. One female, who disclosed that her parents were activists in the American Indian Movement, commented that teachers were totally unaware of the education children received outside the schoolroom. Nearly one-third of the women in this study voiced similar opinions. One college graduate reported, "I mean, . . . here we were, in the sixth grade, and still cutting out black cats and pumpkins for Halloween, pilgrims and Indians for Thanksgiving, and Santa Claus for Christmas. None of these things were meaningful to us. All of these holidays were important to the white man, so they just brought them to the reservation and plopped them into our schools. At home, we were learning about treaties, the history of our people, the wrongs that were done to our tribes, . . . and at school, we were cutting out black cats and singing Christmas carols."

Many women reported losing interest in school for the same reasons. Another college graduate related, "I always struggled in school to maintain an interest. . . . There was very little for me. My escape was the library. . . . I read every book three or four times. The teachers expected very little from us, so the classes were boring. Most of them seemed bored as well. . . . Few of them were well read. Their perspectives were very limited. . . . Most came from around here and didn't like Indians and certainly didn't encourage us to do much. Educated, informed Indians are a real threat to the white people on this reservation—but our time has come."

The specifics of curriculum were addressed by a high school graduate: "You know, there is a lot of controversy on this reservation about the curriculum. I don't go along with a lot of what people are saying. What kids study is not nearly as important as how kids are treated. Sure, it's important to know about your tribe, the government, and things like that, but that kind of a curriculum is not going to get us a job. What we need are caring teachers—teachers who understand that, although our values may be different, we aren't different when it comes to learning. They just have to adapt their ways a little bit when they are teaching us."

Another high school graduate elaborated on these comments:

> I have good memories about school and some very bad ones. My worst memories concern teachers and administrators who did not understand how Indian children are taught to behave and interact. Teachers would scold us for helping others in the classroom. I use to get F's for telling my friends the answers to math problems. Another teacher gave out "red marks" if she caught you helping someone else. It is really hard to trust teachers who punish you for the things you are taught to value in the home, such as helping others. Actually, what happens is that you are forced to choose between your parents' way and the teacher's way. I always chose what my parents taught me. It seemed to be the right way. Unfortunately, it didn't help me much in school—but it has helped me a lot in life.

One college graduate, who was herself an educator, spoke about trust and bonding within the school environment:

> I've read a number of journal articles about the importance of bonding between the school and the child—developing a trusting relationship with teachers. When I was in school, I don't think I ever trusted teachers. For the most part, I always felt it was "us" against "them." I don't think the idea ever occurred to teachers, either. Now that I have a child who will be entering school next year, I worry about this issue. I don't want him to be alienated by teachers. I don't want my experiences to influence him, so we talk about school and how important it is. I want him to believe that school is a caring place, where children and teachers learn and grow together. I hope I am doing the right thing.

Only 3 percent of the women in this study reported that academic difficulty was probably the major reason for their dropping out of school. Others, while admitting to problems in school, did not perceive academics as the primary reason. Most felt that they could do the work if they had wanted to do it. Of this group, the majority felt that their grades suffered for other reasons, especially as these related to uncaring teachers.

When asked if they had dropped out as a result of boredom related to an inappropriate curriculum, less than 2 percent of the women confirmed they had.

One high school dropout spoke about the boredom of school, which began very early in her school years and culminated in repeated absences and skipping: "We just did the same thing, day in and day out. Read and write. Always seat work. There was nothing exciting—nothing, anyway, that caught my interest. I never liked school. It was confining. I lived for the weekends so I could do things. When I got older, I skipped school so I could do things."

Many of the women in the study talked about having chosen not to do well in school. One high school graduate suggested that a combination of peer pressure and her home experiences contributed directly to the way she achieved in school: "Among my friends, doing well in school was frowned on. If you made an A, you were trying to be good or trying to be 'white.' I chose not to do well in school, because I didn't want to be made fun of. Staying in the middle was a safe place to be. Making C's, a few B's was OK. So that's what I did. At home, I was never told I could do better. My parents were just happy that I was passing."

Many women spoke about the importance of not trying to do better than other students. One woman, who had graduated from college, explained her perceptions of this type of behavior:

> When I was in high school, my boyfriend was the star of the basketball team. Everyone knew it, but to be a star is not good among Indians. You have to share the glory. So he would do things to make himself look bad—not show up to practice, not get to a ball game on time, not follow the rules of the coach. You see, if you are really a star, you have to be good. So he would do things to detract from his star quality. I think a lot of Indian kids play that game. In the classroom, you may do such things as not turn in a homework paper or give a wrong answer to the teacher on purpose. Indian kids learn early that to be a star is not what counts. It's better for the whole group to succeed or the whole group to fail than for one to stand out. If you are a star, you are acting like a white person.

Other women noted the importance of the family in terms of success and how it is viewed. One college graduate commented:

> If you come from a family where success is expected, there is a lot more of an opportunity for students to stand out in terms of school achievement or athletic achievement without being criticized. I see this [as] particularly true of children who come from mixed-racial marriages. Many of those kids do extremely well, whether it's school sports, rodeo competitions, or schoolwork. They may be criticized by some kids in school, but they get the encouragement at home to ignore these criticisms and to be the best they can be. Family attitudes are extremely important. We need to get across to our children that being successful in school is not "being white," or being a rodeo champion is not "being white."

We should teach our children to be the very best they can be. That's the issue, not whether they are acting like whites. But the fact that many of these children come from mixed marriages and are part white themselves has contributed to the idea that if you are successful, you must be white—or, in the case of our children, at least part white.

Another college graduate, who admittedly had one-fourth white blood, spoke to this issue as well:

Some researchers have studied "breeds" and "full-bloods" and have demonstrated that "breeds" do better in school. This to me is racist research, based on the old genetic defects theory. They have failed to look beyond genetic factors. For example, if "breeds" do better in school, it may be because teachers treat "breeds" differently than "full-bloods." It may be that if you are more white in appearance, you don't face racism or prejudice as frequently. It may be that your family, which is obviously more acculturated, values success of the individual more than success for the group.

Other women talked about the competitiveness of school and the frustration they felt in the classroom. A college graduate related:

All the teachers in the school knew I was smart. . . . They expected a lot of me, including going to college. They used to say, "When you grow up, you can go to college, make lots of money, and live in a big house." They never realized that I did not have those aspirations for myself. If they had told me that I could help out my family if I went to college, it would have been much more meaningful. We aren't raised to outdo one another. Our success is measured in helping each other. I can have a nice car and house—that's OK—but I can't let my relatives go hungry in order to do that. I suppose I could have a lot more if I lived off the reservation. Out there, nobody helps one another out.

One respondent discussed the insensitivities of the school to Indian students:

Everything was conformity—stand in line, salute the flag, be a good American. We read books written by white men, telling white men's history and about their lives. If an Indian was brought up in class, it was always one who had helped the white man—Pocahontas, Sacajawea. We never learned, and our kids never learned, what really happened to the indigenous people in this country . . . or the contributions they made. We were taught to be hardworking and successful so we could have more than our neighbor. Those were our teachers' values, not our values. No wonder our lives are so screwed up now. We feel guilt if we are successful; we feel guilt when we aren't.

Some researchers have suggested that many dropouts maintain a lifelong grudge against school in general and that this attitude persists when their own children go to school, thus perpetuating the dropout syndrome into the next generation. When the women were questioned about this syndrome, their responses were mixed. Many of the women attributed problems in school to their parents' attitudes toward school. Nearly half of the women in this study, however, reported that even though they may have had bad experiences in school, they were more aware of parents' and children's rights than their parents before them had been, and that they were committed to seeing their children did not suffer the same experiences. When the female respondents were asked about their goals for their children, 100 percent reported wanting them to graduate from high school, and 94 percent said they wanted their children to go to college. When asked how they would help their children avoid the disenchantment with school that many of them voiced, the majority of the women stated that they were going to be more involved in their children's education. One dropout commented, "I may have dropped out of school, but I'm not dumb. When I was in school, I had no one to turn to with my problems. No one spoke out for me. My kids will have me. I will not hesitate to talk to teachers, go to the school board. I think my generation is much more knowledgeable about our rights and the role of the school than our parents were. I will not let a teacher or the school destroy my child's future."

Not all women viewed themselves as able to be an advocate for their children. One woman spoke of her fears of confronting the educational system:

> When I was in school, the teachers could have killed me . . . and my parents wouldn't have done anything about it. When I complained, they offered no solutions. They were resolved to that kind of a situation. My first-grader is scared to death of her teacher. She yells, she throws things, and she has been known to jerk kids around. My sister wants me to go up there and tell her to either straighten up or I'm going to do something about it. I am afraid to do it. I went to a parent-teacher conference, and I really had a hard time talking to her. This bad feeling came over me, and I didn't know what to say; I just wanted to get out of there. My daughter makes up excuses not to go to school. She gets sick a lot. I don't make her go to school, either. I feel sick whenever I think about that teacher.

Approximately one-fifth of the women who had school-age children reported similar experiences between their children and a teacher. Less than one-half of that group admitted to trying to do anything about it. One parent commented that school officials "label" parents who try to take action: "I have a reputation at that school for being a troublemaker. Maybe I am, but there is no way I'm going to let a teacher get away with punishing my kid every day. She puts him in the corner. She keeps him in at recess.

She humiliates him in front of the other kids. I told her that one of these days, I am going to catch her away from the school and beat her up. She reported me to the police. She doesn't treat him so bad anymore. If she does it again, I'll be right back up there. I won't be so nice the next time. [She winks and laughs.]"

When the women were asked if they were moved from one school to another during their school years, almost half reported attending more than one school system. In 33 percent of the cases, girls were placed in boarding schools or attended other reservation schools. In the remaining cases, women attended off-reservation public schools when their parents moved in order to further their education or to seek employment. One-fifth of the dropouts reported changing schools five times or more during their school years. When asked if changing schools affected their academic achievement, the majority reported that doing so had little or no effect; however, most of the women said that social and emotional factors resulting from leaving friends, having different teachers, and moving away from relatives did have a major impact on their adjustment to new schools. Over half of those who were in boarding schools reported "hating dormitory living" and loneliness. As reported in chapter 15, 29 percent of the women who attended boarding schools disclosed abuse from teachers and dormitory personnel, including physical punishment, verbal abuse, withdrawal of meals, solitary confinement, and sexual harassment and abuse. One high school graduate, who had attended eleven different schools before she graduated from high school, stated, "It was very difficult for me in school. My parents were always moving around and putting me in another school. Sometimes I missed weeks of school at a time. Teachers resent kids who move from one place to another. They don't take time to find out if you can learn anything. They figure we won't stay there very long anyway, so why bother with us? It is a serious problem for a child, who has no control over the behavior of parents. Teachers aren't sympathetic to that. We are just another problem."

Other women described similar attitudes among teachers, counselors, and school administrators. One college graduate reported, "I know that my parents weren't the most responsible people in the world when it came to keeping us in school. But the schools take that behavior out on the children. When I'd show up to enroll, I might hear something like, 'Oh, it's you again.' Or, 'How long are you going to stay this time?' It was like it was my fault that my dad moved us around all the time. I hated going to school, for that reason. I only went because my dad said that he would be put in jail if I didn't. At least that kept me in school, and somehow I learned regardless of the bad circumstances."

One of the major problems cited in the literature concerning American Indian dropouts is the high rate of truancy and absenteeism. Parents who frequently keep children out of school or who fail to get them to school on time are often regarded as permissive and irresponsible. This has been an ongoing battle between the home and the school.

Throughout this study, women expressed reasons for parents taking them out of school or for keeping them at home. The reasons ranged from helping parents complete forms, to reading legal materials, to caring for younger siblings. A majority of the women from dysfunctional homes often missed school because of family responsibilities or were unable to deal with school because of home problems. Almost all of the women, whether dropout or graduate, reported missing school because of family responsibilities.

One dropout reported missing school every Monday as a result of the weekend "parties" at her home: "I really liked school, but my teachers thought I didn't. Every Tuesday, they'd comment about my long weekend or my extended vacation. I could hardly say that I was cleaning up after drunks all weekend and taking care of kids. Finally, I just gave up . . . I quit. I couldn't take their harassment anymore."

Other women talked about the differences between the values of the school and those of their families, including misunderstandings that occurred when they were taken out of school or missed school as a result of a family obligation. One female described a scenario that was commonly reported by other women: "I never went to school on Fridays. . . . That was payday. My mom didn't drive, so she always had to get a ride to town with her older sister. We had no money for baby-sitters. I had to go along to supervise the younger ones. I loved those days. My teachers hated to see Fridays come. . . . They thought our parents were irresponsible for taking us out of school; others did it, too. It wasn't that I didn't like school, but I loved to go to town and help out my mom and auntie. It made me feel important."

One nineteen-year-old female dropout scoffed at the irony of in-school suspensions:

> I had five in-school suspensions my sophomore year. They were all because I had three unexcused absences. I never felt they were unexcused. My parents were both alcoholics, and I stayed home to take care of the kids, . . . to keep them from burning down the house, . . . from killing each other. The most ridiculous thing about in-school suspension . . . [is] you're not allowed to go to class. You just sit in a room with other people. The teacher is a warden—generally the dumbest and meanest in the school. He doesn't know enough to help you with algebra or biology, let alone write a sentence or pick out a noun or verb in a sentence. So you get further behind. Schools are supposed to exist for kids. . . . Instead, they exist for teachers and administrators. If I were a principal, I'd do away with in-school suspensions. I'd keep kids in class every minute I could. They wouldn't be missing more class time by being in suspension.

There appears to be another reason for absenteeism that, rightfully so, may also be charged to irresponsible parenting. When women were asked how many had stayed home because they simply wanted a day off from school, over half admitted that their parents allowed them to take days off from school.

When the women were asked if they missed school on a regular basis (once a month or more), nearly one-fourth admitted that they missed school at least that frequently. Of this group, over half eventually dropped out.

When asked if their grades suffered as a result of missing days of school, 37 percent of the women reported receiving failing grades from teachers, having percentage points taken off their grades, and experiencing refusal on the part of teachers to allow them to make up work, take tests, or be provided with additional assistance when they missed school. One high school dropout, who later completed a GED and obtained an associate degree from the tribal college, explained:

> You see, we [those who missed school] didn't matter. Teachers considered us losers. We were never going to amount to anything. They never cared or even tried to understand the hell we lived. . . . Instead, they judged us by some sanctimonious standard. You were only worthy if you attended school every day. They didn't care that I had to get seven kids off to school every morning— that I had to care for them, bathe them, sing them to sleep, listen to their problems. Most of the time, I was too tired or too worried [about her drinking parents] to do my homework. I got some of it done in study halls; the rest I didn't do. After trying so hard and no one even caring, I dropped out.

Another dropout, who completed her GED and graduated from secretarial school, shared the stress and enormous responsibilities of a girl living in a dysfunctional home:

> I was the oldest. My mom and dad were divorced when I was little. My mom wanted to be married. . . . She was always lonely. Sometimes she'd cry for companionship [when she drank], . . . [and] sometimes she'd go to bars and not come home for days or even weeks. During those times, I filled in for her. I kept it all a secret. . . . I didn't want the younger ones placed in a foster home. I learned to lie and to make up stories about my mom's absences.
> It became too difficult to take care of the kids and go to school. Teachers asked too many questions. I couldn't go anywhere with my friends. I had to stay home to take care of my brothers and sisters. I kept up that front until the youngest one got through high school, . . . then I got my GED.

Nineteen percent of the women reported punishment by school officials for missing school—which translated into ineligibility to participate in school activities, including such events as pizza parties, swimming parties, movie trips, "fun days" (regular school activities canceled and other activities scheduled), field trips, and class trips. Since these activities were often directly related to daily attendance, girls who missed school were prevented from participation. To girls who missed school as a result of family responsibilities, such standards were unfair and contributed to their dissatisfaction and disillusionment with school. One college-educated female spoke about the disappointment of being excluded from a school activity because of her absences. She felt that such exclusion often produced the opposite effect from what the school was trying to accomplish—a feeling often expressed by others:

> It was not uncommon for me to miss at least one day of school a week because of some family responsibility. Even though I always tried to catch up and keep my grades up, the principal was always on my back about attendance. I remember that he called me into his office one day, just before my class was to go on a trip, and told me that I had missed too many days and that the teachers had a meeting and decided that I couldn't go. I was crushed. I had been looking forward to this trip. The idea never occurred to any of them [the teachers or administration] that those of us who had so many responsibilities at home needed this trip more than anyone else. To this day, I have been unable to forget . . . or to forgive. The first year I taught school [respondent is a teacher], I was in a school with the same kind of policy. I raised so much hell that the rule was changed. All kids got to go on the class trip. It may work to reward kids for attendance in some settings, but I don't think it works for Indians. There are too many of us who have no control over our lives. Besides, such rewards set a precedent. Once you give a reward for attendance, then it is expected that you give rewards for everything—good behavior, good grades. We need to establish an environment where kids want to come to school because it is important to them. . . . We need to understand those who can't come every day and give special attention to them. I survived this system. As a teacher, my goal is to help others to survive—particularly those girls who grew up like I did— and believe me, there are many of them.

Discussion

Recent research on dropouts suggests that schools and teachers contribute to students dropping out of school. Clearly, in the case of many American Indian girls, it appears that schools and teachers may have been the deciding factor in whether a girl at risk of dropping out actually did so.

FINDING: Retention does not appear to be a major cause of American Indian girls dropping out of school.

Although many of the women in the study reported failing at least one class during their school experience, less than 1 percent of the 991 women in the study were retained in school. Whereas research on urban Indian students has suggested that retention is a major reason for dropping out, that does not appear to be the case with reservation females. Few are retained, and if we are to believe the participants, few felt that retention was even regarded as an option for teachers in Indian schools in reservation communities.

FINDING: Fear of "acting white" appears to contribute to Native American girls' lack of achievement in school.

Generally, all of the women in the study felt that they could have performed better in school had they chosen to do so. Even the women who dropped out felt that they could have succeeded academically had they chosen to stay in school. Most of the women reported that students received passing grades as long as they attended school, accepted the school rules for behavior, and made a minimal effort. In almost all cases, the women attributed "passing" Indian students, regardless of achievement or mastery level, to teachers' lack of expectations. However, "passing" and achieving to the best of one's ability were two very different things. Students who excelled were labeled as "being white" or "acting white," and nearly one-half of the women in this study spoke of compromising achievement in order to avoid harassment by their peers. The women also reported that rebelling against rules of the classroom was acceptable, because if you were "good," you were in fact accepting the standards set by white teachers and white administrators. Breaking rules and passing or failing were more acceptable than being overtly successful or a "star."

It is evident that poor academic achievement affected some of the women in this study and directly impacted their decision to drop out; however, throughout their discussions of academics, the majority of the women reported confidence in their ability to succeed had they chosen that route. From this information, it can be concluded that many chose not to succeed in school or, because of other circumstances, decided to drop out.

FINDING: During preadolescence, American Indian girls often have difficulty forming trusting relationships with teachers or bonding with others in the school.

Nearly half of the women in this study reported that somewhere between the sixth grade and junior high school, they began experiencing "difficulties in school." These "difficulties," which rarely had to do with academic performance, most often centered on behavioral expectations of the teachers, including unrealistic rules, and on teachers who were judgmental, racist, prejudiced, or unfair.

Many researchers have reported on the dramatic physical and psychological changes that, for most children, take place during the adolescent years. Rejection of school rules, teachers, and class work, if it does occur, most often takes place during this period. With American Indian girls, however, this rejection and questioning appears to occur at an earlier age. Perhaps, as the women of this study so aptly stated, it comes from maturing at a much earlier age than girls in mainstream society. Child care and family responsibilities are often delegated to Indian girls as young as five. For those girls growing up in dysfunctional homes, many of them assume the role of the mother and major caretaker of younger children (and often their parents) at a very early age. Add to these conditions the abusive environment of some homes—alcoholism, drug abuse, poverty, the lack of positive role models—and it is understandable why one female commented, "By the time Indian girls are ten, they have done it all, seen it all."

When one examines these issues within the structure of the family and child-rearing practices of American Indian families, it is evident that Indian children become independent very early in life. As small children, they are exposed to adult conversation and adult problems. Perhaps it is not at all unusual to find girls becoming disenchanted with a school curriculum or classroom rules they view as inappropriate for their needs. Furthermore, it is certainly not unusual to find girls rebelling against rules they consider to be for "children," when they already live, function, and survive in an adult world. It is important for educators to realize that the world of the majority of preadolescent American Indian girls is not dance classes, Girl Scouts, and birthday parties. Instead, for many of them it is dealing with adult problems and adult responsibilities at a very early age. Curricula, rules, and teacher behaviors should be adapted to address these problems and the special needs of the American Indian female.

Finally, girls who perceive teachers as uncaring often develop a resistance to school or a general distrust of school. This attitude appears to emerge at a very early age, and subsequent encounters with uncaring or insensitive teachers serve to reinforce their negative attitudes toward teachers and school. In many cases, these encounters result in girls eventually dropping out of school.

FINDING: Transferring from one school to another may impact an American Indian girl's decision to leave school before graduation.

It is quite obvious that transferring from one school to another had a detrimental effect on the social and emotional adjustment of Indian females in this study. Dropout literature often focuses on the academic disruption for students who transfer. In the case of American Indian girls, it appears that being uprooted from a familiar environment has a much more devastating effect on their social and emotional well-being than on their academic performance—at least, in their opinion.

Parents need to be aware of the negative impact of moving children from one school to another, particularly when those moves persist over a number of years. Women in this study who graduated from high school and college had less mobile parents and remained in a school and community environment where they felt safe.

Teachers and school administrators must be more sensitive to the issue of mobility of Indian parents as well. Women in this study were blamed, humiliated, and ignored by teachers, counselors, and administrators who in fact had "given up" on them because their parents relocated frequently. This hostile environment created many problems for the women in the study, and in many cases resulted in their dropping out of school.

FINDING: American Indian women who are high school dropouts hold high expectations for their children to succeed in school.

It is often reported in the literature that parents who are dropouts frequently harbor resentment against the school and therefore influence their own children to drop out, thus perpetuating the dropout syndrome into the next generation. Although many of the women in this study admittedly harbor resentment toward teachers and schools, there was no evidence that such resentments impact these women's desire for their children to learn and be successful in school. In fact, all of the respondents said that they wanted their children to graduate from high school, and 94 percent had expectations that their children go to college.

Although many of the women held bitterness toward the school, and particularly the teachers and administrators whom they perceived as uncaring, they did not believe that their experiences should prevent their children from succeeding in school. In fact, there was an almost unanimous belief among the female parents that their experiences would help them help their children. Half the women in this study perceived themselves to be much more vocal regarding injustices than their parents' generation. In addition, many of the women, because of their experiences, felt they were in a better position to detect problems.

Although it is clear that Indian women want their children to be successful in school, the question becomes whether or not that desire is communicated to the child. If parents truly want their goals to be realized, they must communicate those expectations to their children and they must demand that the teachers in the school have similar expectations. Fearing teachers and administrators and allowing children to stay home from school as an alternative to confronting difficult situations communicate to children an inappropriate method for dealing with problems.

FINDING: Conflicts with undesirable teachers have resulted in a number of American Indian girls dropping out of school.

Nearly one-fifth of the women in this study reported conflicts or problems with teachers that resulted in their leaving school prematurely. Nearly one-third of the women claimed that the reservation attracted undesirable teachers. From their descriptions, their assessments may be correct. Women described teachers who had sexually harassed them, sexually abused them, verbally and physically abused them, psychologically abused them, and introduced them to drugs and alcohol. Many described a school system that was indifferent, administrators who did not want to hear their complaints and punished them if they brought charges against teachers, alienation in a setting where their family situation or cultural traditions were not understood, and repeated injustices and lack of consistency in rules and regulations.

FINDING: Encouragement and support from caring teachers have resulted in American Indian girls staying in school and graduating.

Nearly one-fourth of the women who graduated from high school or college reported having a teacher who made a positive impact on their decision to stay in school and graduate. Clearly, research shows that caring teachers are critical to keeping adolescents in school.

Furthermore, research demonstrates that one of the resiliency factors for keeping at-risk students in school is a caring adult. Women spoke fondly of teachers who cared and believed in them. These teachers not only had high expectations for themselves, but also set high expectations for the women. In other words, these positive role models believed in them, encouraged them, and reminded them as often as necessary, both in word and deed, that they were competent, capable individuals.

FINDING: For American Indian girls, excessive absence from school is linked to dropping out.

American Indian girls are frequently absent from school. Absences and tardiness are often not of their choosing. Although many girls admitted to skipping school or staying home from school on occasion, this behavior was not the norm.

Whether it is actually the absence from school that results in decreased academic performance or whether it is the home situation or personal problems that result in lack of interest in school is hard to delineate. Certainly, for some women the lack of trust or bonding with a teacher results in excessive absences. As children, the women in this study did not want to go to school if they felt threatened by their teacher, and in the majority of the cases, they were not forced to go to school by their parents.

Summary

Although general research on schools and dropouts suggests that the primary school-related reason for students leaving school early is that they are attempting to escape failure, this does not appear to be the case with American Indian girls. It appears that for American Indian girls, the decision to drop out stems from an accumulation of school factors. Many of the women in this study who dropped out of school left behind a history of humiliation, perceived lack of caring on the part of school personnel, lack of individual attention, and an atmosphere of indifference toward them as individuals. Although academic performance may be impacted by these factors, this was not always the case with the women in this study. Clearly, in many cases, school rules were considered foreign and absurd. The values of the home and the school were different, resulting in miscommunication between student and teacher that led to anger and frustration on the part of both parties.

Women repeatedly spoke of situations in which the teachers treated them as though they were irresponsible, or treated them with lack of respect or with indifference. In many cases, this set into motion the self-fulfilling prophecy of failure and rejection. Repeated offenses resulted in distancing from the teacher and the school, in a loss of trust and lack of bonding with the school, and finally in dropping out. When school is viewed as a hostile environment, skipping school and absenteeism are frequent practices.

Indian schools attract all types of teachers. Some are undesirables. Within reservation schools, those undesirables may constitute a greater proportion of the faculty than in nonreservation schools. It is generally agreed that, for a number of reasons, 5 to 10 percent of the teachers in mainstream schools are poor teachers. It appears, at least from the testimony of the women in this study, that American Indian schools attract two to three times that many. Part of the reason is a bureaucratic system that inhibits dismissal of teachers within the BIA, and often in the public schools. Another contributor is the isolation of many reservations. Recruitment of outstanding teachers is often difficult, as the reservation has little to offer in terms of spouse employment, recreational activities, and community involvement for teachers. Further, many reservation schools employ teachers "from nearby towns." Many of those same people have been raised with prejudiced and stereotypical views of Indian students, but return to their hometowns to teach because of ranches and farm holdings owned by their families. They bring those prejudices and stereotypes into the classroom, often perpetuating a cycle of bias and racism.

Indian school boards and administrators must become attentive to these issues. Teachers must be screened very carefully. At a minimum, they should be trained to work with at-risk youth, and at a minimum, they should be required to do more than teach. Teachers who refuse to become involved in the school and the lives of students and their extracurricular activities should be removed. American Indian people can no longer afford to entrust their children to the debilitating influence of these "undesirable" teachers.

Based on the responses of the 991 women in this study, it is obvious that there are some very good teachers in Indian schools and many very bad teachers. School boards and administrators might consider identifying those "good teachers" who impact the lives of students and offering special incentives for them to remain on the reservation, such as paid sabbaticals, release time to counsel students, and time to train and mentor teachers new to the system. There is a desperate need to capitalize on what "good teachers" are doing to affect the lives of children.

Part 3

The Search for a Solution

Chapter 17

What Does It All Mean?

Introduction

When I began this study, I hoped to find "a critical element" that other researchers had missed when trying to explain why nearly half of the American Indian students who enter kindergarten will not graduate from high school. By the time this study was completed, I had actually found that dropping out is a multifaceted issue. Through no fault of their own, American Indian girls set out on the path to school failure, often very early in life. As they encounter one disappointment, failure, and humiliation after another, they eventually drop out. In some cases, the family condition is a critical element, but more importantly, the schools themselves contribute significantly to American Indian girls dropping out of school.

As a bilingual educator, I found it both enlightening and interesting to discover that cultural discontinuity, which so often has been cited in the research as the major cause for dropping out, is in truth only one factor impacting the educational career of a female American Indian student. Certainly, the solution many researchers have proposed for discontinuity—"a culturally relevant curriculum"—does not appear to be the answer. In this study, the main factor as it related to discontinuity was students' lack of adjustment, upon entering school, to teacher behaviors, communication styles, and expectations. Although this lack of adjustment was often rooted in the cultural differences between teachers and students, the content of the school curriculum did not appear to be a primary issue. Clearly, this study demonstrated that the teachers and students discussed herein communicated from very different perspectives, and this created feelings of alienation among students.

Moreover, I completed this study with a renewed sense of pride in being a "Sister in the Blood." The women in this study demonstrated a striking ethos of family support, independence and interdependence (not dependence), and resourcefulness. Many of them shouldered the burden of family responsibilities, often at great cost to any personal ambition. And however painful their personal experiences were and are, they have maintained their commitment to family and, in the majority of cases, to their traditional values and cultures. They accept willingly their role as harbingers of their culture. The majority of them understand that no matter how hard they work or how well they are prepared, there will always be limited opportunities for them. Yet they are universally in agreement that education is necessary and critical for the survival of their people.

In order to make a difference in the lives of American Indian students, educators must first recognize that being American Indian sets children apart. It is much harder for American Indian students to succeed academically when the schools, including those on Indian reservations, are insensitive to the children's needs or misinterpret the issues examined in this book, particularly such concerns as racism, stereotyping, discrimination, teacher expectations, suspension and retention, cultural insensitivity, and family relationships.

Unfortunately, there were too many instances where the women in this study reported lack of expectations on the part of teachers, stereotyping in the schools, and racist attitudes for me to ignore those reports. These accounts were not confined to one state or one reservation; they were found to exist among women of all the tribal groups represented in this study.

As parents, we must realize that we are the first teachers of our children and that children learn from us both the good and the bad. We share the responsibility with the school of ensuring that our children are bicultural, that they are proud of their heritage, and that they can indeed make a difference, if not in the world, then at least on their reservation and within their families.

As members of tribal groups, we must insist that our children be assured of better health care, better housing, and better nutrition, elements that will enable them to go to school and to participate in a way that creates a healthy body, mind, and spirit. Tribal leaders must lay aside internal politics and tribal differences and work to promote economic growth and stability on reservations, which in turn will reduce the poverty conditions for our children. Furthermore, tribal groups have the responsibility of deciding where they fit in the scheme of America, determining what it really means to be a member of a particular tribe, and articulating those ideas to their membership. We can no longer allow outsiders to define who is Indian, or ultimately there will be no Indians. We have to stand steadfast in defense of our language and culture if that is what is important to the people of the reservation. We cannot assume that others will protect those interests for us.

In this chapter, I hope to shatter the disturbing silence about Indian education and contribute to the discussion of how school districts, states, and the nation can advance the educational and vocational opportunities of one of their least visible segments—the most rapidly growing and most vulnerable segment of the adolescent population: American Indian youth. Further, this chapter not only will examine the major factors involved in dropping out, but also will address the major factors involved in remaining in school.

What the Dropouts Said about Why They Left School

This study of the dropout phenomenon among American Indian women showed that dropping out is a multifaceted problem. It starts early, often in kindergarten or the first grade; it has many factors; and it grows incrementally worse with each successive year a student is in school. A series of negative school experiences sets in place a growing sense of dislocation, alienation, and frustration on the part of students. As a result, many of the women in this study reported seeing themselves as misfits or rebels at very early ages and began to blame themselves for their inability to function within the classroom setting.

Furthermore, the study revealed that dropping out is not confined to a handful of students who cannot learn. In fact, ability has little to do with whether or not an American Indian female will drop out.

Perhaps more interesting was that almost all of the dropouts reported that when they entered junior high school or high school, they had every intention of graduating. For the most part, the women expected to graduate. Many of them planned to go to college. Even when they dropped out, many of them held on to their dreams; many obtained GEDs, and some even graduated from college.

In order to understand this phenomenon, it is important to examine the causes of dropping out as candidly identified by the women themselves.

Uncaring, Insensitive Teachers

The study clearly showed that the women held very high expectations for their teachers. In fact, it was not enough, according to the women in the study, for their teachers to be "nice" or "friendly"; they preferred teachers who had the ability to teach and who displayed a sense of optimism in dealing with the slower students, as well as with the good students. These expectations on the part of the women in this study unmistakably showed their willingness and desire to learn and to participate in education. Unfortunately, many of the women did not encounter those kinds of teachers. In fact, most of the women spoke of encounters with teachers who had low expectations of both their students and themselves.

Many women reported negative experiences with teachers who put them down. They were called "dumb," "squaws," "baby factories," or "wild Indians." They reported teachers who "yelled," "screamed," or "hit." They described teachers who humiliated them, nagged them, and lost control when students didn't understand something. In some cases, they described teachers who violated the trust associated with the teacher-student relationship by engaging in such dysfunctional behaviors as physically and sexually abusing the student or introducing alcohol and drugs to the student and her peer group. Others spoke quite eloquently about racism, prejudice, and stereotyping. They felt helpless and confused as to why school boards did not protect them from teachers who obviously held contempt for Indian people and their cultures.

Other women described experiences that can best be identified as invisible barriers to student performance. These were most often reported through descriptions of interactions between the teacher and the student within the classroom setting. These interactions were described in terms of teachers who blatantly had "favorites," teachers who "praised good students and ignored the poor students," and teachers who "ignored poor students who held up their hands to ask questions." Others talked of teachers' body language and facial expressions sending covert messages of "rejection," "contempt," or "dislike."

As these experiences mounted up, the women in this study began to disengage psychologically from school. Many of them outwardly rebelled by walking out of class, while others "skipped" school or simply refused to participate in class activities. In most cases, skipping school was not fun. Perhaps more devastating was returning to school and finding out they had not been missed. Although skipping affected their grade performance to some degree, most "passed" their classes, thereby receiving further reinforcement of the idea that the teachers really didn't care whether they learned or not, but instead just wanted to pass them and get rid of them.

Oppressive School Policies and Poor School Climate

The majority of the 991 women in this study related negative school experiences. As these negative experiences accumulated, they began to outweigh the positive experiences. As a result, the students' perceptions of themselves and the school began to plummet and the women began to doubt whether they belonged in school. Although many of the women addressed negative school experiences with teachers, counselors, and administrators, many of them also talked about other conflicts within the school environment.

Women wished for a school environment where students "did not fight," "did not make fun of each other," or "did not call each other names." Others longed for an environment where students were treated fairly and consistently, and not on the basis of "who your family is" or "how much Indian you are."

Others talked about school policies, especially regarding out-of-school suspension—which the women most often referred to as a "three-day vacation"—and about their feelings of alienation regarding such policies. Although out-of-school suspension rests on the belief that temporary exclusion from school will somehow miraculously motivate students to change their behavior, the women in this study reported that it amounted to no more than a reinforcement of the idea that the schools wanted "to get rid of them." Others called in-school suspension a "farce" or a "joke." All too often, in-school suspensions are used to reduce the number of out-of-school suspensions and appear to be a way of concealing the number of students still being excluded from a teacher's classroom. In many cases, the women in this study felt that their teachers used in-school suspension as a "dumping ground" for students they didn't want in class. Many of the women described in-school suspension as "a place where they give you busywork that they don't even bother to check," or as "a punishment room" where students write that they "will not chew gum," "will not speak out in class," or "will do [their] homework" several hundred times before being released. In the majority of cases, the women talked about other punishments related to in-school suspension, such as not being allowed to go to the lunchroom, talk with other students during the lunch break, or take more than two bathroom breaks during the entire school day. Many of the women confided they had found asking for a bathroom break embarrassing and simply remained in their seats all day.

Others talked about school practices that literally prevented students from attending school. For example, some schools had policies prohibiting students from entering a classroom if they were tardy; others required a letter or visit from a parent; and still others required a visit to the principal. Many of the women reported that, when faced with such classroom exclusions, they resorted to "roaming the halls," "sitting in the bathroom," or "leaving school." Several of the females explained that it was "less hassle" to stay out for one class and go to the next, since "the teachers seldom checked up when you didn't return." Others said such exclusions were another way of "getting rid of you for the day."

A majority of the women spoke about school practices regarding absences. Few of them felt that the school was sensitive to the personal conditions that contributed to their excessive absences. For example, many of the women in the study reported conflicting obligations to their families, requiring them to care for younger siblings or to assist with family business. Others talked about staying home from school because they didn't want to deal with a particular teacher or to face humiliation. Many of these women reported "sleeping through class," or remarked that "school was boring," or "school was not for me."

A majority of the women talked about the enormity and inaneness of classroom rules, which ranged from "no gum chewing," "standing in line," "raising your hand," "no talking," and "no getting out of your seat," to obtaining permission to perform even the necessary tasks associated with learning, such as sharpening a pencil or getting a dictionary. Many of them found such controls in junior high and senior high inappropriate to their maturation levels and expressed their disapproval by breaking the rules.

As other researchers on the dropout problem have reported, dropping out is complex because the act of rejecting school is also accompanied by the belief that the institution has rejected the person. Whether school policies and teacher rules communicate implicitly or explicitly that certain students are not desirable or welcome in school, students respond by developing a set of negative perceptions and beliefs about themselves and the school. This is reinforced by ongoing negative school experiences, further undermining students' attitudes toward school. When school policies and teacher expectations negatively interact with students' perceptions about themselves and of school in general, it creates alienation. As one negative experience leads to another, these experiences ultimately combine to destroy a student's hopes, dreams, and aspirations about education. School personnel caught up in this vicious circle are often ambivalent about students and their perceptions.

Teen Pregnancy

Without question, the most common concrete reason for American Indian girls dropping out of school is pregnancy. Slightly more than half (51 percent) of the women in the study reported that pregnancy was more or less "the straw that broke the camel's back." Unlike other adolescent girls in American society (half of whom choose abortion), Indian girls choose to give birth.

Although in this study, a contributing factor to adolescent pregnancy was the degree to which a girl felt loved at home and appreciated and accepted by her teachers and peers, it is very difficult to determine to what extent those factors impacted premature sexual activity. Clearly, it would appear that by the women's own admission, sex was most often mistaken for love. Consequently, the "search for love and acceptance," which many of them so desperately needed, and which was absent from their home life and at school, often resulted in premature sexual activity and pregnancy.

Although many of the women were totally unprepared for motherhood, many who dropped out of school because of pregnancy reported that they were "on the verge of dropping out anyway," or that pregnancy was "a good excuse to get out of there." Other women, however, stated that even though pregnancy may have delayed their education for a period of time, having a child motivated them to get a GED. Others completed their GEDs and attended college. Some graduated from college and ended up better off financially by their late twenties and early thirties than their peers who had delayed childbearing. Many of the women explained that as a parent, completing their education took on a different meaning. For others, motherhood was an escape from a history of failures, disappointments, and humiliations associated with school, and returning to school was not seen as an option.

Due to the nature of the extended families within American Indian cultures, many of the women who had children prior to high school graduation found themselves afforded a "second chance" by parents or other relatives who took the responsibility for child-rearing. This is not to suggest that all of the women took advantage of the opportunity; nor does it mean that the behavior was not repeated. It does mean, however, that the stigma of being forced to accept the responsibility of child-rearing as a "punishment" for the erring female was almost nonexistent among the women in this study. Further, such attitudes toward pregnancy and child-rearing appear to be a common thread among all tribal groups.

Lack of Adjustment to School

Being able to adjust to school and its demands is one of the most critical elements for children who enter school for the first time. Students must be able to successfully make the transition from home to the school setting. In many cases, the American Indian female appears to have difficulty very early in making that transition. This transition places new demands on students, who are forced to adjust to a setting that is different from and more impersonal than the home environment. A particular impediment to adjustment to school for American Indian girls is incongruence between the expectations of those in the home and those in the school. The problem of incongruence occurs when American Indian girls who have been raised to behave and perform in one culture suddenly confront the white middle-class value structure of the school. Failure to make that transition in the early years continues to create problems of incongruence that may eventually lead to dropping out.

Therefore, when women spoke of "uncaring" lower-elementary teachers who "wouldn't answer your questions unless you held up your hand," or teachers who "wouldn't let us help each other," or teachers who "wouldn't let us talk to our friends," they were in actuality encountering school adjustment problems resulting from an incongruence between acceptable home behaviors and acceptable school behaviors.

Girls who were unprepared prior to school to make this adjustment, or those who were unable to adapt their behaviors to the school, felt "out of place" in their early school years. This alienation promoted a continued lack of adjustment to the school that compounded over the years, with many of these girls being labeled as "incorrigible," "troublemakers," "rebels," or "misfits" by their teachers.

Peer Pressure and Peer Groups

Although peer pressure certainly impacted the behavior of the women in this study, and in some cases resulted in dropping out, peer pressure for American Indian females in many ways takes a unique form. For example, it is a given that one's peers may influence an individual to use alcohol and drugs, smoke cigarettes, or skip school, but American Indian women seem to be caught up in a web of peer pressure that is unlike the situation in mainstream society and may itself contribute to their alienation from school. This behavior, which generally begins in junior high school, often escalates until either the student has "pushed herself into a corner," at which point she finally gives up and drops out, or the school has "pushed the student out."

For example, the women candidly admitted to participating in group activities that were inappropriate for a school setting. Teachers, on the other hand, consciously or unconsciously became willing or unwilling participants in these activities. Women openly discussed "rebellion" against unfair, inconsistent, racist, and prejudiced teachers. Group punishment or the humiliation of an individual by teachers was totally unacceptable to the women in this study. Out of peer loyalty, which in more cases than not was family loyalty, the women spoke of total class rejection of a teacher. This rejection was manifested in a refusal to do class work, to do homework, to pay attention, and to engage in other behaviors the teacher might expect. Although these activities were no more than a rejection by the powerless of the standards of the power group, they served little purpose, in that the majority of the women suffered punishment from those in power, such as out-of-school suspension, in-school suspension, and trips to the principal's office. In many cases, parents who felt helpless to deal with the inappropriate behaviors of the teachers felt even more helpless in dealing with the unhappiness of their children and thus allowed them to stay home from school.

Further, peer groups seemed to set the standards for identification of who was "Indian" and who was "white." "Going along with a teacher," "not participating in some plot against a teacher," "getting good grades," or "not skipping school" could be interpreted by the peer group as "being white." Many women in the study spoke of falling victim to this type of group control. For many, there was no greater rejection than being labeled "white" by their peers. Even many of those who were of "mixed heritage" sought to prove their "Indianness" by conforming to group standards when their ethnicity or loyalties were tested by the group. Only those women who had a strong support group of family or friends, were involved in school activities, and had a firm sense of their own personal identity seemed not to fall prey to such pressure.

Conditions of Poverty

Poverty for American Indian girls is not just the socioeconomic status of family. It involves a whole range of behaviors often associated with reservation life and is erroneously attributed by many experts to being "part of the Indian culture." It is part of the everyday lives of a people who have remained the "poorest of the poor" throughout the history of this country. Poverty involves living in communities where alcoholism, drug abuse, lack of job opportunities, welfare, and inadequate housing are often the norm, rather than the exception.

Poverty is part of growing up in a family where the parents are preoccupied or even consumed by immediate survival needs, such as putting food on the table, providing shelter, and paying the utility bills— and have little energy left for loving, playing, nurturing, or teaching. It is part of learning that if you are poor, you are often rejected—rejected by your peers and rejected by your teachers. It is part of learning that if you are poor, you settle for what others do not want. It is part of learning that you do not expect much of yourself or of others. It is part of not expecting to have a better life than your parents. It is part of accepting that the schools are not going to teach you, and when they do not meet your needs, it only reaffirms your beliefs.

Growing up poor places American Indian girls at high risk of dropping out of school. Inadequate nutrition, clothing, and shelter contribute to their personal and family problems. Growing up poor often results in girls not feeling very good about themselves. Growing up poor in many cases stifles motivation and dreams and results in broken promises and loss of will.

Growing up the "poorest of the poor," even on an Indian reservation, where the average income is below the national poverty level, contributes to girls leaving school prematurely. In fact, it may be the root of many of the problems girls encounter in school. Yet rather than confronting the problem of poverty, anthropologists, researchers, and educators have chosen instead to mislabel the conditions of poverty as conditions of culture and have explained away many of the behaviors of students as an "Indian thing," rather than a "poverty thing." As a result, various remedies for the "cultural conflict" experienced by students in school have been devised, with little attention paid to the poverty conditions that have created the problems in the first place.

What the Graduates Said about Why They Stayed in School

One of the issues that has historically puzzled educators about American Indian students is why some students succeed in school and others give up on school when they come from the same cultural groups, the same environment, and, in many cases, the same family. In other words, if we assume that the environmental, cultural, and family conditions are similar for all students, why is it that some students succeed in school and others fail? What are the factors that enable success for one child in a family and failure for another? These questions were the second focus of this research, and every attempt was made to identify the factors of success. In using this approach, I hope that other researchers will actively move toward research that helps identify what successful students do to resist the negative experiences and what makes them resilient. In effect, looking at resiliency factors will help us discover ways to produce more positive outcomes for all students. In using this approach, I found four major commonalities among the women who graduated from high school or college.

A Caring Adult, Role Model, or Mentor

From this study, it is clear that the single most important factor as to whether a girl stayed in school and graduated was the linkage with a caring, competent adult who not only modeled appropriate behaviors but also encouraged the adolescent and served as an advocate when necessary. Women who were able to weather the painful attacks on their personal identities and self-esteem, women who were able to remain in school despite the poverty conditions of the home life or the abusive nature of their relationships with others, almost always reported a close, nonexploitative relationship with a caring adult. In some cases, the adult was a parent, a grandparent, an aunt, or another sensitive adult in the community. In many cases, the adult was an open, caring, nonjudgmental teacher.

Just as uncaring, insensitive teachers were a significant factor in whether a girl dropped out of school, caring, sensitive teachers were a factor in keeping girls in school. Teachers who were accountable for student success, teachers who displayed a sense of optimism and caring for slower students or the most hard-to-teach students, were praised by the women in this study. These teachers seemed to set high expectations for themselves, as well as for their students. They took a personal interest in their students and took the time to praise, encourage, and support students. Many of the women spoke about teachers who took a special interest in them and understood their personal problems. Others talked about teachers who made a special effort to help them with a myriad of personal problems or who took the time to make them feel they were important.

In other cases, many of the women had developed linkages with family members who helped them survive the stresses of school and their personal lives. These women, despite the problems encountered, developed a sense of purpose that helped them discount or disregard negative experiences. Other females, such as mothers, grandmothers, and aunts, most often provided that adult linkage. In some cases, the women spoke of a female they had emulated simply out of a desire to "be like that individual." Often, the female who was being emulated was unaware of the linkage.

Clearly, the impact of a caring adult, role model, or mentor cannot be underrated when it comes to the resiliency of American Indian females.

Effective Schools and Teachers

When women spoke about the schools, generally the conversation turned to one or two teachers who had made a tremendous difference in their lives. Many of the women spoke of teachers they admired and respected and described them as "firm but fair," having "a good sense of humor and respect for students' rights," teachers who set high expectations and "never let us get away with a thing," teachers who "would go out of their way to help us," teachers who "listened instead of talking all the time," and teachers who clearly enjoyed their job and "loved teaching."

Others spoke fondly of teachers who had become their advocates and had intervened with other teachers and administrators in their behalf when a situation seemed unfair or inconsistent. Some told of teachers who became their personal advocates, saving them from abusive home situations or abusive relationships with peers.

Of the women who stayed in school and graduated, but who at some point in their lives considered dropping out, the majority spoke of a teacher who intervened and helped them stay in school. In some cases, these teachers went far beyond offering encouragement; they became active advocates for students caught up in the bureaucracy of school policies or the unfair practices of other teachers. Some of the women related situations where teachers actually "put their jobs on the line" for them. Several spoke of lifelong relationships with teachers who had made a difference in their lives.

One of the unique characteristics of teachers who made a difference in the lives of these female students was that they assisted students whose self-esteem was constantly under attack from other teachers or peers. For example, some of the women talked about teachers who intervened in the classroom when they became the target of humiliation by other students. In other words, teachers not only modeled the behaviors they expected of students, but they openly encouraged communication among peer groups about feelings, stresses, and attitudes that impacted individual students.

Throughout the interviews with the graduates, it became obvious that there are some very good teachers in Indian schools, teachers who view teaching as more than a job, teachers who treat students with respect, and teachers who believe that students can learn regardless of their family background or their race. Teachers who regarded teaching as a process of dealing with the "whole child" did indeed make a difference in the lives of many of the women in this study. As one of the women stated, "They are the real teachers. The others are just putting in time and taking up space."

In addition, some schools had created a climate that was more conducive to student adjustment and happiness in school. In such cases, administrators and school board members were viewed in a much more positive light. Rules were seen as necessary for safety and order, not as attempts to maintain rigorous control over student movement and behavior. Moreover, these schools had not developed a system of rewards and punishments that further isolated students. The school was viewed as a happy place where students were encouraged to become involved in activities and where, according to one graduate, "there was something for everyone." In particular, this graduate was speaking of a school environment that recognized that not all students were going to be athletes or scholars, but provided a variety of activities that were not competitive-based.

Perhaps one of the most revealing findings was that, in spite of a myriad of negative experiences in school, as well as in their personal lives, the women in this study were very slow to give up on school. Those who found some type of support within the school generally never gave up.

A Strong Sense of Spirituality

One of the greatest sources of resiliency for the women in this study was their sense of spirituality. When using the term *spirituality*, I am referring not only to the belief in a "higher being" or "higher authority," whether through an organized Christian church or through connectedness with the various American Indian religious beliefs and ceremonies—but to the spirituality that also results in taking responsibility for one's place in the scheme of things. For the women in this study, their spirituality had nothing to do with being able to speak a Native language or with the degree of their Indian blood; rather, it manifested itself in a strong, moral purpose of life and an "inner voice" that guided the individual. In some cases, women spoke with an enlightened view of the purpose of life on earth and how each individual was born for a special destiny. For many of them, they felt that their "purpose" was to help their people.

The women often spoke of this spirituality and inner peace in abstract terms. For example, many women said they always knew they would succeed, even when others didn't believe it. Others reported rejecting negative experiences and telling themselves, "What goes around comes around. My time will come." Many spoke of an inner voice that helped them reject personal attacks upon their self-esteem. One woman stated, "I just told myself, 'You know who you are. What does she know, or what does he know?'" Many of these women adamantly believed that children are born with this resiliency and that some children nurture it and perfect it, while others fail to use it as a resource. "It all depends on whether you listen to that inner voice when you are a child and keep it with you or you let it go," said one female, a woman who had dropped out of high school but eventually graduated from college.

Low Family Stress

There were a number of family stresses that both the graduates and the dropouts held in common. However, the one intervening factor appeared to be how the family dealt with those stresses. Poverty was a strong stress factor for many of the women who were successful in school, and yet in many of their homes, poverty was not viewed as hopeless. Women who came from poverty and who graduated from school spoke of parents who strongly encouraged them to stay in school and improve their personal conditions; they described parents who, despite the hardships of poverty, outwardly showered them with love, affection, encouragement, and support. Many of the women spoke of parents who, despite their economic condition, always put the children first, parents who played with them, had fun with them, and had time for them.

In almost all of the homes with low family stress, alcohol and drugs were totally absent. Domestic violence and child abuse were absent. The fear of abandonment or psychological separation from the parents was absent. It is particularly important to note that for the graduates, growing up in a nontraditional family with only a single parent did not increase stress levels.

With this in mind, it is essential for parents and other family members to realize that by maintaining a home atmosphere where children feel safe, loved, and wanted, they can contribute immensely to a girl's success in school and to the realization of her potential.

Chapter 18

Using the Past as a Path to the Future

The American Indian female generally comes from a cultural environment where she understands her immediate world and where her learning begins quite early. She learns at a very young age what is important to her family, how she should behave in this familiar setting, and what is valued not only by her family, but by her relatives and the people within the community. None of this learning requires intellectual tools, structured rules, or punitive disciplinary methods. She learns by observing, imitating, and practicing.

On the other hand, at the age of five or thereabouts, the young American Indian girl is thrown into another setting, where she is asked to make a leap from the familiar culture of the home to the unfamiliar culture of the school. She is expected to do this without having any transitional or adjustment experiences. She has little assistance in formulating an understanding of what is expected of her in this new environment. More often than not, she encounters teachers who do not take the time to facilitate her transition and she finds herself lost, confused, detached, frustrated, and angry. Furthermore, she may encounter a system that labels her familiar mode of behavior as "aberrant" and in need of being corrected, without any understanding on her part as to why her behavior is suspect.

Half of these five-year-olds who enter this school culture will graduate from high school, and sadly, half will not. To effect a positive change in these statistics, there are a number of basic approaches that all Indian schools should consider implementing. Some of these approaches may result in a reordering of priorities and resources, but if we are to reach at-risk youth, there is really no alternative. These approaches include the following:

- Ensure a school climate that promotes a positive, humanistic approach to dealing with children and their problems.
- Employ only highly committed teachers who are willing to take on the roles of teacher, counselor, parent, and advocate and to deal with the problems of the "whole child," including a sensitivity to the problems the child may be experiencing at home, as well as at school.
- Implement careful, extensive monitoring and supervision of daily instructional activities.
- Investigate student and parent complaints in a timely, impartial, and consistent manner.

- Establish expectations wherein all children can succeed and wherein teachers are held professionally accountable for the success of students.
- Identify and remediate academic failures of students at each grade level so that any such problems do not persist.
- Offer night school and summer remediation programs for students who fall behind in their classes, regardless of the reason.
- Establish an alternative school, a "school within a school," with a faculty of four or five highly committed teachers who work with a limited number of students (approximately fifty to sixty) so that the students will be involved in a nurturing, caring environment that tends not only to their academic needs but to their emotional, social, and psychological needs.
- Work with community agencies, including the tribal police and judicial system, to help students from dysfunctional families or those in trouble with the law.
- Establish a peer counseling program and a peer tutoring program so that older children can develop responsibility while working with younger children.
- Establish rules that ensure a positive atmosphere and a supportive peer culture.
- Inform and provide inservice to teachers about the problems of the at-risk child and require them to be alert to student needs and problems and to report those concerns.
- Establish a postsecondary planning program that uses computer labs and in-class activities for mock employment situations and offers career exploration projects to motivate students to begin thinking about careers, postsecondary education, and employment.
- Form a community task force on at-risk students to determine how the community can help the schools in meeting students' needs.

Although the above list of components should be a minimum plan for meeting students' needs, any reform in Indian education and effort to reduce the dropout rate should not proceed without an affirmation of what is really meant when we speak of Indian education.

The history of Indian education has basically reflected the goals and interests of American education in general. Currently, there is no evidence that Indian education is working on a broad scale. It has failed to produce teachers, managers, leaders, doctors, nurses, and other professional and technical personnel in sufficient numbers to allow tribes complete sovereignty or independence from experts outside the Indian community. It has not succeeded in keeping half of the students in school, let alone developing a citizenry that has an opportunity to be gainfully employed or can realize its dreams and be hopeful of a better future for its children or grandchildren.

On the other hand, Indian education has succeeded to some degree in the construction of a new generation of Indians who have pulled themselves up from poverty and racism "by their own bootstraps"—which is a crucial complement to those in power for the continuation of the present educational system. Educators and politicians have used the basic "bootstrap" mythology of individual advancement in defense of the inadequacies of Indian education. This approach has overshadowed many of the long-term problems that have existed, such as poverty, inadequate nutrition, poor health care, substandard housing, and an inadequately educated population, and has resulted in American Indians blaming themselves for their failure and personal conditions, rather than protesting the causes of the failure and asserting the need for restructuring Indian schools and Indian communities.

Compounding the problem in Indian education is the fact that American Indians are a small minority in a nation of many larger minority groups, and fragmentation has resulted. In many cases, Indian school districts may have more non-Indians on the school board than Indians. In other cases, school districts and political districts have been gerrymandered in order to deter elections of American Indians to school boards and state governments. As a result, Indian schools often are not operating in the interest of the American Indians within their own communities, but are instead promoting the interests of those outside the Indian community.

In 1966, Norman Chansky wrote about the "untapped good" of high school dropouts, wherein he likened the dropout to a seed. In his analogy, he suggested that just as seeds must have good soil and adequate moisture to sprout and flourish, so must schools provide a nurturing environment for children to learn. If weeds endanger the growth of the "sprouts," they must be eliminated; so must the problems endangering the child's success. In applying Chansky's philosophy to Indian education, it is time for Indian people to eliminate the "weeds" that have endangered tribal groups and the education of Indian youth since the beginning of their interaction with Euro-Americans.[1]

For starters, we must redefine Indian education from the perspective of Indians. We must develop an educational program that gives meaning to our lives as Indians and to our culture, while at the same time instructing students in the underlying ideas of the American culture and providing the intellectual tools needed to survive in a contemporary, global society.

We must listen to our youth. If there is to be a change in Indian education, it must involve them. Contemporary Indian youth are overburdened with the messages we have given them. On the one hand, we tell them we want them to stay in school and do well, even go to college and graduate, but at the same time we tell them not to assimilate or they will be rejected by their own people. We tell them we want them to learn their own language, and yet as adults, we speak English to them—listing innumerable excuses as to why we do not speak or choose not to learn our own Native languages. We raise them to believe that they have a purpose in life and a responsibility to their people, but we fail to guide them in developing goals and purpose and in becoming responsible.

We must listen to our elders who have experienced the past and who tell us that Indian education today is no more than a continuation of the education of a century or two centuries or even three centuries ago. We must learn from them so that we will not continue to repeat the tragedies of the past.

We must challenge ourselves as Indian educators to question our roles within the schools. Many of us, whether intentionally or unintentionally, have become caught up in a struggle between the Indian community and the non-Indian majority who administer our schools. In many cases, we find ourselves not serving as advocates of our communities, but struggling to preserve a system we know does not work.

As tribal groups, we must challenge ourselves to make some very tough decisions about the direction of Indian education. We must decide, first of all, if the Native language is important to our cultural heritage and our identity; and if it is, we must devise a plan to ensure that it will not vanish within the next generation or two. It may be that many tribes will decide that language renewal and restoration is insignificant to their identity as a tribal people. If a tribe decides otherwise, however, it must set in motion a plan for language renewal wherein tribal members take the responsibility for developing it and causing it to flourish as a part of their identity. If the Native language is essential, it should be taught in the schools from kindergarten through high school—not as a foreign language, but as a language children are expected to learn and speak. In doing so, the adults must recognize that they cannot expect of their children what they them-selves are unwilling to do. To expect the schools to be the sole purveyors of the language will most likely guarantee its demise. Therefore, major steps must be taken to ensure that the tribe, the community, the parents, and the schools are involved.

A redefined plan for Indian education will require a broad-based approach from Indian teachers, Indian administrators, Indian researchers, community agencies, tribal governments, and youth and parents working together as a team. There is no one solution to the problems confronting Indian students and no one answer as to why students are dropping out; however, this study does identify four resiliency factors that could be used as a starting point for developing a dropout intervention/prevention program for American Indian students.

Key features of a comprehensive program must include commitment, coordination, awareness, allocation of resources, and individualized attention for American Indian students at risk. The first step is to make parents, teachers, administrators, and school board members aware of the problem, its causes and consequences, and the resiliency factors common to students who are successful. With an understanding of these issues, educators and parents will be in a better position to make a commitment to deal with the problems encountered by American Indian girls.

Recommendations

With these thoughts in mind, I offer the following recommendations for reducing the dropout rate for all American Indian students, male and female:

RECOMMENDATION 1: I believe Indian schools should be restructured to include three "transitional phases" that enable students to adjust to the demands of an academic environment and to develop an understanding of themselves and what their tribal groups expect of them as adults.

Although this recommendation will require that students spend an increased amount of time in completing a high school education, it would appear that the extra time spent would be offset by increased graduation rates, a better-prepared work force, and a population of young people who have a good understanding of themselves and the needs of their tribes.

These transitional phases would occur three times during students' elementary and secondary years. The initial phase would begin when students first enter school. Instead of a full year of kindergarten, students should first be placed in a school setting where they have an opportunity to learn how to interact, communicate, and respond to the expectations of an academic environment. During this period, parents and elders would work with the teachers in developing a school adjustment plan for Indian students, with respect to both the culture of the home and the culture of the school. Teachers within the school would be required to implement teaching strategies that complement the learning environment of the home, while at the same time ensuring that students have a period of time to experiment, explore, and adjust to the use of learning tools, such as books, paper, pencils, and crayons, and to improve communication skills to ensure better student-teacher interaction. Once students leave this transitional phase and move into kindergarten, an emphasis should be placed on vocabulary development to better prepare them for the demands of reading and writing in the lower-elementary years.

The second transitional phase would occur at the end of the fourth grade, prior to the time students enter a middle school environment. From past experience, we know that American Indian students' test scores, achievement tests, and attendance levels begin to plummet during preadolescence. Discipline may become a problem. Attitudes may change. It is during this time that students experience increased negative messages from the school and teachers about their abilities and worth. As these messages accumulate, students begin to disengage from school. It is also during this time that students are changing emotionally, physically, and psychologically. They are gaining independence and maturity. As they come to terms with their changing bodies, their changing roles, their intellectual abilities, their perceptions of themselves, their peers, and their relationships, their world begins to change as well. It is during this time of change for students that schools should also change. A transitional phase at this time should focus on the involvement of elders, other responsible community leaders, parents, and teachers in resolving the conflicts experienced by preadolescents, while at the same time providing an opportunity for students to learn more about themselves and their culture. During this stage, female students could be guided by female elders and male students by male elders, who would teach them about the traditional gender roles within the society, their ceremonies, and tribal lore and history, while simultaneously using traditional counseling methods to allow for social and psychological adjustment.

The third transitional phase would take place following the completion of the eighth grade. It would provide an opportunity for students to continue their training in traditional roles and expectations under the guidance of tribal elders, while also providing them with an opportunity to perfect their basic skills in math, reading, and writing. Completion of this phase would better prepare students to face the academic rigors of high school courses, while at the same time reinforcing their roles within a tribal community and helping them set goals for their roles as adults.

I believe that such a school structure not only would allow students to be better prepared to handle the stresses of school and to be more academically prepared, but would also nurture the child's own "spirituality" and tribal identity through the involvement with elders and other tribal people.

RECOMMENDATION 2: I believe Indian schools should implement a thorough screening and employment process for personnel to guarantee that Indian students are no longer subjected to psychological and physical abuse. This screening process would also ensure that teachers who are employed have demonstrated excellence or the potential for excellence.

Indian school districts should implement immediately a screening and employment process for all school personnel, whether professional, paraprofessional, or other support staff. This screening should not only incorporate a thorough background check, including references, but also require drug and alcohol testing of each potential employee. School boards should be especially discriminating when it comes to applicants who "ricochet" about Indian country, from one reservation to another and from one Indian school to another, like stray bullets. Many of those individuals, who have been found incompetent or unworthy to serve in one Indian district, find employment in another Indian district. This is often the result of districts obtaining unchallenged resignations for the promise of providing future recommendations. In addition, it may be necessary for school boards to implement a policy of a two-year "provisional employment" for all school personnel in order to determine if an individual is suitable to teach or work in a reservation setting. During that time, personnel would be required to become "culturally sensitive" through training and involvement within the community. Moreover, residency and involvement within the reservation community should be a requirement, not an option. Teachers who are unwilling or unable to comply with these expectations should be dismissed or, better yet, not employed in the first place.

Further, Indian people should cease regarding the school system as an "employment bureau" in which school board members are expected to reward family members and other constituents by providing employment within the school. Politics and family loyalties must cease to guide school policies and employment procedures.

In addition, the number of Indian employees should be increased in the schools. Districts should seek out community elders and other respected community persons who can act in a professional capacity (e.g., do traditional counseling) without the requirements of degrees and certification. Furthermore, Indian communities should aggressively seek out young people who demonstrate an interest in and potential for working with children, and provide opportunities for them to go to college and to obtain teaching degrees.

The number of teachers, counselors, and administrators within the schools who are specifically trained to work with high-risk minority children should be increased. American Indians should demand that universities and colleges within their respective states respond to the needs of Indian education, and should boycott those which do not.

In the event that a tribal college is located on a reservation, the school district, community, and tribal leaders should work toward assisting that college in developing four-year degree programs that would allow students the opportunity to remain at home and complete their college degrees. These students, in turn, would be more likely to stay within the community and serve in professional roles.

RECOMMENDATION 3: I believe school district policies should be redesigned so that they are aimed at keeping students in schools, rather than at keeping them out.

A redesign of school district policies should involve school personnel, parents, and students. Many of the current policies regarding discipline, attendance, truancies, and tardies keep students out of school. School boards, teachers, and administrators should be aware that districts with too many rules are simply asking for those rules to be broken. In essence, districts and their personnel are sending out the message that "we expect you to misbehave." It should be emphasized that expectations among school personnel may constitute a self-fulfilling prophecy for children and that harsh disciplinary rules about suspension and expulsion may be interpreted by students as an invitation to drop out. Furthermore, in-class disciplinary rules that promote failing grades, such as the refusal to accept homework under certain conditions, should cease. Classroom discipline and management rules should be kept to a minimum and should facilitate the student's ability to move about the room and within the school in order to take care of personal and academic needs, as long as the student's behavior does not interfere with or hurt his/her learning or another's learning. District and classroom rules should allow students within a reservation community and school to develop a classroom "family relationship." This would encourage students to be supportive of each other and would allow them to work out problems jointly. In this way, they will learn that rules are important and in their own interest.

RECOMMENDATION 4: I believe an "Adopt-a-Student" program should be implemented among faculty, elders, and other responsible community persons to ensure that each at-risk child has a nonexploitative relationship with at least one adult on a daily basis.

School districts cannot afford to ignore the research demonstrating unquestionably that Indian children who succeed in school generally have at least one nonexploitative adult relationship. This individual would have the responsibility of encouraging at-risk students, supporting them, and counseling them. Furthermore, this individual would, when needed, be an advocate on the part of students with the school and other teachers, and would assist in ensuring that students are receiving proper services from other agencies.

It cannot be assumed that these relationships develop on their own; nor can it be assumed that students will initiate such relationships. Within a school setting, "adoptive students" could be assigned through either volunteering or random drawing. Teachers would then be trained in ways of supporting at-risk youth. As a result, the district could be assured that on a daily basis, there would be at least one adult providing positive attention to the at-risk child. Obviously, a critical element of such a plan would include teacher confidentiality with regard to the identity of the "adoptive student." For such a plan to work, the at-risk child should not know that s/he has been "chosen."

The elder volunteers and community persons could serve as advisers and mentors to the students on an "as needed" basis, to ensure that at-risk students have an advocate within the community, as well as in the school. Tribal advocates could help students in ways that teachers may not be able to help. For example, students who experience racism from their peers, problems involving family loyalties, or other problems directly related to their tribal identity may be best served by a tribal member. This plan would also allow for the further nurturing and motivation of the student and could in fact complement the development of a "spirituality" found in students who are most likely to graduate from school.

RECOMMENDATION 5: I believe Indian schools must establish a nontraditional curriculum as an option for students who are at risk, and incorporate within the implementation process a strong dropout retrieval plan.

Despite all the other recommendations I have suggested, the fact is that there will always be a percentage of students who will remain at high risk and will not graduate unless other options are available to them. At this point, no body of research clearly substantiates that a "culturally relevant" curriculum will make a difference in reducing the dropout rate of Indian students. However, a nontraditional curriculum, with an individualized approach in courses like English and math, holds tremendous promise. In addition, the development of semester-long, self-paced course packets in required courses for students who are homebound due to illness or pregnancy, students who are in drug and alcohol rehabilitation programs, and so on, holds great potential for keeping at-risk youth in school. The use of such a nontraditional curriculum could also be combined with the use of cooperative learning components and, where possible, "real-life" reservation examples and problems. Students could be provided with experiential educational opportunities wherein they would receive credit toward graduation by participating in programs within their communities, such as assisting with an elderly program, a child care center, or a Head Start program, or tutoring younger students in the school. Such experiences would not only give at-risk students a greater sense of purpose, but also orient them to the needs of their communities and the world of work.

Furthermore, reservation schools should establish a child care center within the school for girls with children and offer special classes in child development, nutrition, and care, as well as counseling for teenage mothers. Specific to this training should be discussions regarding child abuse. This program should coincide with a program addressing the consequences and responsibilities of teen fatherhood.

In addition to the nontraditional curriculum, school districts should develop a plan for dropout retrieval so as to encourage those students who have dropped out of school to return to school in a way that is nonthreatening to their self-esteem.

A Final Note

In this chapter, I have tried to provide tribal leaders, school leaders, educators, parents, and community persons within Indian communities with a forum for discussion and with suggestions for reevaluating and redefining Indian education. Perhaps as you critique these ideas, you will find that not all of the suggestions are appropriate for your schools or that there are other components that should be initiated in addition to those offered. It is my sincerest hope that this study and the results presented here will, at a minimum, provide a basis for discussion about Indian education.

We can no longer conceal student failure under the guise of cultural discontinuity or socioeconomic status of the family. We can no longer blame our children for their failures. We cannot continue to place the failure of the past three centuries on a government bureaucracy that has not always had our best interests at heart. We must be willing to protest and change the conditions of our schools and bring about the needed reforms on a community-by-community basis.

Moreover, we should fight any attempts to define ourselves and our cultures by anything but those traits, values, traditions, and characteristics which have been passed down by our ancestors. To submit to or embrace outside interpretations serves no purposes but to fuel the fires of racial prejudices, lower our own sense of self-worth, and inhibit the development and potential of ourselves and our children.

In the end, it is up to us, as American Indian people, to hold ourselves accountable for what happens to our schools and in our schools during the next century. We should make it clear that those who are currently teaching in our schools and running our schools really have no choice but to accept the needed reforms. Admittedly, this may be considered a controversial plan of action, but if we as American Indians are serious about the education of our children, we truly have no alternative.

Notes

Chapter 1

1. J.S. Catterall and E. Cota-Robies, "The Educationally At-Risk: What the Numbers Mean," *Accelerating the Education of At-Risk Students* (Stanford, CA: Stanford University, Center for Educational Research at Stanford, 1988), 6–7.
2. H.M. Levin, *The Educationally Disadvantaged: A National Crisis*, Working Paper No. 6, State Youth Initiatives Project (Philadelphia: Public/Private Ventures, 1985), 1.
3. Ibid.; H.L. Hodgkinson, *All One System: Demographics of Education, Kindergarten through Graduate School* (Washington, DC: Institute for Educational Leadership, 1985); S.S. Peng and R.T. Takai, *High School Dropouts: Descriptive Information from High School and Beyond*, Bulletin (Washington, DC: National Center for Educational Statistics, 1983), 1–9; A.J. Kolstad and J.A. Owings, "High School Dropouts Who Change Their Minds about School" (Paper presented at the Annual Meeting of the American Education Association, San Francisco, CA, April 1986).
4. J.L. Kaplan and E.C. Luck, "The Dropout Phenomenon as a Social Problem," *Educational Forum* 42 (1977): 41–56; H.M. Levin, *The Educationally Disadvantaged: A National Crisis*, Working Paper No. 6, State Youth Initiatives Project (Philadelphia: Public/Private Ventures, 1985).
5. K. Polk, "The New Marginal Youth," *Crime and Delinquency* (Englewood Cliffs, NJ: Prentice Hall, 1984); P. Baker, "A Report on the National Longitudinal Surveys of Youth Labor Market Experience in 1982," *Pathways to the Future*, Report No. 4 (Worthington, OH: Ohio State University, Center for Human Resource Research, 1984); D. Mann, "Can We Help Dropouts?" *Teachers College Record* 87 (1986): 307–23.
6. J.S. Catterall, *On the Social Costs of Dropping out of School* (Stanford, CA: Stanford University, Educational Policy Institute, School of Education, 1985); T. Thornberry, M. Moore, and R.L. Christian, "The Effect of Dropping out of High School on Subsequent Criminal Behavior," *Criminology* 23 (1985): 3–18.
7. H.L. Hodgkinson, *All One System: Demographics of Education, Kindergarten through Graduate School* (Washington, DC: Institute for Educational Leadership, 1985); Centers for Disease Control Study, "One-Fourth Infants Born to Single Moms" (AP Wire Service, Washington, DC), *Bozeman* [MT] *Daily Chronicle*, 3 August 1990, pp. 1, 3.
8. M. Fine and P. Rosenberg, "Dropping out of High School: The Ideology of School and Work," *Journal of Education* 165 (1983): 257–72.
9. S.S. Peng and R.T. Takai, *High School Dropouts: Descriptive Information from High School and Beyond*, Bulletin (Washington, DC: National Center for Educational Statistics, 1983), 1–9; S.M. Barro, *The Incidences of Dropping Out: A Descriptive*

Analysis (Washington, DC: SMB Economic Research, Inc., 1984); R.B. Ekstrom, M.E. Goertz, J.M. Pollack, and D.A. Rock, "Who Drops out of High School and Why? Findings from a National Survey," *Teachers College Record* 87, no. 3 (1986): 356–73; G.G. Wehlage and R.A. Rutter, "Dropping Out: How Do Schools Contribute to the Problem?" *Teachers College Record* 87 (1986): 374–92; R.W. Rumberger, "Dropping out of High School: The Influence of Race, Sex, and Family Background," *American Educational Research Journal* 20, no. 2 (1983): 199–220; L. Smulyan, "Gender Differences in Classroom Adolescence" (Paper presented at the Annual Conference of Research on Women in Education, Howard University, Washington, DC, 1986); D. Sadker and M. Sadker, "Exploding Zepezauer's Mini-Mind Field," *Phi Delta Kappan* 63, no. 4 (1981): 272–73; C. Dweck, T.E. Goetz, and N. Strauss, "Sex Differences in Learned Helplessness, IV: An Experimental and Naturalistic Study of Failure Generalization and Its Mediators," *Journal of Personality and Social Psychology* 38 (1980): 441–52.

10. L. Smulyan, "Gender Differences in Classroom Adolescence" (Paper presented at the Annual Conference of Research on Women in Education, Howard University, Washington, DC, 1986); J.R. Mokros, "Hidden Inequities Can Be Overcome," *Voc Ed* 59 (May 1984): 39–41.

11. D. Sadker and M. Sadker, "Exploding Zepezauer's Mini-Mind Field," *Phi Delta Kappan* 63, no. 4 (1981): 272–73.

12. E.H. Erikson, *Identity: Youth and Crisis* (New York: W.W. Norton and Co., 1968); C. Gilligan, *In a Different Voice: Psychological Theory and Women's Development* (Cambridge, MA: Harvard University Press, 1982); L. Smulyan, "Gender Differences in Classroom Adolescence" (Paper presented at the Annual Conference of Research on Women in Education, Howard University, Washington, DC, 1986).

13. S. Malcolm, *Equity and Excellence: Compatible Goals. An Assessment of Programs That Facilitate Increased Access and Achievement of Females and Minorities in K–12 Mathematics and Science Education* (Washington, DC: American Association for the Advancement of Science, Office of Opportunities in Science, 1984).

14. F. Erickson, "Transformation and School Success: The Politics and Culture of Educational Achievement," *Anthropology and Education Quarterly* 18 (1987): 335–56; K.N. Giles, *Indian High School Dropout: A Perspective* (Milwaukee: University of Wisconsin—Milwaukee, Midwest National Origin Desegregation Assistance Center, 1985); S.V. Goldman and R. McDermott, "The Culture of Competition in American Schools," *Interpretive Ethnography of Education*, ed. G. Spindler and L. Spindler (Hillsdale, NJ: Lawrence Erlbaum Associates, 1987).

15. M. Gibson, "Punjabi Immigrants in an American High School," *Interpretive Ethnography of Education*, ed. G. Spindler and L. Spindler (Hillsdale, NJ: Lawrence Erlbaum Associates, 1987); W. Mahood, "Born Losers: Dropouts and Pushouts," *NASSP Bulletin* 65 (1981): 54–57; H.M. Levin, *The Costs to the Nation of Inadequate Education*, Report to the U.S. Senate Select Committee on Equal Education Opportunity (Washington, DC: GPO, 1972); S. Bowles and H. Gintis, *Schooling in Capitalist America* (New York: Basic Books, 1976); T.P. Carter, *Mexican-Americans in School: A History of Educational Neglect* (New York: College Entrance Examination Board, 1970).

16. H.M. Bahr, B.A. Chadwick, and R.C. Day, eds., *Native Americans Today: Sociological Perspectives* (New York: Harper and Row Publishers, Inc., 1972); A.R. Jensen, *Straight Talk about Mental Tests* (New York: Free Press, 1981); L.M. Dunn, *Bilingual Hispanic Children on the U.S. Mainland: A Review of Research on Their Cognitive, Linguistic, and Scholastic Development* (Circle Pines, MN: AGS, 1987); J. Ogbu, *Minority Education and Caste: The American System in Cross-Cultural Perspective* (New York: Academic Press, 1978); H. Trueba, *Raising Silent Voices: Educating the Linguistic Minorities for the 21st Century* (New York: Harper and Row Publishers, Inc., 1988); F. Erickson, "Transformation and School Success: The Politics and Culture of Educational Achievement," *Anthropology and Education Quarterly* 18 (1987): 335–56.

17. K.H. Au and C. Jordan, "Teaching Reading to Hawaiian Children: Finding a Culturally Appropriate Solution," *Culture and Bilingual Classroom: Studies in Classroom Ethnography*, ed. H. Trueba, G. Guthrie, and K. Au (Boston, MA: Newbury House, 1981); H. Trueba, *Raising Silent Voices: Educating the Linguistic Minorities for the 21st Century* (New York: Harper and Row Publishers, Inc., 1988); R. Tharp and R. Gallimore, *Rousing Minds to Life: Teaching, Learning, and Schooling in Social Context* (New York: Cambridge University Press, 1988); J. Richards, "Learning Spanish and Classroom Dynamics: School Failure in a Guatemalan Maya Community," *Success or Failure? Learning and the Language Minority Student*, ed. H. Trueba (New York: Newbury Publishers, 1987); N. Hornberger, "Iman Chay? Quechua Children in Peru's Schools," *School and Society: Learning Content through Culture*, ed. H. Trueba and C. Delgado-Gaitan (New York: Praeger Publishers, 1988); D. Deyhle, "Learning Failure: Tests as Gatekeepers and the Culturally Different Child," *Success or Failure? Learning and the Language Minority Child*, ed. H. Trueba (New York: Newbury Publishers, 1987).

18. G. Austin, *Drugs and Minorities*, NIDA Research Issues, Series 21, DHEW Pub. (ADM) (Washington, DC: GPO, 1977), 78-507; B. Hanson, "Drug Treatment Effectiveness: The Case of Racial and Ethnic Minorities in America—Some Research Questions and Proposals," *International Journal of the Addictions* 20 (1985): 99–137; P. Iiyama, M.S. Nishi, and B. Johnson, *Drug Use and Abuse among U.S. Minorities* (New York: Praeger Publishers, 1976); J.E. Trimble, A. Padilla, and C. Bell, *Drug Abuse among Ethnic Minorities*, NIDA Office of Science Monographs, DHHS Pub. (ADM) (Washington, DC: GPO, 1987), 48-1474; M.B. Tucker, "U.S. Ethnic Minorities and Drug Abuse: An Assessment of the Science and Practice," *International Journal of the Addictions* 20 (1985): 1021–47; J.W. Welte and G.M. Barnes, "Alcohol Use among Adolescent Minority Groups," *Quarterly Journal of Studies on Alcohol* 48 (1987): 329–36; R. Wright and T.D. Watts, "Alcohol and Minority Youth," *Journal of Drug Issues* 18 (1988): 1–6.

19. S. Fordham and J.C. Ogbu, "Black Students' School Success: Coping with the 'Burden of Acting White,'" *The Urban Review* 18, no. 3 (1986): 176–206.

20. H.M. Bahr, B.A. Chadwick, and R.C. Day, eds., *Native Americans Today: Sociological Perspectives* (New York: Harper and Row Publishers, Inc., 1972); J.F. Bryde, *The Sioux Indian Student: A Study of Scholastic Failure and Personality Conflict* (Vermillion, SD: Dakota Press, 1970); E.A. Fuchs and R.J. Havighurst,

To Live on This Earth: American Indian Education (Albuquerque, NM: University of New Mexico Press, 1983).

Chapter 2

1. B. Berry, *The Education of American Indians: A Survey of the Literature* (Washington, DC: GPO, 1968).
2. F.P. Prucha, *Documents of United States Indian Policy* (Lincoln, NE: University of Nebraska Press, 1975), 110–14.
3. G.E. Faye, ed., *Charters, Laws, and Congressional Acts for Indian Tribes in North America* (Greeley, CO: Colorado State College Press, 1967), 763.
4. Indian Peace Commission, *Report to Congress, 1868* (Washington, DC: GPO, 1868), 1643.
5. Board of Indian Commissioners, *Report to Congress, 1873* (Washington, DC: GPO, 1874), 2493.
6. U.S. Senate and House Indian Affairs Committees, *First Annual Report to the Congress of the United States* (Washington, DC: GPO, 1874), 104.
7. Quoted in L.W. Wittstock, "Native American Women: Twilight of a Long Maidenhood," *Comparative Perspectives of Third World Women: The Impact of Race, Sex, and Class,* ed. Beverly Lindsay (New York: Praeger Publishers, 1980), 219.
8. R.A. Roessel, Jr., *Handbook for Indian Education* (Los Angeles: Amerindian, 1962), 5.
9. C.G. Foster, S.A. Boloz, and D. Salas, eds., *Reservation Schools and 95-561: The Administrator and the Curriculum* (Flagstaff, AZ: Northern Arizona University, 1980); P. Little, *River of People* (Omaha, NE: Interstate Printing Co., 1983).
10. M. Crow Dog and R. Erdoes, *Lakota Woman* (New York: Grove Weidenfeld, 1990), 31.
11. Quoted in C. Hamilton, ed., *Cry of the Thunderbird: The American Indian's Own Story* (Norman, OK: University of Oklahoma Press, 1972), 246.
12. R.M. Utley, *Last Days of the Sioux Nation* (New Haven, CT: Yale University Press, 1963), 59.
13. Quoted in E.A. Fuchs and R.J. Havighurst, *To Live on This Earth: American Indian Education* (Albuquerque, NM: University of New Mexico Press, 1983), 303.
14. U.S. Department of the Interior, Bureau of Indian Affairs, *Annual Report for Fiscal Year Ended June 30, 1903* (Washington, DC: GPO, 1904), 77.
15. L. Meriam, R.A. Brown, H. Cloud, E. Dale, E. Duke, H. Edwards, F. McKenzie, M. Mark, W.C. Ryan, Jr., and W.J. Spillman, *The Problem of Indian Administration* (Baltimore: Johns Hopkins Press, 1928), 403.
16. Ibid., 21.
17. Ibid., 51.
18. F.P. Prucha, *Documents of United States Indian Policy* (Lincoln, NE: University of Nebraska Press, 1975), 239.
19. H. Aurbach and E. Fuchs (with G. Macgregor), *An Extensive Survey of American Indian Education* (College Park, PA: Pennsylvania State University, 1969), 14.

20. A.M. Josephy, Jr., *The Indian Heritage of America* (New York: Bantam Books, Inc., 1969), 1442.
21. Ibid., 1500.
22. F.P. Prucha, *The Indians in American Society: From the Revolutionary War to the Present* (Berkeley, CA: University of California, 1985).
23. U.S. Congress, Senate Committee on Labor and Public Welfare, Special Sub-committee on Indian Education, *Indian Education: A National Tragedy—A National Challenge*, Report No. 90-501, 91st Cong., 1st sess. (Washington, DC: GPO, 1969), 157.
24. R.M. Nixon, *Message from President Richard Nixon: Recommendations for Indian Policy*, Doc. No. 91-363, 91st Cong., 2nd sess., 8 July 1970, 21.
25. Quoted in J. Noriega, "American Indian Education in the United States: Indoctrination for Subordination to Colonialism," *The State of Native America: Genocide, Colonization, and Resistance*, ed. M.A. Jaimes (Boston: South End Press, 1992), 387.
26. "Excerpts from an Interview with Secretary of the Interior James Watt," *Akwesasne Notes* 23 (Winter 1983): 1–3.
27. E.A. Fuchs and R.J. Havighurst, *To Live on This Earth: American Indian Education* (Albuquerque, NM: University of New Mexico Press, 1983).
28. D. Duston, "Senate Panel Asks Lujan for Action to Help Indians" (AP Wire Service, Washington, DC), *Bozeman* [MT] *Daily Chronicle*, 8 June 1989, p. 3.
29. Quoted in J. Noriega, "American Indian Education in the United States: Indoctrination for Subordination to Colonialism," *The State of Native America: Genocide, Colonization, and Resistance*, ed. M.A. Jaimes (Boston: South End Press, 1992), 388.
30. "Federal Program Funding Continues Downward Spiral," *Lakota Times*, 2 September 1992, p. 1.
31. E.A. Fuchs and R.J. Havighurst, *To Live on This Earth: American Indian Education* (Albuquerque, NM: University of New Mexico Press, 1983), xxiii.

Chapter 3

1. R.H. Pearce, *Savagism and Civilization* (Baltimore: Johns Hopkins Press, 1965); R. Slotkin, *Regeneration through Violence: The Mythology of the American Frontier, 1600–1860* (Middletown, CT: Wesleyan University Press, 1973).
2. C.M. Segal and D.C. Stineback, *Puritans, Indians, and Manifest Destiny* (New York: G.P. Putnam & Sons, 1977); R.F. Berkhofer, Jr., *The White Man's Indian* (New York: Alfred A. Knopf, 1978).
3. R.A. Trennert, Jr., *Alternatives to Extinction: Federal Indian Policy and the Beginnings of the Reservation System* (Philadelphia: Temple University Press, 1975).
4. R.H. Pearce, *Savagism and Civilization* (Baltimore: Johns Hopkins Press, 1965).
5. C.M. Harger, "The Indian's Last Stand," *Outlook* 70 (January 1902): 222–25.
6. Zitkala-Sa, "An Indian Teacher among Indians," *Atlantic Monthly*, March 1900, p. 386.
7. F.E. Hoxie, "Beyond Savagery: The Campaign to Assimilate the American Indians" (Ph.D. diss., Brandeis University, Waltham, [MA], 1977).

8. O.L. Graham, *The Great Campaigns: Reform and War in America, 1900–1928* (Englewood Cliffs, NJ: Prentice Hall, 1971).

9. L.I. Deitch, "The Impact of Tourism upon the Arts and Crafts of the Indians of the Southwestern United States," *Hosts and Guests: The Anthropology of Tourism*, ed. V.L. Smith (Philadelphia: University of Pennsylvania Press, 1977).

10. C.M. Harvey, "The Indians of To-day and To-morrow," *American Review of Reviews* 33 (June 1906): 703–7.

11. E.S. Cahn, ed., *Our Brother's Keeper: The Indian in White America* (Washington, DC: New Community Press, 1969), 5, 8.

12. W.H. Cohen and P. Mause, "The Indian: The Forgotten American," *Harvard Law Review* 81, no. 8 (1968): 1820.

13. E.H. Cherrington, *The Evolution of Prohibition in the United States of America* (Westerville, OH: American Issue Press, 1920), 12.

14. P.A. May, "Alcohol Legalization and Native Americans: A Sociological Inquiry" (Ph.D. diss., University of Montana, Missoula, 1976), 3.

15. C. MacAndrew and R.B. Edgerton, *Drunken Comportment: A Social Explanation* (Chicago: Aldine, 1969).

16. J. Westermeyer, "The Drunken Indian: Myths and Realities," *Psychiatric Annals* 4 (November 1974): 31.

17. Ibid.

18. M. Omi and H. Winant, *Racial Formation in the United States: From the 1960s to the 1980s* (New York: Routledge & Kegan Paul, 1986), 58.

19. G. Riley, *Women and Indians on the Frontier, 1825–1915* (Albuquerque, NM: University of New Mexico Press, 1984), 183–4.

20. E.C. Deloria, *Speaking of Indians* (New York: Friendship Press, 1944), 39–40.

21. G.M. Bataille and C.L.P. Silet, "Economic and Psychic Exploitation of American Indians," *Explorations in Ethnic Studies* 6 (1983): 8–23; J.A. Price, "The Stereotyping of North American Indians in Motion Pictures," *Ethnohistory* 20 (1973): 153–71.

22. C.A. Heidenreich, "Alcohol and Drug Use and Abuse among Indian-Americans: A Review of Issues and Sources," *Journal of Drug Issues* 6, no. 3 (1976): 256–72.

23. W.H. Oswalt, *This Land Was Theirs* (New York: John Wiley and Sons, 1966).

24. R.L. West, "The Adjustment of the American Indian in Detroit: A Descriptive Study" (Master's thesis, Wayne State University, Detroit, 1950).

25. B. Berry, *The Education of American Indians: A Survey of the Literature* (Washington, DC: GPO, 1968): 63-64.

26. E.P. Dozier, "Toward a Background for the Teacher of Indian Students," *Teaching Multi-cultural Populations*, ed. J.C. Stone and D.P. DeNeir (New York: Litton Educational Publishing, 1971); K. Polacca, "Ways of Working with the Navajos Who Have Not Learned the White Man's Ways," *Journal of American Indian Education* 2, no. 1 (1962): 4–16; J.F. Bryde, *Modern Indian Psychology* (Vermillion, SD: Institute of Indian Studies, 1971); R.A. Roessel, Jr., "The Indian Child and His Culture," *Teaching Multi-Cultural Populations*, ed. J.C. Stone and D.P. DeNeir (New York: Litton Educational Publishing, 1971); G.D. Spindler and L.S. Spindler, "American Indian Personality Types and Their Sociocultural Roots," *The Annals of the American Academy of Political and Social Science* 311 (May 1957): 147–57.

27. M.L. Wax, R.H. Wax, and R.V. Dumont, Jr., *Formal Education in an American Indian Community*, Monograph (Kalamazoo, MI: The Society for the Study of Social Problems, 1964).

28. E.S. Cahn, ed., *Our Brother's Keeper: The Indian in White America* (Washington, DC: New Community Press, 1969), 43.

29. J. Morse, *A Report on the Secretary of War of the United States on Indian Affairs* (New York: A.M. Kelley, 1970), 74.

30. T. L. McKenney and J. Hall, *The Indian Tribes of North America with Biographical Sketches and Anecdotes of the Principal Chiefs*, vol. 3 (Edinburgh: J. Grant, 1934), 249.

31. G.D. Spindler and L.S. Spindler, "American Indian Personality Types and Their Sociocultural Roots," *The Annals of the American Academy of Political and Social Science* 311 (May 1957): 147–57.

32. L. Kickingbird, "A Portrait of Indian People in Indian Lands," *American Indian Journal* 9, no. 2 (1986): 23–25.

Chapter 4

1. L.M. Coombs, "The Indian Student Is Not Low Man on the Totem Pole," *Journal of American Indian Education* 9 (1970): 1.

2. K.N. Giles, *Indian High School Dropout: A Perspective* (Milwaukee: University of Wisconsin—Milwaukee, Midwest National Origin Desegregation Assistance Center, 1985).

3. M.L. Mizen, *Federal Facilities for Indians: Tribal Relations with the Federal Government* (Washington, DC: GPO, 1966).

4. A.D. Selinger, *The American Indian High School Dropout: The Magnitude of the Problem* (Portland, OR: Northwest Regional Educational Laboratory, 1968), ERIC ED 026-164.

5. Ibid.; C.S. Owens and W.P. Bass, *The American Indian High School Dropout in the Southwest* (Albuquerque, NM: Southwest Cooperative Educational Lab, 1969), ERIC ED 026-195.

6. T. Coladarci, "High School Dropout among Native Americans," *Journal of American Indian Education* 23, no. 1 (1983): 15–22.

7. D. Chavers, "Indian Education: Dealing with a Disaster," *Principal* 70, no. 3 (1991): 28–29; J. Crawford, "One-third of Navajos Drop out Annually," *Education Week* 1 (1986): 1–3; D. Little Bear, "Effective Language Education Practices and Native Language Survival," *Effective Language Education Practices and Native Language Survival*, ed. J. Reyhner (Proceedings of the Ninth Annual International Native American Language Issues [NALI] Institute, Billings, MT, 8–9 June 1989); N. Hill, "American Indian Student Retention: Pedagogy and Self-Determination," *Opening the Montana Pipeline: American Indian Higher Education in the Nineties*, ed. D. LaCounte, W. Stein, and P. Weasel Head (Sacramento, CA: Tribal College Press, 1991), 46–53; National Center for Education Statistics, *Analysis Report: Dropout Rates in the United States: 1988*, Office of Educational Research and Improvement, U.S. Department of Educa-

tion, NCES 89-609 (Washington, DC: GPO, September 1989); K.G. Swisher, M. Hoisch, and D.M. Pavel, *American Indian/Alaska Native Dropout Study* (Washington, DC: National Education Association, 1991).

8. S.S. Peng and R.T. Takai, *High School Dropouts: Descriptive Information from High School and Beyond*, Bulletin (Washington, DC: National Center for Educational Statistics, 1983), 1–9.

9. W. Renfroe, *Early School Leavers: High School Students Who Left before Graduating*, Publication No. 428 (Los Angeles: Los Angeles Unified School District, Research and Evaluation Branch, 1983); T. Coladarci, "High School Dropout among Native Americans," *Journal of American Indian Education* 23, no. 1 (1983): 15–22.

10. M.M. McBee, *Dropout Report for the 1985–86 School Year* (Oklahoma City: Oklahoma City Public Schools, Department of Planning, Research, and Evaluation, 1986); J.C. Cavatta, *New Mexico Dropout Study: 1981–82 School Year* (Santa Fe, NM: New Mexico State Department of Education, Evaluation, Assessment, and Testing Unit, 1982); J.C. Cavatta and A.S. Gomez, *New Mexico Dropout Study: 1983–84 School Year* (Santa Fe, NM: New Mexico State Department of Education, Evaluation, Assessment, and Testing Unit, 1984).

11. E. Currie and J.H. Skolnick, *America's Problems: Social Issues and Public Policy* (Boston: Little, Brown and Company, 1984), 187.

12. K.N. Giles, *Indian High School Dropout: A Perspective* (Milwaukee: University of Wisconsin—Milwaukee, Midwest National Origin Desegregation Assistance Center, 1985), 6.

13. N. Hill, "American Indian Student Retention: Pedagogy and Self-Determination," *Opening the Montana Pipeline: American Indian Higher Education in the Nineties*, ed. D. LaCounte, W. Stein, and P. Weasel Head (Sacramento, CA: Tribal College Press, 1991), 47, 51.

14. S.S. Peng and R.T. Takai, *High School Dropouts: Descriptive Information from High School and Beyond*, Bulletin (Washington, DC: National Center for Educational Statistics, 1983), 1–9.

15. D. Chavers, "Indian Education: Dealing with a Disaster," *Principal* 70, no. 3 (1991): 28–29.

16. U.S. Census, 1980 (Washington, DC: GPO, 1980).

17. A.G. Sargent, *Beyond Sex Roles* (St. Paul, MN: West Publishing Co., 1977).

18. U.S. Census, 1980 (Washington, DC: GPO, 1980).

19. L. Kickingbird, "A Portrait of Indian People in Indian Lands," *American Indian Journal* 9, no. 2 (1986): 23–25.

20. E.A. Fuchs and R.J. Havighurst, *To Live on This Earth: American Indian Education* (Albuquerque, NM: University of New Mexico Press, 1983); A.D. Selinger, *The American Indian Graduate: After High School, What?* (Portland, OR: Northwest Regional Educational Laboratory, 1968); J.L. Delk, "Dropouts from an American Indian Reservation: A Possible Prevention Program," *Journal of Community Psychology* 2, no. 1 (1974): 15–17; C.S. Owens and W.P. Bass, *The American Indian High School Dropout in the Southwest* (Albuquerque, NM: Southwest Cooperative Educational Lab, 1969), ERIC ED 026-195.

21. E.A. Fuchs and R.J. Havighurst, *To Live on This Earth: American Indian Education* (Albuquerque, NM: University of New Mexico Press, 1983); E.P. Mason,

"Cross-Validation Study of Personality Characteristics of Junior High Students from American Indian, Mexican, and Caucasian Ethnic Backgrounds," *Journal of Social Psychology* 77 (1969): 15–24; A. Burnap, "An Analysis of Self-Esteem in Reservation Indian Youth as Measured by Coopersmith's Self-Esteem Inventory" (Master's thesis, Northern State College, Havre [MT], 1972); F.V. Corrigan, "A Comparison of Self-Concepts of American Indian Students from Public or Federal School Background" (Ph.D. diss., George Washington University, Washington, DC, 1970).

22. T. Coladarci, "High School Dropout among Native Americans," *Journal of American Indian Education* 23, no. 1 (1983): 15–22.

23. R. Clawson, "Death by Drink: An Indian Battle," [Butte] *Montana Standard*, 7 January 1990, p. 5; J.O. Whittaker, "Alcohol and the Standing Rock Sioux Tribe, II: Psychodynamic and Cultural Factors in Drinking," *Quarterly Journal of Studies on Alcohol* 24 (1963): 80–90; D.L. Cahalan and H.M. Crossley, *American Drinking Practices: A National Study of Drinking Behaviors and Attitudes*, Monograph No. 6 (New Brunswick, NJ: Rutgers Center for Alcohol Studies, 1969); W.B. Clark, L. Midanik, and G. Knupfer, *Report on the 1979 National Survey* (Berkeley, CA: Social Research Group, 1981); W.C. Cockerham, "Drinking Attitudes and Practices among Wind River Reservation Youth," *Quarterly Journal of Studies on Alcohol* 36 (1975): 321–26; T.W. Hill, "Life Styles and Drinking Patterns of Urban Indians," *Journal of Drug Issues* 10 (1980): 257–72.

24. R. Clawson, "Death by Drink: An Indian Battle," [Butte] *Montana Standard*, 7 January 1990, p. 5; P.A. May, "Epidemiology of Fetal Alcohol Syndrome among American Indians of the Southwest," *Social Biology* 30 (1983): 374–87.

Chapter 5

1. H.L. Hodgkinson, *The Demographics of American Indians: One Percent of the People—Fifty Percent of the Diversity* (Washington, DC: Institute for Educational Leadership, 1990).

2. H.M. Bahr, B.A. Chadwick, and R.C. Day, eds., *Native Americans Today: Sociological Perspectives* (New York: Harper and Row Publishers, Inc., 1972); M.L. Wax, R.H. Wax, and R.V. Dumont, Jr., *Formal Education in an American Indian Community*, Monograph (Kalamazoo, MI: The Society for the Study of Social Problems, 1964).

3. K.N. Giles, *Indian High School Dropout: A Perspective* (Milwaukee: University of Wisconsin—Milwaukee, Midwest National Origin Desegregation Assistance Center, 1985); E. O'Malley, *American Indian Education Handbook* (Sacramento: California State Department of Education, 1982); J.W. Olson, "The Urban Indian as Viewed by an Indian Caseworker," *The American Indian in Urban Society*, ed. J.O. Waddell and O.M. Watson (Boston: Little, Brown and Company, 1971); S.U. Philips, *The Invisible Culture* (New York: Longman Press, 1983).

4. J.E. Trimble, A. Padilla, and C. Bell, *Drug Abuse among Ethnic Minorities*, NIDA Office of Science Monographs, DHHS Pub. (ADM) (Washington, DC: GPO, 1987), 48-1474; E.R. Oetting, F. Beauvais, R. Edwards, M. Waters, J. Velarde,

and G. Goldstein, *Drug Use among Native American Youth: Summary of Findings (1975–1981)*, NIDA Project Report, Project No. 5, ROIDA1853 (Fort Collins, CO: Colorado State University, 1983).

5. J.O. Okwumabua and E.J. Duryea, "Age of Onset, Periods of Risk, and Patterns of Progression in Drug Use among American Indian High School Students," *International Journal of the Addictions* 22, no. 12 (1987): 1269–76; F. Beauvais and E.R. Oetting, "Inhalant Abuse by Young Children," *Epidemiology of Inhalant Abuse: An Update*, ed. R. Crider and B. Rouse, NIDA Research Monograph No. 85 (Washington, DC: GPO, 1988), 30–33; P.A. May, "Alcohol and Drug Misuse Prevention Programs for American Indians: Needs and Opportunities," *Journal of Studies on Alcohol* 47, no. 3 (1986): 187–95.

6. J. Weibel and T. Weisner, *The Ethnography of Rural and Urban Drinking Practices in California*, Annual Statistical Analysis Report for the California Department of Alcohol and Drug Abuse Programs, Sacramento, CA, 1980; E.D. Edwards and M.E. Edwards, "Alcoholism Prevention/Treatment and Native American Youth: A Community Approach," *Journal of Drug Issues* 18, no. 10 (1988): 103–15; S. Schinke, G. Botvin, J.E. Trimble, M.A. Orlandi, L.D. Gilchrist, and V.S. Locklear, "Preventing Substance Abuse among American Indian Adolescents: A Bicultural Competence Skills Approach," *Journal of Counseling Psychology* 35, no. 1 (1988): 87–90.

7. R. Lin, "The Promise and Problems of Native American Students: A Comparative Study of High School Students on the Reservation and Surrounding Areas," *Journal of American Indian Education* 25, no. 1 (1985): 6–16; R. Clawson, "Death by Drink: An Indian Battle," [Butte] *Montana Standard*, 7 January 1990, p. 5; T. Coladarci, "High School Dropout among Native Americans," *Journal of American Indian Education* 23, no. 1 (1983): 15–22; J.E. Trimble, A. Padilla, and C. Bell, *Drug Abuse among Ethnic Minorities*, NIDA Office of Science Monographs, DHHS Pub. (ADM) (Washington, DC: GPO, 1987), 48-1474.

8. L.B. Boyer, "Folk Psychiatry of the Apaches of the Mescalero Indian Reservation," *Magic, Faith, and Healing*, ed. A. Kiev (New York: Free Press of Glencoe, 1964); J.H. Hamer, "Guardian Spirits, Alcohol, and Cultural Defense Mechanisms," *Anthropologica* 11 (1969): 215–41; T.D. Graves, "Acculturation, Access, and Alcohol in a Tri-Ethnic Community," *American Anthropologist* 69 (1967): 306–21; J.E. Trimble, A. Padilla, and C. Bell, *Drug Abuse among Ethnic Minorities*, NIDA Office of Science Monographs, DHHS Pub. (ADM) (Washington, DC: GPO, 1987), 192; E.R. Oetting, F. Beauvais, and R. Edwards, "Alcohol and Indian Youth: Social and Psychological Correlates and Prevention," *Journal of Drug Issues* 18, no. 1 (1988): 87–101; P.A. May, "Substance Abuse and American Indians: Prevalence and Susceptibility," *International Journal of the Addictions* 17 (1982): 1185–1209.

9. E. Maynard, "Drinking as a Part of an Adjustment Syndrome among Oglala Sioux," *Pine Ridge Research Bulletin* 9 (1969): 40.

10. R.A. White, "The Lower-Class 'Culture of Excitement' among the Contemporary Sioux," *The Modern Sioux*, ed. E. Nurge (Lincoln, NE: University of Nebraska Press, 1970), 175–97; J.O. Whittaker, "Alcohol and the Standing Rock Sioux Tribe, I: The Pattern of Drinking," *Quarterly Journal of Studies on Alcohol* 23 (1962): 468–79.

11. J.A. Stevens, "Social and Cultural Factors Related to Drinking Patterns among the Blackfeet" (Master's thesis, University of Montana, Missoula, 1969), 55.
12. W.C. Cockerham, M.A. Forslund, and R.M. Raboin, "Drug Use among White and American Indian High School Youth," *International Journal of the Addictions* 11 (1976): 209–20; C. Vanderwagen, R.D. Mason, and T.C. Owan, eds., *IHS Alcoholism/Substance Abuse Prevention Initiative: Background, Plenary Session, and Action Plan* (Washington, DC: U.S. Department of Health and Human Services, Indian Health Service, 1987); E.R. Oetting, F. Beauvais, and R. Edwards, "Alcohol and Indian Youth: Social and Psychological Correlates and Prevention," *Journal of Drug Issues* 18, no. 1 (1988): 87–101; R. Carpenter, C.A. Lyons, and W.R. Miller, "Peer-managed Self-Control Programs for Prevention of Alcohol Abuse in American Indian High School Students: A Pilot Evaluation Study," *International Journal of the Addictions* 20, no. 2 (1985): 299–310.
13. G. Mohatt, "The Sacred Water: The Quest for Personal Power through Drinking among the Teton Sioux," *The Drinking Man*, ed. D.C. McClelland, W.N. Davis, R. Kalin, and E. Wanner (New York: Free Press, 1972), 261–75; E.D. Edwards and M.E. Edwards, "Alcoholism Prevention/Treatment and Native American Youth: A Community Approach," *Journal of Drug Issues* 18, no. 10 (1988): 103–15; A. Binion, C. Miller, F. Beauvais, and E.R. Oetting, "Rationales for the Use of Alcohol, Marijuana, and Other Drugs by Eighth Grade Native American and Anglo Youth," *International Journal of the Addictions* 23, no. 1 (1988): 47–64.
14. E.D. Edwards and M.E. Edwards, "Alcoholism Prevention/Treatment and Native American Youth: A Community Approach," *Journal of Drug Issues* 18, no. 10 (1988): 103–15; S. Schinke, M.Y. Bebel, M.A. Orlandi, and G. Botvin, "Prevention Strategies for Vulnerable Pupils: School Social Work Practices to Prevent Substance Abuse," *Urban Education* 22, no. 4 (1988): 510–19; D. Jones-Saumty, L. Hochhaus, R. Dru, and A. Zeiner, "Psychological Factors of Familial Alcoholism in American Indians and Caucasians," *Journal of Clinical Psychology* 39 (1983): 783–90; P.A. May, "Alcohol and Drug Misuse Prevention Programs for American Indians: Needs and Opportunities," *Journal of Studies on Alcohol* 47, no. 3 (1986): 187–95; T.E. Malone, *Report of the Secretary's Task Force on Black and Minority Health, Vol. 1: Executive Summary* (Washington, DC: GPO, 1985); J. Trimble, "Drug Abuse Prevention Research Needs among American Indians and Alaska Natives," *White Cloud Journal of American Indian Mental Health* 3, no. 3 (1984): 22–34; F. Beauvais and S. LaBoueff, "Drug and Alcohol Abuse Intervention in American Indian Communities," *International Journal of the Addictions* 20, no. 1 (1985): 139–71.
15. E.R. Oetting, F. Beauvais, and R. Edwards, "Alcohol and Indian Youth: Social and Psychological Correlates and Prevention," *Journal of Drug Issues* 18, no. 1 (1988): 87–101; E.R. Rhoades, M. Marshall, C. Attneave, M. Echohawk, J. Bjork, and M. Beiser, "Mental Health Problems of American Indians Seen in Outpatient Facilities of the Indian Health Service, 1975," *Public Health Reports* 96, no. 4 (1980): 329–35; P.A. May, "Alcohol and Drug Misuse Prevention Programs for American Indians: Needs and Opportunities," *Journal of Studies on Alcohol* 47, no. 3 (1986): 187–95.

16. L.T. Winfree and C.T. Griffiths, "Youth at Risk: Marijuana Use among Native American and Caucasian Youths," *International Journal of the Addictions* 18, no. 1 (1983): 65.

17. D. Moore, "Reducing Alcohol and Drug Use among Native American Youth," *Prevention Pipeline* 1, no. 5 (1988): 6–7; F. Beauvais, E.R. Oetting, and R.W. Edwards, "Trends in Drug Use of Indian Adolescents Living on Reservations: 1975–1983," *American Journal of Drug and Alcohol Abuse* 11 (1985): 209–29; A. Kaufman, "Gasoline Sniffing among Children in a Pueblo Indian Village," *Pediatrics* 51 (1973): 1060–64; D.C. McBride and J.B. Page, "Adolescent Indian Substance Abuse: Ecological and Sociocultural Factors," *Youth and Society* 11, no. 4 (1980): 475–92; J. Weibel-Orlando, "Substance Abuse among American Indian Youth: A Continuing Crisis," *Journal of Drug Issues* 2 (1984): 313–35; T.J. Young, "Inhalant Use among American Indian Youth," *Child Psychiatry and Human Development* 18, no. 1 (1987): 36–46; P.A. May, "Alcohol and Drug Misuse Prevention Programs for American Indians: Needs and Opportunities," *Journal of Studies on Alcohol* 47, no. 3 (1986): 187–95.

18. R. Crider and B. Rouse, eds., *Epidemiology of Inhalant Abuse: An Update*, NIDA Research Monograph No. 85 (Washington, DC: GPO, 1988); E.R. Oetting, F. Beauvais, and R. Edwards, "Alcohol and Indian Youth: Social and Psychological Correlates and Prevention," *Journal of Drug Issues* 18, no. 1 (1988): 87–101.

19. L. Gilchrist, S. Schinke, J.E. Trimble, and G.T. Cvetovich, "Skills Enhancement to Prevent Substance Abuse among American Indian Adolescents," *International Journal of the Addictions* 22, no. 19 (1987): 871–72.

20. L.T. Winfree and C.T. Griffiths, "Youth at Risk: Marijuana Use among Native American and Caucasian Youths," *International Journal of the Addictions* 18, no. 1 (1983): 53–70.

21. M.D. Topper, "Drinking Patterns, Cultural Changes, Sociability, and Navajo Adolescents," *Addictive Disease* 1 (1974): 97–116; R.F. Bales, "Cultural Differences in Rates of Alcoholism," *Quarterly Journal of Studies on Alcohol* 6, no. 4 (1946): 480–99; F. Streit and M.J. Nicolich, "Myths versus Data on American Indian Drug Abuse," *Journal of Drug Education* 7 (1977): 117–22; E.R. Oetting, F. Beauvais, and R. Edwards, "Alcohol and Indian Youth: Social and Psychological Correlates and Prevention," *Journal of Drug Issues* 18, no. 1 (1988): 87–101.

22. W.C. Cockerham, M.A. Forslund, and R.M. Raboin, "Drug Use among White and American Indian High School Youth," *International Journal of the Addictions* 11 (1976): 209–20; E.R. Oetting and G.C. Goldstein, "Drug Use among Native American Adolescents," *Youth Drug Abuse: Problems, Issues, and Treatment*, ed. G.M. Beschner and A.S. Friedman (Lexington, MA: Lexington Books, 1979); C. Vanderwagen, R.D. Mason, and T.C. Owan, eds., *IHS Alcoholism/Substance Abuse Prevention Initiative: Background, Plenary Session, and Action Plan* (Washington, DC: U.S. Department of Health and Human Services, Indian Health Service, 1987); F. Beauvais and S. LaBoueff, "Drug and Alcohol Abuse Intervention in American Indian Communities," *International Journal of the Addictions* 20, no. 1 (1985): 139–71; L.T. Winfree and C.T. Griffiths, "Youth at Risk: Marijuana Use among Native American and Caucasian Youths," *International Journal of the Addictions* 18, no. 1 (1983): 53–70; J. Weibel-Orlando,

"Substance Abuse among American Indian Youth: A Continuing Crisis," *Journal of Drug Issues* 2 (1984): 313–35; V. Garcia-Mason, "Relationship of Drug Use and Self-Concept among American Indian Youth" (Ph.D. diss., University of New Mexico, Albuquerque, 1985); D.W. Swanson, A.P. Bratrude, and E.M. Brown, "Alcohol Abuse in a Population of Indian Children," *Diseases of the Nervous System* 31 (1971): 835–42; E.R. Oetting, F. Beauvais, and R. Edwards, "Alcohol and Indian Youth: Social and Psychological Correlates and Prevention," *Journal of Drug Issues* 18, no. 1 (1988): 87–101; T. Red Horse, "American Indian Families: Research Perspectives," *The American Indian Family: Strengths and Stresses*, ed. F. Hoffman (Proceedings of the Conference on Research Issues, Isleta, NM, 1980): 1–11; L. Longclaws, G. Barnes, L. Grieve, and R. Dumoff, "Alcohol and Drug Abuse among the Brokenhead Ojibwa," *Journal of Studies on Alcohol* 41, no. 1 (1980): 21–36.
23. R. Crider and B. Rouse, eds., *Epidemiology of Inhalant Abuse: An Update*, NIDA Research Monograph No. 85 (Washington, DC: GPO, 1988); E.D. Edwards and M.E. Edwards, "Alcoholism Prevention/Treatment and Native American Youth: A Community Approach," *Journal of Drug Issues* 18, no. 10 (1988): 103–15; A. Binion, C. Miller, F. Beauvais, and E.R. Oetting, "Rationales for the Use of Alcohol, Marijuana, and Other Drugs by Eighth Grade Native American and Anglo Youth," *International Journal of the Addictions* 23, no. 1 (1988): 47–64.
24. Quoted in S. Steiner, *The New Indians* (New York: Harper and Row Publishers, Inc., 1968), 150.
25. Ibid., 151–52.
26. C. Reasons, "Crime and the American Indian," *Native Americans Today: Sociological Perspectives*, ed. H.M. Bahr, B.A. Chadwick, and R.C. Day (New York: Harper and Row Publishers, Inc., 1972), 319–26; E. Lemert, "Drinking among American Indians," *Alcohol, Science, and Society Revisited*, ed. E. Gomberg, H. White, and J. Carpenter (Ann Arbor, MI: University of Michigan Press, 1982).
27. E.H. Richardson, "Cultural and Historical Perspectives in Counseling American Indians," *Counseling the Culturally Different: Theory and Practice*, ed. D.W. Sue (New York: John Wiley and Sons, 1981); H.L. Hodgkinson, *The Demographics of American Indians: One Percent of the People—Fifty Percent of the Diversity* (Washington, DC: Institute for Educational Leadership, 1990).
28. W.O. Farber, P.A. Odeen, and R.A. Tschelter, *Indians, Law Enforcement, and Local Government* (Brookings, SD: Government Research Bureau of South Dakota, 1957); M. Minnis, "The Relationship of the Social Structure of an Indian Community to Adult and Juvenile Delinquency," *Social Forces* 41 (1963): 395–403; C. Reasons, "Crime and the American Indian," *Native Americans Today: Sociological Perspectives*, ed. H.M. Bahr, B.A. Chadwick, and R.C. Day (New York: Harper and Row Publishers, Inc., 1972), 319–26; E.M. Lemert, "The Use of Alcohol in Three Salish Indian Tribes," *Quarterly Journal of Studies on Alcohol* 19 (1958): 90–107; A.S. Riffenburgh, "Cultural Influences and Crime among Indian-Americans of the Southwest," *Federal Probation* 23 (1964): 38–46; E.P. Dozier, "Problem Drinking among American Indians," *Quarterly Journal of Studies on Alcohol* 27 (1966): 72–87; C. Trillin, "U.S. Journal: Gallop, New Mexico (Drunken Indians)," *New Yorker*, 25 September 1971, 108–14; M.A. Forslund

and V.A. Cranston, "A Self-Report Comparison of Indian and Anglo Delinquency in Wyoming," *Criminology* 13, no. 2 (1975): 193–98; T.D. Graves, "The Personal Adjustment of Navajo Indian Migrants to Denver, Colorado," *American Anthropologist* 72, no. 1 (1970): 35–54; L. French and J. Hornbuckle, "An Analysis of Indian Violence: The Cherokee Example," *American Indian Quarterly* 3, no. 4 (1977): 335–56.

29. G.F. Jensen, H. Stauss, and V.W. Harris, "Crime, Delinquency, and the American Indian," *Human Organization* 36, no. 3 (1977): 252–57; M. Minnis, "The Relationship of the Social Structure of an Indian Community to Adult and Juvenile Delinquency," *Social Forces* 41 (1963): 395–403.

30. J.S. Kleinfeld and J. Bloom, "Boarding Schools: Effects on the Mental Health of Eskimo Adolescents," *American Journal of Psychiatry* 134, no. 4 (1977): 411–17.

31. B. Mendelsohn and W. Richards, "Alaska Native Adolescents' Descriptions of Their Mental Health Problems" (Paper presented at the Eighth Joint Meeting of the Professional Associations of the U.S. Public Health Service, Phoenix, AZ, 1973); G.F. Jensen, H. Stauss, and V.W. Harris, "Crime, Delinquency, and the American Indian," *Human Organization* 36, no. 3 (1977): 252–57; P.A. May, "Substance Abuse and American Indians: Prevalence and Susceptibility," *International Journal of the Addictions* 17 (1982): 1185–1209.

32. P.A. May, "Arrests, Alcohol, and Alcohol Legislation among an American Indian Tribe," *Plains Anthropologist* 20 (1975): 129–34; C.A. Heidenreich, "Alcohol and Drug Use and Abuse among Indian-Americans: A Review of Issues and Sources," *Journal of Drug Issues* 6, no. 3 (1976): 256–72; H.M. Bahr, B.A. Chadwick, and J.H. Strauss, *American Ethnicity* (Lexington, MA: D.C. Heath and Co., 1979); M. Minnis, "The Relationship of the Social Structure of an Indian Community to Adult and Juvenile Delinquency," *Social Forces* 41 (1963): 395–403; L.A. Ackerman, "Marital Instability and Juvenile Delinquency among the Nez Perces," *American Anthropologist* 73, no. 3 (1971): 595–603.

33. M.A. Forslund, *A Self-Concept Comparison of Indian and Anglo Delinquency in Wyoming* (Laramie, WY: Governor's Planning Committee on Criminal Administration, 1974); M.A. Forslund and R.E. Meyers, "Delinquency among Wind River Indian Reservation Youth," *Criminology* 12, no. 1 (1974): 97–106.

34. T.W. Hill, "Life Styles and Drinking Patterns of Urban Indians," *Journal of Drug Issues* 10 (1980): 257–72; J. Westermeyer, "The Drunken Indian: Myths and Realities," *Psychiatric Annals* 4 (November 1974): 29–36.

35. G. MacGregor, *Warriors without Weapons: A Study of the Society and Personality Development of the Pine Ridge Sioux* (Chicago: University of Chicago Press, 1946); M.L. Wax, R.H. Wax, and R.V. Dumont, Jr., *Formal Education in an American Indian Community*, Monograph (Kalamazoo, MI: The Society for the Study of Social Problems, 1964); G.F. Jensen, H. Stauss, and V.W. Harris, "Crime, Delinquency, and the American Indian," *Human Organization* 36, no. 3 (1977): 252–57.

36. South Dakota Advisory Committee (SDAC) of the U.S. Commission on Civil Rights, *Liberty and Justice for All* (Washington, DC: GPO, 1977).

37. A. Randall and B. Randall, "Criminal Justice and the American Indian," *Indian Historian* 11, no. 2 (1978): 42–48.

38. L. French, "An Analysis of Contemporary Indian Justice and Correctional Treatment," *Federal Probation* 44 (1980): 19–23; L.E. Williams, B.A. Chadwick, and H.M. Bahr, "Antecedents of Self-reported Arrest for Americans in Seattle," *Phylon* 40 (1979): 243–52; E.L. Hall and A.A. Simkus, "Inequality in the Types of Sentences Received by Native Americans and Whites," *Criminology* 13, no. 2 (1975): 199–222.

39. H.M. Bahr, B.A. Chadwick, and R.C. Day, eds., *Native Americans Today: Sociological Perspectives* (New York: Harper and Row Publishers, Inc., 1972), 140; J.S. Coleman, *Equality of Educational Opportunity* (Washington, DC: GPO, 1966).

40. B.G. Rosenthal, "Development of Self-Identification in Relation to Attitudes toward Self in Chippewa Indians," *Genetic Psychology Monographs* 90 (1974): 43–141; H.D. Thornburg, "An Investigation of a Dropout Program among Arizona's Minority Youth," *Education* 94 (1974): 249–65; R.A. Clifton, "Self Concept and Attitudes: A Comparison of Canadian Indian and Non-Indian Students," *Canadian Review of Sociology and Anthropology* 12 (1975): 577–84; H.P. Lefley, "Acculturation, Child-Rearing, and Self-Esteem in Two North American Indian Tribes," *Ethos* 4 (1976): 385–401; G. Halpin, G. Halpin, and T. Whiddon, "Locus of Control and Self-Esteem among Indians and Whites: A Cross-Cultural Comparison," *Psychological Reports* 48 (1981): 91–98.

41. R. Carlson, "On the Structure of Self Esteem: Comments on Ziller's Formulations," *Journal of Consulting and Clinical Psychology* 34 (1970): 264–68; R.C. Wylie, *The Self-Concept*, 2nd ed., rev. (Lincoln, NE: University of Nebraska Press, 1979); G.G. Wehlage and R.A. Rutter, "Dropping Out: How Do Schools Contribute to the Problem?" *Teachers College Record* 87 (1986): 374–92; M. Fine, "Why Urban Adolescents Drop into and out of Public High School," *Teachers College Record* 87 (1987): 3.

42. K.N. Giles, *Indian High School Dropout: A Perspective* (Milwaukee: University of Wisconsin—Milwaukee, Midwest National Origin Desegregation Assistance Center, 1985).

43. E.A. Fuchs and R.J. Havighurst, *To Live on This Earth: American Indian Education* (Albuquerque, NM: University of New Mexico Press, 1983).

44. P.H. Dreyer and R.J. Havighurst, *The Self-Esteem of American Indian Youth: The Personal-Social Adjustment of American Indian Youth* (1970), ERIC ED 045-273: 147.

45. J.F. Bryde, *The Sioux Indian Student: A Study of Scholastic Failure and Personality Conflict* (Vermillion, SD: Dakota Press, 1970).

46. J.F. Bryde, *Modern Indians*, National Institute of Mental Health (Washington, DC: GPO, 1969); M.L. Wax, R.H. Wax, and R.V. Dumont, Jr., *Formal Education in an American Indian Community*, Monograph (Kalamazoo, MI: The Society for the Study of Social Problems, 1964).

47. H.L. Hodgkinson, *The Demographics of American Indians: One Percent of the People—Fifty Percent of the Diversity* (Washington, DC: Institute for Educational Leadership, 1990).

48. D. McNickle, *Indians in the Land of Plenty* (1965), ERIC ED 012-191.

49. E.H. Erikson, *Childhood and Society*, 2nd ed. (New York: W.W. Norton and Co., 1963).

50. J. Bynum, "Suicide and the American Indian: An Analysis of Recent Trends," *Native Americans Today: Sociological Perspectives*, ed. H.M. Bahr, B.A. Chadwick, and R.C. Day (New York: Harper and Row Publishers, Inc., 1972), 367–77.

51. J.F. Bryde, *The Sioux Indian Student: A Study of Scholastic Failure and Personality Conflict* (Vermillion, SD: Dakota Press, 1970), 24.

52. G.D. Spindler and L.S. Spindler, "American Indian Personality Types and Their Sociocultural Roots," *The Annals of the American Academy of Political and Social Science* 311 (May 1957): 147–57; F. Voget, "Acculturation at Caughnawaga: A Note on the Native-modified Group," *American Anthropologist* 53 (1951): 220–31.

53. P. Roy, "The Measurement of Assimilation: The Spokane Indians," *Native Americans Today: Sociological Perspectives*, ed. M. Bahr, B.A. Chadwick, and R.C. Day (New York: Harper and Row Publishers, Inc., 1972), 225–39; L.C. White and B.A. Chadwick, "Urban Residence, Assimilation, and Identity of the Spokane Indian," *Native Americans Today: Sociological Perspectives*, ed. H.M. Bahr, B.A. Chadwick, and R.C. Day (New York: Harper and Row Publishers, Inc., 1972), 239–49.

54. C.A. Hammerschlag, *Identity Groups with American Indian Adolescents* (1974), ERIC ED 098-451: 11.

55. P. Katz, "Saulteaux-Ojibwa Adolescents: The Adolescent Process amidst a Clash of Cultures," *Psychiatric Journal of the University of Ottawa* 4 (1979): 315–21; D.M. George and R.D. Hoppe, "Racial Identification, Preference, and Self-Concept: Canadian Indian and White Schoolchildren," *Journal of Cross-Cultural Psychology* 10, no. 1 (1979): 85–100; H. Saslow and M. Harrover, "Research on the Psychosocial Adjustment of Indian Youth," *American Journal of Psychiatry* 125 (1968): 120–27.

56. L.C. White and B.A. Chadwick, "Urban Residence, Assimilation, and Identity of the Spokane Indian," *Native Americans Today: Sociological Perspectives*, ed. H.M. Bahr, B.A. Chadwick, and R.C. Day (New York: Harper and Row Publishers, Inc., 1972), 239–49; R.M. Wintrob and P.S. Sindell, *Education and Identity Conflict among Cree Indian Youth: A Preliminary Report* (1968), ERIC ED 039-063.

57. N. Malbin, S. LaTurner, and B.A. Spilke, "Longitudinal Study of Educational Performance among Oglala Sioux Students" (Paper presented at the Annual Meeting of the Rocky Mountain Psychological Association, Denver, CO, May 1971).

58. M.M. Helper and S.L. Garfield, "Use of the Semantic Differential to Study Acculturation in American Indian Adolescents," *Journal of Personality and Social Psychology* 2 (1965): 817–22.

59. G. Leitka, "Search for Identity Creates Problems for Indian Students," *Journal of American Indian Education* 11, no. 1 (1971): 7.

60. D. Vallo, *Indian in the Red*, U.S. Department of Health and Human Services, DHHS Pub. (ADM) (Washington, DC: GPO, 1980), 81-492; Y. Takie, P. Lynch, and G.M. Charleston, "To Drink or Not to Drink: The Indian Adolescent's Choice between Friends and Family," *Journal of American Indian Education* 27 (1988): 1–9.

61. T. Coladarci, "High School Dropout among Native Americans," *Journal of American Indian Education* 23, no. 1 (1983): 15–22; J. Trimble, "Drug Abuse Prevention Research Needs among American Indians and Alaska Natives," *White Cloud Journal of American Indian Mental Health* 3, no. 3 (1984): 22–34; E. Maynard, "Drinking as a Part of an Adjustment Syndrome among Oglala Sioux," *Pine Ridge Research Bulletin* 9 (1969): 35–51; R. Kuttner and A. Lorincz, "Alcoholism and Addiction in Urbanized Sioux Indians," *Mental Hygiene* 51 (1967): 530–42.

62. W.C. Cockerham, M.A. Forslund, and R.M. Raboin, "Drug Use among White and American Indian High School Youth," *International Journal of the Addictions* 11 (1976): 209–20; D.C. McBride and J.B. Page, "Adolescent Indian Substance Abuse: Ecological and Sociocultural Factors," *Youth and Society* 11, no. 4 (1980): 475–92; E.R. Oetting and G.C. Goldstein, "Drug Use among Native American Adolescents," *Youth Drug Abuse: Problems, Issues, and Treatment*, ed. G.M. Beschner and A.S. Friedman (Lexington, MA: Lexington Books, 1979); R.B. Hassrick, *The Sioux: Life and Customs of a Warrior Society* (Norman, OK: University of Oklahoma Press, 1964); G. MacGregor, *Warriors without Weapons: A Study of the Society and Personality Development of the Pine Ridge Sioux* (Chicago: University of Chicago Press, 1946).

63. R.H. Wax, *The Warrior Dropouts* (Lawrence, KS: The University of Kansas Press, 1967); M.L. Wax, R.H. Wax, and R.V. Dumont, Jr., *Formal Education in an American Indian Community*, Monograph (Kalamazoo, MI: The Society for the Study of Social Problems, 1964).

64. F.N. Anderson, "A Mental Hygiene Survey of Problem Indian Children in Oklahoma," *Mental Hygiene* 20 (1936): 472–76; R. Wallis, "The Overt Fears of Dakota Indian Children," *Child Development* 25, no. 3 (1954): 185–92; D. Sydiaha and J. Rempel, "Motivation and Attitudinal Characteristics of Indian School Children as Measured by the Thermatic Apperception Test," *Canadian Psychologist* 5a, no. 3 (1964): 139–48; T.P. Krush, J. Bjork, P. Sindell, and J. Nelle, "Some Thoughts on the Formation of Personality Disorder: Study of an Indian Boarding School Population," *American Journal of Psychiatry* 122 (1966): 875; R.R. Cocking, "Fantasy Confession among Arapaho Indian Children," *Journal of Genetic Psychology* 114 (1969): 229–35; H. Saslow and M. Harrover, "Research on the Psychosocial Adjustment of Indian Youth," *American Journal of Psychiatry* 125 (1968): 120–27; J.S. Kleinfeld and J. Bloom, "Boarding Schools: Effects on the Mental Health of Eskimo Adolescents," *American Journal of Psychiatry* 134, no. 4 (1977): 411–17.

65. E.A. Fuchs and R.J. Havighurst, *To Live on This Earth: American Indian Education* (Albuquerque, NM: University of New Mexico Press, 1983); H. Gilliland, "The Need for an Adopted Curriculum," *Teaching the Indian Child: A Bilingual/Multicultural Approach*, ed. J. Reyhner (Billings, MT: Eastern Montana College, 1986), 1–11; P.A. May and L.H. Dizmang, "Suicide and the American Indian," *Psychiatric Annals* 4, no. 9 (1974): 22–23, 27–28; M. Ogden, M.I. Spector, and C.A. Hill, Jr., "Suicides and Homicides among Indians," *Public Health Report* 85 (1970): 75–80; L.H. Dizmang, "Suicide among Cheyenne Indians," *Bulletin of Suicidology* 1 (1967): 8–11; S.I. Miller and L.S. Schoenfield, "Suicide Attempt Patterns among Navajo Indians," *International Journal of Social Psychiatry* 17,

no. 3 (1971): 189–93; C. Frederick, *Suicide, Homicide, and Alcoholism among American Indians*, DHEW Pub. No. ADM 76-92, Department of Health, Education, and Welfare (Washington, DC: GPO, 1975); R.D. Conrad and M. Kahn, "An Epidemiological Study of Suicide and Attempted Suicide among the Papago Indians," *American Journal of Psychiatry* 131, no. 1 (1974): 69–72; E.B. Harvey, L. Gazay, and B. Samuels, "Utilization of a Psychiatric–Social Work Team in an Alaska Native Secondary Boarding School," *Journal of Child Psychiatry* 15, no. 3 (1976): 558–74; L.H. Dizmang, J. Watson, P.A. May, and J. Bopp, "Adolescent Suicide at an Indian Reservation," *American Journal of Orthopsychiatry* 44, no. 1 (1974): 43–49.

66. L.H. Dizmang, J. Watson, P.A. May, and J. Bopp, "Adolescent Suicide at Fort Hall Reservation" (Paper presented at the Annual Meeting of the American Psychiatric Association, May 1970), 12.

67. J.H. Shore, "Suicide and Suicide Attempts among American Indians of the Pacific Northwest," *International Journal of Social Psychiatry* 18, no. 2 (1972): 91–96; J. Weibel-Orlando, "Substance Abuse among American Indian Youth: A Continuing Crisis," *Journal of Drug Issues* 2 (1984): 313-35; J.A. Stevens, "Social and Cultural Factors Related to Drinking Patterns among the Blackfeet" (Master's thesis, University of Montana, Missoula, 1969).

68. P.A. May, *Suicide and Suicide Attempts on the Pine Ridge Reservation* (Pine Ridge, SD: U.S. Public Health Service, Community Mental Health Program, 1973); J.H. Shore, "Suicide and Suicide Attempts among American Indians of the Pacific Northwest," *International Journal of Social Psychiatry* 18, no. 2 (1972): 91–96; E.A. Fuchs and R.J. Havighurst, *To Live on This Earth: American Indian Education* (Albuquerque, NM: University of New Mexico Press, 1983); L.H. Dizmang, "Suicide among Cheyenne Indians," *Bulletin of Suicidology* 1 (1967): 8–11; H.L. Hodgkinson, *The Demographics of American Indians: One Percent of the People—Fifty Percent of the Diversity* (Washington, DC: Institute for Educational Leadership, 1990).

69. B. Medicine, "The Changing Dakota Family and the Stresses Therein," *Pine Ridge Research Bulletin* 9 (1969): 11.

70. P.A. May, "Epidemiology of Fetal Alcohol Syndrome among American Indians of the Southwest," *Social Biology* 30 (1983): 374–87.

71. M. Dorris, *The Broken Cord* (New York: Harper and Row Publishers, Inc., 1989).

72. B. Anquoe "Indians Fall in Poverty Stats," *The Lakota Times*, 29 July 1992, p.1.

73. M.L. Mizen, *Federal Facilities for Indians: Tribal Relations with the Federal Government* (Washington, DC: GPO, 1966); S.R. Rist, "Shoshone Indian Education: A Descriptive Study Based on Certain Influential Factors Affecting Academic Achievement of Shoshone Indian Students, Wind River Reservation, Wyoming" (Master's thesis, Montana State University, Bozeman, 1961); R.J. Felber, "Factors Influencing the Educational Attainments of Indian Pupils in Sisseton, South Dakota" (Master's thesis, University of Wyoming, Laramie, 1955); E.A. Parmee, *Formal Education and Culture Change: A Modern Apache Indian Community and Government Education Programs* (Tucson, AZ: University of Arizona Press, 1968); A. Yates, "Current Status and Future Directions of Research on the American Indian Child," *American Journal of Psychiatry* 144 (1987): 1135–42.

74. E.A. Fuchs and R.J. Havighurst, *To Live on This Earth: American Indian Education* (Albuquerque, NM: University of New Mexico Press, 1983).
75. B.F. Lund, "A Survey of Comparative Achievement and Scholarship Records of California Indian Children in the Auburn Public Schools" (Master's thesis, Sacramento State College, Sacramento, 1963).
76. H.J. Miller, *The Effects of Integration of Rural Indian Pupils: Final Report* (Washington, DC: Department of Health, Education, and Welfare, Office of Education, 1968); G.A. Just, "American Indian Attitudes toward Education in Select Areas of South Dakota" (Master's thesis, University of South Dakota, Vermillion, 1970).
77. U.S. Congress, Senate Committee on Labor and Human Resources, Subcommittee on Employment and Productivity, *Guaranteed Job Opportunity Act*, 100th Cong., 1st sess., S. Doc. 777, 3 March 1987 and 3 April 1987.
78. U.S. Department of the Interior, *American Indians Today: Answers to Your Questions*, Bureau of Indian Affairs (Washington, DC: GPO, 1988); U.S. Department of the Interior, *Indian Service Population and Labor Force Estimates*, Bureau of Indian Affairs (Washington, DC: GPO, 1989).
79. R.L. Brod and J.M. McQuiston, "American Indian Adult Education and Literacy: The First Annual Survey," *Journal of American Indian Education* 1, no. 22 (1983): 1–16.
80. U.S. Department of Commerce, "American Indians, Eskimos, and Aleuts on Identified Reservations and in the Historic Areas of Oklahoma (Excluding Urbanized Areas)," *1980 Census of Population*, U.S. Department of Commerce Report No. PC80-2-1D, Part 1 (Washington, DC: GPO, November 1985), 1–3.
81. E.A. Fuchs and R.J. Havighurst, *To Live on This Earth: American Indian Education* (Albuquerque, NM: University of New Mexico Press, 1983).
82. Quoted in M.E. Layman, *A History of Indian Education in the United States* (Ph.D. diss., University of Minnesota, 1942), Minneapolis, 21.
83. B. Spilka, *Alienation and Achievement among Oglala Sioux Indian Secondary School Students* (1970), ERIC ED 945-225.
84. R.J. Havighurst and B.L. Neugarten, *American Indian and White Children: A Sociopsychological Investigation* (Chicago: University of Chicago Press, 1955), 79.
85. B. Spilka, *Alienation and Achievement among Oglala Sioux Indian Secondary School Students* (1970), ERIC ED 945-225.
86. S.U. Philips, *The Invisible Culture* (New York: Longman Press, 1983).
87. J.F. Bryde, *Modern Indian Psychology* (Vermillion, SD: Institute of Indian Studies, 1971).
88. S.U. Philips, "Participant Structures and Communicative Competence: Warm Springs Children in Community and Classroom," *Functions of Language in the Classroom*, ed. C.B. Cazden, V.P. John, and D. Hymes (New York: Teachers College Press, 1972), 392.
89. W.L. Larson, *A Comparative Analysis of Indian and Non-Indian Parents' Influence on Educational Aspirations, Expectations, Preferences, and Behavior of Indian and Non-Indian Students in Four High Schools*, AES Bulletin 660 (Bozeman, MT: Montana State Agricultural Experiment Station, 1971); A. Berger, "Nine Families and Forty Children," *Journal of American Indian Education* 12, no. 3 (1973): 1–8; G. Anderson and D. Safar, "The Influence of Differential Community

Perceptions on the Provision of Equal Educational Opportunities," *Sociology of Education* 40, no. 2 (1967): 219–30; H. Zenter, "Parental Behavior and Student Attitudes towards Further Training among Indian and Non-Indian Students in Oregon and Alberta," *Alberta Journal of Educational Resources* 9, no. 1 (1963): 22–30.

90. D. Little Bear, "Teachers and Parents Working Together," *Teaching the Indian Child: A Bilingual/Multicultural Approach*, ed. J. Reyhner (Billings, MT: Eastern Montana College, 1986), 223–25.

91. H. Wolcott, *A Kwakiuti Village and School* (New York: Holt, Rinehart, and Winston, 1967); A. Joseph, R. Spicer, and J. Chesky, *The Desert People* (Chicago: University of Chicago Press, 1949); D. Leighton and C. Kluckhohn, *Children of the People* (Cambridge, MA: Harvard University Press, 1948); G. MacGregor, *Warriors without Weapons: A Study of the Society and Personality Development of the Pine Ridge Sioux* (Chicago: University of Chicago Press, 1946); H. Thompson, *Education for Cross-Cultural Enrichment* (Lawrence, KS: Haskell Institute, 1964).

92. T. Garcia, "A Study of the Effects of Education on the Wind River Reservation" (Master's thesis, University of Wyoming, Laramie, 1965); S.R. Rist, "Shoshone Indian Education: A Descriptive Study Based on Certain Influential Factors Affecting Academic Achievement of Shoshone Indian Students, Wind River Reservation, Wyoming" (Master's thesis, Montana State University, Bozeman, 1961).

93. R.H. Wax, *The Warrior Dropouts* (Lawrence, KS: The University of Kansas Press, 1967).

94. T.W. Hill, "Life Styles and Drinking Patterns of Urban Indians," *Journal of Drug Issues* 10 (1980): 257–72; J.A. Stevens, "Social and Cultural Factors Related to Drinking Patterns among the Blackfeet" (Master's thesis, University of Montana, Missoula, 1969).

95. L. Kickingbird, "A Portrait of Indian People in Indian Lands," *American Indian Journal* 9, no. 2 (1986): 23–25.

96. P.A. May and L.H. Dizmang, "Suicide and the American Indian," *Psychiatric Annals* 4, no. 9 (1974): 22–23, 27–28.

97. G.C. Lang, "Survival Strategies of Chippewa Drinkers in Minneapolis," *Central Issues in Anthropology* 1, no. 2 (1979): 19–40; J. Westermeyer, "Options regarding Alcohol Use among the Chippewa," *American Journal of Orthopsychiatry* 42 (1972): 398–403.

98. C. Lujan, L. DeBruyn, P. May, and M. Bird, "Profile of Abused and Neglected American Indian Children in the Southwest," *Child Abuse and Neglect* 13 (1989): 449–61; R.S. Fischler, "Child Abuse and Neglect in American Indians," *The IHS Primary Care Provider* 8 (1983): 1–7; R.S. Fischler, "Child Abuse and Neglect in American Indian Communities," *Child Abuse and Neglect* 9 (1985): 95–106; R. White and D. Cornely, "Navajo Child Abuse and Neglect Study: A Comparison Group Examination of Abuse and Neglect of Navajo Children," *Child Abuse and Neglect* 5 (1981): 9–17.

99. M. Pagelow, *Family Violence* (New York: Praeger Publishers, 1984).

100. R.J. Gelles and J.B. Lancaster, eds., *Child Abuse and Neglect: Biosocial Dimensions* (New York: Aldine DeGruyter, 1987); K.A. Long, "Cultural Considerations in the Assessment and Treatment of Intrafamilial Abuse," *American Journal of Orthopsychiatry* 56 (1986): 131–36.

101. C. Lujan, L. DeBruyn, P. May, and M. Bird, "Profile of Abused and Neglected American Indian Children in the Southwest," *Child Abuse and Neglect* 13 (1989): 450.

102. D. Jones, "Child Welfare Problems in an Alaskan Native Village," *Social Service Review* 43 (1969): 297–309.

103. H. Ishisaka, "American Indians and Foster Care: Culture Factors and Separation," *Child Welfare* 57, no. 5 (1978): 299–307.

104. R.S. Fischler, "Child Abuse and Neglect in American Indian Communities," *Child Abuse and Neglect* 9 (1985): 95–106; R. White, *Navajo Child Abuse and Neglect Study* (Baltimore: Johns Hopkins University, Department of Maternal and Child Health, 1977); C. Wischlacz, J. Lane, and C. Kempe, "Indian Child Welfare: A Community Team Approach to Protective Services," *Child Abuse and Neglect* 2 (1978): 29–35.

105. J.A. Stevens, "Social and Cultural Factors Related to Drinking Patterns among the Blackfeet" (Master's thesis, University of Montana, Missoula, 1969).

106. P. Old Dog Cross, "Sexual Abuse: A New Threat to the Native American Woman," *The Listening Post* 6, no. 2 (1982): 17–23. Albuquerque, NM: Indian Health Service.

107. L. Oakland and R.L. Kane, "The Working Mother and Child Neglect on the Navajo Reservation," *Pediatrics* 51, no. 5 (1973): 849–53.

108. H.M. Bahr, B.A. Chadwick, and R.C. Day, eds., *Native Americans Today: Sociological Perspectives* (New York: Harper and Row Publishers, Inc., 1972); C.A. Heidenreich, "Alcohol and Drug Use and Abuse among Indian-Americans: A Review of Issues and Sources," *Journal of Drug Issues* 6, no. 3 (1976): 256–72.

109. I. Berlin, "Psychopathology and Its Antecedents among American Indian Adolescents," *Advances in Clinical Psychology* 9 (1986): 125–51; J.E. Levy and S.J. Kunitz, "A Suicide Prevention Program for Hopi Youth," *Social Science and Medicine* 25 (1987): 931–40; A.M. Shkilnyk, *A Poison Stronger than Love: The Destruction of an Ojibwa Community* (New Haven, CT: Yale University Press, 1985).

110. T. Brod, "Alcoholism as a Mental Health Problem of Native Americans: A Review of the Literature," *Archives of General Psychiatry* 32 (1975): 1385–91; H. Hoffman and A. Noem, "Alcoholism and Abstinence among Relatives of American Indian Alcoholics," *Journal of Studies in Alcohol* 36 (1975): 165–70; D. Jones-Saumty, L. Hochhaus, R. Dru, and A. Zeiner, "Psychological Factors of Familial Alcoholism in American Indians and Caucasians," *Journal of Clinical Psychology* 39 (1983): 783–90.

111. C. Lujan, L. DeBruyn, P. May, and M. Bird, "Profile of Abused and Neglected American Indian Children in the Southwest," *Child Abuse and Neglect* 13 (1989): 449–61.

112. C.F. Lummis, "My Brother's Keeper," *Land of Sunshine* 11 (1899): 334.

113. U.S. Commissioner of Indian Affairs, *Annual Report of the Commissioner of Indian Affairs* (Washington, DC, 1887), xxi.

114. U.S. Commissioner of Indian Affairs, *Annual Report of the Commissioner of Indian Affairs* (Washington, DC, 1894), 134.

115. P. Weeks and J.B. Gidney, *Subjugation and Dishonor: A Brief History of the Travail of the Native Americans* (Huntington, NY: Robert E. Krieger, 1981), 119.

116. U.S. Commissioner of Indian Affairs, *Annual Report of the Commissioner of Indian Affairs* (Washington, DC, 1887), xxiii–xxiv.

117. H. Thompson, *Education for Cross-Cultural Enrichment* (Lawrence, KS: Haskell Institute, 1964), 408.

118. B. Gaarder, *Education of American Indian Children* (Report presented at the Annual Conference of the Southwest Council of Foreign Language Teachers, El Paso, TX, November 1967, and in testimony before the U.S. House of Representatives Subcommittee on Education, Washington, DC, June 1967), ERIC ED 018-299.

119. M. Heatherington, *How Language Works* (Cambridge, MA: Winthrop, 1980), 216.

120. F. Ahenakew, "Text Based Grammars in Cree Language Education," *Proceedings: Selected Papers and Biographies*, ed. S. Weryackwe (Choctaw, OK: Sixth Annual International Native American Language Issues Institute, 1986), 1–3.

121. K.L. Deissler, "A Study of South Dakota Indian Achievement Problems," *Journal of American Indian Education* 1, no. 3 (1962): 19–21; W.D. Conway, "A Transformational Analysis of the Written and Oral Syntax of Fourth, Sixth, and Eighth Grade Omaha Indian Children" (Ph.D. diss., University of Nebraska, Lincoln, 1971).

122. A.D. Bowd, "Some Determinants of School Achievement in Several Indian Groups," *Alberta Journal of Educational Research* 18, no. 2 (1972): 69–81.

123. G. Blossom, "A New Approach to an Old Problem," *Journal of American Indian Education* 1, no. 2 (1962): 13–14.

124. L.M. Coombs, *The Educational Disadvantage of the Indian American Student* (Las Cruces, NM: New Mexico State University, 1970), 60–61.

125. W. Holm, "Community School Charts Achievements," *Indian Affairs* 108 (1985): 2–4.

126. K. Hakuta, *Mirror of Language: The Debate on Bilingualism* (New York: Basic Books, 1986).

127. W. Holm, "Community School Charts Achievements," *Indian Affairs* 108 (1985): 2–4; K. Hakuta, *Mirror of Language: The Debate on Bilingualism* (New York: Basic Books, 1986); J. Cummins, "Empowering Minority Students: A Framework for Intervention," *Harvard Educational Review* 56 (1986): 18–36.

128. W.L. Leap, "Roles for the Linguist in Indian Bilingual Education," *Language Renewal among American Indian Tribes: Issues, Problems, and Prospects*, ed. R. St. Clair and W. Leap (Rosslyn, VA: National Clearinghouse for Bilingual Education, 1982).

129. E.H. Erikson, "Observations on Sioux Education," *Journal of Psychology* 7 (1939): 101–56.

130. G. MacGregor, *Warriors without Weapons: A Study of the Society and Personality Development of the Pine Ridge Sioux* (Chicago: University of Chicago Press, 1946); R.J. Havighurst and B.L. Neugarten, *American Indian and White Children: A Sociopsychological Investigation* (Chicago: University of Chicago Press, 1955); M.L. Wax, R.H. Wax, and R.V. Dumont, Jr., *Formal Education in an American Indian Community*, Monograph (Kalamazoo, MI: The Society for the Study of Social Problems, 1964).

131. E.A. Fuchs and R.J. Havighurst, *To Live on This Earth: American Indian Education* (Albuquerque, NM: University of New Mexico Press, 1983).

132. P. Katz, "Saulteaux-Ojibwa Adolescents: The Adolescent Process amidst a Clash of Cultures," *Psychiatric Journal of the University of Ottawa* 4 (1979): 315–21.

133. Ibid.

134. R.H. Wax, *The Warrior Dropouts* (Lawrence, KS: The University of Kansas Press, 1967).

135. B. Albaugh and P. Albaugh, "Alcoholism and Substance Sniffing among the Cheyenne and Arapaho Indians of Oklahoma," *International Journal of the Addictions* 14, no. 7 (1979): 1001–7.

136. J. Westermeyer, "The Drunken Indian: Myths and Realities," *Psychiatric Annals* 4 (November 1974): 29–36.

137. W. Patton and E. Edington, "Factors Related to the Persistence of Indian Students at College Level," *Indian Education* 12 (1973): 19–23; M. Wienberg, *A Chance to Learn: A History of Race and Education in the United States* (London: Cambridge University Press, 1977).

138. A.G. Miller, "Integration and Acculturation of Cooperative Behavior among Blackfoot Indian and Non-Indian Canadian Children," *Journal of Cross-Cultural Psychology* 4, no. 3 (1973): 347–80.

139. P.A. May and L.H. Dizmang, "Suicide and the American Indian," *Psychiatric Annals* 4, no. 9 (1974): 27.

140. B. Berry, *The Education of American Indians: A Survey of the Literature* (Washington, DC: GPO, 1968), 70.

141. E.H. Erikson, *Childhood and Society* (New York: W.W. Norton and Co., 1950); E.H. Erikson, "Observations on Sioux Education," *Journal of Psychology* 7 (1939): 101–56; H. Saslow and M. Harrover, "Research on the Psychosocial Adjustment of Indian Youth," *American Journal of Psychiatry* 125 (1968): 120–27.

142. J.E. Trimble, A. Padilla, and C. Bell, *Drug Abuse among Ethnic Minorities*, NIDA Office of Science Monographs, DHHS Pub. (ADM) (Washington, DC: GPO, 1987), 2.

143. S. Polgar, "Biculturation of Mesquakine Teenage Boys," *American Anthropologist* 62 (1960): 217–35; M. McFee, "The 150% Man: A Product of Blackfeet Acculturation," *American Anthropologist* 70 (1968): 1096–1103.

144. J. Bynum, "Suicide and the American Indian: An Analysis of Recent Trends," *Native Americans Today: Sociological Perspectives*, ed. H.M. Bahr, B.A. Chadwick, and R.C. Day (New York: Harper and Row Publishers, Inc., 1972), 375.

145. C.A. Bowers and D.J. Flanders, *Responsive Teaching: An Ecological Approach to Classroom Patterns of Language, Culture, and Thought* (New York: Teachers College Press, 1990); E. Jacob and C. Jordan, "Explaining the School Performance of Minority Students," *Anthropology and Education Quarterly* 18, no. 4 (1987): 259–392; G.D. Spindler, "Why Have Minority Groups in North America Been Disadvantaged in Their Schools?" *Education and Cultural Process: Anthropological Approaches*, ed. G.D. Spindler (Prospect Heights, IL: Waveland, 1987), 160–72.

146. J.U. Ogbu, *The Next Generation* (New York: Academic Press, 1974); J.U. Ogbu, *Minority Education and Caste: The American System in Cross-Cultural Perspective*

(New York: Academic Press, 1978); J.U. Ogbu, "Cultural Discontinuities and Schooling," *Anthropology and Education Quarterly* 13 (1982): 290–307; J.U. Ogbu, "Minority Status and Schooling in Plural Societies," *Comparative Education Review* 27 (1983): 168–90; J.U. Ogbu, "Variability in Minority School Performance: A Problem in Search of an Explanation," *Anthropology and Education Quarterly* 18 (1987): 312–34.

147. K.N. Giles, *Indian High School Dropout: A Perspective* (Milwaukee: University of Wisconsin—Milwaukee, Midwest National Origin Desegregation Assistance Center, 1985), 2.

148. T. Coladarci, "High School Dropout among Native Americans," *Journal of American Indian Education* 23, no. 1 (1983): 15–22.

149. D.R. Eberhard, "American Indian Education: A Study of Dropouts, 1980–1987," *Journal of American Indian Education* 19, no. 1 (1989): 32–40.

150. E.A. Fuchs and R.J. Havighurst, *To Live on This Earth: American Indian Education* (Albuquerque, NM: University of New Mexico Press, 1983).

151. D.E. Milone, "American Indian Student Reasons for Dropping out and Attitude toward School" (Master's thesis, Arizona State University, Tempe, 1983).

152. D. Deyhle, "Pushouts and Pullouts: Navajo and Ute School Leavers," *Journal of Navajo Education* 6, no. 2 (1989): 36–51.

153. Ibid.; Platero Paperwork, Inc., *Executive Summary: Navajo Area Student Dropout Study* (Window Rock, AZ: Navajo Division of Education, the Navajo Nation, 1986). For a discussion of traditional college students, see R.L. Lin, "Perceptions of Family Background and Personal Characteristics among Indian College Students," *Journal of American Indian Education* 29, no. 3 (1990): 19–28.

154. E. Rowe, "Five Hundred Forty-Seven and Two Hundred Sixty-Eight Indian Children Tested by the Binet-Simon Tests," *The Pedagogical Seminary* 21 (1914): 454-68; O. Klineberg, "Racial Differences in Speed and Accuracy," *Journal of Abnormal and Social Psychology* 22 (1928): 273–77.

155. J. Rohrer, "Test Intelligence of Osage Indians," *Journal of Social Psychology* 16 (1942): 99–105; E. Evvard, "A New Concept on the Navajo," *Journal of American Indian Education* 5, no. 3 (1966): 1–17.

156. J.F. Bryde, *Modern Indians*, National Institute of Mental Health (Washington, DC: GPO, 1969); U.S. Senate, *Indian Education: A National Tragedy—A National Challenge*, Report of the Committee on Labor and Public Welfare, Special Subcommittee on Indian Education, Report No. 90-501, 91st Cong., 1st sess. (Washington, DC: GPO, 1969); R.H. Wax, *The Warrior Dropouts* (Lawrence, KS: The University of Kansas Press, 1967).

157. E.A. Fuchs and R.J. Havighurst, *To Live on This Earth: American Indian Education* (Albuquerque, NM: University of New Mexico Press, 1983); H. Saslow and M. Harrover, "Research on the Psychosocial Adjustment of Indian Youth," *American Journal of Psychiatry* 125 (1968): 120–27.

158. J.F. Bryde, *Modern Indians*, National Institute of Mental Health (Washington, DC: GPO, 1969).

159. R.W. Rhodes, "Standardized Testing of Minority Students: Navajo and Hopi Examples," *Journal of Navajo Education* 6, no. 2 (1989): 29–35; J. Oakes, *Keeping Track: How Schools Structure Inequality* (New Haven, CT: Yale University Press, 1985); B.S. Bloom, *All Our Children Learning* (New York: McGraw-Hill, 1981).

160. O.L. Taylor and D.L. Lee, "Standardized Tests and African-American Children," *The Negro Educational Review* 38 (1987): 67–80.

161. L.M. Coombs, R. Kron, E. Collister, and K. Anderson, *The Indian Child Goes to School* (Lawrence, KS: U.S. Bureau of Indian Affairs, Haskell Institute, 1958).

162. J.F. Bryde, *Modern Indians*, National Institute of Mental Health (Washington, DC: GPO, 1969).

163. K. Levensky, "The Performance of American Indian Children on the Draw-a-Man Test," *The National Study of American Indian Education* 1, no. 2 (1970): 1–21; J.S. Kleinfeld, "Intellectual Strengths in Culturally Different Groups: An Eskimo Illustration," *Review of Educational Research* 43 (1973): 341–59; P. Suppes, J.D. Fletcher, and M. Zanotti, "Performance Models of American Indian Students on Computer-assisted Instruction in Elementary Mathematics," *Instructional Science* 4 (1975): 303–13; P. Rosier and W. Holm, *The Rock Point Experience: A Longitudinal Study of the Navajo School Program* (Washington, DC: Center for Applied Linguistics, 1980), ERIC ED 195–363.

164. H.L. Bacon, G.D. Kidd, and J.J. Seaberg, "The Effectiveness of Bilingual Instruction with Cherokee Indian Students," *Journal of American Indian Education* 21 (1982): 34–43; B. Anderson, "A Comparative Study in Estimating Time," *Journal of American Indian Education* 19 (1980): 1–4.

165. L. Burd, J. Dodd, and P. Grassl, "A Comparison of Reservation Native American and Public School Children's Time Estimation Skills," *Child Study Journal* 11 (1981): 247–52.

166. J.F. Bryde, *Modern Indians*, National Institute of Mental Health (Washington, DC: GPO, 1969).

167. J.N. Cress and J.P. O'Donnell, "Indiannness, Sex, and Grade Differences on Behavior and Personality Measures among Oglala Sioux Adolescents," *Psychology in the Schools* 11, no. 3 (1974): 306–9; B. Spilka, *Alienation and Achievement among Oglala Sioux Indian Secondary School Students* (1970), ERIC ED 945-225.

168. V.P. Collier, "How Long? A Synthesis of Research on Academic Achievement in a Second Language," *TESOL Quarterly* 23 (1989): 509–31; J. Cummins, *Empowering Minority Students* (Sacramento, CA: California Association for Bilingual Education, 1989).

169. National Commission on Excellence in Education, *A Nation at Risk: The Imperative for Educational Reform* (Washington, DC: GPO, 1983).

170. L. Weis, E. Farrar, and H.G. Petrie, eds., *Dropouts from School: Issues, Dilemmas, and Solutions* (Albany, NY: State University of New York, 1989).

171. L.A. Shepard and M.L. Smith, eds., *Flunking Grades: Research and Policies on Retention* (New York: Falmer Press, 1989).

172. L.J. Bearden, W.A. Spencer, and J.C. Moracco, "A Study of High School Dropouts," *The School Counselor* 37 (1989): 113–20.

173. G.G. Wehlage and R.A. Rutter, "Dropping Out: How Do Schools Contribute to the Problem?" *Teachers College Record* 87 (1986): 374–92.

174. Ibid.

175. L. Misiaszek, "The Cultural Dilemma of American Indians," *Social Education* 33, no. 4 (1969): 438–46; E.P. Dozier, "Toward a Background for the Teacher of Indian Students," *Teaching Multi-cultural Populations*, ed. J.C. Stone and D.P.

DeNeir (New York: Litton Educational Publishing, 1971); B. Chadwick, H. Bahr, and J. Strauss, "Indian Education in the City: Correlates of Academic Performance," *Journal of Educational Research* 70, no. 3 (1977): 135–41; J.J. Westermeyer, "Indian Powerlessness in Minnesota," *Society* 10, no. 3 (1973): 45–52.

176. S.W. Johnson and R. Suetopka-Duerre, "Contributory Factors in Alaska Native Educational Success: A Research Strategy," *Educational Research Quarterly* 8, no. 4 (1984): 49.

177. H.L. Hodgkinson, *The Demographics of American Indians: One Percent of the People—Fifty Percent of the Diversity* (Washington, DC: Institute for Educational Leadership, 1990).

178. D. Chavers, "Indian Education: Dealing with a Disaster," *Principal* 70, no. 3 (1991): 28–29.

179. H. Gilliland, "Discipline and the Indian Student," *Teaching the Indian Child: A Bilingual/Multicultural Approach*, ed. J. Reyhner (Billings, MT: Eastern Montana College, 1986), 232–41.

180. L. Olson and R. Edwards, *Push Out, Step Out: A Report on California Public School Dropouts* (Oakland, CA: Citizens Policy Center, 1982).

181. J.M. Gonzalez, "Renegotiating Society's Contract with the Public Schools," *Carnegie Quarterly*, Carnegie Corporation of New York, 1985, 1–4.

182. G.G. Wehlage and R.A. Rutter, "Dropping Out: How Do Schools Contribute to the Problem?" *Teachers College Record* 87 (1986): 374–92.

183. G. Golden, *Red Moon Called Me: Memoirs of a Schoolteacher in the Government Indian Service*, ed. C. Dryden (San Antonio, TX: Naylor, 1954); F.G. Iliff, *People of the Blue Water* (New York: Harper and Brothers, 1954); A.H. Kneale, *Indian Agent* (Caldwell, ID: Caxton, 1950).

184. Office of Indian Education Programs, *Report on BIA Education: Excellence in Indian Education through the Effective School Process*, Bureau of Indian Affairs, U.S. Department of the Interior (Washington, DC: GPO, 1988).

185. H. Gilliland, "The Need for an Adopted Curriculum," *Teaching the Indian Child: A Bilingual/Multicultural Approach*, ed. J. Reyhner (Billings, MT: Eastern Montana College, 1986), 5.

186. R.J. Havighurst, "Indian Education since 1960," *American Academy of Political and Social Science Annals* 436 (1978): 13–26.

187. E.S. Cahn, ed., *Our Brother's Keeper: The Indian in White America* (Washington, DC: New Community Press, 1969), 30.

188. M. Zintz, *The Indian Research Study: The Adjustment of Indian and Non-Indian Children to the Public Schools of New Mexico* (Albuquerque, NM: University of New Mexico, College of Education, 1960).

189. G. Heath, *Red, Brown, and Black Demands for Better Education* (Philadelphia: Westminster Press, 1972), 26.

190. H. Gilliland, "The Need for an Adopted Curriculum," *Teaching the Indian Child: A Bilingual/Multicultural Approach*, ed. J. Reyhner (Billings, MT: Eastern Montana College, 1986), 5–6.

191. D. Little Bear, "Teachers and Parents Working Together," *Teaching the Indian Child: A Bilingual/Multicultural Approach*, ed. J. Reyhner (Billings, MT: Eastern Montana College, 1986), 222.

192. E.A. Fuchs and R.J. Havighurst, *To Live on This Earth: American Indian Education* (Albuquerque, NM: University of New Mexico Press, 1983).

193. E.P. Dozier, "Toward a Background for the Teacher of Indian Students," *Teaching Multi-cultural Populations*, ed. J.C. Stone and D.P. DeNeir (New York: Litton Educational Publishing, 1971); R. Evans and M. Husband, "Indian Studies in the Classroom," *Journal of American Indian Education* 15 (1975): 4–7.

194. F. Erickson and G. Mohatt, "Cultural Organization of Participation in Two Classrooms of Indian Students," *Doing the Ethnography of Schooling*, ed. G. Spindler (New York: Holt, Rinehart, and Winston, 1982); A. Brewer, "On Indian Education," *Integrateducation* 15 (1971): 21–23; B. Lockhart, *Cultural Conflict: The Indian Child in the Non-Indian Classroom* (1978), ERIC ED 195-379.

195. A. Brown, "Cherokee Culture and School Achievement," *American Indian Culture and Research Journal* 4 (1980): 55–74.

196. F. Erickson and G. Mohatt, "Cultural Organization of Participation in Two Classrooms of Indian Students," *Doing the Ethnography of Schooling*, ed. G. Spindler (New York: Holt, Rinehart, and Winston, 1982); S.B. Heath, "Question at Home and at School: A Comparative Study," *Doing the Ethnography of Schooling*, ed. G. Spindler (New York: Holt, Rinehart, and Winston, 1982); R.V. Dumont, Jr., "Learning English and How to Be Silent: Studies in Sioux and Cherokee Classrooms," *Functions of Language in the Classroom*, ed. C.B. Cazden, V.P. John, and D. Hymes (New York: Teachers College Press, 1972).

197. E. Longstreet, *Aspects of Ethnicity* (New York: Teachers College Press, 1978); V.P. John, "Styles of Learning—Styles of Teaching: Reflections on the Education of Navajo Children," *Functions of Language in the Classroom*, ed. C.B. Cazden, V.P. John, and D. Hymes (New York: Teachers College Press, 1972).

198. A. Brown, "Cherokee Culture and School Achievement," *American Indian Culture and Research Journal* 4 (1980): 55–74; R.E. Slavin, "Research on Cooperative Learning: Consensus and Controversy," *Educational Leadership* 47 (1989): 52–54.

199. T.C. Wildcat, "Notes on Native Education," *Canadian Journal of Native Education* 9 (1981): 11–13; W.A. Scaldwell, J.E. Frame, and D.G. Cookson, "Individual Intellectual Assessment of Chippewa, Muncey, and Oneida Children Using the WISC-R" (Paper presented at the MOKAKIT Indian Education Research Conference, University of Western Ontario, London, Ontario, 1984).

200. N. Mickelson and C.G. Galloway, "Modification of Behavior Problems of Indian Children," *Elementary School Journal* 72 (1972): 150–55; G. Hurlburt, A. Henjum, and L. Eide, "A Comparison of Academic, Career, and Social Patterns of American Indian Students," *Journal of American Indian Education* 22 (1983): 17–23.

201. R.H. Wax, "The Warrior Dropouts," *Native Americans Today: Sociological Perspectives*, ed. H.M. Bahr, B.A. Chadwick, and R.C. Day (New York: Harper and Row Publishers, Inc., 1972), 149.

202. L. Meriam, R.A. Brown, H. Cloud, E. Dale, E. Duke, H. Edwards, F. McKenzie, M. Mark, W.C. Ryan, Jr., and W.J. Spillman, *The Problem of Indian Administration* (Baltimore: Johns Hopkins Press, 1928).

203. D. Deyhle, "Pushouts and Pullouts: Navajo and Ute School Leavers," *Journal of Navajo Education* 6, no. 2 (1989): 36–51.

204. J. Cummins, *Empowering Minority Students* (Sacramento, CA: California Association for Bilingual Education, 1989).
205. D.G. Savage, "Why Chapter I Hasn't Made a Difference," *Phi Delta Kappan* 68 (1987): 581–84; F. Smith, *Joining the Literacy Club: Further Essays into Literacy* (Portsmouth, NH: Heinemann, 1988).
206. D. Deyhle, "Pushouts and Pullouts: Navajo and Ute School Leavers," *Journal of Navajo Education* 6, no. 2 (1989): 36–51.
207. Senate Special Committee on School Performance, "Helping Schools Succeed at Helping All Children Learn," Fifteenth Alaska Legislature, Fairbanks, AK, 1989.
208. P.R. Platero, E.A. Brandt, G. Witherspoon, and P. Wong, *Navajo Students at Risk: Final Report for the Navajo Area Student Dropout Study* (Window Rock, AZ: Navajo Division of Education, 1986).
209. L.B. Palladino, *Indian and White in the Northwest: A History of Catholicity in Montana* (Lancaster, PA: Wickersham, 1922).
210. J. Oakes, *Keeping Track: How Schools Structure Inequality* (New Haven, CT: Yale University Press, 1985).
211. National Center for Education Statistics, *Analysis Report: Dropout Rates in the United States: 1988*, Office of Educational Research and Improvement, U.S. Department of Education, NCES 89-609 (Washington, DC: GPO, September 1989).
212. J. Oakes, *Keeping Track: How Schools Structure Inequality* (New Haven, CT: Yale University Press, 1985).
213. F. Miller and D.D. Caulkins, "Chippewa Adolescents: A Changing Generation," *Human Organization* 23, no. 2 (1964): 152.
214. E.D. Jackson, "The Teaching of English as a Second Language to Alaskan Native Children of Non-English Speaking Backgrounds on the Kindergarten and First Grade Levels" (Master's thesis, University of Washington, Seattle, 1963); H. Gilliland, "Self Concept and the Indian Student," *Teaching the Indian Child: A Bilingual/Multicultural Approach*, ed. J. Reyhner (Billings, MT: Eastern Montana College, 1986), 62.
215. H. Gilliland, "Self Concept and the Indian Student," *Teaching the Indian Child: A Bilingual/Multicultural Approach*, ed. J. Reyhner (Billings, MT: Eastern Montana College, 1986), 62.
216. E.A. Parmee, *Formal Education and Culture Change: A Modern Apache Indian Community and Government Education Programs* (Tucson, AZ: University of Arizona Press, 1968); M.J. Kennedy, "Contact and Acculturation of the Southwestern Pomo" (Ph.D. diss., University of California, Berkeley, 1955); B.H. Goodman, "An Investigation of the Adjustment of the Apache Indians to the Public Schools of the State of Arizona" (Master's thesis, Arizona State University, Tempe, 1951).
217. E.A. Fuchs and R.J. Havighurst, *To Live on This Earth: American Indian Education* (Albuquerque, NM: University of New Mexico Press, 1983).
218. A.L. Hafner, *National Education Longitudinal Study of 1988: A Profile of the American Eighth Grader*, National Center for Education Statistics, Office of Educational Research and Improvement, U.S. Department of Education (Washington, DC: GPO, 1990).

219. D. Deyhle, "Pushouts and Pullouts: Navajo and Ute School Leavers," *Journal of Navajo Education* 6, no. 2 (1989): 36–51.

220. D. Little Bear, "Teachers and Parents Working Together," *Teaching the Indian Child: A Bilingual/Multicultural Approach*, ed. J. Reyhner (Billings, MT: Eastern Montana College, 1986), 223.

221. Ibid.

222. H. Gilliland, "The Need for an Adopted Curriculum," *Teaching the Indian Child: A Bilingual/Multicultural Approach*, ed. J. Reyhner (Billings, MT: Eastern Montana College, 1986), 9.

223. R. Coles, *Children of Crisis*, vol. 3, *The South Goes North* (Boston: Little, Brown and Company, 1971), 435–36.

224. R. Rosenthal and L. Jacobson, *Pygmalion in the Classroom* (New York: Holt, Rinehart, and Winston, Inc., 1968).

225. W. Chunn, "Sorting Black Students for Success and Failure: The Inequity of Ability Grouping and Tracking," *Urban League Review* 11 (1988): 93–106.

226. K. Alexander, D. Entwisle, and M. Thomson, "School Performance, Status Relations, and the Structure of Sentiment: Bringing the Teacher Back In," *American Sociological Review* 52 (1987): 665–82.

227. K.L. Alexander and D.R. Entwisle, "Achievement in the First 2 Years of School: Patterns and Processes," *Monographs of the Society for Research in Child Development* 53, no. 2, serial no. 218 (1988); R.D. Rist, "Student Social Class and Teachers' Expectations: The Self-fulfilling Prophecy in Ghetto Education," *Harvard Educational Review* 40 (1970): 411–51.

228. R.D. Rist, "Student Social Class and Teachers' Expectations: The Self-fulfilling Prophecy in Ghetto Education," *Harvard Educational Review* 40 (1970): 411–51.

229. Center for Policy Research in Education, *Repeating Grades in School: Current Practice and Research Evidence*, EA021686, U.S. Department of Education (Washington, DC: GPO, 1990), 2–8.

230. A.M. Gallup, "The 18th Annual Gallup Poll of the Public Attitudes toward the Public Schools," *Phi Delta Kappan* 68 (1986): 43–59.

231. C.T. Holmes, "Grade Level Retention Effects: A Meta-Analysis of Research Studies," *Flunking Grades: Research and Policies on Retention*, ed. L.A. Shepard and M.L. Smith (New York: Falmer Press, 1986), 34–63.

232. D.A. Brynes, "Attitudes of Students, Parents, and Educators toward Repeating a Grade," *Flunking Grades: Research and Policies on Retention*, ed. L.A. Shepard and M.L. Smith (New York: Falmer Press, 1989), 180–231.

233. K. Yamamoto, "Children under Stress: The Causes and Cures," Family Weekly, Ogden [UT] *Standard Examiner*, 1980, pp. 6–8.

234. J.E. Parsons, T.F. Adler, and C.M. Kaczala, "Socialization of Achievement Attitudes and Beliefs: Parental Influences," *Child Development* 53 (1982): 310–21.

235. K.L. Alexander, D.R. Entwisle, D. Cadigin, and A. Pallas, "Getting Ready for First Grade: Standards of Deportment in Home and School," *Social Forces* 66 (1987): 57–84.

236. J. Porter, *Black Child, White Child* (Cambridge, MA: Harvard University Press, 1971); T.F. Pettigrew, *A Profile of the Negro American* (Princeton, NJ: D. Van Nostrand Co., 1964).

237. P.H. Dreyer and R.J. Havighurst, *The Self-Esteem of American Indian Youth: The Personal-Social Adjustment of American Indian Youth* (1970), ERIC ED 045-273; E.E. Harris, "Racial and National Identities: An Exploratory Study in Self and 'We Group' Attitudes," *Journal of Negro Education* 34 (1965): 425–30.

238. M. Crow Dog and R. Erdoes, *Lakota Woman* (New York: Grove Weidenfeld, 1990), 38.

239. D. Deyhle, "Pushouts and Pullouts: Navajo and Ute School Leavers," *Journal of American Indian Education* 23, no. 1 (1989): 36–51.

240. T. Giago, "Blood Quantum Is a Degree of Discrimination," *Notes from Indian Country*, vol. 1 (Pierre, SD: State Publishing Company, 1984), 337.

241. R. Means, Speech presented at the Law School of the University of Colorado, Boulder, CO, 19 April 1985.

242. F.A. Ryan, Working paper prepared for the National Advisory Committee on Indian Education, Paper No. 071279, Harvard American Indian Education Program, Harvard University Graduate School of Education, Cambridge, MA, 18 July 1979.

243. V.I. Armstrong, *I Have Spoken: American History through the Voices of the Indians* (New York: Pocket Books, 1975), 175.

244. P.N. Limerick, *The Legacy of Conquest: The Unbroken Past of the American West* (New York: W.W. Norton and Co., 1987), 338.

245. U.S. Department of Health, Education, and Welfare, "A Study of Selected Socio-Economic Characteristics of Ethnic Minorities Based on the 1970 Census," *American Indians*, vol. 3 (Washington, DC: GPO, 1974).

246. U.S. Congress, Office of Technology Assessment, *Indian Health Care*, OTA-H-290 (Washington, DC: GPO, 1986), 78.

247. R. Thorton, *American Indian Holocaust and Survival: A Population History since 1492* (Norman, OK: University of Oklahoma Press, 1987), 199–200.

Chapter 6

1. N. Butterfield, "Transcending the Stereotype: American-Indian Women Embody Modern and Traditional Characteristics," *Ohoyo* (1980): 5; B. Medicine, *The Native American Woman: A Perspective* (Austin, TX: National Educational Laboratory Publishers, 1978); P.C. Albers, "Sioux Women in Transition: A Study of Their Changing Status in Domestic and Capitalist Sectors of Production," *The Hidden Half: Studies of Plains Indian Women*, ed. P. Albers and B. Medicine (Lanham, MD: University Press of America, 1983); P.G. Allen, *The Sacred Hoop: Recovering the Feminine in American Indian Traditions* (Boston: Beacon Press, 1986); S. Steiner, *The New Indians* (New York: Harper and Row Publishers, Inc., 1968).

2. S. Steiner, *The New Indians* (New York: Harper and Row Publishers, Inc., 1968).

Chapter 8

1. Quoted in B. Anquoe, "Indians Fall in Poverty Stats," *Lakota Times*, 29 July 1992, p. 1.
2. R. Coles, *Children of Crisis*, vol. 3: *The South Goes North* (Boston: Little, Brown and Company, 1971), 435.
3. Ibid., 435–36.
4. U.S. Government Accounting Office, *Dropouts: The Extent and Nature of the Problem*, (Washington, DC: GPO, June 1986); S.S. Peng and R.T. Takai, *High School Dropouts: Descriptive Information from High School and Beyond*, Bulletin (Washington, DC: National Center for Educational Statistics 1983); Hispanic Policy Development Project, *Make Something Happen* (Washington, DC: National Commission on Secondary Schooling for Hispanics, 1984); National Foundation for the Improvement of Education, *Dropping Out: The Quiet Killer of the American Dream* (Washington, DC: National Education Association, 1986); S. Peng, *High School Dropouts: A National Concern*, U.S. Department of Education, prepared for the Business Advisory Commission, Education Commission of the States, Denver, CO, March 1985; K.G. Swisher, M. Hoisch, and D.M. Pavel, *American Indian/Alaskan Native Dropout Study* (Washington, DC: National Education Association, 1991).
5. T.R. Sizer, *Horace's Compromise: The Dilemma of the American High School* (Boston: Houghton Mifflin, 1984), 36–37.
6. I.V. Sawhill, "The Underclass: An Overview," *Public Interest* 96 (Summer 1989): 3.
7. Ibid., 5.
8. Ibid.
9. W.J. Wilson, *The Truly Disadvantaged: The Inner-City, the Underclass, and Public Policy* (Chicago: University of Chicago Press, 1987), 6–7.
10. D.T. Ellwood, *Poor Support: Poverty in the American Family* (New York: Basic Books, 1988), 200.
11. J.M. Gonzalez, "Renegotiating Society's Contract with the Public Schools," *Carnegie Quarterly*, Carnegie Corporation of New York, 1985, 4.
12. B.S. Bloom, "Innocence in Education," *School Review* 80 (1972): 333–52.
13. J. Shipman and A. Bussis, "The Impact of the Family," *Disadvantaged Children and Their First School Experience: ETS–OEO Longitudinal Study* (Princeton, NJ: Educational Testing Service, 1968).
14. E.S. Shaefer, "Parents as Educators: Evidence from Cross-Sectional, Longitudinal, and Intervention Research," *The Young Child*, Vol. 2, ed. W.W. Hartup (Washington, DC: National Association for the Education of Young Children, 1976); E.S. Shaefer, "Need for Early and Continuing Education," *Education of the Infant and Young Child*, ed. V.H. Denenberg (New York: Academic Press, 1970).
15. H. Levin, "Work: The Staff of Life" (Paper presented at the American Psychological Association Conference, New York, 1975).
16. N. Hurwitz, "Communications Networks and the Urban Poor," *Equal Opportunity Review* (May 1975): 1–5.

17. Ibid., 4.
18. H.G. Birch and J.D. Gussow, *Disadvantaged Children: Health, Nutrition, and School Failure* (New York: Harcourt, Brace & World, 1970); H.G. Birch, "Malnutrition, Learning, and Intelligence," *American Journal of Public Health* 62 (1972): 773–84.
19. H.G. Birch, "Malnutrition, Learning, and Intelligence," *American Journal of Public Health* 62 (1972): 773–84; J. Brock, *Recent Advances in Human Nutrition* (London: J. & A. Churchill, 1961); H.G. Birch and J.D. Gussow, *Disadvantaged Children: Health, Nutrition, and School Failure* (New York: Harcourt, Brace & World, 1970); M.G. Hertzig, H.G. Birch, S.A. Richardson, and J. Tizard, "Intellectual Levels of School Children Severely Malnourished during the First Two Years of Life," *Pediatrics* 49 (1972): 814–24.

Chapter 9

1. J.U. Ogbu, *The Next Generation* (New York: Academic Press, 1974); J.U. Ogbu, *Minority Education and Caste: The American System in Crosscultural Perspective* (New York: Academic Press, 1978).
2. E. Jacob and C. Jordan, "Explaining the School Performance of Minority Students," *Anthropology and Education Quarterly* 18, no. 4 (1987): 259–392.
3. E. Jacob and C. Jordan, "Explaining the School Performance of Minority Students," *Anthropology and Education Quarterly* 18, no. 4 (1987): 259–392; C.A. Bowers and D.J. Flanders, *Responsive Teaching: An Ecological Approach to Classroom Patterns of Language, Culture, and Thought* (New York: Teachers College Press, 1990); G.D. Spindler, "Why Have Minority Groups in North America Been Disadvantaged in Their Schools?" *Education and Cultural Process: Anthropological Approaches*, ed. G.D. Spindler (Prospect Heights, IL: Waveland, 1987), 160–72.
4. G. Wilkinson, "Educational Problems in the Indian Community: A Comment on Learning as Colonialism," *Integrateducation* 19 (January/April 1981): 46.
5. M. Cole and J. Bruner, "Cultural Differences and Inferences about Psychological Processes," *American Psychologist* 26 (1971): 867–76.
6. D.H. Hymes, "On Ways of Speaking," *Explorations in the Ethnography of Speaking*, ed. P. Bauman and J. Sherzer (New York: Cambridge University Press, 1974).
7. S.U. Philips, *The Invisible Culture* (New York: Longman Press, 1983), 4.
8. W. Labov, "The Logic of Non-Standard English," *Language and Poverty: Perspectives on a Theme*, ed. F. Williams (Chicago: Markham, 1970); S. Baratz and J. Baratz, "Early Childhood Intervention: The Social Science Base of Institutional Racism," *Harvard Educational Review* 40 (1970): 29–50.
9. R. Gallimore, J. Boggs, and C. Jordan, *Culture, Behavior, and Education* (Beverly Hills, CA: Sage, 1974).
10. S. Ledlow, "Is Cultural Discontinuity an Adequate Explanation for Dropping Out?" *Journal of American Indian Education* 31, no. 3 (1992): 21–36.
11. L. Vogt, C. Jordan, and R.G. Tharp, "Explaining School Failure, Producing School Success: Two Cases," *Anthropology and Education Quarterly* 18 (1987): 276–86.

12. Ibid.
13. T. Coladarci, "High School Dropout among Native Americans," *Journal of American Indian Education* 23, no. 1 (1983): 15–22; J. Reyhner, "American Indians out of School: A Review of School-based Causes and Solutions," *Journal of American Indian Education* 31, no. 3 (1992): 21–56.
14. K.S. Chan and B. Osthimer, *Navajo Youth and Early School Withdrawal: A Case Study* (Los Alamitos, CA: National Center for Bilingual Research, 1983).
15. D. Deyhle, "Pushouts and Pullouts: Navajo and Ute School Leavers," *Journal of Navajo Education* 6, no. 2 (1989): 42.
16. J.U. Ogbu, "Cultural Discontinuities and Schooling," *Anthropology and Education Quarterly* 13 (1982): 290–307.
17. Ibid., 291.
18. Ibid., 298.
19. F. Erickson, "Transformation and School Success: The Politics and Culture of Educational Achievement," *Anthropology and Education Quarterly* 18 (1987): 335–56.
20. Ibid., 344.
21. Ibid., 348.
22. Ibid., 354.
23. Ibid., 354–55.
24. G. Wilkinson, "Educational Problems in the Indian Community: A Comment on Learning as Colonialism," *Integrateducation* 19 (January/April 1981): 47.
25. K.S. Chan and B. Osthimer, *Navajo Youth and Early School Withdrawal: A Case Study* (Los Alamitos, CA: National Center for Bilingual Research, 1983); D. Deyhle, "Pushouts and Pullouts: Navajo and Ute School Leavers, " *Journal of Navajo Education* 6, no. 2 (1989): 42.
26. G. Wilkinson, "Educational Problems in the Indian Community: A Comment on Learning as Colonialism," *Integrateducation* 19 (January/April 1981): 49.
27. Ibid., 50.

Chapter 11

1. P.A. May, "Alcohol and Drug Misuse Prevention Programs for American Indians: Needs and Opportunities," *Journal of Studies on Alcohol* 47, no. 3 (1986): 187–95.
2. D.L. Cahalan and H.M. Crossley, *American Drinking Practices: A National Study of Drinking Behaviors and Attitudes*, Monograph No. 6 (New Brunswick, NJ: Rutgers Center for Alcohol Studies, 1969); W.B. Clark, L. Midanik, and G. Knupfer, *Report on the 1979 National Survey* (Berkeley, CA: Social Research Group, 1981).

Chapter 12

1. N. Chodorow, "Family Structure and Feminine Personality," *Woman, Culture, and Society*, ed. M.Z. Rosaldo and L. Lamphere (Stanford, CA: Stanford University Press, 1974), 44.

2. V. Woolf, *A Room of One's Own* (New York: Harcourt, Brace & World, 1929).
3. C. Gilligan, *In a Different Voice: Psychological Theory and Women's Development* (Cambridge, MA: Harvard University Press, 1982), 86.

Chapter 15

1. D. Finkelhor, R.J. Gelles, G.T. Hotaling, and M.A. Straus, eds., *The Dark Side of Families: Current Family Violence Research* (Beverly Hills, CA: Sage, 1983); E. Zigler, "Controlling Child Abuse in America: An Effort Doomed to Failure," *Critical Perspectives on Child Abuse*, ed. R. Bourne and E.H. Newberger (Lexington, MA: Lexington Books, 1979), 171–207.

Chapter 18

1. N. Chansky, *Untapped Good: The Rehabilitation of School Dropouts* (Springfield, IL: Charles C Thomas, 1966).

References

Ackerman, L.A. "Marital Instability and Juvenile Delinquency among the Nez Perces." *American Anthropologist* 73, no. 3 (1971): 595–603.

Ahenakew, F. "Text Based Grammars in Cree Language Education." *Proceedings: Selected Papers and Biographies*. Ed. S. Weryackwe. Choctaw, OK: Sixth Annual International Native American Language Issues Institute, 1986. 1–3.

Albaugh, B., and P. Albaugh. "Alcoholism and Substance Sniffing among the Cheyenne and Arapaho Indians of Oklahoma." *International Journal of the Addictions* 14, no. 7 (1979): 1001–7.

Albers, P.C. "Sioux Women in Transition: A Study of Their Changing Status in Domestic and Capitalist Sectors of Production." *The Hidden Half: Studies of Plains Indian Women*. Eds. P. Albers and B. Medicine. Lanham, MD: University Press of America, 1983.

Alexander, K., D. Entwisle, and M. Thomson. "School Performance, Status Relations, and the Structure of Sentiment: Bringing the Teacher Back In." *American Sociological Review* 52 (1987): 665–82.

Alexander, K.L., and D.R. Entwisle. "Achievement in the First 2 Years of School: Patterns and Processes." *Monographs of the Society for Research in Child Development* 53, no. 2, serial no. 218 (1988).

Alexander, K.L., D.R. Entwisle, D. Cadigin, and A. Pallas. "Getting Ready for First Grade: Standards of Deportment in Home and School." *Social Forces* 66 (1987): 57–84.

Allen, P.G. *The Sacred Hoop: Recovering the Feminine in American Indian Traditions*. Boston: Beacon Press, 1986.

Anderson, B. "A Comparative Study in Estimating Time." *Journal of American Indian Education* 19 (1980): 1–4.

Anderson, F.N. "A Mental Hygiene Survey of Problem Indian Children in Oklahoma." *Mental Hygiene* 20 (1936): 472–76.

Anderson, G., and D. Safar. "The Influence of Differential Community Perceptions on the Provision of Equal Educational Opportunities." *Sociology of Education* 40, no. 2 (1967): 219–30.

Anderson, O., ed. *American Indian–Alaskan Native Women's Caucus Newsletter* (January 1979). Wichita Falls, TX.

Anquoe, B. "Indians Fall in Poverty Stats." *Lakota Times*, 29 July 1992, p. 1.

Armstrong, V.I. *I Have Spoken: American History through the Voices of the Indians*. New York: Pocket Books, 1975.

Au, K.H., and C. Jordan. "Teaching Reading to Hawaiian Children: Finding a Culturally Appropriate Solution." *Culture and Bilingual Classroom: Studies in Classroom Ethnography*. Eds. H. Trueba, G. Guthrie, and K. Au. Boston, MA: Newbury House, 1981.

Aurbach, H., and E. Fuchs (with G. Macgregor). *An Extensive Survey of American Indian Education*. College Park, PA: Pennsylvania State University, 1969.

Austin, G. *Drugs and Minorities*. NIDA Research Issues, Series 21, DHEW Pub. (ADM). Washington, DC: U.S. Government Printing Office, 1977.

Bacon, H.L., G.D. Kidd, and J.J. Seaberg. "The Effectiveness of Bilingual Instruction with Cherokee Indian Students." *Journal of American Indian Education* 21 (1982): 34–43.

Bahr, H.M., B.A. Chadwick, and R.C. Day, eds. *Native Americans Today: Sociological Perspectives*. New York: Harper and Row Publishers, Inc., 1972.

Bahr, H.M., B.A. Chadwick, and J.H. Strauss. *American Ethnicity*. Lexington, MA: D.C. Heath and Co., 1979.

Baker, P. "A Report on the National Longitudinal Surveys of Youth Labor Market Experience in 1982." *Pathways to the Future*. Report No. 4. Worthington, OH: Ohio State University, Center for Human Resource Research, 1984.

Bales, R.F. "Cultural Differences in Rates of Alcoholism." *Quarterly Journal of Studies on Alcohol* 6, no. 4 (1946): 480–99.

Baratz, S., and J. Baratz. "Early Childhood Intervention: The Social Science Base of Institutional Racism." *Harvard Educational Review* 40 (1970): 29–50.

Barro, S.M. *The Incidences of Dropping Out: A Descriptive Analysis*. Washington, DC: SMB Economic Research, Inc., 1984.

Bataille, G.M., and C.L.P. Silet. "Economic and Psychic Exploitation of American Indians." *Explorations in Ethnic Studies* 6 (1983): 8–23.

Bearden, L.J., W.A. Spencer, and J.C. Moracco. "A Study of High School Dropouts." *The School Counselor* 37 (1989): 113–20.

Beauvais, F., and S. LaBoueff. "Drug and Alcohol Abuse Intervention in American Indian Communities." *International Journal of the Addictions* 20, no. 1 (1985): 139–71.

Beauvais, F., and E.R. Oetting. "Inhalant Abuse by Young Children." *Epidemiology of Inhalant Abuse: An Update*. Ed. R. Crider and B. Rouse. NIDA Research Monograph No. 85. Washington, DC: U.S. Government Printing Office, 1988.

Beauvais, F., E.R. Oetting, and R.W. Edwards. "Trends in Drug Use of Indian Adolescents Living on Reservations: 1975–1983." *American Journal of Drug and Alcohol Abuse* 11 (1985): 209–29.

Berger, A. "Nine Families and Forty Children." *Journal of American Indian Education* 12, no. 3 (1973): 1–8.

Berkhofer, R.F., Jr. *The White Man's Indian*. New York: Alfred A. Knopf, 1978.

Berlin, I. "Psychopathology and Its Antecedents among American Indian Adolescents." *Advances in Clinical Psychology* 9 (1986): 125–51.

Berry, B. *The Education of American Indians: A Survey of the Literature*. Washington, DC: U.S. Government Printing Office, 1968.

Binion, A., C. Miller, F. Beauvais, and E.R. Oetting. "Rationales for the Use of Alcohol, Marijuana, and Other Drugs by Eighth Grade Native American and Anglo Youth." *International Journal of the Addictions* 23, no. 1 (1988): 47–64.

Birch, H.G. "Malnutrition, Learning and Intelligence." *American Journal of Public Health* 62 (1972): 773–84.

Birch, H.G., and J.D. Gussow. *Disadvantaged Children: Health, Nutrition, and School Failure*. New York: Harcourt, Brace & World, 1970.

Bloom, B.S. *All Our Children Learning*. New York: McGraw-Hill, 1981.

Bloom, B.S. "Innocence in Education." *School Review* 80 (1972): 333–52.

Blossom, G. "A New Approach to an Old Problem." *Journal of American Indian Education* 1, no. 2 (1962): 13–14.

Board of Indian Commissioners. *Report to Congress, 1873.* Washington, DC: U.S. Government Printing Office, 1874.

Bowd, A.D. "Some Determinants of School Achievement in Several Indian Groups." *Alberta Journal of Educational Research* 18, no. 2 (1972): 69–81.

Bowers, C.A., and D.J. Flanders. *Responsive Teaching: An Ecological Approach to Classroom Patterns of Language, Culture, and Thought.* New York: Teachers College Press, 1990.

Bowles, S., and H. Gintis. *Schooling in Capitalist America.* New York: Basic Books, 1976.

Boyer, L.B. "Folk Psychiatry of the Apaches of the Mescalero Indian Reservation." *Magic, Faith, and Healing.* Ed. A. Kiev. New York: Free Press of Glencoe, 1964.

Brewer, A. "On Indian Education." *Integrateducation* 15 (1971): 21–23.

Brock, J. *Recent Advances in Human Nutrition.* London: J. & A. Churchill, 1961.

Brod, R.L., and J.M. McQuiston. "American Indian Adult Education and Literacy: The First Annual Survey." *Journal of American Indian Education* 1, no. 22 (1983): 1–16.

Brod, T. "Alcoholism as a Mental Health Problem of Native Americans: A Review of the Literature." *Archives of General Psychiatry* 32 (1975): 1385–91.

Brown, A. "Cherokee Culture and School Achievement." *American Indian Culture and Research Journal* 4 (1980): 55–74.

Bryde, J.F. *Modern Indian Psychology.* Vermillion, SD: Institute of Indian Studies, 1971.

Bryde, J.F. *Modern Indians.* National Institute of Mental Health. Washington, DC: U.S. Government Printing Office, 1969.

Bryde, J.F. *The Sioux Indian Student: A Study of Scholastic Failure and Personality Conflict.* Vermillion, SD: Dakota Press, 1970.

Brynes, D.A. "Attitudes of Students, Parents, and Educators toward Repeating a Grade." *Flunking Grades: Research and Policies on Retention.* Ed. L.A. Shepard and M.L. Smith. New York: Falmer Press, 1989. 180–231.

Burd, L., J. Dodd, and P. Grassl. "A Comparison of Reservation Native American and Public School Children's Time Estimation Skills." *Child Study Journal* 11 (1981): 247–52.

Burnap, A. "An Analysis of Self-Esteem in Reservation Indian Youth as Measured by Coopersmith's Self-Esteem Inventory." Master's thesis, Northern State College (MT), 1972.

Butterfield, N. "Transcending the Stereotype: American-Indian Women Embody Modern and Traditional Characteristics." *Ohoyo* (1980): 5.

Bynum, J. "Suicide and the American Indian: An Analysis of Recent Trends." *Native American Indians Today: Sociological Perspectives.* Ed. H.M. Bahr, B.A. Chadwick, and R.C. Day. New York: Harper and Row Publishers, Inc., 1972. 367–77.

Cahalan, D.L., and H.M. Crossley. *American Drinking Practices: A National Study of Drinking Behaviors and Attitudes.* Monograph No. 6. New Brunswick, NJ: Rutgers Center for Alcohol Studies, 1969.

Cahn, E.S., ed. *Our Brother's Keeper: The Indian in White America.* Washington, DC: New Community Press, 1969.

Carlson, R. "On the Structure of Self Esteem: Comments on Ziller's Formulations." *Journal of Consulting and Clinical Psychology* 34 (1970): 264–68.

Carpenter, R., C.A. Lyons, and W.R. Miller. "Peer-managed Self-Control Programs for Prevention of Alcohol Abuse in American Indian High School Students: A Pilot Evaluation Study." *International Journal of the Addictions* 20, no. 2 (1985): 299–310.

Carter, T.P. *Mexican-Americans in School: A History of Educational Neglect.* New York: College Entrance Examination Board, 1970.

Catterall, J.S. *On the Social Costs of Dropping out of School.* Stanford, CA: Stanford University, Educational Policy Institute, School of Education, 1985.

Catterall, J.S., and E. Cota-Robles. "The Educationally At-Risk: What the Numbers Mean." *Accelerating the Education of At-Risk Students.* Stanford, CA: Stanford University, Center for Educational Research at Stanford, 1988. 6–7.

Cavatta, J.C. *New Mexico Dropout Study: 1981–82 School Year.* Santa Fe, NM: New Mexico State Department of Education, Evaluation, Assessment, and Testing Unit, 1982.

Cavatta, J.C., and A.S. Gomez. *New Mexico Dropout Study: 1983–84 School Year.* Santa Fe, NM: New Mexico State Department of Education, Evaluation, Assessment, and Testing Unit, 1984.

Center for Policy Research in Education. *Repeating Grades in School: Current Practice and Research Evidence.* EA021686, U.S. Department of Education. Washington, DC: U.S. Government Printing Office, 1990.

Centers for Disease Control. "One-Fourth Infants Born to Single Moms." (AP Wire Service, Washington, DC). *Bozeman* [MT] *Daily Chronicle,* 3 August 1990, pp. 1, 3.

Chadwick, B., H. Bahr, and J. Strauss. "Indian Education in the City: Correlates of Academic Performance." *Journal of Educational Research* 70, no. 3 (1977): 135–41.

Chan, K.S., and B. Osthimer. *Navajo Youth and Early School Withdrawal: A Case Study.* Los Alamitos, CA: National Center for Bilingual Research, 1983.

Chansky, N. *Untapped Good: The Rehabilitation of School Dropouts.* Springfield, IL: Charles C Thomas, 1966.

Chavers, D. "Indian Education: Dealing with a Disaster." *Principal* 70, no. 3 (1991): 28–29.

Cherrington, E.H. *The Evolution of Prohibition in the United States of America.* Westerville, OH: American Issue Press, 1920.

Chodorow, N. "Family Structure and Feminine Personality." *Woman, Culture, and Society.* Ed. M.Z. Rosaldo and L. Lamphere. Stanford, CA: Stanford University Press, 1974.

Chunn, W. "Sorting Black Students for Success and Failure: The Inequity of Ability Grouping and Tracking." *Urban League Review* 11 (1988): 93–106.

Clark, W.B., L. Midanik, and G. Knupfer. *Report on the 1979 National Survey.* Berkeley, CA: Social Research Group, 1981.

Clawson, R. "Death by Drink: An Indian Battle." [Butte] *Montana Standard,* 7 January 1990, p. 5.

Clifton, R.A. "Self Concept and Attitudes: A Comparison of Canadian Indian and Non-Indian Students." *Canadian Review of Sociology and Anthropology* 12 (1975): 577–84.

Cockerham, W.C. "Drinking Attitudes and Practices among Wind River Reservation Youth." *Quarterly Journal of Studies on Alcohol* 36 (1975): 321–26.

Cockerham, W.C., M.A. Forslund, and R.M. Raboin. "Drug Use among White and American Indian High School Youth." *International Journal of the Addictions* 11 (1976): 209–20.

Cocking, R.R. "Fantasy Confession among Arapaho Indian Children." *Journal of Genetic Psychology* 114 (1969): 229–35.

Cohen, W.H., and P. Mause. "The Indian: The Forgotten American." *Harvard Law Review* 81, no. 8 (1968): 1818–58.

Coladarci, T. "High School Dropout among Native Americans." *Journal of American Indian Education* 23, no. 1 (1983): 15–22.

Cole, M., and J. Bruner. "Cultural Differences and Inferences about Psychological Processes." *American Psychologist* 26 (1971): 867–76.

Coleman, J.S. *Equality of Educational Opportunity.* Washington, DC: U.S. Government Printing Office, 1966.

Coles, R. *Children of Crisis*, vol. 3: *The South Goes North.* Boston: Little, Brown and Company, 1971.

Collier, V.P. "How Long? A Synthesis of Research on Academic Achievement in a Second Language." *TESOL Quarterly* 23 (1989): 509–31.

Conrad, R.D., and M. Kahn. "An Epidemiological Study of Suicide and Attempted Suicide among the Papago Indians." *American Journal of Psychiatry* 131, no. 1 (1974): 69–72.

Conway, W.D. "A Transformational Analysis of the Written and Oral Syntax of Fourth, Sixth, and Eighth Grade Omaha Indian Children." Ph.D. dissertation, University of Nebraska, Lincoln, 1971.

Coombs, L.M. *The Educational Disadvantage of the Indian American Student.* Las Cruces, NM: New Mexico State University, 1970.

Coombs, L.M. "The Indian Student Is Not Low Man on the Totem Pole." *Journal of American Indian Education* 9 (1970): 1–9.

Coombs, L.M., R. Kron, E. Collister, and K. Anderson. *The Indian Child Goes to School.* Lawrence, KS: U.S. Bureau of Indian Affairs, Haskell Institute, 1958.

Corrigan, F.V. "A Comparison of Self-Concepts of American Indian Students from Public or Federal School Background." Ph.D. dissertation, George Washington University, Washington, DC, 1970.

Crawford, J. "One-third of Navajos Drop out Annually." *Education Week* 1 (1986): 1–3.

Cress, J.N., and J.P. O'Donnell. "Indiannness, Sex, and Grade Differences on Behavior and Personality Measures among Oglala Sioux Adolescents." *Psychology in the Schools* 11, no. 3 (1974): 306–9.

Crider, R., and B. Rouse, eds. *Epidemiology of Inhalant Abuse: An Update.* NIDA Research Monograph No. 85. Washington, DC: U.S. Government Printing Office, 1988.

Crow Dog, M., and R. Erdoes. *Lakota Woman.* New York: Grove Weidenfeld, 1990.

Cummins, J. *Empowering Minority Students.* Sacramento, CA: California Association for Bilingual Education, 1989.

Cummins, J. "Empowering Minority Students: A Framework for Intervention." *Harvard Educational Review* 56 (1986): 18–36.

Currie, E., and J.H. Skolnick. *America's Problems: Social Issues and Public Policy.* Boston: Little, Brown and Company, 1984.

Deissler, K.L. "A Study of South Dakota Indian Achievement Problems." *Journal of American Indian Education* 1, no. 3 (1962): 19–21.

Deitch, L.I. "The Impact of Tourism upon the Arts and Crafts of the Indians of the Southwestern United States." *Hosts and Guests: The Anthropology of Tourism.* Ed. V.L. Smith. Philadelphia: University of Pennsylvania Press, 1977.

Delk, J.L. "Dropouts from an American Indian Reservation: A Possible Prevention Program." *Journal of Community Psychology* 2, no. 1 (1974): 15–17.

Deloria, E.C. *Speaking of Indians.* New York: Friendship Press, 1944.

Deyhle, D. "Learning Failure: Tests as Gatekeepers and the Culturally Different Child." *Success or Failure? Learning and the Language Minority Child.* Ed. H. Trueba. New York: Newbury Publishers, 1987.

Deyhle, D. "Pushouts and Pullouts: Navajo and Ute School Leavers." *Journal of Navajo Education* 6, no. 2 (1989): 36–51.

Dizmang, L.H. "Suicide among Cheyenne Indians." *Bulletin of Suicidology* 1 (1967): 8–11.

Dizmang, L.H., J. Watson, P.A. May, and J. Bopp. "Adolescent Suicide at Fort Hall Reservation." Paper presented at the Annual Meeting of the American Psychiatric Association, May 1970.

Dizmang, L.H., J. Watson, P.A. May, and J. Bopp. "Adolescent Suicide at an Indian Reservation." *American Journal of Orthopsychiatry* 44, no. 1 (1974): 43–49.

Dorris, M. *The Broken Cord.* New York: Harper and Row Publishers, Inc., 1989.

Dozier, E.P. "Problem Drinking among American Indians." *Quarterly Journal of Studies on Alcohol* 27 (1966): 72–87.

Dozier, E.P. "Toward a Background for the Teacher of Indian Students." *Teaching Multi-cultural Populations.* Ed. J.C. Stone and D.P. DeNeir. New York: Litton Educational Publishing, 1971.

Dreyer, P.H., and R.J. Havighurst. *The Self-Esteem of American Indian Youth: The Personal-Social Adjustment of American Indian Youth, 1970.* ERIC ED 045-273.

Dumont, R.V., Jr. "Learning English and How to Be Silent: Studies in Sioux and Cherokee Classrooms." *Functions of Language in the Classroom.* Ed. C.B. Cazden, V.P. John, and D. Hymes. New York: Teachers College Press, 1972.

Dunn, L.M. *Bilingual Hispanic Children on the U.S. Mainland: A Review of Research on Their Cognitive, Linguistic, and Scholastic Development.* Circle Pines, MN: AGS, 1987.

Duston, D. "Senate Panel Asks Lujan for Action to Help Indians." (AP Wire Service, Washington, DC). *Bozeman* [MT] *Daily Chronicle,* 8 June 1989, pp. 1, 3.

Dweck, C., T.E. Goetz, and N. Strauss. "Sex Differences in Learned Helplessness, IV: An Experimental and Naturalistic Study of Failure Generalization and Its Mediators." *Journal of Personality and Social Psychology* 38 (1980): 441–52.

Eberhard, D.R. "American Indian Education: A Study of Dropouts, 1980–1987." *Journal of American Indian Education* 19, no. 1 (1989): 32–40.

Edwards, E.D., and M.E. Edwards. "Alcoholism Prevention/Treatment and Native American Youth: A Community Approach." *Journal of Drug Issues* 18, no. 10 (1988): 103–15.

Ekstrom, R.B., M.E. Goertz, J.M. Pollack, and D.A. Rock. "Who Drops out of High School and Why? Findings from a National Survey." *Teachers College Record* 87, no. 3 (1986): 356–73.

Ellwood, D.T. *Poor Support: Poverty in the American Family.* New York: Basic Books, 1988.

Erickson, F. "Transformation and School Success: The Politics and Culture of Educational Achievement." *Anthropology and Education Quarterly* 18 (1987): 335–56.

Erickson, F., and G. Mohatt. "Cultural Organization of Participation in Two Classrooms of Indian Students." *Doing the Ethnography of Schooling.* Ed. G. Spindler. New York: Holt, Rinehart, and Winston, 1982.

Erikson, E.H. *Childhood and Society.* New York: W.W. Norton and Co., 1950.

Erikson, E.H. *Childhood and Society.* 2nd ed. New York: W.W. Norton and Co., 1963.

Erikson, E.H. *Identity: Youth and Crisis.* New York: W.W. Norton and Co., 1968.

Erikson, E.H. "Observations on Sioux Education." *Journal of Psychology* 7 (1939): 101–56.

Evans, R., and M. Husband. "Indian Studies in the Classroom." *Journal of American Indian Education* 15 (1975): 4–7.

Evvard E. "A New Concept on the Navajo." *Journal of American Indian Education* 5, no. 3 (1966): 1–17.

"Excerpts from an Interview with Secretary of the Interior James Watt." *Akwesasne Notes* 23 (Winter 1983): 1–3.

Farber, W.O., P.A. Odeen, and R.A. Tschelter. *Indians, Law Enforcement, and Local Government.* Brookings, SD: Government Research Bureau of South Dakota, 1957.

Faye, G.E., ed. *Charters, Laws, and Congressional Acts for Indian Tribes in North America.* Greeley, CO: Colorado State College Press, 1967.

"Federal Program Funding Continues Downward Spiral." *Lakota Times,* 2 September 1992, p.1.

Felber, R.J. "Factors Influencing the Educational Attainments of Indian Pupils in Sisseton, South Dakota." Master's thesis, University of Wyoming, Laramie, 1955.

Fine, M. "Why Urban Adolescents Drop into and out of Public High School." *Teachers College Record* 87 (1987): 3.

Fine, M., and P. Rosenberg. "Dropping out of High School: The Ideology of School and Work." *Journal of Education* 165 (1983): 257–72.

Finkelhor, D., R.J. Gelles, G.T. Hotaling, and M.A. Straus, eds. *The Dark Side of Families: Current Family Violence Research.* Beverly Hills, CA: Sage, 1983.

Fischler, R.S. "Child Abuse and Neglect in American Indian Communities." *Child Abuse and Neglect* 9 (1985): 95–106.

Fischler, R.S. "Child Abuse and Neglect in American Indians." *The IHS Primary Care Provider* 8 (1983): 1–7.

Fordham, S., and J.C. Ogbu. "Black Students' School Success: Coping with the 'Burden of Acting White.'" *The Urban Review* 18, no. 3 (1986): 176–206.

Forslund, M.A. *A Self-Concept Comparison of Indian and Anglo Delinquency in Wyoming.* Laramie, WY: Governor's Planning Committee on Criminal Administration, 1974.

Forslund, M.A., and V.A. Cranston. "A Self-Report Comparison of Indian and Anglo Delinquency in Wyoming." *Criminology* 13, no. 2 (1975): 193–98.

Forslund, M.A., and R.E. Meyers. "Delinquency among Wind River Indian Reservation Youth." *Criminology* 12, no. 1 (1974): 97–106.

Foster, C.G., S.A. Boloz, and D. Salas, eds. *Reservation Schools and 95-561: The Administrator and the Curriculum.* Flagstaff, AZ: Northern Arizona University, 1980.

Frederick, C. *Suicide, Homicide, and Alcoholism among American Indians.* DHEW Pub. No. ADM 76-92. Department of Health, Education, and Welfare. Washington, DC: U.S. Government Printing Office, 1975.

French, L. "An Analysis of Contemporary Indian Justice and Correctional Treatment." *Federal Probation* 44 (1980): 19–23.

French, L., and J. Hornbuckle. "An Analysis of Indian Violence: The Cherokee Example." *American Indian Quarterly* 3, no. 4 (1977): 335–56.

Fuchs, E.A., and R.J. Havighurst. *To Live on This Earth: American Indian Education.* Albuquerque, NM: University of New Mexico Press, 1983.

Futrell, M.H. "Mission Not Accomplished: Education Reform in Retrospect." *Phi Delta Kappan* 71 (1989): 8–14.

Gaarder, B. *Education of American Indian Children.* Report presented at the Annual Conference of the Southwest Council of Foreign Language Teachers, El Paso, TX, November 1967, and in testimony before the U.S. House of Representatives Subcommittee on Education, Washington, DC, June 1967. ERIC ED 018–299.

Gallimore, R., J. Boggs, and C. Jordan. *Culture, Behavior, and Education.* Beverly Hills, CA: Sage, 1974.

Gallup, A.M. "The 18th Annual Gallup Poll of the Public Attitudes toward the Public Schools." *Phi Delta Kappan* 68 (1986): 43–59.

Garcia, T. "A Study of the Effects of Education on the Wind River Reservation." Master's thesis, University of Wyoming, Laramie, 1965.

Garcia-Mason, V. *Relationship of Drug Use and Self-Concept among American Indian Youth.* Ph.D. dissertation, University of New Mexico, Albuquerque, 1985.

Gelles, R.J., and J.B. Lancaster, eds. *Child Abuse and Neglect: Biosocial Dimensions.* New York: Aldine DeGruyter, 1987.

George, D.M., and R.D. Hoppe. "Racial Identification, Preference, and Self-Concept: Canadian Indian and White Schoolchildren." *Journal of Cross-Cultural Psychology* 10, no. 1 (1979): 85–100.

Giago, T. "Blood Quantum Is a Degree of Discrimination." *Notes from Indian Country.* Vol. 1. Pierre, SD: State Publishing Company, 1984.

Gibson, M. "Punjabi Immigrants in an American High School." *Interpretive Ethnography of Education.* Eds. G. Spindler and L. Spindler. Hillsdale, NJ: Lawrence Erlbaum Associates, 1987.

Gilchrist, L., S. Schinke, J.E. Trimble, and G.T. Cvetovich. "Skills Enhancement to Prevent Substance Abuse among American Indian Adolescents." *International Journal of the Addictions* 22, no. 19 (1987): 869–79.

Giles, K.N. *Indian High School Dropout: A Perspective.* Milwaukee: University of Wisconsin–Milwaukee, Midwest National Origin Desegregation Assistance Center, 1985.

Gilligan, C. *In a Different Voice: Psychological Theory and Women's Development.* Cambridge, MA: Harvard University Press, 1982.

Gilliland, H. "Discipline and the Indian Student." *Teaching the Indian Child: A Bilingual/Multicultural Approach.* Ed. J. Reyhner. Billings, MT: Eastern Montana College, 1986. 232–41.

Gilliland, H. "The Need for an Adopted Curriculum." *Teaching the Indian Child: A Bilingual/Multicultural Approach.* Ed. J. Reyhner. Billings, MT: Eastern Montana College, 1986. 1–11.

Gilliland, H. "Self Concept and the Indian Student." *Teaching the Indian Child: A Bilingual/Multicultural Approach.* Ed. J. Reyhner. Billings, MT: Eastern Montana College, 1986. 57–69.

Golden, G. *Red Moon Called Me: Memoirs of a Schoolteacher in the Government Indian Service.* Ed. C. Dryden. San Antonio, TX: Naylor, 1954.

Goldman, S.V., and R. McDermott. "The Culture of Competition in American Schools." *Interpretive Ethnography of Education.* Eds. G. Spindler and L. Spindler. Hillsdale, NJ: Lawrence Erlbaum Associates, 1987.

Gonzalez, J.M. "Renegotiating Society's Contract with the Public Schools." *Carnegie Quarterly.* Carnegie Corporation of New York, 1985. 1–4.

Goodman, B.H. "An Investigation of the Adjustment of the Apache Indians to the Public Schools of the State of Arizona." Master's thesis, Arizona State University, Tempe, 1951.

Graham, O.L. *The Great Campaigns: Reform and War in America, 1900–1928.* Englewood Cliffs, NJ: Prentice Hall, 1971.

Graves, T.D. "Acculturation, Access, and Alcohol in a Tri-Ethnic Community." *American Anthropologist* 69 (1967): 306–21.

Graves, T.D. "The Personal Adjustment of Navajo Indian Migrants to Denver, Colorado." *American Anthropologist* 72, no. 1 (1970): 35–54.

Hafner, A.L. *National Education Longitudinal Study of 1988: A Profile of the American Eighth Grader.* National Center for Education Statistics, Office of Educational Research and Improvement, U.S. Department of Education. Washington, DC: U.S. Government Printing Office, 1990.

Hakuta, K. *Mirror of Language: The Debate on Bilingualism.* New York: Basic Books, 1986.

Hall, E.L., and A.A. Simkus. "Inequality in the Types of Sentences Received by Native Americans and Whites." *Criminology* 13, no. 2 (1975): 199–222.

Halpin G., G. Halpin, and T. Whiddon. "Locus of Control and Self-Esteem among Indians and Whites: A Cross-Cultural Comparison." *Psychological Reports* 48 (1981): 91–98.

Hamer, J.H. "Guardian Spirits, Alcohol, and Cultural Defense Mechanisms." *Anthropologica* 11 (1969): 215–41.

Hamilton, C., ed. *Cry of the Thunderbird: The American Indian's Own Story.* Norman, OK: University of Oklahoma Press, 1972.

Hammerschlag, C.A. *Identity Groups with American Indian Adolescents,* 1974. ERIC ED 098-451.

Hanson, B. "Drug Treatment Effectiveness: The Case of Racial and Ethnic Minorities in America—Some Research Questions and Proposals." *International Journal of the Addictions* 20 (1985): 99–137.

Harger, C.M. "The Indian's Last Stand." *Outlook* 70 (January 1902): 222–25.

Harris, E.E. "Racial and National Identities: An Exploratory Study in Self and 'We Group' Attitudes." *Journal of Negro Education* 34 (1965): 425–30.

Harvey, C.M. "The Indians of To-day and To-morrow." *American Review of Reviews* 33 (June 1906): 703–7.

Harvey, E.B., L. Gazay, and B. Samuels. "Utilization of a Psychiatric–Social Work Team in an Alaska Native Secondary Boarding School." *Journal of Child Psychiatry* 15, no. 3 (1976): 558–74.

Hassrick, R.B. *The Sioux: Life and Customs of a Warrior Society.* Norman, OK: University of Oklahoma Press, 1964.

Havighurst, R.J. "Indian Education since 1960." *American Academy of Political and Social Science Annals* 436 (1978): 13–26.

Havighurst, R.J., and B.L. Neugarten. *American Indian and White Children: A Sociopsychological Investigation.* Chicago: University of Chicago Press, 1955.

Heath, G. *Red, Brown, and Black Demands for Better Education.* Philadelphia: Westminster Press, 1972.

Heath, S.B. "Question at Home and at School: A Comparative Study." *Doing the Ethnography of Schooling.* Ed. G. Spindler. New York: Holt, Rinehart, and Winston, 1982.

Heatherington, M. *How Language Works.* Cambridge, MA: Winthrop, 1980.

Heidenreich, C.A. "Alcohol and Drug Use and Abuse among Indian-Americans: A Review of Issues and Sources." *Journal of Drug Issues* 6, no. 3 (1976): 256–72.

Helper, M.M., and S.L. Garfield. "Use of the Semantic Differential to Study Acculturation in American Indian Adolescents." *Journal of Personality and Social Psychology* 2 (1965): 817–22.

Hertzig, M.G., H.G. Birch, S.A. Richardson, and J. Tizard. "Intellectual Levels of School Children Severely Malnourished during the First Two Years of Life." *Pediatrics* 49 (1972): 814–24.

Hill, N. "American Indian Student Retention: Pedagogy and Self-Determination." *Opening the Montana Pipeline: American Indian Higher Education in the Nineties.* Ed. D. LaCounte, W. Stein, and P. Weasel Head. Sacramento, CA: Tribal College Press, 1991. 46–53.

Hill, T.W. "Life Styles and Drinking Patterns of Urban Indians." *Journal of Drug Issues* 10 (1980): 257–72.

Hispanic Policy Development Project. *Make Something Happen.* Washington, DC: National Commission on Secondary Schooling for Hispanics, 1984.

Hodgkinson, H.L. *All One System: Demographics of Education, Kindergarten through Graduate School.* Washington, DC: Institute for Educational Leadership, 1985.

Hodgkinson, H.L. *The Demographics of American Indians: One Percent of the People— Fifty Percent of the Diversity.* Washington, DC: Institute for Educational Leadership, 1990.

Hoffman, D.K. "Relationship of Self-Concept and Academic Aspirations of Underprivileged Adolescent Indians." *Dissertation Abstracts* 30 (1969): 1226B–1227B, UM 69–11, 302.

Hoffman, H., and A. Noem. "Alcoholism and Abstinence among Relatives of American Indian Alcoholics." *Journal of Studies in Alcohol* 36 (1975): 165–70.

Holm, W. "Community School Charts Achievements." *Indian Affairs* 108 (1985): 2–4.

Holmes, C.T. "Grade Level Retention Effects: A Meta-Analysis of Research Studies." *Flunking Grades: Research and Policies on Retention.* Ed. L.A. Shepard and M.L. Smith. New York: Falmer Press, 1989. 34–63.

Hornberger, N. "Iman Chay? Quechua Children in Peru's Schools." *School and Society: Learning Content through Culture.* Ed. H. Trueba and C. Delgado-Gaitan. New York: Praeger Publishers, 1988.

Hoxie, F.E. "Beyond Savagery: The Campaign to Assimilate the American Indians." Ph.D. dissertation, Brandeis University, 1977.

Hurlburt, G., A. Henjum, and L. Eide. "A Comparison of Academic, Career, and Social Patterns of American Indian Students." *Journal of American Indian Education* 22 (1983): 17–23.

Hurwitz, N. "Communications Networks and the Urban Poor." *Equal Opportunity Review* (May 1975): 1–5.

Hymes, D.H. "On Ways of Speaking." *Explorations in the Ethnography of Speaking.* Ed. P. Bauman and J. Sherzer. New York: Cambridge University Press, 1974.

Iiyama, P., M.S. Nishi, and B. Johnson. *Drug Use and Abuse among U.S. Minorities.* New York: Praeger Publishers, 1976.

Iliff, F.G. *People of the Blue Water.* New York: Harper and Brothers, 1954.

Indian Peace Commission. *Report to Congress, 1868.* Washington, DC: U.S. Government Printing Office, 1868. 1643.

Ishisaka, H. "American Indians and Foster Care: Culture Factors and Separation." *Child Welfare* 57, no. 5 (1978): 299–307.

Jackson, E.D. "The Teaching of English as a Second Language to Alaskan Native Children of Non-English Speaking Backgrounds on the Kindergarten and First Grade Levels." Master's thesis, University of Washington, Seattle, 1963.

Jacob, E., and C. Jordan. "Explaining the School Performance of Minority Students." *Anthropology and Education Quarterly* 18, no. 4 (1987): 259–392.

Jensen, A.R. *Straight Talk about Mental Tests.* New York: Free Press, 1981.

Jensen, G.F., H. Stauss, and V.W. Harris. "Crime, Delinquency, and the American Indian." *Human Organization* 36, no. 3 (1977): 252–57.

John, V.P. "Styles of Learning—Styles of Teaching: Reflections on the Education of Navajo Children." *Functions of Language in the Classroom.* Ed. C.B. Cazden, V.P. John, and D. Hymes. New York: Teachers College Press, 1972.

Johnson, S.W., and R. Suetopka-Duerre. "Contributory Factors in Alaska Native Educational Success: A Research Strategy." *Educational Research Quarterly* 8, no. 4 (1984): 44–51.

Jones, D. "Child Welfare Problems in an Alaskan Native Village." *Social Service Review* 43 (1969): 297–309.

Jones–Saumty, D., L. Hochhaus, R. Dru, and A. Zeiner. "Psychological Factors of Familial Alcoholism in American Indians and Caucasians." *Journal of Clinical Psychology* 39 (1983): 783–90.

Joseph, A., R. Spicer, and J. Chesky. *The Desert People.* Chicago: University of Chicago Press, 1949.

Josephy, A.M., Jr. *The Indian Heritage of America.* New York: Bantam Books, Inc., 1969.

Just, G.A. "American Indian Attitudes toward Education in Select Areas of South Dakota." Master's thesis, University of South Dakota, Vermillion, 1970.

Kaplan, J.L., and E.C. Luck. "The Dropout Phenomenon as a Social Problem." *Educational Forum* 42 (1977): 41–56.

Katz, P. "Saulteaux-Ojibwa Adolescents: The Adolescent Process amidst a Clash of Cultures." *Psychiatric Journal of the University of Ottawa* 4 (1979): 315–21.

Kaufman, A. "Gasoline Sniffing among Children in a Pueblo Indian Village." *Pediatrics* 51 (1973): 1060–64.

Kennedy, M.J. "Contact and Acculturation of the Southwestern Pomo." Ph.D. dissertation, University of California, Berkeley, 1955.

Kickingbird, L. "A Portrait of Indian People in Indian Lands." *American Indian Journal* 9, no. 2 (1986): 23–25.

Kleinfeld, J.S. "Intellectual Strengths in Culturally Different Groups: An Eskimo Illustration." *Review of Educational Research* 43 (1973): 341–59.

Kleinfeld, J.S., and J. Bloom. "Boarding Schools: Effects on the Mental Health of Eskimo Adolescents." *American Journal of Psychiatry* 134, no. 4 (1977): 411–17.

Klineberg, O. "Racial Differences in Speed and Accuracy." *Journal of Abnormal and Social Psychology* 22 (1928): 273–77.

Kneale, A.H. *Indian Agent.* Caldwell, ID: Caxton, 1950.

Kolstad, A.J., and J.A. Owings. "High School Dropouts Who Change Their Minds about School." Paper presented at the Annual Meeting of the American Education Association, San Francisco, CA, April 1986.

Krush, T.P., J. Bjork, P. Sindell, and J. Nelle. "Some Thoughts on the Formation of Personality Disorder: Study of an Indian Boarding School Population." *American Journal of Psychiatry* 122 (1966): 868–76.

Kuttner, R., and A. Lorincz. "Alcoholism and Addiction in Urbanized Sioux Indians." *Mental Hygiene* 51 (1967): 530–42.

Labov, W. "The Logic of Non-Standard English." *Language and Poverty: Perspectives on a Theme.* Ed. F. Williams. Chicago: Markham, 1970.

Lang, G.C. "Survival Strategies of Chippewa Drinkers in Minneapolis." *Central Issues in Anthropology* 1, no. 2 (1979): 19–40.

Larson, W.L. *A Comparative Analysis of Indian and Non-Indian Parents' Influence on Educational Aspirations, Expectations, Preferences, and Behavior of Indian and Non-Indian Students in Four High Schools.* AES Bulletin 660. Bozeman, MT: Montana State Agricultural Experiment Station, 1971.

Layman, M.E. *A History of Indian Education in the United States.* Ph.D. dissertation, University of Minnesota, 1942.

Leap, W.L. "Roles for the Linguist in Indian Bilingual Education." *Language Renewal among American Indian Tribes: Issues, Problems, and Prospects.* Ed. R. St. Clair and W. Leap. Rosslyn, VA: National Clearinghouse for Bilingual Education, 1982.

Ledlow, S. "Is Cultural Discontinuity an Adequate Explanation for Dropping Out?" *Journal of American Indian Education* 31, no. 3 (1992): 21–36.

Lefley, H.P. "Acculturation, Child-Rearing, and Self-Esteem in Two North American Indian Tribes." *Ethos* 4 (1976): 385–401.

Leighton, D., and C. Kluckhohn. *Children of the People.* Cambridge, MA: Harvard University Press, 1948.

Leitka, G. "Search for Identity Creates Problems for Indian Students." *Journal of American Indian Education* 11, no. 1 (1971): 7–10.

Lemert, E. "Drinking among American Indians." *Alcohol, Science, and Society Revisited*. Ed. E. Gomberg, H. White, and J. Carpenter. Ann Arbor, MI: University of Michigan Press, 1982.

Lemert, E.M. "The Use of Alcohol in Three Salish Indian Tribes." *Quarterly Journal of Studies on Alcohol* 19 (1958): 90–107.

Levensky, K. "The Performance of American Indian Children on the Draw-a-Man Test." *The National Study of American Indian Education* 1, no. 2 (1970): 1–21.

Levin, H. "Work: The Staff of Life." Paper presented at the American Psychological Association Conference, New York, 1975.

Levin, H.M. *The Costs to the Nation of Inadequate Education*. Report to the U.S. Senate Select Committee on Equal Education Opportunity. Washington, DC: U.S. Government Printing Office, 1972.

Levin, H.M. *The Educationally Disadvantaged: A National Crisis*. Working Paper No. 6, State Youth Initiatives Project. Philadelphia: Public/Private Ventures, 1985.

Levy, J.E., and S.J. Kunitz. "A Suicide Prevention Program for Hopi Youth." *Social Science and Medicine* 25 (1987): 931–40.

Limerick, P.N. *The Legacy of Conquest: The Unbroken Past of the American West*. New York: W.W. Norton and Co., 1987.

Lin, R. "The Promise and Problems of Native American Students: A Comparative Study of High School Students on the Reservation and Surrounding Areas." *Journal of American Indian Education* 25, no. 1 (1985): 6–16.

Lin, R.L. "Perceptions of Family Background and Personal Characteristics among Indian College Students. *Journal of American Indian Education* 29, no. 3 (1990): 19–28.

Little, P. *River of People*. Omaha, NE: Interstate Printing Co., 1983.

Little Bear, D. "Effective Language Education Practices and Native Language Survival." *Effective Language Education Practices and Native Language Survival*. Ed. J. Reyhner. Proceedings of the Ninth Annual International Native American Language Issues (NALI) Institute, Billings, MT, 8–9 June 1989.

Little Bear, D. "Teachers and Parents Working Together." *Teaching the Indian Child: A Bilingual/Multicultural Approach*. Ed. J. Reyhner. Billings, MT: Eastern Montana College, 1986. 222–31.

Lockhart, B. *Cultural Conflict: The Indian Child in the Non-Indian Classroom*, 1978. ERIC ED 195-379.

Long, K.A. "Cultural Considerations in the Assessment and Treatment of Intrafamilial Abuse." *American Journal of Orthopsychiatry* 56 (1986): 131–36.

Longclaws, L., G. Barnes, L. Grieve, and R. Dumoff. "Alcohol and Drug Abuse among the Brokenhead Ojibwa." *Journal of Studies on Alcohol* 41, no. 1 (1980): 21–36.

Longstreet, E. *Aspects of Ethnicity*. New York: Teachers College Press, 1978.

Lujan, C., L. DeBruyn, P. May, and M. Bird. "Profile of Abused and Neglected American Indian Children in the Southwest." *Child Abuse and Neglect* 13 (1989): 449–61.

Lummis, C.F. "My Brother's Keeper." *Land of Sunshine* 11 (1899): 333–35.

Lund, B.F. "A Survey of Comparative Achievement and Scholarship Records of California Indian Children in the Auburn Public Schools." Master's thesis, Sacramento State College, 1963.

MacAndrew C., and R.B. Edgerton. *Drunken Comportment: A Social Explanation.* Chicago: Aldine, 1969.

MacGregor, G. *Warriors without Weapons: A Study of the Society and Personality Development of the Pine Ridge Sioux.* Chicago: University of Chicago Press, 1946.

Mahood, W. "Born Losers: Dropouts and Pushouts." *NASSP Bulletin* 65 (1981): 54–57.

Malbin, N., S. LaTurner, and B.A. Spilke. "Longitudinal Study of Educational Performance among Oglala Sioux Students." Paper presented at the Annual Meeting of the Rocky Mountain Psychological Association, Denver, CO, May 1971.

Malcolm, S. *Equity and Excellence: Compatible Goals. An Assessment of Programs That Facilitate Increased Access and Achievement of Females and Minorities in K–12 Mathematics and Science Education.* Washington, DC: American Association for the Advancement of Science, Office of Opportunities in Science, 1984.

Malone, T.E. *Report of the Secretary's Task Force on Black and Minority Health.* Vol. 1: *Executive Summary.* Washington, DC: U.S. Government Printing Office, 1985.

Mann, D. "Can We Help Dropouts?" *Teachers College Record* 87 (1986): 307–23.

Mason, E.P. "Cross-Validation Study of Personality Characteristics of Junior High Students from American Indian, Mexican, and Caucasian Ethnic Backgrounds." *Journal of Social Psychology* 77 (1969): 15–24.

May, P.A. "Alcohol and Drug Misuse Prevention Programs for American Indians: Needs and Opportunities." *Journal of Studies on Alcohol* 47, no. 3 (1986): 187–95.

May, P.A. "Alcohol Legalization and Native Americans: A Sociological Inquiry." Ph.D. dissertation, University of Montana, Missoula, 1976.

May, P.A. "Arrests, Alcohol, and Alcohol Legislation among an American Indian Tribe." *Plains Anthropologist* 20 (1975): 129–34.

May, P.A. "Epidemiology of Fetal Alcohol Syndrome among American Indians of the Southwest." *Social Biology* 30 (1983): 374–87.

May, P.A. "Substance Abuse and American Indians: Prevalence and Susceptibility." *International Journal of the Addictions* 17 (1982): 1185–1209.

May, P.A. *Suicide and Suicide Attempts on the Pine Ridge Reservation.* Pine Ridge, SD: U.S. Public Health Service, Community Mental Health Program, 1973.

May, P.A., and L.H. Dizmang. "Suicide and the American Indian." *Psychiatric Annals* 4, no. 9 (1974): 22–23, 27–28.

Maynard, E. "Drinking as a Part of an Adjustment Syndrome among Oglala Sioux." *Pine Ridge Research Bulletin* 9 (1969): 35–51.

McBee, M.M. *Dropout Report for the 1985–86 School Year.* Oklahoma City: Oklahoma City Public Schools, Department of Planning, Research, and Evaluation, 1986.

McBride, D.C., and J.B. Page. "Adolescent Indian Substance Abuse: Ecological and Sociocultural Factors." *Youth and Society* 11, no. 4 (1980): 475–92.

McDavid, J. "The Teacher as an Agent of Socialization." *Critical Issues in Research Related to Disadvantaged Children.* Ed. E. Grotberg. Princeton, NJ: Educational Testing Service, 1969.

McFee, M. "The 150% Man: A Product of Blackfeet Acculturation." *American Anthropologist* 70 (1968): 1096–1103.

McKenney, T.L., and J. Hall. *The Indian Tribes of North America with Biographical Sketches and Anecdotes of the Principal Chiefs.* Vol. 3. Edinburgh: J. Grant. 1934.

McNickle, D. *Indians in the Land of Plenty,* 1965. ERIC ED 012-191.

Means, R. Speech presented at the Law School of the University of Colorado. Boulder, CO, 19 April 1985.

Medicine, B. "The Changing Dakota Family and the Stresses Therein." *Pine Ridge Research Bulletin* 9 (1969): 1–20.

Medicine, B. *The Native American Woman: A Perspective.* Austin, TX: National Educational Laboratory Publishers, 1978.

Mendelsohn, B., and W. Richards. "Alaska Native Adolescents' Descriptions of Their Mental Health Problems." Paper presented at the Eighth Joint Meeting of the Professional Associations of the U.S. Public Health Service, Phoenix, AZ, 1973.

Meriam, L., R.A. Brown, H. Cloud, E. Dale, E. Duke, H. Edwards, F. McKenzie, M. Mark, W.C. Ryan, Jr., and W.J. Spillman. *The Problem of Indian Administration.* Baltimore: Johns Hopkins Press, 1928.

Mickelson, N., and C.G. Galloway. "Modification of Behavior Problems of Indian Children." *Elementary School Journal* 72 (1972): 150–55.

Miller, A.G. "Integration and Acculturation of Cooperative Behavior among Blackfoot Indian and Non-Indian Canadian Children." *Journal of Cross-Cultural Psychology* 4, no. 3 (1973): 347–80.

Miller, F., and D.D. Caulkins. "Chippewa Adolescents: A Changing Generation." *Human Organization* 23, no. 2 (1964): 150–59.

Miller, H.J. *The Effects of Integration of Rural Indian Pupils: Final Report.* Washington, DC: Department of Health, Education, and Welfare, Office of Education, 1968.

Miller, S.I., and L.S. Schoenfield. "Suicide Attempt Patterns among Navajo Indians." *International Journal of Social Psychiatry* 17, no. 3 (1971): 189–93.

Milone, D.E. "American Indian Student Reasons for Dropping out and Attitude toward School." Master's thesis, Arizona State University, Tempe, 1983.

Minnis, M. "The Relationship of the Social Structure of an Indian Community to Adult and Juvenile Delinquency." *Social Forces* 41 (1963): 395–403.

Misiaszek, L. "The Cultural Dilemma of American Indians." *Social Education* 33, no. 4 (1969): 438–46.

Mizen, M.L. *Federal Facilities for Indians: Tribal Relations with the Federal Government.* Washington, DC: U.S. Government Printing Office, 1966.

Mohatt, G. "The Sacred Water: The Quest for Personal Power through Drinking among the Teton Sioux." *The Drinking Man.* Ed. D.C. McClelland, W.N. Davis, R. Kalin, and E. Wanner. New York: Free Press, 1972. 261–75.

Mokros, J.R. "Hidden Inequities Can Be Overcome." *Voc Ed* 59 (May 1984): 39–41.

Moore, D. "Reducing Alcohol and Drug Use among Native American Youth." *Prevention Pipeline* 1, no. 5 (1988): 6–7.

Morse, J. *A Report on the Secretary of War of the United States on Indian Affairs.* New York: A.M. Kelley, 1970.

National Center for Education Statistics. *Analysis Report: Dropout Rates in the United States: 1988.* Office of Educational Research and Improvement, U.S. Department of Education, NCES 89-609. Washington, DC: U.S. Government Printing Office, September 1989.

National Coalition of Advocates for Students. *Barriers to Excellence: Our Children at Risk.* Boston: The Coalition, 1985.

National Commission on Excellence in Education. *A Nation at Risk: The Imperative for Educational Reform.* Washington, DC: U.S. Government Printing Office, 1983.

National Foundation for the Improvement of Education. *Dropping Out: The Quiet Killer of the American Dream.* Washington, DC: National Education Association, 1986.

Nixon, R.M. *Message from President Richard Nixon: Recommendations for Indian Policy.* Doc. No. 91–363. 91st Congress, 2nd Session, 8 July 1970.

Noriega, J. "American Indian Education in the United States: Indoctrination for Subordination to Colonialism." *The State of Native America: Genocide, Colonization, and Resistance.* Ed. M.A. Jaimes. Boston: South End Press, 1992. 387–88.

Oakes, J. *Keeping Track: How Schools Structure Inequality.* New Haven, CT: Yale University Press, 1985.

Oakland, L., and R.L. Kane. "The Working Mother and Child Neglect on the Navajo Reservation." *Pediatrics* 51, no. 5 (1973): 849–53.

Oetting, E.R., F. Beauvais, and R. Edwards. "Alcohol and Indian Youth: Social and Psychological Correlates and Prevention." *Journal of Drug Issues* 18, no. 1 (1988): 87–101.

Oetting, E.R., F. Beauvais, R. Edwards, M. Waters, J. Velarde, and G. Goldstein. *Drug Use among Native American Youth: Summary of Findings (1975–1981).* NIDA Project Report, Project No. 5, ROIDA1853. Fort Collins, CO: Colorado State University, 1983.

Oetting, E.R., and G.C. Goldstein. "Drug Use among Native American Adolescents." *Youth Drug Abuse: Problems, Issues, and Treatment.* Ed. G.M. Beschner and A.S. Friedman. Lexington, MA: Lexington Books, 1979.

Office of Indian Education Programs. *Report on BIA Education: Excellence in Indian Education through the Effective School Process.* Bureau of Indian Affairs, U.S. Department of the Interior. Washington, DC: U.S. Government Printing Office, 1988.

Ogbu, J.U. "Cultural Discontinuities and Schooling." *Anthropology and Education Quarterly* 13 (1982): 290–307.

Ogbu, J.U. *Minority Education and Caste: The American System in Cross Cultural Perspective.* New York: Academic Press, 1978.

Ogbu, J.U. "Minority Status and Schooling in Plural Societies." *Comparative Education Review* 27 (1983): 168–90.

Ogbu, J.U. *The Next Generation.* New York: Academic Press, 1974.

Ogbu, J.U. "Variability in Minority School Performance: A Problem in Search of an Explanation." *Anthropology and Education Quarterly* 18 (1987): 312–34.

Ogden, M., M.I. Spector, and C.A. Hill, Jr. "Suicides and Homicides among Indians." *Public Health Report* 85 (1970): 75–80.

Okwumabua, J.O., and E.J. Duryea. "Age of Onset, Periods of Risk, and Patterns of Progression in Drug Use among American Indian High School Students." *International Journal of the Addictions* 22, no. 12 (1987): 1269–76.

Old Dog Cross, P. "Sexual Abuse: A New Threat to the Native American Woman." *The Listening Post* 6, no. 2 (1982): 17–23. Albuquerque, NM: Indian Health Service.

Olson, J.W. "The Urban Indian as Viewed by an Indian Caseworker." *The American Indian in Urban Society*. Ed. J.O. Waddell and O.M. Watson. Boston: Little, Brown and Company, 1971.

Olson, L., and R. Edwards. *Push Out, Step Out: A Report on California Public School Dropouts*. Oakland, CA: Citizens Policy Center, 1982.

O'Malley, E. *American Indian Education Handbook*. Sacramento: California State Department of Education, 1982.

Omi, M., and H. Winant. *Racial Formation in the United States: From the 1960s to the 1980s*. New York: Routledge & Kegan Paul, 1986.

Oswalt, W.H. *This Land Was Theirs*. New York: John Wiley and Sons, 1966.

Owens, C.S., and W.P. Bass. *The American Indian High School Dropout in the Southwest*. Albuquerque, NM: Southwest Cooperative Educational Lab, 1969. ERIC ED 026–195.

Pagelow, M. *Family Violence*. New York: Praeger Publishers, 1984.

Palladino, L.B. *Indian and White in the Northwest: A History of Catholicity in Montana*. Lancaster, PA: Wickersham, 1922.

Pallas, A.M., G. Natriello, and E.L. McDill. "The Changing Nature of the Disadvantaged Population: Current Dimensions and Future Trends." *Educational Researcher* 18, no. 5 (1989): 16–22.

Parmee, E.A. *Formal Education and Culture Change: A Modern Apache Indian Community and Government Education Programs*. Tucson, AZ: University of Arizona Press, 1968.

Parsons, J.E., T.F. Adler, and C.M. Kaczala. "Socialization of Achievement Attitudes and Beliefs: Parental Influences." *Child Development* 53 (1982): 310–21.

Patton, W., and E. Edington. "Factors Related to the Persistence of Indian Students at College Level." *Indian Education* 12 (1973): 19–23.

Pearce, R.H. *Savagism and Civilization*. Baltimore: Johns Hopkins Press, 1965.

Peng, S. *High School Dropouts: A National Concern*. U.S. Department of Education. Prepared for the Business Advisory Commission, Education Commission of the States, Denver, CO, March 1985.

Peng, S.S., and R.T. Takai. *High School Dropouts: Descriptive Information from High School and Beyond*. Bulletin. Washington, DC: National Center for Educational Statistics, 1983.

Pettigrew, T.F. *A Profile of the Negro American*. Princeton, NJ: D. Van Nostrand Co., 1964.

Philips, S.U. *The Invisible Culture*. New York: Longman Press, 1983.

Philips, S.U. "Participant Structures and Communicative Competence: Warm Springs Children in Community and Classroom." *Functions of Language in the Classroom*. Ed. C.B. Cazden, V.P. John, and D. Hymes. New York: Teachers College Press, 1972. 370–94.

Platero, P.R., E.A. Brandt, G. Witherspoon, and P. Wong. *Navajo Students at Risk: Final Report for the Navajo Area Student Dropout Study*. Window Rock, AZ: Navajo Division of Education, 1986.

Platero Paperwork, Inc. *Executive Summary: Navajo Area Student Dropout Study*. Window Rock, AZ: Navajo Division of Education, the Navajo Nation, 1986.

Polacca, K. "Ways of Working with the Navajos Who Have Not Learned the White Man's Ways." *Journal of American Indian Education* 2, no. 1 (1962): 4–16.

Polgar, S. "Biculturation of Mesquakine Teenage Boys." *American Anthropologist* 62 (1960): 217–35.

Polk, K. "The New Marginal Youth." *Crime and Delinquency*. Englewood Cliffs, NJ: Prentice Hall, 1984.

Porter, J. *Black Child, White Child*. Cambridge, MA: Harvard University Press, 1971.

Price, J.A. "The Stereotyping of North American Indians in Motion Pictures." *Ethnohistory* 20 (1973): 153–71.

Prucha, F.P. *Documents of United States Indian Policy*. Lincoln, NE: University of Nebraska Press, 1975.

Prucha, F.P. *The Indians in American Society: From the Revolutionary War to the Present*. Berkeley, CA: University of California, 1985.

Randall, A., and B. Randall. "Criminal Justice and the American Indian." *Indian Historian* 11, no. 2 (1978): 42–48.

Reasons, C. "Crime and the American Indian." *Native Americans Today: Sociological Perspectives*. Ed. H.M. Bahr, B.A. Chadwick, and R.C. Day. New York: Harper and Row Publishers, Inc., 1972. 319–26.

Red Horse, T. "American Indian Families: Research Perspectives." *The American Indian Family: Strengths and Stresses*. Ed. F. Hoffman. Proceedings of the Conference on Research Issues, Isleta, NM, 1980. 1–11.

Renfroe, W. *Early School Leavers: High School Students Who Left before Graduating*. Publication No. 428. Los Angeles: Los Angeles Unified School District, Research and Evaluation Branch, 1983.

Reyhner, J. "American Indians out of School: A Review of School-based Causes and Solutions." *Journal of American Indian Education* 31, no. 3 (1992): 21–56.

Rhoades, E.R., M. Marshall, C. Attneave, M. Echohawk, J. Bjork, and M. Beiser. "Mental Health Problems of American Indians Seen in Outpatient Facilities of the Indian Health Service, 1975." *Public Health Reports* 96, no. 4 (1980): 329–35.

Rhodes, R.W. "Standardized Testing of Minority Students: Navajo and Hopi Examples." *Journal of Navajo Education* 6, no. 2 (1989): 29–35.

Richards, J. "Learning Spanish and Classroom Dynamics: School Failure in a Guatemalan Maya Community." *Success or Failure? Learning and the Language Minority Student*. Ed. H. Trueba. New York: Newbury Publishers, 1987.

Richardson, E.H. "Cultural and Historical Perspectives in Counseling American Indians." *Counseling the Culturally Different: Theory and Practice*. Ed. D. W. Sue. New York: John Wiley and Sons, 1981.

Riffenburgh, A.S. "Cultural Influences and Crime among Indian-Americans of the Southwest." *Federal Probation* 23 (1964): 38–46.

Riley, G. *Women and Indians on the Frontier, 1825–1915*. Albuquerque, NM: University of New Mexico Press, 1984.

Rist, R.D. "Student Social Class and Teachers' Expectations: The Self-fulfilling Prophecy in Ghetto Education." *Harvard Educational Review* 40 (1970): 411–51.

Rist, S.R. "Shoshone Indian Education: A Descriptive Study Based on Certain Influential Factors Affecting Academic Achievement of Shoshone Indian Students, Wind River Reservation, Wyoming." Master's thesis, Montana State University, Bozeman, 1961.

Roessel, R.A., Jr. *Handbook for Indian Education*. Los Angeles: Amerindian, 1962.

Roessel, R.A., Jr. "The Indian Child and His Culture." *Teaching Multi-Cultural Populations.* Ed. J.C. Stone and D.P. DeNeir. New York: Litton Educational Publishing, 1971.

Rohrer, J. "Test Intelligence of Osage Indians." *Journal of Social Psychology* 16 (1942): 99–105.

Rosenthal, B.G. "Development of Self-Identification in Relation to Attitudes toward Self in Chippewa Indians." *Genetic Psychology Monographs* 90 (1974): 43–141.

Rosenthal, R., and L. Jacobson. *Pygmalion in the Classroom.* New York: Holt, Rinehart, and Winston, Inc., 1968.

Rosier, P., and W. Holm. *The Rock Point Experience: A Longitudinal Study of the Navajo School Program.* Washington, DC: Center for Applied Linguistics, 1980. ERIC ED 195-363.

Rowe, E. "Five Hundred Forty-seven and Two Hundred Sixty-eight Indian Children Tested by the Binet-Simon Tests." *The Pedagogical Seminary* 21 (1914): 454–68.

Roy, P. "The Measurement of Assimilation: The Spokane Indians." *Native Americans Today: Sociological Perspectives.* Ed. M. Bahr, B.A. Chadwick, and R.C. Day. New York: Harper and Row Publishers, 1972. 225–39.

Rumberger, R.W. "Dropping out of High School: The Influence of Race, Sex, and Family Background." *American Educational Research Journal* 20, no. 2 (1983): 199–220.

Ryan, F.A. Working paper prepared for the National Advisory Committee on Indian Education. Paper No. 071279, Harvard American Indian Education Program, Harvard University Graduate School of Education, Cambridge, MA, 18 July 1979.

Sadker, D., and M. Sadker. "Exploding Zepezauer's Mini-Mind Field." *Phi Delta Kappan* 63, no. 4 (1981): 272–73.

Sargent, A.G. *Beyond Sex Roles.* St. Paul, MN: West Publishing Co., 1977.

Saslow, H., and M. Harrover. "Research on the Psychosocial Adjustment of Indian Youth." *American Journal of Psychiatry* 125 (1968): 120–27.

Savage, D.G. "Why Chapter I Hasn't Made a Difference." *Phi Delta Kappan* 68 (1987): 581–84.

Sawhill, I.V. "The Underclass: An Overview." *Public Interest* 96 (Summer 1989): 3–15.

Scaldwell, W.A., J.E. Frame, and D.G. Cookson. "Individual Intellectual Assessment of Chippewa, Muncey, and Oneida Children Using the WISC–R." Paper presented at the MOKAKIT Indian Education Research Conference, University of Western Ontario, London, Ontario, 1984.

Schinke, S., M.Y. Bebel, M.A. Orlandi, and G. Botvin. "Prevention Strategies for Vulnerable Pupils: School Social Work Practices to Prevent Substance Abuse." *Urban Education* 22, no. 4 (1988): 510–19.

Schinke, S., G. Botvin, J.E. Trimble, M.A. Orlandi, L.D. Gilchrist, and V.S. Locklear. "Preventing Substance Abuse among American Indian Adolescents: A Bicultural Competence Skills Approach." *Journal of Counseling Psychology* 35, no. 1 (1988): 87–90.

Segal, C.M., and D.C. Stineback. *Puritans, Indians, and Manifest Destiny.* New York: G.P. Putnam & Sons, 1977.

Selinger, A.D. *The American Indian High School Dropout: The Magnitude of the Problem.* Portland, OR: Northwest Regional Educational Laboratory, 1968. ERIC ED 026–164.

Selinger, A.D. *The American Indian Graduate: After High School, What?* Portland, OR: Northwest Regional Educational Laboratory, 1968.

Senate Special Committee on School Performance. "Helping Schools Succeed at Helping All Children Learn." Fifteenth Alaska Legislature, Fairbanks, AK, 1989.

Shaefer, E.S. "Need for Early and Continuing Education." *Education of the Infant and Young Child.* Ed. V.H. Denenberg. New York: Academic Press, 1970.

Shaefer, E.S. "Parents as Educators: Evidence from Cross-Sectional, Longitudinal, and Intervention Research." *The Young Child,* Vol. 2. Ed. W.W. Hartup. Washington, DC: National Association for the Education of Young Children, 1976.

Shepard, L.A., and M.L. Smith, eds. *Flunking Grades: Research and Policies on Retention.* New York: Falmer Press, 1989.

Shipman, J., and A. Bussis. "The Impact of the Family." *Disadvantaged Children and Their First School Experience: ETS–OEO Longitudinal Study.* Princeton, NJ: Educational Testing Service, 1968.

Shkilnyk, A.M. *A Poison Stronger than Love: The Destruction of an Ojibwa Community.* New Haven, CT: Yale University Press, 1985.

Shore, J.H. "Suicide and Suicide Attempts among American Indians of the Pacific Northwest." *International Journal of Social Psychiatry* 18, no. 2 (1972): 91–96.

Sizer, T.R. *Horace's Compromise: The Dilemma of the American High School.* Boston: Houghton Mifflin, 1984.

Slavin, R.E. "Research on Cooperative Learning: Consensus and Controversy." *Educational Leadership* 47 (1989): 52–54.

Slotkin, R. *Regeneration through Violence: The Mythology of the American Frontier, 1600–1860.* Middletown, CT: Wesleyan University Press, 1973.

Smith, F. *Joining the Literacy Club: Further Essays into Literacy.* Portsmouth, NH: Heinemann, 1988.

Smulyan, L. "Gender Differences in Classroom Adolescence." Paper presented at the Annual Conference of Research on Women in Education, Howard University, Washington, DC, 1986.

South Dakota Advisory Committee (SDAC) of the U.S. Commission on Civil Rights. *Liberty and Justice for All.* Washington, DC: U.S. Government Printing Office, 1977.

Spilka, B. *Alienation and Achievement among Oglala Sioux Indian Secondary School Students,* 1970. ERIC ED 945–225.

Spindler, G.D. "Why Have Minority Groups in North America Been Disadvantaged in Their Schools?" *Education and Cultural Process: Anthropological Approaches.* Ed. G.D. Spindler. Prospect Heights, IL: Waveland, 1987. 160–72.

Spindler, G.D., and L.S. Spindler. "American Indian Personality Types and Their Sociocultural Roots." *The Annals of the American Academy of Political and Social Science* 311 (May 1957): 147–57.

Steiner, S. *The New Indians.* New York: Harper and Row Publishers, Inc., 1968.

Stevens, J.A. "Social and Cultural Factors Related to Drinking Patterns among the Blackfeet." Master's thesis, University of Montana, Missoula, 1969.

Streit, F., and M.J. Nicolich. "Myths versus Data on American Indian Drug Abuse." *Journal of Drug Education* 7 (1977): 117–22.

Suppes, P., J.D. Fletcher, and M. Zanotti. "Performance Models of American Indian Students on Computer–assisted Instruction in Elementary Mathematics." *Instructional Science* 4 (1975): 303–13.

Swanson, D.W., A.P. Bratrude, and E.M. Brown. "Alcohol Abuse in a Population of Indian Children." *Diseases of the Nervous System* 31 (1971): 835–42.

Swisher, K.G., M. Hoisch, and D.M. Pavel. *American Indian/Alaska Native Dropout Study.* Washington, DC: National Education Association, 1991.

Sydiaha, D., and J. Rempel. "Motivation and Attitudinal Characteristics of Indian School Children as Measured by the Thematic Apperception Test." *Canadian Psychologist* 5a, no. 3 (1964): 139–48.

Takie, Y., P. Lynch, and G.M. Charleston. "To Drink or Not to Drink: The Indian Adolescent's Choice between Friends and Family." *Journal of American Indian Education* 27 (1988): 1–9.

Taylor, O.L., and D.L. Lee. "Standardized Tests and African-American Children." *The Negro Educational Review* 38 (1987): 67–80.

Tharp, R., and R. Gallimore. *Rousing Minds to Life: Teaching, Learning, and Schooling in Social Context.* New York: Cambridge University Press, 1988.

Thompson, H. *Education for Cross-Cultural Enrichment.* Lawrence, KS: Haskell Institute, 1964.

Thornberry, T., M. Moore, and R.L. Christian. "The Effect of Dropping out of High School on Subsequent Criminal Behavior." *Criminology* 23 (1985): 3–18.

Thornburg, H.D. "An Investigation of a Dropout Program among Arizona's Minority Youth." *Education* 94 (1974): 249–65.

Thorton, R. *American Indian Holocaust and Survival: A Population History since 1492.* Norman, OK: University of Oklahoma Press, 1987.

Topper, M.D. "Drinking Patterns, Cultural Changes, Sociability, and Navajo Adolescents." *Addictive Disease* 1 (1974): 97–116.

Trennert, R.A., Jr. *Alternatives to Extinction: Federal Indian Policy and the Beginnings of the Reservation System.* Philadelphia: Temple University Press, 1975.

Trillin, C. "U.S. Journal: Gallop, New Mexico (Drunken Indians)." *New Yorker*, 25 September 1971, 108–14.

Trimble, J. "Drug Abuse Prevention Research Needs among American Indians and Alaska Natives." *White Cloud Journal of American Indian Mental Health* 3, no. 3 (1984): 22–34.

Trimble, J.E., A. Padilla, and C. Bell. *Drug Abuse among Ethnic Minorities.* NIDA Office of Science Monographs, DHHS Pub. (ADM). Washington, DC: U.S. Government Printing Office, 1987.

Trueba, H. *Raising Silent Voices: Educating the Linguistic Minorities for the 21st Century.* New York: Harper and Row Publishers, Inc., 1988.

Tucker, M.B. "U.S. Ethnic Minorities and Drug Abuse: An Assessment of the Science and Practice." *International Journal of the Addictions* 20 (1985): 1021–47.

U.S. Census, 1980. Washington, DC: U.S. Government Printing Office, 1980.

U.S. Commissioner of Indian Affairs. *Annual Report of the Commissioner of Indian Affairs*. Washington, DC, 1887 and 1894.

U.S. Congress, Office of Technology Assessment. *Indian Health Care*. OTA-H-290. Washington, DC: U.S. Government Printing Office, 1986.

U.S. Congress Senate Committee on Labor and Human Resources, Subcommittee on Employment and Productivity. *Guaranteed Job Opportunity Act*. 100th Congress, 1st Session, S. Doc. 777, 3 March 1987 and 3 April 1987.

U.S. Department of Commerce. "American Indians, Eskimos, and Aleuts on Identified Reservations and in the Historic Areas of Oklahoma (Excluding Urbanized Areas)." *1980 Census of Population*. U.S. Department of Commerce Report No. PC80–2–1D, Part 1, pp. 1–3. Washington, DC: U.S. Government Printing Office, November 1985.

U.S. Department of Health, Education, and Welfare. "A Study of Selected Socio-Economic Characteristics of Ethnic Minorities Based on the 1970 Census." *American Indians*. Vol. 3. Washington, DC: U.S. Government Printing Office, 1974.

U.S. Department of the Interior. *American Indians Today: Answers to Your Questions*. Bureau of Indian Affairs. Washington, DC: U.S. Government Printing Office, 1988.

U.S. Department of the Interior. *Indian Service Population and Labor Force Estimates*. Bureau of Indian Affairs. Washington, DC: U.S. Government Printing Office, 1989.

U.S. Department of the Interior, Bureau of Indian Affairs. *Annual Report for Fiscal Year Ended June 30, 1903*. Washington, DC: U.S. Government Printing Office, 1904.

U.S. Government Accounting Office. *Dropouts: The Extent and Nature of the Problem*. Washington, DC: U.S. Government Printing Office, June 1986.

U.S. Senate. *Indian Education: A National Tragedy—A National Challenge*. Report of the Committee on Labor and Public Welfare, Special Subcommittee on Indian Education. Report No. 90–501, 91st Congress, 1st Session. Washington, DC: U.S. Government Printing Office, 1969.

U.S. Senate and House Indian Affairs Committees. *First Annual Report to the Congress of the United States*. Washington, DC: U.S. Government Printing Office, 1874.

Utley, R.M. *Last Days of the Sioux Nation*. New Haven, CT: Yale University Press, 1963.

Vallo, D. *Indian in the Red*. U.S. Department of Health and Human Services, DHHS Pub. (ADM). Washington, DC: U.S. Government Printing Office, 1980.

Vanderwagen, C., R.D. Mason, and T.C. Owan, eds. *IHS Alcoholism/Substance Abuse Prevention Initiative: Background, Plenary Session, and Action Plan*. Washington, DC: U.S. Department of Health and Human Services, Indian Health Service, 1987.

Voget, F. "Acculturation at Caughnawaga: A Note on the Native-modified Group." *American Anthropologist* 53 (1951): 220–31.

Vogt, L., C. Jordan, and R.G. Tharp. "Explaining School Failure, Producing School Success: Two Cases." *Anthropology and Education Quarterly* 18 (1987): 276–86.

Wallis, R. "The Overt Fears of Dakota Indian Children." *Child Development* 25, no. 3 (1954): 185–92.

Wax, M.L. *Indian Americans: Unity and Diversity.* Englewood Cliffs, NJ: Prentice Hall, 1971.

Wax, M.L., R.H. Wax, and R.V. Dumont, Jr. *Formal Education in an American Indian Community.* Monograph. Kalamazoo, MI: The Society for the Study of Social Problems, 1964.

Wax, R.H. *The Warrior Dropouts.* Lawrence, KS: The University of Kansas Press, 1967.

Wax, R.H. "The Warrior Dropouts." *Native Americans Today: Sociological Perspectives.* Ed. H.M. Bahr, B.A. Chadwick, and R.C. Day. New York: Harper and Row Publishers, Inc., 1972. 146–55.

Weeks, P., and J.B. Gidney. *Subjugation and Dishonor: A Brief History of the Travail of the Native Americans.* Huntington, NY: Robert E. Krieger, 1981.

Wehlage, G.G., and R.A. Rutter. "Dropping Out: How Do Schools Contribute to the Problem?" *Teachers College Record* 87 (1986): 374–92.

Weibel, J., and T. Weisner. *The Ethnography of Rural and Urban Drinking Practices in California.* Annual Statistical Analysis Report for the California Department of Alcohol and Drug Abuse Programs, Sacramento, CA, 1980.

Weibel-Orlando, J. "Substance Abuse among American Indian Youth: A Continuing Crisis." *Journal of Drug Issues* 2 (1984): 313–35.

Weis, L., E. Farrar, and H.G. Petrie, eds. *Dropouts from School: Issues, Dilemmas, and Solutions.* Albany, NY: State University of New York, 1989.

Welte, J.W., and G.M. Barnes. "Alcohol Use among Adolescent Minority Groups." *Quarterly Journal of Studies on Alcohol* 48 (1987): 329–36.

West, R.L. "The Adjustment of the American Indian in Detroit: A Descriptive Study." Master's thesis, Wayne State University, Detroit, MI, 1950.

Westermeyer, J. "The Drunken Indian: Myths and Realities." *Psychiatric Annals* 4 (November 1974): 29–36.

Westermeyer, J. "Options regarding Alcohol Use among the Chippewa." *American Journal of Orthopsychiatry* 42 (1972): 398–403.

Westermeyer, J.J. "Indian Powerlessness in Minnesota." *Society* 10, no. 3 (1973): 45–52.

White, L.C., and B.A. Chadwick. "Urban Residence, Assimilation, and Identity of the Spokane Indian." *Native American Indians Today: Sociological Perspectives.* Ed. H.M. Bahr, B.A. Chadwick, and R.C. Day. New York: Harper and Row Publishers, Inc., 1972. 239–49.

White, R. *Navajo Child Abuse and Neglect Study.* Baltimore: Johns Hopkins University, Department of Maternal and Child Health, 1977.

White, R.A. "The Lower-Class 'Culture of Excitement' among the Contemporary Sioux." *The Modern Sioux.* Ed. E. Nurge. Lincoln, NE: University of Nebraska Press, 1970. 175–97.

White, R., and D. Cornely. "Navajo Child Abuse and Neglect Study: A Comparison Group Examination of Abuse and Neglect of Navajo Children." *Child Abuse and Neglect* 5 (1981): 9–17.

Whittaker, J.O. "Alcohol and the Standing Rock Sioux Tribe, I: The Pattern of Drinking." *Quarterly Journal of Studies on Alcohol* 23 (1962): 468–79.

Whittaker, J.O. "Alcohol and the Standing Rock Sioux Tribe, II: Psychodynamic and Cultural Factors in Drinking." *Quarterly Journal of Studies on Alcohol* 24 (1963): 80–90.

Wienberg, M. *A Chance to Learn: A History of Race and Education in the United States.* London: Cambridge University Press, 1977.

Wildcat, T.C. "Notes on Native Education." *Canadian Journal of Native Education* 9 (1981): 11–13.

Wilkinson, G. "Educational Problems in the Indian Community: A Comment on Learning as Colonialism," *Integrateducation* 19 (January/April 1981): 46–50.

Williams, L.E., B.A. Chadwick, and H.M. Bahr. "Antecedents of Self–reported Arrest for Americans in Seattle." *Phylon* 40 (1979): 243–52.

Wilson, W.J. *The Truly Disadvantaged: The Inner-City, the Underclass, and Public Policy.* Chicago: University of Chicago Press, 1987.

Winfree, L.T., and C.T. Griffiths. "Youth at Risk: Marijuana Use among Native American and Caucasian Youths." *International Journal of the Addictions* 18, no. 1 (1983): 53–70.

Wintrob, R.M., and P.S. Sindell. *Education and Identity Conflict among Cree Indian Youth: A Preliminary Report*, 1968. ERIC ED 039-063.

Wischlacz, C., J. Lane, and C. Kempe. "Indian Child Welfare: A Community Team Approach to Protective Services." *Child Abuse and Neglect 2* (1978): 29–35.

Wittstock, L.W. "Native American Women: Twilight of a Long Maidenhood." *Comparative Perspectives of Third World Women: The Impact of Race, Sex, and Class.* Ed. Beverly Lindsay. New York: Praeger Publishers, 1980. 207-228.

Wolcott, H. *A Kwakiuti Village and School.* New York: Holt, Rinehart, and Winston, 1967.

Woolf, V. *A Room of One's Own.* New York: Harcourt, Brace & World, 1929.

Wright, R., and T.D. Watts. "Alcohol and Minority Youth." *Journal of Drug Issues* 18 (1988): 1–6.

Wylie, R.C. *The Self-Concept.* 2nd ed., rev. Lincoln, NE: University of Nebraska Press, 1979.

Yamamoto, K. "Children under Stress: The Causes and Cures." Family Weekly. *Ogden* [UT] *Standard Examiner*, 1980: 6–8.

Yates, A. "Current Status and Future Directions of Research on the American Indian Child." *American Journal of Psychiatry* 144 (1987): 1135–42.

Young, T.J. "Inhalant Use among American Indian Youth." *Child Psychiatry and Human Development* 18, no. 1 (1987): 36–46.

Zenter, H. "Parental Behavior and Student Attitudes towards Further Training among Indian and Non-Indian Students in Oregon and Alberta." *Alberta Journal of Educational Resources* 9, no. 1 (1963): 22–30.

Zigler, E. "Controlling Child Abuse in America: An Effort Doomed to Failure." *Critical Perspectives on Child Abuse.* Ed. R. Bourne and E.H. Newberger. Lexington, MA: Lexington Books, 1979. 171–207.

Zintz, M. *The Indian Research Study: The Adjustment of Indian and Non-Indian Children to the Public Schools of New Mexico.* Albuquerque, NM: University of New Mexico, College of Education, 1960.

Zitkala-Sa. "An Indian Teacher among Indians." *Atlantic Monthly* 85, March 1900, 386.

Index

Abortion, 208, 211–12

AIDS, 209

Alcohol use: adolescent vs. adult, 194; and child abuse and neglect, 77, 236, 240; and dropout, 48, 54–57, 189, 194; and early sexual activity, 209; gender issues, 55–56, 195–99; and health issues, 49; parent attitudes toward, 83, 192–94, 205, 227; and peer pressure, 67, 203, 227–29, 230, 231; and perception of level of drinking, 189–91, 205; and self-reporting on level of drinking, 190–91, 205; as a social activity, 58–59, 83, 191–92, 194, 195, 199, 227; stereotypes about, 32–33, 190–91; and suicide, 69, 70; among teachers, 248–49. *See also* Dropout, American Indian: and alcohol use; Dropout, general: and alcohol use

Allotment Act (1887). *See* Dawes Severalty Act

Allotment period, 18–21

American Indian culture: and cooperative learning, 92, 93; distinguishing features of, 41; federal efforts to suppress, 16, 17, 24, 31, 39; and the media, 181–82; "pan-Indian" vs. tribal affiliation, 37–38; in school curricula, 31, 39, 42, 85, 86, 154–55, 165, 173, 250, 289; school sensitivity to, 153, 164; teacher knowledge of, 91. *See also* Cultural discontinuity; Dropout, American Indian: and cultural discontinuity

American Indian education: and Bureau of Indian Affairs, 18, 22, 23, 25, 26, 28; and "civilization," 13, 14, 15, 16, 19, 20, 30, 31, 39, 99; and colonization, 13–14, 25; community involvement in, 16, 21, 23, 24, 25, 41; and "degree of Indian blood" policies, 20, 99; effects of Indian Self-Determination Act of 1975, 42; federal goals for, 14, 16, 17, 19, 21, 25, 27, 40, 106, 174; federal policy toward and administration of, 18, 20, 21–23, 24, 25, 27, 40, 41–42; funding for, 15, 16, 18, 25; history of, 13–28; and poverty, 125–50; state administration of, 19; student resistance to, 155. *See also* Allotment period; Curricula; Missionary period; Termination period; Treaty period

American Indian Freedom of Religion Act (1978), 25

American Indian Movement (AIM), 23, 25, 164; International Indian Treaty Council, 27

American Indian schools: Bureau of Indian Affairs controlled, 19–21, 23, 24, 25, 26, 27, 28, 43; child abuse in, 27, 239, 242, 255, 286–87; existing, 13, 17; federal administration of, 18, 20, 21–22, 23, 26; and gender segregation, 40; and grade retention, 245; origins of, 13–14; parent attitudes toward, 17, 18; recommendations to improve, 281–290; and self-esteem, 48; Survival Schools, 25; teacher selection and qualifications, 14, 15, 18, 20, 21, 24, 25, 26, 91, 263–64, 286–87; tribal colleges, 25, 287; tribally controlled, 25, 26, 28. *See also* Boarding schools; Curricula; Day schools

Assimilation, 42, 182; as a colonial policy, 14; effects of policy, 24; as a federal policy, 15, 16, 17–21, 26, 174; myth of, 101; school role in promoting, 17, 106, 174